DESIGNING
CHARACTER-BASED
CONSOLE GAMES

DESIGNING CHARACTER-BASED CONSOLE GAMES

MARK DAVIES

CHARLES RIVER MEDIA

Boston, Massachusetts

Cover Design: Tyler Creative
Cover Image: Denise Tyler

CHARLES RIVER MEDIA
25 Thomson Place
Boston, Massachusetts 02210
617-757-7900
617-757-7969 (FAX)
crm.info@thomson.com
www.charlesriver.com

This book is printed on acid-free paper.

Mark Davies. *Designing Character-Based Console Games.*
ISBN: 1-58450-521-4
ISBN-13: 978-1-58450-521-1

Library of Congress Cataloging-in-Publication Data
Davies, Mark, 1977-
  Designing character-based console games / Mark Davies. -- 1st ed.
     p. cm.
  Includes index.
  ISBN 1-58450-521-4 (pbk. with cd : alk. paper)
  1. Computer games--Design. 2. Computer games--Programming. I. Title.
  QA76.76.C672D387 2007
  794.8'1526--dc22

2006038168

Printed in the United States of America
07 7 6 5 4 3 2 First Edition

Dedicated to my beautiful wife, Lexi, and baby, Isaac.

CONTENTS

PREFACE   xiii

ACKNOWLEDGMENTS   xv

PART 1   **CONCEPTS**   1

CHAPTER 1   **THE CONSOLE DESIGN PROCESS**   3

Conception   4
Turning Ideas into Reality   7
Production   9
The Console Submission Process   19
Summary   22

CHAPTER 2   **GAMEPLAY**   25

Defining Gameplay   26
Types of Gameplay   33
Gameplay Pace   37
Goals   38
Emotions in Gameplay   39
Game Duration   42
Multiplayer Gameplay   44
Summary   48

CHAPTER 3   **NARRATIVE**   51

Game versus Story   52
Setting   54

	Story	58
	Characters	75
	Summary	82
CHAPTER 4	**GAME STRUCTURE**	**85**
	Logical Structure	86
	Physical Structure	93
	Summary	100
PART 2	**GAME MECHANICS**	**103**
CHAPTER 5	**CHARACTER CONTROL**	**105**
	Control Input	106
	Standard Movement	114
	Advanced Movement	115
	Object Interaction	124
	Quick Time Events	125
	Summary	129
CHAPTER 6	**VIEWPOINTS AND CAMERAS**	**133**
	Viewpoints	134
	Camera Basics	139
	Game Cameras	142
	Animated Cameras	164
	Multiplayer Game Cameras	164
	Summary	165
CHAPTER 7	**COMBAT FUNDAMENTALS**	**169**
	The Basics of Combat	170
	The Combat Procedure	172
	Basic Combat Dynamics	176
	Aiming and Targeting	180
	Summary	189
CHAPTER 8	**MELEE COMBAT DYNAMICS**	**191**
	Combat Control Systems	192
	Melee Combat Balance	194
	Melee Weapons	195

Attack Parameters   196
Attack Windows   199
Types of Moves   202
Changing Attack Sets   206
Combos   207
Defensive Moves   212
Weapon Trails   215
Summary   215

CHAPTER 9   RANGED COMBAT DYNAMICS   219
Projectile Weapons   220
Beam Weapons   229
Mine Weapons   231
Defense Against Ranged Attacks   233
Ranged Combat Animation   233
Summary   236

CHAPTER 10   DAMAGE AND IMPACT   239
The Hit Test   240
Damage   247
Impacts and Hit Reactions   255
Summary   262

CHAPTER 11   ECONOMIES   265
Character Economies   266
Progression   273
Wealth   279
Inventory   282
Rating   295
Time   298
Lives and Saves   300
Summary   303

PART 3   WORLD BUILDING   307

CHAPTER 12   LEVEL-DESIGN PRINCIPLES   309
Function   310
Form   312

	Flow	319
	Summary	331
Chapter 13	**Level Implementation**	**333**
	Design Methodologies	334
	The Level Design Pipeline	336
	Logical Structures	343
	Construction Methods	356
	Tools	358
	Summary	360
Chapter 14	**Artificial Intelligence Fundamentals**	**363**
	AI Components	364
	AI Communication	366
	Methods of Choice	367
	AI Construction Methods	374
	The Mechanics of Actions	376
	Group Management	392
	Summary	394
Chapter 15	**Implementing AI Actors**	**397**
	Player Expectation and Feedback	398
	Enemies	399
	Nonplayer Characters	414
	Allies	427
	Bot AI	433
	Summary	434
Chapter 16	**Physics**	**437**
	Physics Simulation	438
	Physics in Gameplay	444
	Summary	448
Chapter 17	**Audio**	**451**
	Designing with Sound	452
	Types of Sound	453
	Summary	461

PART 4	**USER INTERFACE**	**463**
CHAPTER 18	**THE FRONT END**	**465**
	Front End Elements	466
	Flow Schemas	473
	Visual Style	476
	Technical Requirements	478
	The Back End	479
	Summary	480
CHAPTER 19	**IN-GAME INTERFACE**	**481**
	HUD (Head up Display)	482
	Pause Menu	488
	Inventory Screen	489
	Treasure or Experience Screen	490
	Map Screen	490
	Objectives Screen or Quest Log	491
	Information Screens	491
	Game Hints	491
	Character Advancement Screen	492
	Save Games	492
	Store or Merchant Screens	494
	Summary	494
PART 5	**BALANCING**	**497**
CHAPTER 20	**GAME BALANCE PRINCIPLES AND PRACTICE**	**499**
	Difficulty	500
	Motivation	509
	Component Balance	511
	Summary	519
CHAPTER 21	**THE ACT OF BALANCING**	**521**
	Preparation	522
	Game Walkthrough	522
	Spreadsheet Modeling	523
	Paper Prototyping	524

Playtesting   524
Summary   526

APPENDIX   **527**

REFERENCES   **529**

INDEX   **533**

PREFACE

Games design offers a world of possibilities, but just as many pitfalls are waiting for the unwary or inexperienced. This book aims to show some of the ways games can be designed and ways to avoid common mistakes. This is by no means the definitive way to design games—it's just too rich a subject and developing too quickly to ever encapsulate every facet and idea that has ever been and ever will be. What this book does offer is a starting point for any budding designer, a point of reference for anyone who wants to learn more about how games are made, and a few choice nuggets of information for the expert.

The scope of the book has been narrowed to concentrate on character-based console games, which is a large subject that also includes the broader aspects of design that apply to all types of games. Throughout the book you will learn the key aspects of game design.

Concepts: The processes and theory behind game design from game-play and narrative to the actual structure of the game itself

Game mechanics: The mechanisms that make up a character-based console game, from character control and cameras to combat and game economies

World building: The creation of levels and methods of implementation, the use of artificial intelligence to create believable characters, and the integration of physics and audio into a game world

User interface: The design of menus and in-game systems to relay information to the player

Game balance: The principles of game balance and the methods used in performing game balancing

I'd like to thank the people who have sparked ideas and shared knowledge that has influenced much of what lies in this book—people with whom I have worked closely on projects in the past and people from the industry at large. It is an industry I am proud to be part of and one that I hope continues to evolve and innovate for many years to come.

ACKNOWLEDGMENTS

I'd like to take this opportunity to thank all the people who I've worked with at Climax and Ninja Theory, many of whom have taught me much about making games.

Thanks to Dan Attwell, Bill Green, Eamon Murtagh, Chris Rundell, Elco Vossers, Chris G., Pete Maton, James Lane, Sam Barlow, Tom Colvin, Tim Swann, Tim Adams, Treena Seymour, Matt Cooper, Mark Wilson, Pete, Rudi, Wilmot, Gareth Noyce, and the rest of the people at Climax with whom I have had the pleasure to work. Thanks also to Tameem Antoniades, Mike Ball, Nina Kristensen, Geoff Scott, Matt Hart, Stan, Beaners, Attila, Martin, Tom, John, Dario and all the rest of the *Heavenly Sword* team. Thanks especially to Wil Driver for allowing me to use his idea of a component-based camera system. To anyone I may have missed—sorry!

Thanks to family and friends.

A very special thanks to Joseph Cavalla for giving me my break into the industry.

Also a very big thank you to Jenifer Niles for making this book a reality.

CONCEPTS

Before we can start to look at character-based game design in depth, we must first learn about some core concepts. These concepts will set in our mind the design processes we must go through when designing games and provide the theory that will form the basis of game systems and mechanics.

Console design is a very different beast from other forms of game design for several reasons, as we shall investigate in the first chapter of the book. This design process has become a fairly standard process throughout the games industry, although every company will have its own particular methods of writing documents and building prototypes.

With a process in place, there are still other aspects with which every designer needs to be familiar. First is the importance of gameplay. The emphasis in producing a game design should always be on gameplay. It should always be at the forefront of the game designer's mind. We will investigate several concepts of gameplay in the second chapter.

Our emphasis on character-based games means that our game will have a narrative. The third chapter of this book investigates forms of narrative and how they can be applied to a game design. We will also investigate every aspect of narrative from the story and the setting to the characters that make up our narrative.

Finally, we will look at game structure, both the logical structure of game content into game modes and level structures, and the physical structure of the systems that are required to create a game.

THE CONSOLE DESIGN PROCESS

In This Chapter

- Conception
- Turning Ideas into Reality
- Production
- The Console Submission Process

Not all that long ago a game design could have been scribbled on the back of an envelope. Simple games with simple mechanics gave birth to the industry, as the lack of technological power of the machines facilitated the need for abstraction. Even the role of the game designer is relatively new. Games were generally the work of one individual—a lone coder creating the design as he went along.

Things are very different now. Projects cost millions of dollars and have large teams of people building them. The designer is now a dedicated individual whose only concern is the design itself.

Game design is tricky to explain to industry outsiders. There are many common misconceptions:

Guy on Street:	So you make the graphics?
Game Designer:	No—that's the artist's job.
Guy on Street:	Ah! So you write the code!
Game Designer:	No—that would be the programmers.
Guy on Street:	Oh! You play games all day!
Game Designer:	I wish . . .

There are several facets to the design role, and not every company regards design in the same manner.

In this chapter we will learn about several aspects of the designer's role in making a game through the life cycle of a project:

- Conception
- Turning ideas into reality
- Production
- The Console submission process

CONCEPTION

This is the most free and organic part of the process, and it can be daunting. Searching for the idea can be very difficult; it is all too easy to copy what has been done before. Creating a whole new IP (Intellectual Property) from scratch can be particularly daunting and very costly to market to the right audience, but the rewards are often great.

There are ways to start with an advantage. Licensed property can be fairly expensive, but the right license will guarantee interest from a certain market and should result in increased sales. Licensed games have, in the past, made a bad reputation for themselves by being poorly conceived and cheaply produced. However, the quality of licensed games these days is much higher than it used to be.

The subject of this book is focused on a narrow subsection of games that are based on the use of characters and developed on game consoles. In reality, this is far from a narrow field, but to encompass the vast field of game design would be a truly mammoth task. Character-based games are the predominant type of game made and sold throughout the world, and game consoles are the most popular platform on which they are played, so there is a huge market for such a title. Conversely, this can make it harder to get noticed in a saturated market. The recipe for success is in making a solid game, marketing it well, and having some good luck.

For the purposes of this book, a character-based game can be classified as having a number of elements that might not be found in every other type of game:

- A narrative that drives the player through the game
- A number of characters that interact with each other in different ways
- Gameplay that is based around the movement of a particular character or small group of characters

What kind of game does this encompass? While the above may seem a very narrow list of requirements, a huge number of games and game genres that would fall under this umbrella:

Action–adventure games: This very broad genre encompasses all manner of games—the classic style of point and click adventures such as *Monkey Island*®; modern action games such as *Splinter Cell*™, *Metal Gear Solid*®, and numerous other titles; exploration games such as *Tomb Raider*™; freeform world games such as *Grand Theft Auto*™ (shown in Figure 1.1); and many, many more.

FIGURE 1.1   *Grand Theft Auto: Vice City Stories*™. © Rockstar Games.
All Rights Reserved

Beat 'em ups: The beat 'em up was once a towering giant of the games industry, with acres of arcade space reserved for side-scrolling beat 'em ups such as *Golden Axe*™. They have now become much more focused on one-on-one fighting since the granddaddy of the genre, *Street Fighter*® *II*, made it so popular. The one-on-one fighter remains popular today with titles such as *Virtua Fighter*™, *Tekken*®, and *Dead or Alive*®.

Platformers: Another previous giant of a genre, the platformer, involves lots of acrobatic action. The classic games of the 8- and 16-bit era such as *Sonic the Hedgehog*™ and *Super Mario Bros*® still hold up today, but they are joined by more wide-ranging titles such as the new *Prince of Persia*™ series.

First-person shooters: The current fad genre is without a doubt the first-person shooter (FPS), originally brought into the spotlight by *DOOM®*. The genre continues to evolve with titles that redefine the genre such as *Half-Life®* and *Half-Life 2*, and plenty of others that are content to emulate their peers.

Role-playing games: Large worlds and extensive stories tend to characterize role-playing games (RPGs), as they often have a group of playable characters as opposed to a single avatar. The two main branches of RPGs are divided by which part of the world they come from. Eastern RPGs tend to have a predefined bunch of characters and a very strong, generally linear narrative, such as in the *Final Fantasy®* series. Western RPGs tend to have characters that are user created and worlds that allow free exploration, often with a branching narrative structure, such as *Diablo®* and *Neverwinter Nights™*.

Whether creating an original IP or a licensed product, the designer should take several steps when coming up with the basis of the game concept:

- General research
- Brainstorming
- Market research

General Research

It is rare, if not impossible, that perfect game ideas simply pop into a game designer's head. They have to emerge and be nurtured before they become workable, and that means doing some research. The most valuable time a designer can spend away from actual game development is in the research of ideas and concepts.

Looking at other games and "reverse engineering" gives the designer invaluable information for future game designs, but the good designer will not stop at looking at other games. Inspiration can strike the designer from the most unlikely of places. Indulge in other mass media, read literature, take a look at the world around you right now—there is a game idea nestling there somewhere.

Brainstorming

Brainstorming with groups of people is a useful way to generate ideas. Ideas suggested by one person may spark a whole other series of ideas from another person. Make sure that detailed notes are taken during such a session, as almost any idea may influence a design later. However, limit brainstorming to the initial stages of design only. Making the whole game design by committee is dangerous and rarely results in a good end result. It often takes one person with vision to make decisions; otherwise, the result is a watered down mish-mash of ideas and opinions.

Market Research

Market research tends to be an expensive and time consuming process and is not without its pitfalls. Essentially, you need to find out what your audience likes, what they might want (which is often very different from what they think they want), and what they play now.

There are many ways of doing this:

Surveys: Polling the marketplace is a good way to gather information about a potential audience. However, a survey will produce a lot of bad data when people fill out misleading answers. The data needs to be sorted and the results taken with a slight pinch of salt. It should be used as guidance rather than gospel.

Focus groups: Gathering a group of people together to review existing games is a great way to discover information about an audience, but getting good data from a focus test requires a good deal of research and preparation beforehand. The right people have to be chosen for the test, and the right games need to be selected to be played. Targeting specific parts of an audience will allow you to gather some invaluable information, but it is all too easy to produce misleading data if the focus group is not properly organized and well targeted.

Using other people's data: Often the easiest method of market research is to borrow from people who have already conducted the research. While this is the simplest option, there are no guarantees as to how accurate the data is, whether it will suit the particular target market you are seeking, or whether it asks the right questions for your needs. Just like scientific research, the results are utterly dependent on how the data was handled.

TURNING IDEAS INTO REALITY

Ideas are only the tip of a very large iceberg. Lots of people say they have an amazing idea for a game. Anyone can have an idea for a game—even a very good one. The hard part is making the idea a reality.

The Proposal

Writing the proposal for the game is an essential part of the process, whether pitching for a licensed game or trying to sell an original idea. The proposal document is the initial contact with a publisher—generally the publisher will be the main source of funding for the game. The proposal also serves as a great document to solidify the basis of the game. What you are aiming to do is sum up the game as briefly as possible. You need to get across the main point—the USPs (ultimate selling points)—and the vision for the game.

The proposal needs to be brief, as it is going to be used by many individuals, such as marketing personnel. Keep it succinct and craft it to a fine degree. This needs to hit people in the face and make them want to play the game then and there. Electronic Arts (EA) uses a system called the X, where the game is summed up in one word that acts as a slogan for the game.

ON THE CD

The file Design-GameProposal.doc on the companion CD-ROM shows an example of a game proposal.

Concept Approval

Developing for a console platform is a more involved and difficult process than people may first imagine. There are quite a few differences between developing a game for a console and developing for the PC. Some aspects are easier; others more difficult.

The first hurdle any potential developer will encounter is getting permission to develop for a particular console. Unlike the PC environment, where anyone can publish pretty much whatever they like, console manufacturers require a review of the concept and must give approval before the developer will be allowed to create a game for that console. This process is in place to maintain the integrity and image of the console, as manufacturers look to appeal to certain markets. Nintendo® was notoriously strict about the content they would allow to be released on their earlier consoles, as it would tarnish their family company image, but they have relaxed the rules a little bit in more recent times.

Concept approval is generally little more than a formality. The developer must fill out an application form that is sent to the console manufacturer. Each manufacturer's form is different, but they generally require information about the type of content that will be featured and the target audience. Once the concept has been approved, the developer will be able to get development kits to start creating the game on the target platform. A development kit is a version of the console that allows the developer to connect to and debug the code being run on it. These tend to be extremely expensive items, traditionally making it prohibitively expensive for small teams. This barrier to development is changing, as smaller games are being released through online services such as Xbox Live® Arcade, allowing smaller teams to produce games for the latest generation of games without prohibitively expensive development costs. Microsoft has taken this opening up of console development a step further with the release of XNA and Game Studio Express, which allows the hobbyist game developer to develop for the Xbox 360 for very little expense.

Preproduction

The trend of game development now seems to be that publishers are generally unwilling to fork out millions of dollars on the basis of a proposal. Instead publishers tend to fund many small preproduction phases and then choose the best of those that fit within their portfolio, or a developer will have to self-fund a demo to gain interest. Publishers want a fairly wide spectrum of games, so you may be competing against many similar game concepts. Your idea needs to work, and it needs to be proven in the preproduction phase.

The results of preproduction tend to be a macro design document and a prototype. Some publishers may request a more polished prototype, often referred to as a vertical slice.

Macro Design

The macro design is a document that covers all the core concepts of the game without going into great detail. It should explain the more individual aspects of the game and demonstrate those elements that make the game stand out from its competition.

The ideal size of a macro design document is highly debatable. Many say it should not exceed 10 pages, but many games require more than that to explain all the essential features in sufficient detail. For a fairly complex game you could be looking at 30 pages. Adjust the size of the macro design document to suit the size and scope of the project. Include only what is needed.

Never underestimate the usefulness of paper design. Many people overlook it and move straight on to the prototype. However, there are very strong advantages:

Solid documentation: Having your designs written down means you have a great form of communicable design that you can show to the team. Of course, it must be communicated well to be understood by others. A few scrawls on the back of an envelope is not proper documentation.

A preliminary vision: Writing a paper design enables you to work logically through problems and catch a number of possible pitfalls before you get to the development stage. However, as great as a paper design may be, the designer must always be ready to change designs during implementation. What looks good on paper may not feel right when implemented.

Prototype

Prototyping is the act of making a rough and ready version of the game mechanics to allow the designers to tweak the gameplay to make it as fun as possible. Prototyping is a hugely useful step that often gets overlooked in the development process because of time constraints, but it is such an effective tool that it really shouldn't be skipped.

The development of a demo is now also becoming a vital tool in securing a project, so design of exactly what goes into the prototype is essential. A prototype should demonstrate all of the core features of the game—particularly quirky or unusual mechanics that have not been attempted before.

The benefits of prototyping are many:

Proof of concept: Creating a prototype can prove that the game concept works and sometimes proves that it doesn't. Finding out that something doesn't work can be a blessing in disguise—better to find this out at the very start of the project than months (and thousands of dollars) down the line.

Immediate feedback: Assuming the concept holds up well, the prototype enables the developers to refine the gameplay. The benefit of having a well-built prototype is that the developers can change various aspects of the gameplay and get immediate feedback on the results.

Vertical Slice

The vertical slice is a buzzword used to describe the creation of a fully playable "slice" of the game. This somewhat silly terminology is based on the idea of the complete game being a cake. If you were to take a slice of this, then you get an idea of how the finished cake will be.

The vertical slice is a step beyond the prototype, in that it is no longer rough and ready, but is a complete representation of how the final game should be in art style, gameplay, and so on. Many publishers demand this as a deliverable from preproduction before they will approve a project to go into full production.

PRODUCTION

Once a project is signed on, the game enters full production. Now everyone begins to move toward a common goal, and a clear design is required. The huge size of many modern games requires meticulous planning from both a creative and managerial perspective. It is the designers' job to put in place a solid creative vision—to specify exactly how the game will function.

To develop a game on a console, the developer will need to procure development kits (assuming the concept was approved by the manufacturer). The one great advantage of console development is that the target hardware is a known quantity. The biggest problem for PC development is the sheer breadth of hardware combinations that face the developer. It's almost impossible to know exactly what a target consumer will have in his machine. This makes testing a nightmare and makes designing the game difficult when you are not entirely sure of the control system the end user might have (though they are very likely to own a mouse and keyboard, this isn't really the ideal gaming device for many game genres of game). With console development, every box has pretty much the same kit inside. The same can be said for the control input device; every console is sold with a default controller. However, while controllers are great for games, they are a little harder for user interfaces, such as menu systems or entering names. Getting user interfaces right on a joypad can be quite a tricky task.

Things also get tricky when developing for more than one platform at once. In this instance the developer will have to take account of the differences in architecture in two or more different machines, which may be radically different in the way they work, particularly with parallel processing architecture becoming increasingly prevalent.

Bearing all these facts in mind, the designer must start to develop the game in earnest. There are several tasks for the designers during the production phase:

- Functional specification
- Content
- Implementation
- Localization
- Testing

Functional Specification

The functional specification (aka micro design) is an in-depth document that details all the needed design elements. This document contains all aspects of the game that concern the game systems (other documents specify other features, such as the technical design document, which contains the game architecture).

This is an important document, as it instructs all members of the team as to exactly how the vision will be realized. Often people do not pay enough attention to the documentation of a project and make design decisions as they go along. This is a very dangerous route to follow, as not everyone has a clear view of all the decisions that were made, and they often get lost or forgotten.

It is essential that the design document be kept up to date throughout the course of a project. At the beginning you cannot foresee all the design issues that will occur over the course of a project. Thus, it is essential that the design documents remain flexible. If the document itself is not kept up to date, then someone reading the document will not know the current state of the design—meaning the document is pretty much useless.

The other problem with design documentation is that it can often be very large. A document should be easy to navigate and easy to read; otherwise, the team simply won't bother. Look at ways of improving delivery of information to the team, such as wiki pages.

Content

Once the main gameplay elements of the game, such as character control, combat, and so on, have been determined, it is the perfect time to begin designing the content of the game. This means all of the levels, the characters, the equipment, and the story of the game.

This should only be done after the core mechanics are finalized, if possible, as many of these mechanics will have a significant impact on the content.

The design of content should be documented meticulously and always planned on paper before implementation is undertaken, but as with the main design document, it should remain organic and free so it can be changed as necessary.

Implementation

The first step of implementation is to throw out the prototype. You might be a bit perplexed by that last sentence, but allow me to explain. A prototype is created in a short time and is often built on old technology. You have proved that the concept works. Now you must build it properly. If you build on top of the old prototype code, you will only cause problems for yourself later down the line because of earlier short cuts and oversights.

As soon as you have a working game, nail down the mechanics. This stage of the prototype still holds true. This should be done before any implementation is started and really should be done before much content design is complete. Many elements of the core structure impact on the content, and changing these fundamental elements late in the game can have devastating effects on a project's schedule.

With the core mechanics in place, you can get on with the serious business of taking content from the page and putting it into the game. This is generally done with some kind of editing tool or scripting language. Usually these are specifically tailored to the game and should be developed early in order to be stable and good enough to use to actually build the game.

Often the designers form many great ideas as they familiarize themselves with the technology. Putting these ideas into the game requires thought. If they are simple to implement, then it may be easy to add them into the game. If, however, they require extra functionality from the game, then it is important to consider the consequences. Is the new feature worth the effort of implementing it? If this feature could be used in many different circumstances, then the answer may well be yes. If the feature can only really be applied in one area, then it may not be worth doing, unless the feature is such a stupendously good idea that it would be madness not to use it.

One should also consider the stage of the project. If it is late in the game development cycle, then it may be a bad idea to try to push more content in. When more features are pushed in at the end of a project, it is termed "feature creep" and can often send a project way over schedule.

Localization

Localization is the act of converting game content or technology to suit the requirements of a specific country or market. Games are sold in a number of territories around the world. There were traditionally three main territories, though the popularity of games in Korea has boosted it to the unofficial status of a fourth key territory:

Japan: At one time the biggest consumer and developer of games was Japan. Japanese tastes are diverse, and much of their output is translated for the other markets, but there are many games that would only sell to the Japanese market. Many Western games are not met with a warm response, as the Japanese gaming culture is markedly different than the Western ideal.

North America: The market in North America has become the driving force for the whole industry. Success here guarantees good sales and will often translate to success in other territories.

Europe: Europe is widely considered the hardest territory to develop for, as it has the widest concentration of languages in a small space and has different broadcasting standards than the other two territories. It nevertheless remains a key territory to develop for.

Korea: Korea has become gaming obsessed, particularly with massively multiplayer online games. However, piracy is so rife in this territory that actually selling games here is difficult at present (hence the prevalence of subscription-based gaming).

Localization is an important and oft-overlooked aspect of game development that requires meticulous planning and consideration from the beginning of a project. All too often a poor localization job is done, or it is a task that becomes overly complicated, simply because it is not considered till the end of a project.

Good localization is essential to releasing a product across a number of different territories and creating a highly successful game. Games often lose much of their charm and appeal because of poor localization, which severely affects their sales potential in territories other than the original development.

There are key issues that the developer will have to consider when it comes to localization:

- Technology
- Language
- Censorship and ratings
- Culture

Technology

The world is a large place, where technology has spread in different ways. Although we are moving toward globalization, there are inevitably still substantial technology differences between countries.

Broadcast Standards

TV broadcasting standards are one area where there are a number of differences. Since many consoles are hooked up to traditional TV sets, knowledge of the different broadcasting standards is useful. Three main types of traditional broadcast standards are used in various parts of the globe:

> **NTSC (National Television System Committee):** The North American standard displays images at 30 Hz. It has been adopted by eastern countries such as Japan and South Korea, as well as much of South America.
>
> **PAL (Phase Alteration Line):** A European system developed from the NTSC standard. It displays a higher-resolution image than NTSC, with superior color at 25 Hz. It is used in the United Kingdom, Western Europe, many parts of Asia, the Middle East, and parts of Africa and South America.
>
> **SECAM (Systeme Electronique Couleur avec Memoire):** A system developed by the French and adopted by Russia and many Eastern European countries. When designing for SECAM, it is generally treated the same as the PAL system, as it features the same number of scan lines and refresh rate.

Refresh rates and picture sizes can be very different where these three systems are used. NTSC has a higher refresh rate than the PAL system, which can cause significant issues with conversion, usually meaning a poorer framerate. The smaller image also means bars are often added to fill out a PAL display, so the benefit of the larger picture is lost. The refresh rate is less of a problem with the existence of multisynch

TV sets, but is still an issue. NTSC suffers from a poor color display (it is nicknamed Never The Same Color), especially when displaying bright red values, which tend to bleed heavily.

HDTV

High-definition TV (HDTV) is the great hope of the next generation (at the time of writing). HDTV is supposed to offer a crisp, solid image equivalent to a computer monitor and solve the broadcasting standard niggles of previous systems (although at present the problem has been made worse as several companies jostle to set theirs as the de facto standard).

Both Xbox 360 and PlayStation® 3 (PS3) are capable of outputting HD images. The Xbox 360 can output 720p and 1080i images (p stands for progressive, meaning it draws the whole image every frame, unlike interlaced—i). The PS3 can output images at 1080p, but such images are potentially very expensive in terms of memory, and at present few TVs are capable of displaying at this resolution.

While HDTV is doing well in North America, uptake in Europe so far has been fairly slow. It remains to be seen how popular HDTV will become and how much of a role consoles will play in pushing the technology into people's homes.

Controllers

Often different controllers may be sold across different territories to account for different tastes or ergonomic requirements. Take the original XBox control pad that was adapted for the Japanese market to fit a smaller hand size (ironically the pad proved much more effective and became the standard for all territories). This pad had a different layout of the white and black buttons, meaning that a carefully designed control pad layout for the original pad might not work with the new pad.

It is important to test a control layout with all available controllers and ensure that a layout will work with all of these. If not, then provide the option to change the control layout to suit these differences.

Language

The largest and most complex task of localization is translating various parts of the game into different languages. Though this task is not one that is fulfilled by the design team (it is generally done out-of-house by specialized localization teams), it is something that designers should be aware of from the start, so that they know about any restrictions posed by localization requirements.

Different territories have different demands for language. North America is mainly English, but Spanish is often included to accommodate the large Hispanic population. French might also be included for the Canadian market. Japan requires Japanese, obviously, and tends not to have many if any other translations. The European market is the most demanding, having such a broad range of languages in such a small area. There are five or six main languages that are usually accommodated for in the European market: English, French, German, Italian, Spanish, and often Dutch. However, as the games market increases, more languages are becoming more popular, such as Scandinavian and Eastern European languages.

Translation Elements

There are more elements to translate in a game than may first meet the eye and several pitfalls the development team can fall into.

Text Translation: Text translation is an essential element, since if you cannot read menus, then it can be difficult to even start the game. There are many text-based elements within a game:

- Front-end menus
- HUD (Heads-Up Display) information
- Dialog
- Mission objectives
- Help hints and information

To localize this text, it is essential that it is easily accessible. Having text hard-coded into the game will prove to be an absolute nightmare. What is needed is a basic database where text regions are coded, so that different languages will select the appropriate phrases and automatically insert them into their places.

One aspect that is very costly to localize is language within textures applied to the environment—a signpost, for example. To localize this would require an alternate texture for each language. This is obviously time consuming and a waste of resources. Text like this should either not be included and icons used instead, should offer some kind of interaction to provide text translation, or should not be used for any essential information.

Another important consideration is that languages are not necessarily composed of similar length words and sentences. For instance, German text is on average 30% longer than the equivalent English text. This means text holder elements need to fit these larger sizes. Without careful consideration, they could overrun or suffer from very poor layout. Converting to languages with non-Western character sets can also pose potential problems with layout.

Speech Translation: Speech translation is needed in games that use speech for the bulk of communication, which is the norm these days. In fairly simple action games this is not too difficult a challenge, but in games with reams of dialog this can present absolutely massive problems. First, there is the sheer volume of resources required. Games with large pools of voice recording are difficult enough with one language to contend with. There is also the cost of hiring whole new groups of voice actors for each language. Then there are the technical limitations of having to stream off the disk. With a large amount of dialog, it is feasible that Voice Over (VO) resources for six languages would easily fill a DVD—probably even several.

If speech translation is unlikely to be a viable option, subtitles are an appropriate substitute. The beauty of these is that they are relatively easy to implement and they keep the original performance, so there are no dubbing issues where the voice and mouth movements don't match.

Translation Quality

Literal translations are quite often utter gibberish. Translating is a skilled and difficult job, as the words must keep context and meaning from one language to the next. Cultural references do not translate well, particularly humor, which can be very different from country to country. Proverbs, sayings, slang, and other colloquialisms are also unlikely to make sense in translation. It is also essential that the correct terminology is used for a subject across each language.

The result of bad translation can be seen in many games, such as the first *Resident Evil*, though it has become much less of an issue as more money has come into the industry. It has been a while since laughable translations such as the infamous "All your base are belong to us" from the Japanese game *Zero Wing*.

There are other aspects to translation quality. Original-language speech may have been done with expensive, well-known actors and may have resulted in good performances, but this can often come undone when different-language actors come in. The whole tone of the performance can easily be lost, especially if costs are cut from the original-language performance. The result is often a much poorer experience for players in other languages.

Censorship and Ratings

Games are evil. At least that's what many would have you believe. Like the music videos in the 1980s, games have become something of a scapegoat for a perceived lack of moral fiber in today's youth.

Like it or loath it, censorship exists, though in the games industry this is in a mostly self-regulating form. Ratings are applied by industry bodies such as the Entertainment Software Ratings Board (ESRB) according to the content in a game, which can have a profound impact on the sales of the game. Interestingly an Adult rating can lead to poor sales of the game because of family-based retail chains such as WalMart refusing to stock Adult rated titles. This leads to a somewhat naïve attitude of removing blood in order to get a lower Teen rating to get the product on the shelf. Simply removing blood doesn't remove the act of violence behind it, so this seems a pretty weak attempt at self-regulation.

Different countries have different moral and legal standpoints on game content. Violence is frowned upon in Germany and Australia. In Germany the use of red blood is banned. Australia famously took the step of banning *Grand Theft Auto: San Andreas* because of its content. In the United States sex is a big no-no. These restrictions seem somewhat extreme, as the average age of a gamer has risen dramatically, meaning there is a large market for more mature content.

The Hot Coffee mod for *Grand Theft Auto: San Andreas* unlocks sexually explicit content, which is relatively crude and hardly titillating, yet it caused a massive furor, in the United States particularly, where the rating was pushed up from Mature to Adult, causing it to be removed from the shelves of many major retailers. This is somewhat ludicrous considering this was hidden content, when the rest of the game involves crime, drugs, and the ability to fumble with hookers in the back of a stolen car and then beat them to death with a dildo to get your cash back. On reflection, the sexually explicit scenes with your various girlfriends in the game are somewhat tame.

Culture

Culture is a much more far reaching problem for the designer, in that it may affect the whole design of the game itself. Much research has been done by independent studies as to the differences in gaming culture across the globe. Nowhere is the divide more evident than between East and West .

Gaming Culture

The different approaches to gaming between Eastern and Western markets is notably different. The Western audience loves competitive games—games with strong elements of freedom and free-form worlds. They like the freedom of choice and often like the opportunity to customize their characters. First-person games are popular, as the players can believe themselves to be in the world.

Eastern audiences prefer more cooperative, social gameplay and prefer playing against AI than a human opponent. They tend to take on the role of a predefined character rather than creating a character of their own, and too much freedom in a game can be off-putting [Edge04].

Cultural Taboos

Different cultures regard different acts as taboo. What one culture may find horrific, another may find perfectly valid. Sex and violence are the two main areas where problems are likely to arise, but the use of certain language or actions that may appear innocuous to you may cause great offence in another culture. If you are releasing into a particular territory, it is worth making sure that your game is not going to offend great swathes of the populous.

Music

Popular music tastes tend to differ from country to country. While it is unlikely that changing a bespoke score for each country is a worthwhile endeavor, if licensed music tracks are being used, it may be worth looking at localizing them.

Different styles of music and different artists are popular in different regions. For example, dance music is very popular in the United Kingdom, but is far less popular than rock and country in America. Offering familiar music to players will often encourage them to take a look at the game.

Advertising and Product Placement

Advertisements and product placement are becoming much more prevalent in gaming and offers more potential sources of revenue for developers. We're some way away from having advertising breaks in the middle of gameplay (let's hope that will never happen), but product placement is a very popular feature in contemporary games where it is actually fitting to find such items.

However, different products are sold in different territories, and not all advertising will be global. The ability to localize advertising may be of great benefit to the advertisers themselves.

Sometimes a product is even used as a gameplay feature. *Worms 3D* featured Red Bull as an item that increases the player's health. For those that know that Red Bull is an energy drink this makes perfect sense, but in countries where Red Bull is not sold, this is not going to make any sense at all.

Testing

The most immediate thought people have when testing is mentioned is bug testing—trying to find errors in the game. However, there are a number of types of testing that may occur during the course of the project.

Focus Testing

Focus testing is the act of gauging public opinion about aspects of your game and using that feedback to make improvements. Large publishing houses often use this technique to make their games appeal to a wide audience.

Focus testing occurs during the early stages of a project. Focus testers are drawn from the general public from different demographics. They are shown concept drawings and early builds of the game and then questioned about various aspects such as the visual style, elements of the story, the setting, and the gameplay.

There are benefits to focus testing if used appropriately, but results can be applied overzealously, resulting in a watered-down, insipid style for the game. The general public tend to like the familiar, and canvassing a large group of people results in half the quality of each particular style. Uniqueness should be nurtured and encouraged and ultimately results in much more memorable experiences for the audience. Design by committee never really works.

Quality Control

Being a commercial product means that it has to adhere to certain standards so that people will part with their hard earned cash to buy it. This is especially applicable when making games for consoles. In the PC world there is no real limit as to what can be released, save what a publisher is willing to publish and what is legally accepted in the country of sale. Console games, on the other hand, are subject to a number of different requirements, mainly because of the console manufacturer's demands about what they will or will not allow on their consoles. Releasing a bug-ridden mess of a game is not going to do anyone any favors, so quality control is a necessary phase of development.

On a console title there are generally three phases of bug testing and fixing:

- Development testing
- Alpha
- Beta

Development Testing

Often a test team is not put on a project until it is near completion, when bug fixing really kicks in. However, a project can definitely benefit from having a few testers onboard much earlier in the development cycle.

At earlier stages testers can seek out areas where there are underlying problems with mechanics and push certain areas to try to find crash bugs. However, it is essential that the test team know exactly where the level is in development so they are not bringing up problems with elements that have not been fully realized. They must also bear in mind that placeholder elements may exist and require the ability to see beyond the rough work to visualize the mechanics behind it.

Get this stage right, and issues can be caught early and solved before they become a major problems. Get it wrong, and the development team could become frustrated and disillusioned with the testing team, which can have devastating consequences later in development. Often testing is sneered upon by members of the development team, but it must be remembered that testing is an essential aspect of creating a good game.

Alpha

Alpha is usually deemed to be content complete; that is, all content should be in the game. During this stage the game balancing will enter its intense phase, as extensive playtesting and tweaking occurs. However, there is usually slippage, meaning that content is still going in or, worse still, the dreaded feature creep has occurred. Feature creep is the addition of features as the game progresses that take it beyond the original design. Some feature creep early in the project is often desirable, but by the time Alpha comes along, everything should be finalized or problems are going to ensue.

At this point a lot of playtesting, bug testing, and bug fixing will be occurring alongside the game balancing. This is usually a very hectic time in the project lifecycle.

Beta

Once Beta occurs, all content is locked down and frozen. Only bug fixing should be occurring. Letting balancing slip into Beta can be risky, as it can have several knock-on effects. Often at this point in the game much of the team has moved on to the next project, and those left behind have become honorary testers (designers often fall into this category).

Bugs are often classed according to severity, for example, A-type bugs being crashes or game blockers, B being major bugs, and C being minor bugs. Beta-phase bug fixing concentrates on removing A- and B-type bugs and catching as many C-type bugs as time allows. Often there are accepted limits of bugs that can be put in the final game, though A-type bugs should never be allowed through.

The result of the completion of the Beta phase should be a version of the game ready to enter the submission phase.

Playtesting

Playtesting (and a usability study) is a vital stage for game balancing that provides designers with information on how players perceive the game and allows them to fine-tune the experience. Playtesting is discussed in detail in the later game balancing chapter.

THE CONSOLE SUBMISSION PROCESS

The submission process is a required stage of console development, where the finalized game is sent to a quality control division at the console manufacturer to gain permission to publish on that console. This process usually takes a few weeks for the manufacturer to properly assess the game and will result in either a pass or a fail. Ideally a developer would like a game to go through console submission the first time and pass, as this will save them several weeks' work and a lot of panic. In order to achieve this the game must adhere to the manufacturer's technical requirements and be free of crashes or game-breaking bugs.

Technical Requirements

The manufacturer's quality control team tests the game to find errors and game-breaking situations in a similar manner to the quality control for the developer or publisher, but the game is also tested against a number of technical requirements laid down by the manufacturer. If any of these stages fail, the game will fail submission (although some minor faults may be let through).

Games often fail because of not meeting one of the technical requirements laid down in the documents that are supplied to the developer. Spending some design time reviewing these documents is a good way of saving lots of headaches later in the project development cycle.

Each console manufacturer's demands tend to be different and change over the lifetime of a console. Guidelines may even differ between various territories. It can be problematic for a developer working on a multiplatform title that requires several different technical requirements to be fulfilled. In this instance particular care will have to be taken when managing the technical requirements and when beginning the console submission process (often the submissions may be staggered to each of the different manufacturers).

There are many aspects that Technical Requirements cover. Many of these are only really applicable to the programming team, but other requirements will have a direct effect on the design of the game itself.

Basic Requirements

There are several basic requirements to any game:

Free of bugs: The game should not crash, lock up, or contain game-breaking scenarios.

Aging: The game should be able to play for extended periods without problems (e.g., the dreaded memory leak).

Error messages: The game should display the correct information when particular errors occur.

System

System requirements specify set methods of accessing basic components of the console and the libraries supplied. This is to prevent bad use of the hardware leading to data loss or corruption. It is unlikely the designers will need to concern themselves with the details of these requirements, as they are integral to the core architecture of the code itself.

Data Storage

Data storage is one of the areas where submissions often fail, as there are strict guidelines on how data is stored and messages that are displayed to the player when reading and writing data.

File size: Data must fit on the storage device (obviously).

Free space: The memory card interface should indicate if there is not enough space and allow the player to free some up if necessary. The players should also be able to continue the game without saving but must be warned that they cannot save again.

Memory card format: The game should warn the player if the memory card is incorrectly formatted.

Warning messages: Messages should be displayed whenever loading from or saving to the card, warning the player not to turn off the console or remove the memory card during the load or save.

Error messages: Messages should be displayed if a save or load goes wrong and allow the player to retry the operation. Corrupted or damaged data should also present their own specific warnings.

Progress bar: Progress bars for loading and saving to the memory card are encouraged.

Load times: There should not be a blank screen for a prolonged period of time when loading.

Peripherals

A number of typical requirements are associated with peripherals such as controllers:

Vibration: Vibration must be able to be switched off.

Disconnection: If the peripheral is accidentally disconnected, the game should pause and a warning message be displayed to allow the player to reconnect the peripheral.

Bespoke peripherals: Menu systems should allow navigation with the traditional controller as well as with the bespoke peripheral.

Calibration: If peripherals need calibration, options to calibrate them must be implemented.

User Interface

Manufacturers like to encourage a number of standards for products released on their consoles to unify the products available and make menu control, in particular, instantly familiar to the consumer.

Navigation: Often specific buttons are assigned to OK and Cancel actions.

Feedback: Audio and visual feedback to UI elements is desired, such as a highlight bar to show selection.

Prompts: Button prompts should be shown on menu screens to indicate the possible inputs.

Volume: Music and audio effects should be individually adjustable.

Terminology: Specific phrases should be used when referring to various parts of the hardware such as the console itself, the controller, buttons on the console, Input/Output ports, memory cards, operating system screens, and so on.

Submission Fail

Should submission fail, there will be a list of reasons why that submission has failed. At this point the team will need to work flat out to get the failure points fixed so that the game can be resubmitted.

Failure of submission can be a fairly demoralizing experience, but it happens on many games, so it is by no means a rare occurrence. It does mean the team will have to pull together for one last push to get the game out the door. Remember that you will learn more from the projects that have problems than those that go smoothly from start to finish.

Submission Pass

So your game has passed submission! Congratulations are definitely the order of the day. Time for a well-earned rest and a little recuperation, as the crunch of the previous weeks have probably taken their toll on the team. The game itself now goes into the manufacturing process, where the final discs and boxes are created and packaged, which then enter the distribution channels to wing their way around the world and onto game store shelves.

What happens now? At this point the team is likely to start ramping up on the next project, perhaps a sequel or maybe something completely new. However, there are always some loose ends that should be tied up from the previous project. One very useful task to perform is a postmortem of the project to see what went wrong and what went right. This knowledge will put you in good stead for the next project. And so the process begins all over again.

SUMMARY

In this chapter we learned about the console design process. This design process has become fairly standard across the industry, as it produces results. The process typically includes the following steps:

Conception: Game ideas can come from all manner of inspiration, but there are several processes that a designer should go through when developing a concept:

- **General research:** Looking at other games and other types of media for inspiration and ideas.
- **Brainstorming:** Getting together to thrash out ideas and refine particular designs.
- **Market research:** Surveys, focus groups, and other people's data can give insight into what the game consumers want.

The Proposal: Whether writing a pitch document for a licensed game or a sales document for an original concept, the proposal helps solidify the vision for the game and acts as a point of reference for the development team.

Concept Approval: An essential part of the process is the application to the console manufacturer for concept approval. This is generally all but a formality to allow the development team access to development kits.

Preproduction: The first stage of actual game development is to establish the main functional aspects of the game design.

- **Macro design:** An overview of the game mechanics and the content of the game.
- **Prototype:** A proof of concept for game mechanics that provides immediate feedback to the developers.
- **Vertical slice:** A much more polished area of the game to give a feel of the final product.

Production: Once production begins, development begins in earnest. For the designers there are several elements that will be produced during this stage:

- **Function specification (aka micro design):** A detailed breakdown of the game mechanics and their functionality.
- **Content:** Documents outlining in detail all the content that will be produced for the game—animation lists, level designs, and so on.

- **Implementation:** For the designers this will mean tying together all the various aspects of the game as they come together in a world editor and may mean scripting all the various scenarios as well.
- **Localization:** The process of localizing language is not done by the designers, but must be kept in mind when designing the game itself.
- **Testing:** The game will go through several stages of testing. Focus testing allows designers to refine the game design to suit the marketplace. Playtesting improves and helps balance the game once it has come together. Finally quality control is performed by the test department to ensure that a decent product is produced and is free of bugs.

The console submission process: A final stage that is unique to console development is the submission process, where the final game is tested by the console manufacturer to ensure that the product is suitable for release.

Following this process in developing your game should ensure that all the necessary steps are taken to get a game design from initial conception to its place on the game store shelf.

However, the way in which games are produced is likely to start changing in the near future as digital distribution is becoming a reality on game consoles. This will remove the whole manufacturing and distribution process from the product lifecycle of game development, meaning we may see changes in the needs of publishers. It could mean the removal of the game publisher altogether for smaller games, as the developer will now be able to sell directly to the customer. In short, it is an exciting time to become a game developer, as a new future is being shaped at this very moment.

GAMEPLAY

In This Chapter

- Defining Gameplay
- Game Rules
- Types of Gameplay
- Gameplay Pace
- Goals
- Emotions in Gameplay
- Game Duration
- Multiplayer Gameplay

Throughout the defining characteristic of a game in comparison to other forms of media is the nature of its interactivity—commonly called gameplay. It is gameplay that is the draw for many players. The prettiest graphics and most involving narratives in the world won't count for anything if the gameplay does not engage its players.

In this book we are looking at gameplay in character-based games. This narrows our focus a little, but there are still plenty of facets of gameplay to be explored:

- Defining gameplay
- Game rules
- Types of gameplay
- Gameplay pace
- Goals
- Emotions in gameplay
- Game duration
- Multiplayer gameplay

DEFINING GAMEPLAY

Many studies of both games and play have been conducted over the years, but not many discuss how to design gameplay. Gameplay can be thought of in simple terms as the amount of enjoyment a player experiences while playing a game. For a more in-depth look at this area, read *Rules of Play: Game Design Fundamentals*, by Katie Salen and Eric Zimmermann [SalenZimmerman04]. Every designer should have this book in his collection. Much of what is discussed in this section can be found in much greater detail there, as they strive to set down a formal method for the theoretical discussion of games.

Defining a Game

We have all played games at some point in our life—from whiling away hours playing board games to the physical activity of playing a game of football or tennis. Just what is it that defines a game?

A game is a system that is defined by its rules. In playing a game, players engage in some form of conflict. From this conflict there is an outcome (such as win, lose, or draw) [SalenZimmerman04].

This definition presents us with several points that outline the boundaries that separate games from everyday activities:

- Players interact with a system, meaning that all games are systems.
- There is artificial conflict. Any dangers or conflict that occurs will not cause harm to the players in reality.
- Rules bound the players of the game. All game systems are formed by rules that govern how players can behave within the game and limit their interactions.
- Each game has a quantifiable outcome or goal. This goal may be a clear winner, defined as a score, the progression of a character, or beating the game design to complete a narrative.

Defining the Act of Play

Play is an integral part of human nature that has come to be regarded by modern Western society as childish. However, play is an essential part of our continued intellectual and emotional development and continues to permeate all aspects of our lives in adulthood. Parlor games, board games, computer games, sport—nearly all forms of recreation—involve some element of play. It is how we relax and unwind, and it can also help us to learn.

Play is a broad term that can exist outside the paradigm of a game. However, as game designers, it is the play of games that intrigues us. Four types of play are described in the work of sociologist Roger Caillois, which has become an accepted model for game designers:

Agon: Competition to determine an ultimate winner
Alea: Chance and the act of gambling on chance
Mimicry: Assuming another personality or playing a role
Ilinx: The feeling of vertigo due to physical movement such as acceleration

These types of play are applied to computer games to varying degrees. Agon and mimicry are the most immediately obvious, as all games feature some form of conflict and place the player in some form of virtual world. Alea plays more of a supporting role, as randomness is a delicate balance: too little and the game will always play the same, too much and the game can descend into chaos. Ilinx, on the other hand, is a more difficult type of play to replicate. While console games cannot recreate the direct experience of acceleration and movement, the sensations of speed and acceleration can be mimicked, resulting in a slight sensation of the real thing.

Furthermore, play can be structured into two extremes: spontaneous play (paidia) and structured play (ludus). Bateman and Boon define these two groups as improvised toyplay and structured gameplay [BatemanBoon05].

While we talk extensively about gameplay, toyplay also exists in games where the players define their own goals within the structure of the game rules. Sim games are a prime example of the popularity of toyplay in computer games, but toyplay also pervades more narrative-based games such as *Grand Theft Auto*. Here a whole city environment is created to let the players run freely and interact almost as they please. The result is a very free-form experience. Toyplay is often called sandbox play.

GAME RULES

Rules are an essential part of any game; a game does not exist without rules. They define the boundaries of play and determine how players interact with the game world. A computer game is essentially entirely composed of rules—the code that defines the game. A well-designed set of rules is conducive to the creation of good gameplay, as in turn ineffective or poorly designed rules will shatter the feel of the game. Rules are only part of the story, but they provide the foundations upon which everything else is built. Thus, they need careful design and serious consideration from the very outset.

Simulation and Abstraction

Simulation is the act of modeling a system in order to replicate its behavior in software. Abstraction is the act of simplifying a system so that it can be modeled. Abstraction is therefore a natural process of simulation.

The level of abstraction will define the depth of the simulation. A system that is highly abstracted will result in a simulation that is not as deep as one in which abstraction is at a much lower level. A fine balance exists between the desire to create an accurate simulation and the desire to have a high level of abstraction to simplify the system.

Goals of Simulation

A simulation is created to model a real or fictional system. The goal is to create a simulation that makes the system believable to the player and fun to play. Two main factors drive the believability: realism and expectation.

Realism

Achieving realism means trying to accurately recreate the system so that it represents exactly what would happen in reality. Initially this would seem to be an ideal goal, as it suggests the most believability. Several issues are involved with trying to attain realism. First, real life tends not to be much fun a lot of the time, meaning a completely true-to-life game experience is not going to be much fun either. Games condense a lot of action into a small space to keep the game flowing. Second, the players may have only experienced the actions they will perform through other media such as film. The firing of a real gun is a very different experience from the sounds and sights of a gun firing on film. This makes realism again seem flat and dull.

Expectations

Much of a game simulation is based on player expectations rather than realism. So much of our experience is shaped by what we read, hear, or watch in today's media that we have come to expect certain elements from experiences we have never encountered first hand.

Thus, we have preconceptions about how the world may behave and how certain systems ought to work. If these expectations are not met, the players may feel that the game is not believable or is too flat and uninteresting. The solution is to research perceptions of a possible system as well as to observe reality, so that any preconceptions can be woven into the simulation and thus improve its believability.

Reasons for Abstraction

While a deep simulation is likely to provide a believable experience, abstraction may be required for several reasons:

- Technical limitations
- Budget restrictions
- Redundancy
- Clarity

Technical Limitations

Unfortunately processing power still imposes heavy restrictions on the depth of a simulation. It will be a very long time before a game simulation would model the world atom by atom (a pretty pointless exercise anyway). Thus, many abstractions are made so that the game can physically be constructed. These kinds of abstractions are numerous, such as fading out dead bodies to free up space for new entities.

As technology marches ever forward, many of these abstractions may fall by the wayside, but there will always be some physical limits as to what can be done with the technology available, and thus we need abstractions to deal with these problems.

Another aspect of the technical limitations is the running of the simulation on areas of the game that the player cannot even see. Anything outside of the scope of the player's range can simply be switched off until it is required. This is usually done by some form of sectorizing system.

Budget Restrictions

Time, money and manpower are limited resources on any project. Deep simulation requires a lot of resources. Hence, abstractions are often made to scale the simulation to a feasible level. For example, it would be nice if every game could have multiple interactions with every object in the world, but doing so can mean huge demands on already strained resources. Defining abstractions to keep the level of interactions reasonable ensures that a project will be delivered on time and within budget.

Redundancy

A simulation could be taken to crazy depths (within the bounds of technology) and have very little or even no impact on the player. A programmer was once heard to say that he would model the constellations in the sky so that they were accurately positioned for that time period. This kind of simulation depth in a game is redundant, as it has absolutely no bearing on the game itself, and it's unlikely that any player would ever notice it anyway.

This is an extreme example, but there are much more down-to-earth simulation depths that are just as redundant. Often complex simulations can have the same impact as a clever abstraction. For example, it is perfectly feasible to accurately model wind blowing through trees, but a simple animation or procedural movement will have exactly the same effect with much less processing power required. Knowing which aspects of a simulation require depth and which do not will ensure that time is spent concentrating on aspects of the simulation that will have greater return for the game.

Clarity

A complex simulation is all very well, but if it is ineffectively communicated to the player, then it is next to useless. By abstracting an element, it can be simplified so that it is more readily understood or stands out from its surroundings to be more visible.

Rules of the World

In creating virtual worlds, some elements of the real world must be simulated, and abstractions must be made for technical reasons.

Physics

Physics is a simulation of the natural laws of the universe. Therefore, a game will contain some elements of this model in some form. Some games have extremely simplified simulations of physics with a very basic model of gravity and collision detection. Other games attempt to recreate much more complex physics to accurately model complex collisions, dynamics, and so on. However, game physics simulations are still pretty much in their infancy, and there are plenty more aspects that can be modeled to improve the simulation. At present many of the more complex simulations such as fluid dynamics are limited by processing power, but these barriers will inevitably be overcome.

Time

Two aspects of time need to be considered in a virtual world: passage of time and persistence.

Passage of Time

As yet it seems that no one has invented a time machine, so in reality the passage of time is a constant fixed element. However, in a single-player game at least, the passage of time in the game world does not have to match the passage of time in the real world. We can manipulate time in a number of ways:

Skip time: Removing boring sections or suggesting the passage of time between level loads or cutscenes. This could be any length of time. For instance, we might jump from a character's youth to his mature years from one level to another.

Time dilation: The slowing down or speeding up of time.

Time distortion: Having two time lines occurring in one space (for instance, the player being at normal speed while those around are in slow motion).

Time reverse: Rewinding sections of time to correct mistakes.

Persistence

Persistence is the lifetime of an object and exists as an abstraction because of technical limitations. When we are out of range of an object, we can stop running the simulation and even remove the object entirely. Persistence is an important part of level design and is dealt with in depth in Part 3, "World Building."

Space

Owing to both technical and budget restrictions, the size of a world is limited; only a limited amount of data will fit into memory at any one time, and only a certain amount of data will be created over the course of the project.

The technical limitations of memory also mean that the world needs to be split into separate chunks, often called "levels" or "missions." These can be distinct chunks of time and space utterly separate from one another or may be made to flow from one to the next. The division of space is covered in more detail in Part 3.

Rules of the Game

The rules of the game are the limitations placed on the objects within the world and, more specifically, the available interactions between them.

Interactivity

Interactivity is what defines the scope of gameplay. It defines exactly what the player is able to do in that world. A game without interactivity no longer is a game, but simply a show for the player to watch.

Choice

For a meaningful action to exist, there needs to be some element of choice involved. This choice may be as simple as choosing whether to interact with the object or not, but can become much more complex if multiple choices are offered for interaction with an entity or situation.

When a choice is made, a response is given by the system—known as feedback or reaction. The depth of an interaction is defined by the relationship between the choice and the response. Every interactive action within a game represents a choice, from the choice to press the trigger to the choice of what to say to a nonplayer character (NPC). Some choices occur extremely frequently, such as which direction to move in. Others happen much more rarely, such as using a ladder.

Action, Reaction and Feedback

For meaningful interactivity, every action performed in the game needs to have an outcome—a reaction. An action does not have to have an immediately visible reaction, but without any form of feedback to the player, it is almost impossible to gauge the result of that action. Therefore, having some feedback, whether it be visual, aural, or through rumble in the controller, is essential for the players to feel that they are having an impact on the world.

Feedback can suffer from two problems: noise and overcomplexity. Noise is extraneous information that confuses the player. Hence, important information needs to stand out or be isolated from all other action. Overcomplex feedback gives back too much information, much of which may be redundant. For the best translation of information, the feedback should be short and to the point—only necessary information. For example, a verbose mission objective is likely to confuse a player, whereas a short, snappy line will get the objective across immediately.

Player Abilities

Player abilities are the physical interactions the player can make within the world. There are several possible interactions for the player in an action–adventure game:

Movement set: The various movements, acrobatics, and physical attacks the player character can perform

Useable objects: The switches, levers, and other mechanisms that the player can operate within the world (though they might need a specific skill to interact with them)

Pickups: The keys, weapons, health, power-ups, and other inventory items that can be collected and stored or used immediately

Skills: Latent abilities the player character may have, such as magic, or skills that enable him to use objects in the world, such as a lock-picking skill to open doors

Conversations: The interactive dialog the player character might have with other characters in the game (much of the dialog in a game tends to be non-interactive, for example, during cutscenes.)

Consistency

One very important factor in the design of good rules for a game is consistency. Having a consistent set of rules enforces a solid game language that the player can understand. When the player comes to perform an interaction with consistent rules in place, he knows the likely outcome of his actions. An unexpected result of an action may occur if this is not the case, breaking the knowledge the player has gained and more than likely causing frustration. Let's say, for example, that we have a lever next to a door. When we pull this lever, we expect the door to open. If this has happened every time, we have a consistent rule. If, however, pulling one particular lever sets off an explosion that kills the player, the consistency is broken and the player is likely to be annoyed.

There is an exception to this rule, however. We can break consistency if we provide a clue to the possible outcome of the action. If our explosive lever is surrounded by scorch marks and dead bodies, the player might be a little more suspicious before pulling the lever (even so, instant death is a pretty harsh punishment for such a simple action).

Emergence

Emergent gameplay defines elements that, when they come together, create gameplay that the designer was not expecting. This can create beneficial emergence, where a really exciting gameplay element is discovered, or detrimental emergence, where an unwanted result occurs. The hope is to maximize beneficial emergence and remove all detrimental elements.

TYPES OF GAMEPLAY

There are different types of gameplay—structures that form rules for particular interactions. All of these types are constructed from two basic forms: conflict and experience.

Conflict

All games feature some kind of conflict. The player must work as an individual or as part of a team to resolve this conflict. They may work alone or cooperatively with other players against a computer-controlled scenario or fight competitively against other players. Without some form of conflict, there is no reason for structure—no set goals for the player to pursue. It becomes toyplay as opposed to gameplay.

In *Rules of Play* Salen and Zimmerman identify three types of conflict: territorial, economic, and knowledge [SalenZimmerman04]. These can be applied to a number of types of gameplay we might expect to find in an action–adventure game.

Territorial Conflict

A strategy game has a very visual and instantly appreciable territorial conflict (the players are literally fighting for control of territory), but in an action–adventure game territory is a little more abstract.

While the player is not usually directly fighting to gain control of territory, he is trying to progress through the game world. The conflict arises owing to obstacles placed in the way of this progress that must be overcome. The structure of these obstacles defines exactly what the core mechanics of the game will be—the key interactions of the system.

Skill-Based Obstacles

Skill-based obstacles require the player to perform dexterous maneuvers. These can have several different forms:

Real-time Combat: Combat is perhaps the most obvious form of conflict. In its real-time form it will require dexterity from the player to perform the required moves or to aim and fire successfully.

Acrobatics: Using a variety of complex maneuvers to negotiate a carefully laid out space. This has been brought to a high level by the *Prince of Persia* series, which features all sorts of acrobatic moves such as wall runs, pole swinging, and so on.

Timing: Timing-skill obstacles challenge the player to pick a precise moment to perform an action in order to avoid the obstacle. For example, it might mean dodging an axe swinging like a pendulum.

Rhythm: Rhythm-based challenges require the player to follow a pattern and match it as closely as possible.

Reaction: Reaction skills put the player in a situation that requires him to respond quickly to avoid danger or to deal with a sudden action.

Stealth: Stealth requires trying to avoid detection by enemy entities such as guards or security cameras. This is like a game of cat and mouse. Stealth may use elements of noise, light, and movement as mechanics for detecting the player's presence. Stealth gameplay also features cerebral elements and pattern recognition.

Race: Move to the front to be the first to cross the finish line. Races may be against other characters or players or a race to finish in the fastest time, but there must be some form of competition involved.

Cerebral Obstacles

Cerebral obstacles are very often called puzzles. The use of a cerebral puzzle obstacle usually results in a very different pace for the gameplay—often much slower and more methodic. However, this pace can be picked up by enforcing time restrictions on an obstacle.

A few pitfalls can occur with cerebral obstacles. They might be able to enter a broken state, where the player cannot continue the game because the puzzle is no longer solvable. It is important to have some kind of reset to allow players to return to a default state if they get too confused or ensure that the puzzle can never enter a broken state. Another problem is that elements can be destroyed or lost. Often there will need to be some kind of respawning item to ensure that the puzzle can be completed.

Whether pace is affected or not, there are lots of possibilities for puzzles in a game:

Turn-based combat: While real-time combat requires various strategies, it is very much a skill-based type of gameplay. Turn-based combat, on the other hand, is not about reaction and dexterity, but instead about choosing the right tactics and formulating a strategy. As such, it could be considered to be very cerebrally orientated.

Spatial: Many puzzles such as block pushing appear to be skill based, but are in fact much more cerebrally orientated. Others such as acrobatic traversal blend the two, so there is a lot of skill and thinking involved. Any puzzle in which there is some traversal of the environment or manipulation of space to access previously inaccessible areas can be said to be a spatial puzzle.

Codes and ciphers: Codes are a common obstacle placed in the way of a player's progress. Codes will each have different ways of deciphering them. Some puzzles are not immediately obvious as being codes, such as a puzzle to link up two lines by rotating pieces on a board or turning the hands on a clock face to a particular time. However, these are forms of codes. A code needs to either be easy to crack (which in real life would be a pretty useless code) or needs a cipher—instructions for decoding the corresponding code. Some game elements may appear to be codes, such as a keypad that you need to acquire the number for, but are in fact just memory tests or require collection.

Logic: Logic puzzles require logical thought to arrive at a conclusion. This may be mathematical, word play, or some similar form of puzzle that the player has to calculate or determine. They can be difficult to use, as there is generally only one solution and the player may well not be able to solve it.

Cooperative: These skill puzzles require two or more characters or players to work together to help each other solve the puzzle. For example, one character holds open a door for another to enter.

Economic Conflict

Economic conflict occurs with the acquisition or loss of resources or commodities. Such conflict can contain a lot of changing variables within any period of time or may concern a very limited element at any one moment. Several forms of gameplay fit within the economic conflict category:

Combat: While combat is an obstacle to progression, it also contains economic conflict with battles for health, ammunition, and so on.

Collection: A large part of economic conflict is the acquisition of items. Collection is generally performed through either exploration or combat. Collection can entail the acquisition of items, score, ratings, and so on. Items such as a key might be required for progression. This makes them territorial conflicts as well as economic.

Trading: Collecting might be performed for the sheer pleasure of accumulation, but it is generally performed to engage in trading. The conflict arises from the need to collect enough of a particular resource such as money to be able to exchange it for another item.

Gambling: The player may have to trust in luck (and perhaps a little skill) to try to receive gains. The conflict is in knowing the odds and taking risks in the hope that they pay off.

Construction: The player may have to create or build an object. This tends to be part of strategy or management games rather than action–adventure games but may be featured in mechanics such as character creation.

Management: The player may have to control and tweak particular elements. Again this tends to be a very large part of strategy and, of course, management games, but does appear in various guises in action–adventure games. For example, the game might feature detailed inventory management.

Conflicts of Knowledge

Conflicts of knowledge are those that require acquisition and utilization of information. Several forms of gameplay are based around this:

Memory: Memory-based puzzles require the player to remember information to solve the puzzle or use it for exploiting a weakness in the case of a boss fight. Memory puzzles that block progress can also be considered to have territorial conflict. The problem with a memory-based puzzle is that it can be terminal if the player has forgotten the information. There should be some way of finding the clue again, but having the clue immediately to hand will make it no longer a memory test, but simple information regurgitation.

Knowledge test: This is a test of the player's knowledge of information in the game world (intrinsic) or outside the game (extrinsic). Examining the game world for information may consist of simply looking but might also involve more meaningful interaction such as text being displayed that explains specific elements in the world. Much of this information will just enhance the narrative, but it might also be used for the process of deduction. The use of extrinsic knowledge is not always a good idea. In a contemporary setting it may work, but it relies on the player's knowledge (or ability to research). In many cases it breaks the fourth wall and feels out of place.

Deduction: Some puzzles offer clues to the players and ask them to deduce the answer. Deduction-based gameplay suffers from one very large problem, in that if the player is unable to make the deductions, then he is unable to complete the puzzle. If this is an obstacle to progression, the player will be stuck and will have to cheat by looking elsewhere for the answer to the problem, which is not particularly desirable.

Interrogation and interview: This requires conversing with game characters to acquire knowledge. It may involve choosing the right things to ask, a skill-based puzzle, or elements of chance against a player attribute to extract information.

Experience

While conflict tends to be the driving force for much of the gameplay, experience is also a huge and essential part of most games. For many types of player, the experience is more important than the challenge [BatemanBoon05].

Experience encompasses a number of elements of narrative: story, setting, ambience, as well as more utilitarian constructs such as the user interface. The gameplay that arises can be split into a few basic types:

Exploration: Exploration is a key element for many players. The ability to discover new areas and to progress through the game world can be a very enticing part of the game experience. Different game structures will affect the exploration potential in different ways. Very linear games restrict this to the progression though the laid-out line. Free-form worlds allow the players to discover the world for themselves, but a far less rigid game structure can make it difficult to create challenge.

Narrative progression: Much of the joy of a game can be experienced through the progression of a narrative. Players often want to follow a well-written plot through to its conclusion. However, a poorly structured and badly executed narrative can be off-putting.

Character growth: The building and advancement of a character can provide a wealth of opportunity for player satisfaction. A lot of growth is performed through economic conflict, but for many it is the experience of customizing and nurturing their characters that holds the most pleasure.

Sandbox and toyplay: In free-form worlds players are much more able to set their own goals and agendas and make their own rules to define their play. Often this kind of play tends to be short lived but can be fulfilling. *Grand Theft Auto* is a good example of a game that offers good opportunities for sandbox play thanks to its free-form world. At any point the player can engage in all manner of activities, such as driving, shooting, or just causing general mayhem.

Sensory experience: Games can be visually and aurally stunning, which leads to the play of games to experience these sensory wonders. The only problem with this is that the constant march of technology can very quickly make a jaw dropping game become the norm and eventually make it look dated.

Moral choices: Players may be made to make moral decisions that will have an outcome either on characters in the world or the player characters themselves. In some games the consequence of a moral decision will take the player through different paths in the game. Both *Black & White*® and *Fable*®, two very different styles of game from developer Lionhead Studios, feature moral choice throughout the course of the game. While in *Black & White* the player takes on the role of a benevolent or malevolent god, in *Fable* the player is free to guide his avatar on the course of good or evil as he sees fit.

GAMEPLAY PACE

The pace of a game is an important element in defining its feel. Pacing is influenced by a number of factors:

Type of gameplay: Each type of gameplay has a natural pace of its own.

Speed of the action: Within an action section the speed of character movement will determine how fast the pace is.

Number of threats: The more danger the player is in, the more adrenaline will be pumping and the faster the pace of action will seem.

Interaction breaks: Cinematic cutscenes and similar sequences that remove control from the player allow a stop in interaction for a few moments. Though these can be fast paced in themselves, they still offer a break from the concentration required in controlling the game.

Pacing the game correctly is an important design skill. High-action sections can be exhilarating, but if they go on for too long, they can become tiring or monotonous. The solution is to pace the game carefully by mixing types of gameplay—having moments of intense action tempered with quiet moments to allow the players to take stock and collect their thoughts. More sedate adventure games will have long sections of relaxed gameplay punctuated with moments of sudden or intense action. Ultimately, the pacing of the game needs to suit the style of the game.

ON THE CD
The file Balance-LevelPace.xls on the companion CD-ROM shows an example of changing pace over the course of a level. This file can be used to graph a visual representation of what a player might be feeling across the breadth of a level.

Two forms of pacing occur in gameplay:

Natural pacing: This is the natural feel of a type of gameplay, based only on the defining structures of that type. High-action gameplay is naturally faster paced than stealthy, cerebral, or exploring gameplay.

Forced pacing: The gameplay pace is altered by forcing a constraint onto the dynamic, such as a time limit or reduction in health. This forces the pace to become faster than it would be naturally and can turn even slow-paced cerebral gameplay into an adrenaline ride. Forced pacing can work well in certain situations, but, if used poorly, can cause some serious frustration. Ensure that such sections are easy to replay if failed (place a checkpoint just before them).

GOALS

Goals are the reason we play games. They are the targets we aim to reach, the carrot dangling ahead that keeps us playing. Goals act as a marker for progress, letting us know how well (or how badly) we are performing.

Types of Goal

Within the structure of gameplay there are two basic types of goal:

Embedded goals: Those defined by the designers—the core mechanics of the game; pre-scripted challenges and targets that the player must complete.

User-defined goals: Those created by the players as they play the game. More free-form games allow much larger scope for user-defined goals.

Motivation

Goals are driven by a number of different motivations. Different people have different needs and desires that they want to fulfill when playing games:

Desire to win: Nearly everyone wants success, but some people desire winning more than others. The act of achieving a goal is winning in itself. However, the feeling of satisfaction is usually proportional to the challenge required to achieve the goal.

Desire to learn: We all like to expand our knowledge and skills. This desire leads us to want to become better at the game, so that ultimately we can win.

Desire to experience: The fun of becoming immersed in an experience is often one of the greatest draws for players.

Desire to control: Our mastery over others or over a system is a strong motivational force.

Desire to create: The feeling of creation and subsequent ownership can be a very strong motivational element.

Desire to share: People who like to socialize, compete, or cooperate will want to interact with other people and enjoy a shared experience.

Desire to accumulate: Many of us like to accumulate commodities. Usually this is to gain something we desire. For some it may be for the act of accumulation itself (collectors).

Goals should be designed to satisfy one or more of these motivations; otherwise, they will not have any purpose for the player. However, different players will respond in different ways to different goals.

Levels of Goal

Goals can be split into three levels according to approximate timescale, although these boundaries are fairly fuzzy:

Low-level goals: Immediate, moment-to-moment gameplay such as choosing which direction to move in or what action to perform.

Mid-level goals: Short-term goals such as completing a challenge, meeting a mission objective, defeating a particular group of enemies or finishing a level.

High-level goals: Long-term goals such as completing the game, exploring every nook and cranny, and collecting every object.

The definitions for each type of goal differ from game to game. In a single-player game the mid-level goals might be to complete a level or mission, and long-term goals might be to complete the game. In a multiplayer match-based game the mid-level goal would be to win a round, and the high-level goal would be to win the match. The timescale of each goal is based on the time frame of a complete narrative unit.

Narrative context is applied to each of these goals to change it from being a cold mechanical system to a goal that makes sense within the world. For example, the goal of completing the game is given meaning, becoming "defeat the evil wizard" or something similar.

EMOTIONS IN GAMEPLAY

Game designers have been striving to imbue games with emotion for years, and slowly we are succeeding to involve players more and more on an emotional level as they play a game. There are two categories of emotions we can appeal to:

- Positive emotions
- Negative emotions

Positive Emotions

In gameplay a fairly limited number of positive emotions can be expressed. Of course there is (we hope) the pleasure achieved through playing the game, but embedded within the mechanics of the game it is difficult to embody certain positive emotions. Some are a core part of gameplay, however.

Power

Power is a very important emotion used in games. Making the players feel powerful will massage their egos and make them feel good about playing the game.

Imagine entering a combat arena with 10 other guys, and you alone take them on. Twisting and turning through the air, you pull off some astounding moves that would make Bruce Lee's jaw drop. You feel powerful; you feel good, because you know that never in a million years could you do all this in real life. That is essentially why we play games—to escape reality and do things that we could never do in our daily life.

However, it is always important to ensure that the player is still challenged; otherwise, the game can quickly become too easy and thus rather dull. Short plateaus of player power will make them feel like they have reached a new level of skill. This can be done by leveling out the difficulty for a section so that players have time to master the gameplay. Just as they are starting to feel like they have truly mastered the game, you can start to challenge them again on the way to the next plateau.

Glory

As well as making players feel powerful, the designer might also want them to feel they have triumphed under difficult circumstances. This triumph is the feeling of glory when a battle is hard won (also called fiero). However, not everyone experiences this in the same way. The challenge must meet the player's abilities; he will experience frustration if the challenge is too great or boredom if it is too little.

Love

Beyond power and glory, a few other positive emotions are embedded into the game mechanics. There have been attempts at creating emotional bonds through gameplay. One such area is the buddy system—an artificial intelligence (AI)–controlled ally that helps the player or must be protected. In most cases the buddy is more of a hindrance than a help, so the only emotional experience is one of frustration. Often the babysitting nature of the interaction can lead to players not caring about the fate of their charges, but rather wishing they didn't have to bother with them.

Love can also occur when the player invests time in creating or customizing characters. Once the player has a lot of time invested in this character, he starts to form an emotional bond (to the degree where there has been real-life violence to protagonists of the victim's virtual avatar in online games).

Humor

Laughter is a powerful force that gives us joy, a powerful emotion but also an incredibly subjective one. What makes one person laugh is unlikely to do the same for everyone.

So far humor in games has been limited to fairly immature or very basic levels of comedic understanding (with only a few notable exceptions). This is partly a limitation of the medium but has more to do with poor writing skills.

Good comedy is very difficult to get right—even more so when trying to appeal to a broad audience. Varying forms of humor also tend to be received very differently by different cultures.

The interactive nature of video games makes certain forms of comedy very difficult, as it breaks the viability of one of the key rules of comedy—timing. Slapstick is perhaps the easiest form of humor to integrate into gameplay, by using elements in the environment to set up comedic moments, because it is a very action-orientated form of humor. Other forms of humor tend to get written into the dialog or are created from the personality or appearance of particular characters in the game.

Negative Emotions

Many of our reaction processes are hardwired to our sensory organs, so that we can react to a situation without our brain having to preprocess the information. This survival instinct means that many of the negative emotions such as fear are more deeply engrained than many positive emotions. This makes using such emotions relatively easy.

Fear

Fear is perhaps the most powerful emotion yet used in games. If used well, it can become the main element of gameplay. Games such as *Resident Evil*®, *Silent Hill*®, *Project Zero*, and *F.E.A.R.*™ use it to great effect.

However, it is important to remember that playing on fear too much will cause the player to become desensitized. An important balance must be struck: play on their fear but don't make them jump around every corner or it will soon become normality. Pace is important. Make the players jump when they least expect it. Use the tricks of classic horror films; prey on every sense possible, both sound and vision (touch, taste, and smell are somewhat difficult to convey in digital form). Use false scary moments to keep the players on their toes and build up their tension. Remember that fear of the unknown is the most frightening of all.

Stealth games also utilize a player's fear—the fear of getting caught. Standing only a few meters away from a patrolling guard will really get the player's adrenaline pumping.

Panic

Panic is very much like fear, but it is not the overriding element of gameplay. Panic could be described as a short burst of fear that causes the player to make decisions under duress.

The chase sequence is a great method of changing game pace suddenly and provoking a reaction of panic in the player. Sudden chase sequences get the adrenaline pumping and provide a different element of gameplay, but such high-tension moments are best used sparingly and for short periods of time; otherwise, they can quickly become monotonous and lose the feeling of panic.

Anger

Anger as a reaction to a game is usually due to frustration with bad design or overly difficult sections of play. However, there are perhaps times when anger can be a useful emotion for gameplay.

Imagine having built up your character for many hours of gameplay and collected the best weapon in the game, only for some thief to run off with it just as you're about to use it. This anger is a great drive for the player to get his own back. If you dangle the carrot, the player will follow, as long as at the end of this angry journey the player gets to take out his rage on the cause of his stress.

Be careful with this one. Anger can quickly turn to frustration if you don't design it well.

GAME DURATION

The duration of a game is a contentious issue. Just how much game time should be provided to a player? How can we extend the life of a game without having to create reams of extra content?

Game Length

A single-player narrative-based game will be of a fairly fixed length, although of course, some players will take longer to complete a game than others. The issue of how long a game should be is a hotly debated one that many people have opinions on. Deciding roughly how long a game should be is a difficult task. One fact that should be kept in mind is that many game stores have a return policy of a certain number of days. If the game doesn't entice the player to keep the game for longer than this period, then the amount of returns for a game is likely to be high—and therefore profits low.

Game length also varies by genre. Simple action games usually clock in at 10 hours or more. Heavily story-based games can often clock in at twice this value. RPGs can have up to 100 hours of gameplay in some titles. A game below 10 hours is usually considered to be short. Anything below 5 hours is probably too short to justify the expense.

Whatever the game length, the truth is that a short good game experience is still better than a long dull one. Too many games have long filler sections inserted to artificially boost the game length. Ultimately it can sully the whole feel of the game.

Replayability

Certain types of game are naturally replayable, such as multiplayer matches or simple arcade experiences. Single-player, narrative-based experiences tend to be something people only play through once, meaning the longevity of the game is only as long as the narrative.

Improving the longevity of a single-player game requires adding attractive replayability incentives. Several elements can be used to increase the replayability of a game:

Secrets: Hidden locations within the levels that contain rewards such as extra items, collectibles, and so on. Just finding all the secrets can be an incentive for playing through again.

Score: Having some kind of score or rating is a great incentive to get players to try to better their previous attempts.

Time: Having a time value for each level allows players to complete levels in the quickest times possible. Some players get very obsessive about such challenges.

Collectibles: A variety of collectible items throughout the level can encourage players to try to find all of them. Offering rewards for doing so will provide further inspiration. They might be simple rewards such as concept art or may be more expansive such as opening up new game modes.

Revisit: You can enable the player to return to previous levels and use new skills to access previously inaccessible areas. This encourages players to explore as fully as possible.

New characters: Having finished the game, the player can play through with a new character that may have different skills and abilities or even have different story branches. This is a very good method of encouraging replay but is also expensive in terms of the amount of resources it may require.

Funny cheat modes: A good reward is to give the player a funny cheat mode such as big head, squeaky voices, and so on. They can be fairly simple to do and, while fairly limited in longevity, they provide a source of amusement.

While all these methods can encourage players to replay all or parts of the game, the only surefire way to encourage replayability is by crafting a good gameplay experience from the outset. Good narrative will also help get the player to reinvest time in playing the game through again. However, bear in mind that most people do not even complete games the first time round, so much of this work is done to satiate the hardcore, which could be a minority of the audience. Make sure you invest your time wisely and don't add replayability for its own sake. If it is easy to add to the game or if you have plenty of time to do it, then adding replayability will boost the gameplay experience.

MULTIPLAYER GAMEPLAY

Multiplayer gaming has been popular for a long time. Originally people crowded round one machine and shared a single screen to indulge in multiplayer action. While this kind of multiplayer gaming is still popular, the advent of the Internet has enabled people thousands of miles away to play against each other from their own homes.

Multiplayer gaming online using a PC has been popular for years, but until recently consoles have not managed to be particularly popular online. However, Microsoft's Xbox Live service has changed the face of multiplayer console gaming, and the other major manufacturers are swiftly following in their footsteps to provide online services. The future of console gaming online is looking very bright indeed.

Multiplayer gameplay for action–adventure games falls into two basic categories: cooperative and competitive.

Cooperative Gameplay

Co-operative games are usually based on the single-player game mode, allowing two players to work together to complete the narrative. Some games have this cooperative mode as their main game mechanic (*Final Fantasy Crystal Chronicles*™ or *The Legend of Zelda*®: *Four Swords* for example).

Gameplay created specifically for cooperative play can utilize several elements:

Linked actions: One player performs an action to help the other player, such as giving them a boost up to a higher ledge.

Linked attacks: Players are able to perform linked moves that initiate special attacks against their opponents.

Cooperative puzzles: The players encounter puzzles that require them to work together.

Protection: One player provides protection for the other player while he performs some action.

Some of these elements could not be incorporated into a single-player game unless the player can swap between characters or is supported by an ally AI character. Whole new sections would have to be created or tailored for a cooperative game if these gameplay elements are desired. Many games simply tack on cooperative play without any concessions to improving gameplay.

Many problems can occur when two players must be monitored rather than one. For example, a trigger that slams a door shut could lock the other character on the wrong side. Some games will need major reworking to fix these issues or will have to "cheat" a little. The above problem can be solved by teleporting the second player to a location near the player that activated the trigger.

Competitive Gameplay

Competitive gameplay is the most popular multiplayer mechanic. All sorts of games feature some kind of competitive multiplayer options, the most popular being fighting and shooting games.

Rounds

Each competitive multiplayer game is split into a number of rounds. Each round has a winning team or individual. A score may be kept of how many rounds a team or individual has won.

Some games have more hierarchy, so that a match is made up of rounds and score can be kept of how many matches have been won (beat 'em ups like *Tekken*, for example). There could be even more hierarchy than this. Just look at the structure of a tennis match: points, games, sets, and matches.

Rounds are considered to be complete when one of the following demands is met:

- Round time has elapsed.
- A set score target is reached.
- A winner has been found—all opponents have been eliminated.
- A mission objective is complete.

Game Types and Rules

There are plenty of different game types for multiplayer competitive modes, each with various sets of rules:

- Free-for-all
- Territorial
- Mission based

Free-for-All

The basic premise of a free-for-all match is every man for himself. There are a number of popular rule sets for these types of game:

Versus: Two players are pitted against each other. Only one can come out the victor by reaching a certain score or winning a number of rounds.

Death match: Each player competes to "frag" (kill) as many opponents as they can.

Team death match: Similar to death match, but you should only kill the enemy team members.

Last man standing: Every time a player is killed he is out of the round. The winner is the last man left alive.

Hold the flag: Players compete to hold a flag or similar object. The longer a player holds it, the more points he scores.

Pass the bomb: Players compete to get rid of a bomb or similar object. Each time the bomb goes off, the player holding it receives a point. The bomb is then randomly given to another player. The player with the highest points at the end of the round is the loser.

Juggernaught: A pickup makes one player more powerful than the others. Anyone who kills this "juggernaught" takes on these powers. The winner is the person who has been juggernaught for the longest period of time.

Race: Players compete to get from one point to another in the fastest time possible.

Territorial

Territorial games organize players into two or more teams. The goal of the game is to take as much territory as possible. To grab a territory, the players need to stand in a capture zone for a territory for a period of time until it comes under their control (this is to prevent immediate territory switching and to promote a sense of danger). It also encourages battles to occur at these capture points. A territory belongs to either team or is neutral. When enemy territory is captured, it usually has to turn neutral before being turned over to the capturing team. This therefore takes longer than capturing a neutral territory.

There are several variations on territorial rules:

Point accumulation: Capturing territory provides points that are accumulated each second. Different bases can be worth different amounts of points (harder to defend or busier bases tending to be worth higher points). The winning team is the team with the most points at the end of the round.

Conquest: Both teams have a permanent base but must fight for territory in the center of the map. Teams start off with a number of points (called tickets in *Battlefield*™). When they control a majority of territory, then the opponent's points start to tick down until they recapture a territory. The winner is the team with the most points at the end of the round or the team that does not reach zero points.

Biased conquest: Like conquest, but one team has a permanent base and the other does not but has all the territory and starts off with the point advantage. They must fight to keep hold of territories or they will have no place left to respawn.

Push: Territory is formed along a line, and only one territory is allowed to be captured at a time. Holding a territory opens up the next territory toward the enemy. This is like a tug of war to take territory and push toward the enemy base. Points tick down as they do in conquest.

Node linking: *Unreal® Tournament 2004* introduced the idea of node linking, which is really an advanced form of push. Basically, one territory is linked to one or two others. One node in the chain must be captured before any linking nodes can be taken.

Mission Based

Mission-based games require two or more teams to achieve specific objectives. These objectives can be fairly wide-ranging. They cause teams to either attack or defend or possibly both.

Some typical mission-based rules are:

Capture the flag: Each team has a flag. They must try to take the enemy's flag and bring it back to their own base. It features both attack and defense for both teams.

Assault: One team is designated attacker while the others defend. The attacking team must reach or destroy a certain objective within a time limit. Teams then swap, and the new attackers must attempt the same objective in a faster time. A similar idea to assault is escape, where one team must reach a point while the other team tries to stop them.

Infiltrate: One team must infiltrate the enemy area and reach some objective. The hugely popular team-based FPS *Counter-Strike®* has a bomb placement objective, where the terrorist team must plant a bomb and the counter-terrorists must try to stop them.

Rescue: One team must rescue a group of AI hostages or objects and return them to a safe zone. *Counter-Strike's* hostage rescue maps require the counter-terrorist team to rescue hostages and bring them back to the extraction point.

VIP: One team must escort a VIP or movable object through enemy territory to reach safety. The other team tries to take out the VIP or capture the object before the defending team reaches the safe zone.

Respawning

Respawning is the act of resurrecting a player once he is dead. The manner in which a character is respawned differs from game type to game type but is usually one of four methods:

Immediately: The player can respawn immediately on pressing a button. This is mainly used in free-for-all games.

Spawn delay: The player must wait for a specified time before he can respawn. This is often used in territorial or team-based games.

Scheduled reinforcements: Respawning is only allowed at a specified time. These are schedules that occur across the length of a round (simulating reinforcements arriving in battle). When players die, they might be lucky and have little time to wait or may have to wait several seconds for the next schedule (schedules shouldn't be too long in duration).

No respawn: The harshest of all is to be out for the rest of a round. If round times are short, then this is not too bad. It promotes caution and diligence, as the penalty for failure is so great (it makes for some heart in the mouth moments but also extreme frustration). *Counter-Strike* used this method very successfully.

The place a player respawns is also dependant on game type. There are basic respawn positions:

Predetermined: Spawn points are scattered at various points on a map by the designers. When being respawned, a player is placed as far away from other players as possible so he isn't unfairly killed or doesn't become the victim of spawn camping (the act of waiting near spawn points to kill people as they respawn).

Base: Each team has a base. A number of respawn points are available in their base. These are often behind one-way routes so that the enemy cannot spawn camp.

Territory selection: Territory games can let the player select any held territory in which to respawn.

Mobile respawners: Territory games may feature vehicles or objects that can act as respawners to allow tactical deployment of people. These are usually destructible so the enemy has a way of stemming the flow of opponents.

SUMMARY

Gameplay is the primary concern of the designer, as it is what will create the element of fun. In this chapter we have learned the following:

Definition of gameplay: Gameplay can be defined by the amount of enjoyment a player experiences while playing a game. Breaking this down further:

- **Game:** Games are systems defined by rules. Players engage in conflict from which there is some outcome: win, lose, or draw.
- **Play:** Four types of play—agon, alea, mimicry, and ilinx—form the two extremes of structured gameplay (ludus) and improvised toyplay (paidia).

Rules: Rules form the basis of all gameplay. These rules are of certain types:

- **Simulation and abstraction:** Simulation seeks to model real systems to replicate their behavior. Abstraction is the process of simplifying a system to allow it to be modeled. The level to which abstraction is performed determines the depth of the simulation. A simulation may try to achieve realism, but this can often fall short of expectations that players may have from seeing films, reading books, and so on. Abstraction may be made because of technical limitations, budget restrictions, redundancy, or for the sake of clarity.
- **Rules of the world:** Several systems are modeled in every game, such as some degree of physics, as well as the application of time and space.
- **Rules of the game:** Every game has rules that apply to interactivity, player abilities, and consistency that describe what players can do in the game world. From this may develop emergence—gameplay that the designer was not expecting.

Types of gameplay: There are two forms of gameplay:

- **Conflict:** Split into three types—territorial, economic, and conflicts of knowledge.
- **Experience:** Encompasses narrative elements such as story, setting, and ambience, as well as aspects of the user interface.

Gameplay pace: Pace is an important element in defining the feel of a game. This is based on the type of gameplay, the speed of the action, the number of threats, and breaks in interaction. There are two forms of pacing—natural and forced.

Goals: Goals are why we play games. There are two types of goal—embedded and user-defined. Goals are driven by different motivations and can be split into three levels: low, mid, and high.

Emotions in gameplay: Often we want to trigger particular emotions in the player—either positive or negative. We explored several techniques for doing this.

Game duration: The length of a game is a complex topic, but there are techniques for increasing the longevity of a game through replayability.

Multiplayer gameplay: Multiplayer games are either competitive or cooperative, or possibly both. Competitive games are structured around matches. Cooperative games usually require players to work together through the main narrative.

Gameplay will always continue to evolve. Much emphasis is placed on creating original concepts within the development community. In actuality evolution has a much greater role to play in game design than innovation. Innovation is required to keep us pushing into new territory, but evolution of existing concepts pushes gameplay further forward with each iteration. A good balance of both will ensure that gameplay will get better and better in the future.

NARRATIVE

In This Chapter

- Game versus Story
- Setting
- Story
- Characters

E arlier in the book we declared that one of the defining aspects of a character-based game is a narrative that drives the player through the game. Narrative is not considered vital by all game players, but there is hardly any game that is not touched by some form of narrative, whether it be *PAC-MAN*™ or *Metal Gear Solid*. The sophistication of narrative will continue to increase over the coming years, as designers are finally getting the kinds of technology that make their visions more possible. Movie-quality narrative has become a goal of many designers, but others argue that we should be looking at different ways of tackling narrative within games.

We will cover several aspects of narrative in this chapter:

- Game versus story
- Setting
- Story
- Characters

GAME VERSUS STORY

Within the field of academic game design there have appeared two distinct camps: the ludologists and the narratologists. Ludologists often argue that games should be viewed in terms of their gameplay, whereas narratologists view games as narrative devices. Some bitter battles have been fought between these two camps. In the commercial sector these arguments are pretty much immaterial. Games are composed of both gameplay and narrative elements, and both are essential to the construction of a successful title.

Narrative is not always the starting point for a game, as many games are built around a core game mechanic. However, it is narrative that fleshes out the game world and makes it real. Narrative is often used to describe the story, but there is more than just story driving the narrative of an action–adventure title. There is narrative in every game, even if it is not immediately obvious. Even a driving game such as *Gran Turismo*® has a narrative of sorts: the player's journey through a series of races. In essence, narrative is how the game is structured; it is what pulls the player through the game. According to game designer Marc LeBlanc, there are two forms of narrative [Adams05]:

> **Embedded:** The predefined, designer-created elements that describe the world and the story within it
> **Emergent:** The story told through the player's interactions with the world

Both of these types of narrative are important. The second type of narrative arises from meaningful interactions with and situations in the game world. It is the first definition of narrative that we are concerned with in this section.

There are three important aspects of narrative:

- Suspension of disbelief
- Verisimilitude
- Continuity

Suspension of Disbelief (the Fourth Wall)

An aspect of narrative that has emerged in other media over the years is the notion of the fourth wall—an imaginary boundary between the stage and the audience, which suggests suspension of disbelief by the audience. It is generally accepted that breaking the boundary between game and reality shatters the suspension of disbelief for the player (known as breaking the fourth wall), so every aspect of the game should be acted "in character" so that the player isn't reminded that he is playing a game. Breaking of the fourth wall occurs in most games when the player is instructed to press specific buttons on the controller.

Many designers look for ways of working these breaking the fourth wall issues out of the game, but designers like Hideo Kojima (creator of the *Metal Gear Solid* series) often like to play with this concept, even breaking this fourth wall for the purposes of gameplay. *Metal Gear Solid* on the PlayStation® One had a boss character called Psycho Mantis who was able to "read your mind" and react to your actions. To defeat him you had to switch your joypad to the other port so that he could no longer read your pad input (many found this was far too obscure a puzzle and had to seek help to defeat this boss). *Metal Gear Solid 2* is itself one big narrative about breaking the fourth wall, in which the game becomes the subject of the narrative itself.

Verisimilitude

Verisimilitude describes the ability of a narrative to conform to our sense of reality, or through suspension of disbelief, our ability to believe the world created in a narrative.

A sense of reality is produced when we believe the illusion cast by the narrative to be authentic. Much of our sense of reality has been skewed by past experiences through narrative, so even though guns in the movies don't sound like they do in reality, we believe guns sound that way, as most of us experience these sounds in this manner. Plenty of other conventions present differences between reality and a constructed narrative, but we willingly accept these conventions thanks to our past experiences.

Continuity

Continuity concerns errors of consistency of plot, characters, and the objects, places, and events experienced by the audience.

Visual continuity errors are extremely common in film, where characters' appearances change from one shot to another, the shadows in the scene are different, or objects suddenly leap from one point to another between shots. This is because film scenes are shot at different times. It is very easy for these kind of errors to slip into a scene. In a computer game everything is pretty much set in stone: scenes can be saved at a certain point. However, visual continuity problems can still creep into virtual scenes if they are not carefully controlled, particularly if work is being outsourced to another company.

Plot errors occur when logical inconsistency leaks into the story. These can very easily slip in if the writer does not have absolute control and does not organize the backstory of the piece properly before beginning writing.

SETTING

Many people would immediately begin creating the story as soon as the basic vision for the game is defined. However, the setting should be carefully considered and planned out before the story is fully created. Doing this will give the writer a much stronger base to build upon and will likely prevent gaping holes in the plot or strange anomalies between scenes.

By considering the setting, we create a backstory, a history and a solid set of foundations upon which to build the main thread of the narrative. It also aids in creating characters and determining how they fit within our virtual world.

We should consider several aspects of the setting:

- Geography
- Culture
- History

Geography

The geography of a setting describes the physical space that a player will inhabit while playing the game. Limitless potential spaces might be employed, from forests and mountains, to cities and towns, to particular buildings. Scale plays an important part in the geography of a world. The player might inhabit a realistic representation of world space or might inhabit a geographically condensed world, where a variety of different environments can be experienced.

The geography of an area is usually based on that we see around us on Earth. Often it is a more spectacular version—a hyper-real image of what might appear. Alternatively the world may be completely alien to us, such as being in space or on another planet. Geography in an alien world might be a twisted version of our own reality or might challenge all concepts we have about the construction of the world. We might even represent more abstract spaces such as the human mind or cyberspace.

Culture

Culture defines various aspects of the characters and the events that will occur within the world, as well as the architecture of the space the characters inhabit. When considering culture, there is a vast wealth of real-world examples to draw upon, some which have been examined many times in the past and others that have not been looked at much at all. Of course, this is due to the designer's familiarity with certain cultures over others. A lot of designers' own cultures' traits are likely to be found in their own creations, as these are their direct influences and experiences. It is easy to make mistakes when basing a game on an unfamiliar real-world culture, and some mistakes may even be offensive.

Often real-world cultures are only drawn upon to provide inspiration for a fantasy game. Again there are many clichéd cultures that have already been extensively used as a basis: Roman, Egyptian, Greek, medieval, and so on. There are still plenty of cultures that haven't had the chance to be used to their full potential; for example, few games draw upon the rich history of South America such as the Aztecs, Mayans, or Incas.

A number of aspects should be considered when designing the culture for the game:

- Time period
- Technology
- Fashion
- Beliefs and customs
- Language and dialect
- Morals and laws

Time Period

Almost every action–adventure game, even if it is a fantasy, will be based on some real-world period in history. The game may attempt a contemporary urban cityscape or be set far in the future, the medieval past, Jurassic times, the Wild West, World War II, feudal Japan, and so on. The time period a game is based on will dictate the other aspects of culture, but certain elements may be twisted and changed to mutate the game away from reality and into the realm of fantasy.

In some cases twisting reality can work in your favor. For instance, prehistoric man would never have encountered a dinosaur, but many games and movies pit cavemen against them. Sometimes juxtaposition of realities can create a truly unique game world. Alternate realities also translate well into the game paradigm. What if the Nazis had won the war? What if the ancient Egyptian civilization was still around today? These are rather clichéd, but there are plenty of potential twists that could be explored.

Before getting into details about other aspects of the game's culture it is wise to set the time period and ensure that everything is built around this. If you are making a historically accurate game, it will pay to do as much research as possible into the subject, as it is surprising what players will immediately find wrong.

Technology

Technology is a big part of culture, as it defines the boundaries of progress for a civilization. Putting the wrong technology in the wrong place can feel instantly unsettling. Often games try to be historically accurate but make huge errors in what technology might have been available at that time. Take, for example, the use of railway tracks in ancient cultures, when they only became a reality around 1550 in Germany. Modern railways as we know them now weren't around until 1820. Where games are not trying to be historically accurate or are more fantasy based, this is of much less concern.

Fantasy games can also use technology in different ways, perhaps mimicking real-world modern technologies with different technologies from the past (though steam-based contraptions are rather clichéd these days). Sci-fi settings offer the designer the chance to dream and imagine future technologies, though this always seems to end up as lasers and shiny surfaces or a dystopian *Blade Runner* clone.

Fashion

Clothes say a lot about the people that wear them: what place they live in, what part of society they fit into, how they feel about themselves, and so on. Clothes are often regional. Very often you can tell where in the world people come from by the way they dress. Of course, this is made easier if they dress in national costume, but this can end up looking very stereotyped. The time period the game is set in will also have a massive impact on the fashion that characters will be wearing.

Clothes can indicate a character's profession or lifestyle. Uniforms instantly tell us what a character does for a living and can also empower or repress an individual. Ways of dressing affect how we view someone. A character dressed up like a skinhead projects a very different persona than someone dressed in a suit.

A lot of attention is paid and time lavished on costumes in movies, and there is no reason why the same shouldn't be done in games.

Beliefs and Customs

Every culture has different beliefs and customs that must be obeyed. Religion is not often a subject touched upon in computer games (probably for fear of making the industry's already poor reputation with many religions even worse), but it is a huge influence on a society and is often the cause of conflict.

Every culture has its traditions, ceremonies, festivals, and ways of doing things that have been passed from generation to generation. These customs and traditions can seem strange to those unfamiliar with them. However, a designer can significantly increase the richness of the game world by using them, particularly when creating a fantasy world.

Language and Dialect

Language is a bit of a tricky subject, as for the most part the game will be in one language (the one in which the player chooses to view and listen to it). However, it is perfectly feasible for characters to speak in different languages and subtitle them. A whole fictional language might even be created as was done in *Ico*™. One really nice touch in this game is that both lead characters speak in different fictional languages and neither understands the another. This brings in a narrative element where the two characters have to work together even harder to achieve their goals.

Creating a whole new language is not an easy task, but it creates an alien and dislocated feel for the player. Many fiction writers have created their own languages in their work, for example, George Orwell's Newspeak (*1984*), Frank Herbet's Chakobsa and Fremen (*Dune*) and Anthony Burgess's Nadsat (*A Clockwork Orange*). There are a number of other examples of languages created for games besides *Ico*: Al Bhed (*Final Fantasy X*), Hylian (*The Legend of Zelda*), D'ni (*Myst*®), Gargish (*Ultima*), and many more.

Having your main character speak a different language than those around him can create a feeling of isolation, loneliness, or even a dreamlike surreal world, such as that which Sofia Coppola creates in her film *Lost In Translation*.

While language can be difficult to play with, dialects are much easier to incorporate. Accents can dramatically change the feel of a character and place him within a specific group of people. Too many games suffer from using a monotonous, nondescript American accent for all their characters. However it can be taken to the other extreme; too many accents can create a disparate, unconnected mish-mash in which characters are unrelated to one another. A pool of accents should be attributed to like characters, so that a unified feel is created for every element of society, and the choice of accent for a character doesn't feel arbitrary.

Slang and other colloquialisms are tough to incorporate, as they will have little meaning when translated for other markets, so we would suggest not using slang unless it is well known across a wide audience. Creating new slang for your game world can work well if you explain clearly what each word or phrase means.

Morals and Laws

Different cultures have differing opinions on what is right and wrong. These moral principles may define concepts of honor and duty and define the laws by which a society lives (or at least attempts to).

Having a strong sense of morals and laws within a game culture can enrich the experience for the player. Moral decisions and breaking of laws are often integrated into gameplay. For example, in *Grand Theft Auto*, the player knows that certain actions are illegal and will result in police attention, though not all laws have been modeled for gameplay purposes; for example, speeding is ignored by the police. Games that feature laws of their own that might be unfamiliar to the player will need to explain the possible consequences of breaking those laws.

History

History is an important element of the setting for a game, as it establishes a backstory that defines many of the elements within it. Games based on real-world environments require less work in terms of developing a history for the world, as it already exists.

Contemporary games based on recent historical events require the least effort in communicating a sense of history, as many of the elements within it will be familiar to those observing them. Earlier time periods have to be explained more to the player, as many of these historical events may not be known. Of course, games are not always historically accurate. Often events will be based on real events but twisted to suit the needs of the narrative. Be careful with tampering with real history, or you may end up insulting or annoying specific audiences. Take, for example, the film *U-571*, which depicted the Americans capturing the Enigma machine, when in fact it was British forces that did so, a fact that was not lost on British audiences.

In a fantasy game a whole different scope of history has to be created. A whole history can be invented from scratch. One of the main reasons for the success of J.R.R. Tolkien's books was the enormous sense of history he invoked within their pages. A fantasy world does not necessarily need Tolkien's levels of depth but will definitely benefit from the creation of a backstory beyond the arc of the main story. This history may be as simple as a time line, which defines dates of major relevance, or may be as deep as a tome on the history of various characters or peoples within the world. Many fantasy histories are based on real-world cultures such as the Greeks, Romans, Egyptians, and so on and draw upon characters and events within their folklore. Basing a fantasy history around these tales is a good method of creating complex histories.

STORY

For many people, the narrative *is* the story. This is the tale weaved by the script writers to set the scene for the gameplay. Story is only really relevant to single or cooperative experiences. Competitive multiplayer games' narratives are generally defined by their settings and the actions of the players.

The story in a game can often provide the drive for players to keep playing, as they unravel each stage of the plot. Writing a good story will draw the players in and immerse them in the game world.

Creative writing is a skill. If you are not a skilled writer, then the best solution is to get someone on board who is. It is not a skill that can be mastered with ease, and it requires a great deal of natural talent. You've probably either got it or you haven't. It is a common failing of game designers to think that they can easily write a story. Frankly, in most games this lack of ability shows. Writers are keen and eager to work in the field of games and, by working with them, we will produce better narratives in games [PratchettWhitta04].

It is, however, essential that every designer have a basic grasp of how to create compelling stories and, more importantly, how to weave the story into the gameplay. Studying the structure of the story allows the designer to use the key elements of storytelling to maximum advantage and merge them more easily with gameplay.

Narrative Elements

Many studies of narrative have been conducted over the years that attempt to break narrative down into its constituent parts—its base elements.

Mimesis and Diegesis

There are two strains of storytelling: show (mimesis) and tell (diegesis). Most of a computer game's story is divulged through mimesis, visually displaying the story to the player—acting it out, so to speak. As film writers are often told, "Show, don't tell." The same methodology is often applied to computer game stories.

Diegesis is used in game stories through the act of narration, displaying backstory or interim text. Another form of this may occur within the game world itself, where the player might pick up a book and be able to read a selection of text from it. Telling rather than showing presents a danger of information overload, which is often boring and generally unnecessary. Providing an audience with just enough information should keep the story flowing, though the option to allow the players to explore further if they wish can enrich the experience for players who want to discover more of the backstory. The *Resident Evil* series of survival horror games uses scraps of information within the world to allow the player to do just this. Information placed in the world like this is known as diegetic, whereas narration and displayed text that does not appear within the context of the game world is known as non-diegetic.

Barthes' Codes

One enduring method of breaking a narrative down was constructed by Roland Barthes in his book *S/Z*. Here he suggests five codes (elements) that relate to various aspects of the narrative [Felluga03]. Consideration of these codes is a good starting point for knowing what elements are needed to craft a story.

Hermeneutic Code (Enigma Code)

Any element in a story that poses a question and does not immediately answer it is classed as a hermeneutic code. The withholding of information from the audience is one of the two main ways of building dramatic tensions or suspense in the audience (the other being a proairetic code—an action). An audience is likely to feel unsatisfied with a story unless these questions are answered by the end. Barthes also describes a number of ways to play with the audience when a truth is to be revealed:

Snares: Deliberately avoiding the truth
Equivocations: A mixture of the truth and a snare
Partial answers: Providing only part of the solution
Jammings: Acknowledging the difficulty or impossibility of the answer

A prime example of the hermeneutic code in action is the detective story genre. Here a variety of clues are assembled during the course of the story, but the complete picture is not revealed until the very end.

Proairetic Code (Action Code)

The second element that builds dramatic tension or suspense in the audience is a proairetic code, or an action code. This element defines any action and a reaction, or response. The possible outcome of this action may be known to the audience (unlike a hermeneutic code element), but there may be a number of possible outcomes. It is the wait for the choice of outcome that determines the tension.

Hermeneutic codes and proairetic codes only make sense in order. If studied out of order, they will become confusing and ambiguous. Take the film *Memento*, for example. In this film we witness a story in reverse chronological order to ultimately find out what the protagonist has forgotten. This film only works in this order because our protagonist has amnesia. In effect, we build up to the moment of discovery, even though time is moving backward. Indeed, this film wouldn't work if played forward, because we'd get all the answers to our questions in the first scene.

Semantic Code

The semantic code deals with the meaning of the words used, their connotations, and often additional meanings. These connotations can apply character traits to people, places, and objects. For example, a person may have traits such as being honorable or untrustworthy. As Spoors notes in his essay "Narrative and Interaction in Computer Games: Codes of Computer Gameplay" [Spoors], the semantic code used in computer games can be applied to character attributes such as strength, health, dexterity, and so on. These may function thematically to associate a character with the setting.

Symbolic Code

The symbolic code is tied to the semantic code in that it is a structural form that organizes semantic meanings according to similarity and difference. Binary oppositions are pairs of opposites such as good and evil within which semantic elements can be aligned. Some proairetic elements can also be treated in a similar manner, such as an action that will have an outcome aligned with good or evil.

Cultural Code

A cultural code element refers to knowledge outside of the present narrative—knowledge we have of the real world or of particular constructs. This knowledge could be historical, physical, psychological, literary, and so on, and, in the case of a game, may have a number of abstractions based on knowledge of gaming conventions that have accumulated over the years.

Narrative Structure

People have studied the structure of narrative for centuries, and a number of different ways of organizing it have been formulated. Different structures apply to different types of story and to the different ways these stories are presented. Each of these structures have their own merits and drawbacks. Some structures are more suited to game design than others.

The study of structure in narrative is part of a movement called structuralism, which seeks to find structure in many different fields. A more recent movement known as post-structuralism is challenging the ideas of structure within narrative. This breaking down of structures results in open-ended narratives, where scenes are held together loosely and endings are very open. This kind of narrative poses a problem for a game story: because the player is investing time in playing the game, he requires a reward on completion. An open ending will not provide much satisfaction for completion and the player may feel as though he has lost. Hence, it is nearly impossible to apply these post-structuralist ideas onto a game narrative without leaving the player feeling somewhat cheated.

Three-Act Structure

The three-act structure is a commonly heralded method of breaking a story into specific sections, or acts. This is often attributed to Aristotle, who specified that a story has a beginning, a middle, and an end but never specifically mentioned three acts.

Celebrated American screenwriting guru Syd Field uses a three-act structure to analyze scripts and suggests it as a tool for creating screenplays. His model breaks a screenplay into Act I: Setup, Act II: Confrontation, and Act III: Resolution [Field72]. However, this model cheats somewhat and should perhaps be considered a four-act model, as Act II is broken into two parts.

The three-act structure has many fierce critics who argue that it is inherently flawed: films do not need acts since there are no intermissions like there would be in a play and the plot points are pretty arbitrary. Some argue that following these rules will result in formulaic, identikit scripts and that the rules quash innovation. However, the structure has become so ingrained into Hollywood bureaucracy that the system is readily accepted by studio executives and the money men.

In terms of computer games, the three-act structure is not particularly useful. Films are set at roughly the same running times. Games, on the other hand, vary tremendously in the amount of time they take to play. The three-act markers are also useless when applied to games, as again there are no set intermissions; players will stop playing when they grow bored or weary or have to return to the real world. The physical divisions of world space generally act as sections of story, and there are invariably more than three levels in any particular game. In short, this is a technique that may be useful for studying the basic structure, but it really shouldn't be used as a definitive tool for the construction of a game story.

Five-Act Structure

Gustav Freytag describes in his book *Technique of Drama*, published in 1863, the breakdown of a story into five acts. This structure has been expressed in a diagram that has become known as Freytag's pyramid [Wikipedia]. This matches time against plot to show the rising and falling drama of the story (see Figure 3.1).

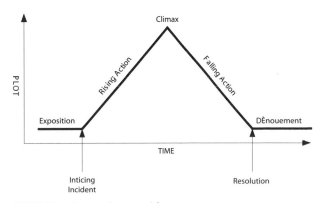

FIGURE 3.1   Freytag's pyramid.

Freytag's analysis is based on dramatic plays and thus is somewhat different than what might occur in many modern stories. However, the structure is fairly generic and does not specify exact moments at which events should occur. This structure is still relevant to modern drama, though some elements may be skipped or brushed over and others embellished further.

Different interpretations of Freytag's work over the years have named the five acts differently. The following act names are a result of a combination of different views and opinions:

- Exposition
- Rising action
- Climax
- Falling action
- Dénouement

Exposition

The main protagonist (in our case the player character) is introduced along with other major characters such as the antagonist. Other major elements are also introduced, such as the setting and the cause of the conflict. The end of this act is marked by the inciting moment—the point at which our journey begins.

Rising Action

The second act introduces further circumstances or problems in relation to the main source of conflict. These are various obstacles and challenges that make the achievement of the protagonist's goal more difficult.

Climax

In the third act the plot reaches its pinnacle, and the climax, or turning point of the story, occurs. If things were going badly, they start to go the protagonist's way; otherwise, things may take a severe turn for the worse.

Falling Action

The conflict moves toward the moment of resolution when the outcome will be decided. Often there is a moment of final suspense, when the outcome may be in some doubt.

Dénouement

The resolution comes at the end of the falling action and determines the conclusion of the story. A story will generally conclude with either the protagonists being better off than they were at the beginning or in catastrophe, where they are worse off than they were at the beginning.

There is a potential problem here for the game designer. Ending a game in catastrophe could be disastrous. The players have invested huge amounts of time and energy into reaching the conclusion of the story and will want their achievements rewarded. To have their labors end in a fruitless situation will demean all of the hard work they have invested and will be at best annoying and at worst utterly insulting. Thus, a game story's conclusion should always have a positive outcome, even if there are negative elements involved.

A technique known as deus ex machina could be used to resolve a seemingly desperate situation. A deus ex machina is a plot device whereby an intervention breaks the internal logic of the plot. For example, the hand of God may come down and pluck our hapless hero out of trouble. The problem with this type of device is that it can very easily break the suspension of disbelief and is often seen as a cop-out. More dangerously in terms of game design, it requires an intervention beyond the player's control, which removes their feeling of accomplishment. Therefore, it is a plot device best ignored when it comes to devising the game plot.

Monomyth (the Hero's Journey)

The monomyth (also known as the hero's journey) is a model described by Joseph Campbell in his seminal work *The Hero with a Thousand Faces* [Campbell49]. This model examines the structure of heroic myths and the journey that these heroes undergo during the course of the story. This model has been applied to analyze many existing works but has also inspired a lot of contemporary mythology. George Lucas was inspired by this model when writing *Star Wars,* and many other examples of modern writing exhibit the monomyth influence. A more recent book by Christopher Vogler, *The Writer's Journey* [Vogler98], interprets this journey further. Many writers refer to Vogler's interpretation, as it is a simpler, refined version of Campbell's work.

The hero's journey is an excellent fit for many computer games, as it encapsulates the essence of the journey the player will take in controlling his avatar. This parallel means that studying the elements of this structure will allow the designer to fit the structure of the story to the journey that the player will experience. Troy Dunniway identifies the use of the hero's journey in game design in his Gamasutra article "Using the Hero's Journey in Games" [Dunniway00].

The monomyth is divided into three sections:

Departure: The hero setting forth on his quest
Initiation: The adventures the hero experiences on his quest
Return: The hero's return home with acquired knowledge and powers

Each of these sections is divided into a number of specific events that occur during the journey.

Departure

The call to adventure: We meet our hero as he exists before the quest. He is
generally troubled in some way; the seeds of needing some kind of quest are

sown. It is at this point that a herald will often arrive to announce the quest to the hero.

Refusal of the call: Generally the hero refuses or is somehow prevented from initially being able to answer the call. This refusal or prevention often leads to some form of tragedy that will act as a catalyst for the hero to realize that the call needs to be answered.

Supernatural aid: Once on his journey, the hero will likely encounter a helper, usually some form of mentor character who will educate or give him powers or objects that will assist him in his quest.

The coming of the first threshold: The hero arrives at the beginning of the dark underworld. He must cross this threshold between the world he knows and loves and the fearsome world that lies ahead of him. This transition often means facing a threshold guardian. This is some challenge, conflict, or choice the hero must complete before being granted passage into the underworld.

The belly of the whale: Now in the underworld, the hero becomes engulfed in the unknown and may enter an almost dream-like world where nothing seems quite real since it is so distant from the world he has left behind.

Initiation

The road of trials: The hero is now faced with obstacles that need to be over-come. With these obstacles come mental and/or physical tests where the hero must prove his worth to himself or others. With these tests complete, he gains new skills and strengths that will help him onward with his quest.

The meeting with the goddess/woman as temptress: The goddess (or possibly a male counterpart if it is the heroine's journey) is a beautiful or motherly figure, who may act as a counterpoint to the hero—the missing part of their whole—or may act as the temptress, plunging the hero back into the belly of the whale if he fails to resist the temptation.

Atonement with the father: A patriarchal figure may need to be reconciled with. Reconciliation will gain the hero understanding of this figure and, by doing so, will help him gain insight into himself.

Apotheosis/the ultimate boon: The hero achieves personal enlightenment. His view of himself and of the world around him has changed. He is capable of new things and has strengths he did not previously know existed within him. These new-found skills and abilities have potential benefits to society.

Return

Refusal of the return: With these new-found skills and abilities and his enlightenment, the hero may be reluctant to return to his previous world with the prize.

The magic flight: The hero returns to his normal world often in an extraordinary way.

Rescue from without: In some journeys the hero may need outside help to assist in bringing the journey to its conclusion.

> **The crossing of the return threshold:** Before the hero returns to his previous world, there may be another threshold guardian to face.
>
> **Freedom to live:** The hero's new-found skills and abilities have potential benefits that can be used to help humanity.

The hero's journey is criticized by many literary experts for being somewhat simplistic and formulaic. Undoubtedly, if everyone rigidly adhered to it, then that would be the case. It is best used as a starting point to give an idea of some elements that will build a good story.

Branching Structure

A branching structure is a much more recent method of organizing narrative and allowing interactivity. Early examples of branching stories are the *Choose Your Own Adventure* series of books, which were not the first but were perhaps the most successful of the interactive fiction novels. These offer the reader a series of different paths through the book.

This kind of structure is extremely useful for game narrative, as it immediately fits the gameplay model of making choices. Text adventures were the first examples of these branching story structures used in computer games and were some of the earliest games to be created. A branching narrative has a number of predetermined paths that can be taken via the actions of the player in the game world. The structure can vary wildly so that there are many branches with many endings or branches that converge back to a single ending.

One important consideration is cost in terms of resources and time. All these branches may require considerable extra work to create. A linear story is guaranteed to be seen, whereas separate branches may never be seen by most players. Choosing to do a branching story calls for much careful consideration, as it can be very costly to weave a good tale and offer varied interaction.

Plot

Plot is not the story as a whole, but rather the events that occur that are then ordered to form the story. Every story should have some form of plot that will interest the player and that has internal consistency so that it does not break the suspension of disbelief. Plot holes and errors can seriously jeopardize a player's enjoyment of the story.

A story will have a main plot (often called an A-plot) and any number of subplots. The subplot structure works well in games, as it often encompasses the mission–level structure with each subplot, while continuing a main plot across all of the missions and levels.

Plot Themes

While there are potentially limitless themes for a plot, a limited number work really well. Many plots are variations on the same theme. According to who you consult, there are many different numbers of potential themes for a plot, varying from 1 to over 60.

A widely recognized list of potential plot themes was constructed by Georges Polti in 1868 in his book *The Thirty Six Dramatic Situations*, though he himself admits this list is fairly arbitrary and there may be more or less than those specified. However, this list remains a useful starting point when considering a plot.

Relatively few plots beyond the tyrannical oppressor, kidnapped girlfriend, and world in peril type of themes have been explored by games. This is mainly because games need some form of dramatic conflict that will encourage a hero to step forth. However, more subtle subplots can easily be worked in alongside main dramatic themes, and there are plenty of dramatic themes beyond the now clichéd video-game plots we have seen again and again over the years.

Chronology

Film director Jean-Luc Goddard once said, "A story should have a beginning, a middle, and an end . . . but not necessarily in that order." The chronology of a story determines in what order time-based elements of the plot are presented. This will have a very large effect on the relaying of information to the audience.

There are several approaches to using time in a story:

Linear: The most standard method of playing out a story is linear time. This may, however, include flashbacks or foreshadowing to show past and future events.

Roaming: A more unusual method of relaying information is to jump fairly randomly between different points in time. Films such as *Pulp Fiction* have used this technique to great effect.

Reverse: In this unusual technique the story is told in chunks of time that progress backward with each time chunk. The film *Memento* uses this technique.

A story will usually be told in a purely linear fashion in computer games. There are very good reasons for this. Unlike with a normal story, the audience is able to interact with the world. As players progress through the game, they will increase in skill and their characters might also progress though attributes, skills, and equipment. A serious paradox ensues when the player flashes back in time to a previous point, where the character would be less proficient than at a later point. However because the player has increased in skill, he is now more proficient in the past than he is in the future in the context of the story. If character progression is being used, then these advances will have to be taken away when transitioning back in time.

These flashback techniques can be put to good use as tutorials for introducing a new skill. A flashback when a new skill is introduced will put that skill into context and allow players to practice before transitioning back to the present time in the story context. They will then be proficient at this skill when the story demands it.

Plot Devices

Plot devices are objects, people, or events used in a story to present information, expand the audience's knowledge, and advance the plot. Poorly used plot devices can seem contrived, cause a rupture in the audience's suspension of disbelief, or cause plot holes. A few plot devices that are particularly relevant to games are discussed below, but many more can be found online on sites such as *tvtropes.org* [TVTropes].

Twists

A twist should be an unexpected event in the plot designed to shock the audience. A good twist will provide some kind of clues or fit within the context of the story. A poor twist will break the suspension of disbelief or will be immediately obvious to most of the audience. Many examples of twists can be seen in a variety of narratives. Film director M. Night Shyamalan is famed for using twist endings for his films *The Sixth Sense, Unbreakable, Signs,* and *The Village.*

A red herring may be used to try to put the audience on the wrong trail and then allow a surprise twist to be sprung upon them.

Flashbacks and Foreshadowing

Flashbacks are used to show past events. They are usually brief glimpses of events that have occurred but may last for longer periods of time. Foreshadowing is a technique of displaying a glimpse of the future so that the player will know what may occur. There are several flashback or foreshadowing techniques that might be used, each of which will have a different impact on the audience:

Dream sequence: A common device for flashbacks and foreshadowing is the use of a dream sequence. Here the audience is shown clues to a future scenario or past events that are often very surreal. In games the dream sequence might be a playable sequence. Third-person shooter game *Max Payne*® used some playable dream sequence sections in which the player entered a surreal black void and had to follow a trail of blood to some new revelation about the main character's past.

Had I but known: This is a foreshadowing technique that shows consequences of an action a character is about to make as a warning of what might happen if he makes the wrong choice.

Future/past glimpse: A very brief glimpse of a future or past event can be used to shock the player or strengthen the impact of a theme. The first-person shooter game *F.E.A.R.* uses a future glimpse technique extensively throughout the game to shock the player, showing some horrible incident that he is about to encounter just up ahead.

Events

Event devices are common elements in films, TV shows, and video games that preclude a particular scenario. There are potentially hundreds of these kinds of events, but many pertain to scenarios that are unlikely to crop up in the story of a typical video game. However, a number of common event devices do occur often in video games:

A god I am: A character gains superpowers or believes he has and develops delusions of grandeur. He will have some flaw that renders him vulnerable. This device might be used for a boss character in an action game.

And your little dog too: The act of the villain performing an evil act just because he can. The phrase comes from *The Wizard of Oz* when the wicked witch threatens the dog as well as Dorothy.

Forced prize fight: A group of allies are forced to fight against each other, often to the death.

Ironic inversion: Two characters enter a challenge, and one seems much more suited to the task. The underdog is the surprise champion.

Miracle rally: A team appears to be at the moment of defeat, but after a pivotal event, such as letting a particular character take the lead, they come back to win.

Secret test of character: The hero is put under a test to reach a particular goal, but during the pursuit of this goal encounters a moral decision. The correct moral decision will make him lose the goal, but in doing so he will actually pass the real goal of the test.

This is something he's got to do himself: The main hero is part of a group when they face up to the main villain. The hero declares that defeating the villain is something that he has to do alone.

Wrecked weapon: The hero's main power or weapon is damaged or lost. This can be particularly emotional if an empathic item is used as the main weapon and the hero has become very attached to it.

Using an event device runs the risk of seeming clichéd, since some of these events have been so extensively used.

Characters

Certain types of characters may appear in a story who are there to perform a very specific function for the plot. These characters are often NPC characters that the players encounters on their travels, but elements of them may be used to create motivations for the players themselves.

Androcles and the lion: Based on an ancient myth in which Androcles befriends a lion. It is used to describe the befriending of a wild animal by aiding it in some way. The creature will later come to rescue the main character in a time of need (basically a form of Chekhov's gun, described later).

Buttmonkey: A character who is the butt of all the jokes or who all the bad stuff happens to.

Fake defector: A character who turns to the opposite side in order to achieve a goal. The side they were originally working for may not realize that they have not actually defected.

Feet of clay: An incredibly talented hero who turns out to be completely useless or an incredibly dangerous villain who turns out to be a total wimp.

I just want to be normal: A character who is different from normal society, or in a comic book universe, a character with superpowers who is reluctant to use them and desperately wants to just be normal. This also can be applied to a non-human character who desperately wants to be human.

Moses in the bullrushes: An lost infant who is brought up by strangers. The child is often destined for greatness. Alternatively, a child of royalty or similarly high status and finds this out later.

Items

A number of different items are used as plot devices. These items can be essential in moving the plot in a specific direction. They may be the main source of the character's motivations or may be the focus of stopping a particular event from happening.

Chekhov's gun: An element introduced early that is used later on. The term originates from Anton Chekhov writing that a rifle should not be put on stage if no one is going to fire it. This is a form of foreshadowing.

Empathic item: An item that is personified and reacts to its wielder. Eastern myths heavily feature weapons that have their own personalities and even grow in strength as their wielder does.

MacGuffin: An object central to the plot that motivates the characters but needs no real explanation, such as the loot in a heist film.

Plot coupon: An element that is essential to resolving the conflict on which the plot hangs. This is a device very often used in games; for example, a number of items must be collected or the various parts of a single item must be reunited to defeat the threat.

Plot voucher: A plot voucher is similar to the coupon, except that is used to get out of a tight spot. Often the use of the voucher will not become clear until the tight spot arises, at which point its use will (or at least should) become clear. A voucher must have a reason for being; otherwise, it becomes a form of deus ex machina that simply solves a problem in a way that breaks the player's suspension of disbelief.

Symbols

Symbols are references within the plot that are used to symbolize particular events. The symbol is generally some kind of visual element, such as a particular object. They may have one or more particular symbolic representations for other elements in the plot [Freeman02]:

Change in character: The symbol reflects a marked change in the character.

Plot event marker: The symbol reflects a big change in the plot such as a twist or new avenue of action.

Emotional symbol: The symbol reflects the current emotion of the plot or the emotional state of a particular character in the story.

Finales

The end of a story may feature some kind of device to resolve the conflict or to set the story up for a sequel.

Cliff-hanger: A cliff-hanger leaves the hero in a predicament in the final scene. This is used in episodic media or is used to force the conclusion of the story in a sequel. It can be dangerous to use this technique in a traditional computer game, as it may leave the player feeling cheated. However, if games are moving toward episodic content, then this device may become more familiar in the future.

Deus ex machina: A deus ex machina is an ending that swoops down like the hand of God to resolve the problems faced by the hero.

Distant finale: A large jump forward in time may occur to show how the characters end up in the future.

Here we go again: An ending can set up the story to begin again in the same manner in the next episode or the sequel.

Twist finale: This is an end scene that uses a twist to shock the audience. This can work very well in a computer game as long as it does not have an impact on the player's progression or is not a deus ex machina.

Interactive Storytelling Issues

The game designer must remember one fundamental difference between games and other storytelling mediums: games are interactive. In his article "Interactive Narratives Revisited: Ten Years of Research" [Adams05], Ernest Adams notes a few issues with interactivity that impact on the ability to tell a story:

Internal consistency: The consistency of a world can be difficult to maintain, with the problem of the player performing actions that do not match the characteristics of their avatar. This is often solved by restricting the player from performing such actions. However, this places limits on the player's freedom that can seem unfair. Sometimes the problem is best solved by doing nothing and hoping players will maintain character themselves.

Amnesia: One seemingly very odd occurrence is that the avatars appear to have developed amnesia, in that they must explore the environment that forms their everyday life—forgetting where they might keep their own things at home, for example. Such issues are simply a part of the experience, and little can be done to solve the issue, except by placing the avatar in an unknown environment.

Narrative flow: The dramatic tension of a story can be shattered by one branch of a narrative not having the same impact as another. This can result in very different experiences for different audiences, depending on the choices they make during their journey. The final climax can be particularly difficult, as dramatic tension can be built up to near the point of climax and then dropped before the event occurs. There is no real solution to the problem; it's really just tough luck for the audience.

Interactivity issues within the story structure are often skipped over by using a linear storyline and avoiding the problems associated with trying to make a branching structure work. This makes things a lot easier but does restrict the potential of the medium. Some very interesting situations can arise when branching structures are used, and there is much greater scope for replayability.

Storytelling Devices in Games

Storytelling can be performed in a variety of ways in a computer game. However, telling a story during sections of interactivity is difficult, so many games tend to remove player interaction during storytelling moments. However, there are ways of telling a story without removing player control, as we shall see.

Sequences

A sequence is the general method of storytelling used in games. This is an acted-out sequence of events that occurs before the player's eyes. A sequence typically features objects, characters, dialog, and scenery.

There are a number of reasons for using a sequence [Hancock02]:

Scene setting: Set the mood of a scene by showing the player the area in a sweeping shot or emphasizing some element of the environment (such as the ubiquitous lightning bolt over a haunted house).

Imparting information: A sequence can be used to give the player information, such as specific points of his mission objective or the result of some action the player has performed (such as pushing a switch to open a door).

Foreshadowing and flashback: These can be used to emphasize a situation or offer the player clues of possible future events.

Victory or failure: These are used to signify victory or failure for the player.

Reward: If the quality of script and animation and motion capture is of a high quality, then the uncovering of the next sequence acts as a reward to the player, as he gets to experience the scene unfolding before his eyes.

Several types of sequence can be used in games:

- Scripted sequence
- Background sequence
- Cutscene
- Interactive cutscene (quick time event [QTE])
- Full motion animation (FMA) and full motion video (FMV)

Scripted Sequence

A scripted sequence is an interactive sequence between actors. As a gameplay device, these are generally preferable to sequences that remove control from the player. They are a much more immersive way to tell the story.

However, there are some major issues with using interactive sequences like this in a game:

Player attention: Because the player is free to move around, he can move to a position where he cannot see the action and thus miss the information being imparted to him.

Interruption: The player can attack, throw an object, or interfere with a sequence in some manner that will break the flow of the scene.

In incidental scenes there is no need to worry about the problems posed by interactive sequences. If they don't get witnessed, then there is no real issue, and interrupting them should just break the character out of the sequence to react to the interruption. However, when important scenes are being played, a number of methods can be employed:

Lockdown: The player is locked into a restricted area, keeping him within a certain distance of the sequence so he can still hear information even if he cannot see it.

Focused directions: Third-person cameras can be directed to view the sequence to ensure that it is seen as much as possible. In a first-person game the sequence can be stalled until the player is looking in a particular direction.

Character following: If only dialog is involved in the scene, then it is perfectly feasible for the character to follow the player to divulge the information.

Picture-in-picture: A smaller window in the picture displays a second camera focused on the desired action. This solves the problem of seeing the action but has a big technical hit on the render engine, as it has to render two scenes.

Action prevention: To prevent the player from performing a potentially scene-breaking action the player can simply be prevented from performing that action. In *Half-Life 2* aiming at an ally will cause the avatar to dip the weapon down, preventing the ally from being shot at.

Sequence branching: Different interactions can be intercepted and dealt with by the script so that there is a sensible outcome for each interruption. This makes for a much more dynamic experience but requires a good deal of work and requires that every possibility is accounted for.

Invulnerability: Important characters that are essential to the continuity of the story need to be made impossible to kill. This can be as simple as not letting them take damage at all (which can look a little ridiculous sometimes) or by reacting to the damage but having unlimited health (this can be difficult to believe if a character is shot in the head).

Background Sequence

While interactive scenes are great in terms of gameplay, the issues associated with them can be difficult to solve. Background sequences are played without removing control from the player or by placing the action behind some kind of barrier (*Half-Life* often uses bulletproof glass for a barrier). A background sequence solves the problem of interrupting the sequence but still poses the problem of player attention.

Background sequences are often used to add color to a scene, to have action in the distance, or to play important scenes that cannot be interrupted. However, in terms of the latter, it can be difficult to have a suitable barrier every time.

Cutscene

A cutscene removes control from the player and displays a predefined sequence that the player simply watches. On completion, the player is returned to normal play.

The cutscene is something of a dilemma in the game designer's world. Some people think they are a vital tool; others see them as a hindrance to interactivity. They do have a useful purpose: to explicitly move the story along without any chance of distraction for the player. This can be incredibly important in a narrative-driven game.

Whether they break interactivity and game flow or not, they are a useful tool in the designers toolbox. Judicious use of cutscenes can enhance the story, set the mood, and guide the player through new mechanics and paths through the game. The designer should always be careful not to use cutscenes as a crutch for poor design. Keep them fairly short and to the point, and most important of all, *allow the players to skip them if they so wish!* You may have spent ages making all these lovely sequences, but never force the players to sit through something where they don't have control. They'll hate you for it.

Also remember that cutscenes are not gameplay. Don't overuse them or attempt to extend play time with lots of cutscenes, as there will be little meat to the game itself, and the players will be left feeling like they are watching a movie with a little bit of gaming in between.

Interactive Cutscene (QTE)

An interactive cutscene, or QTE sequence allows a limited amount of interaction during the course of a cutscene. These interactions are generally limited to timed button presses and directional movements to correspond to on-screen prompts.

QTEs have the benefit of being cinematic and visually impressive while still engaging the player in terms of gameplay. However, the flaw of most QTEs is that the players are watching the prompts so much that they miss the action. While not really a good basis for an entire game these days (see *Space Ace*® and *Dragon's Lair*® for an example of purely QTE-based games), they are useful for quick or spectacular sequences and have been used in games such as *Fahrenheit*, *God of War*™, and *Resident Evil 4*.

FMA and FMV

FMA and FMV are terms for sequences played as introductions or between sections of a game. They are often longer than in-game cutscenes and are used for very important moments of plot exposition.

FMA is generally authored using the game engine itself, though it may use higher-resolution models than those used during general gameplay. Sometimes the FMA is rendered out to video, where it can be processed and played back as FMV.

FMV uses video playback to display a prerendered video. In the PlayStation® One era it was very much the fashion to render these scenes using traditional rendering methods rather than with the game engine itself. While this resulted in some visually stunning sequences, it often produced a great contrast to the in-game art quality. FMV is now often done by rendering out from the game engine so that it retains the same feel. However, the good thing about prerendering scenes is that the work can be easily outsourced to another company.

Narration and Text Display

A technique that is used fairly rarely in games is using narration or display text to deliver story information. *Prince of Persia: Sands of Time* had a fairly interesting narration technique, where the whole story was pitched as though the player character was recounting his story. This was used to cover up gaps in internal consistency when the player dies. The prince simply says, "No, wait, that's not how it happened" before returning to play. This is the first time we have seen this consistency problem tackled, and it works rather well.

The joy of using voice over narration is that it can be used during play, and control does not need to be taken away from the player. However, many writers consider narration a lazy form of storytelling, and overuse of the technique can make it difficult to allow the player to absorb all of the information.

Displaying text to narrate a particular section is altogether more difficult. The *Star Wars* films use display text at the beginning of each film to impart information to the audience. The problem is that it demands the audience's full concentration, meaning that unless it is extremely succinct, the control will have to be removed from the player if it is used for a game. Too much text at any one point dumps too much information on the players at once. They will likely get bored or not retain much of that information.

Diegetic Story Elements

Diegetic story elements were discussed earlier in this chapter, but to recap, these are elements contained within the game world that can be interacted with to give information that aids the player in his quest. These elements can take many forms, from books to tape recordings, but they will use one of the following techniques to provide information:

   Text: A text description, clue, or backstory on a particular subject. This might be in the form of a book, journal, or email.
   Audio: An audio clip that gives details of a particular event, character, or so on. This might be found in the form of a tape, answering machine message, or other communication.
   Image(s): An image or sequence of images that depict events, plans, or other information. This might appear in the form of a photograph, projected image, or so on.
   Video: A moving picture that might also have an audio track. This might take the form of, for example, a videotape, computer terminal, or closed-circuit TV image.

Diegetic elements are used to form and enrich a deep backstory or as essential clues in the player's quest. Either way, they can be an excellent tool to use in story-telling that can really add to the atmosphere of the game.

Conversations

A very common method of building story into the game world is to have characters that can be conversed with. Talking with a character can glean new information, offer clues, initiate subquests, and so on.

Conversations are discussed in greater depth in Chapter 15, "Implementing AI Actors."

Story Time Line

In a linearly structured game the story will naturally progress as the player moves through the game world. However, in more free-form worlds the player can revisit areas at different points in the story. In order for the world, characters, and objects within that area to match the current position in the story, we need some way to determine the current story position.

This is done with a story time line—an integer value that determines the current position. Every time an event of note occurs, the story time line can be incremented. Then any element that needs to test the story position makes a comparison against this value. It is best to have large values between major events to leave room for expansion of more minor events in between (see Table 3.1).

TABLE 3.1   Example Story Time Line

TIME CODE	ITEM
0000	Game start
0010	First combat
0100	Kill commander boss
0200	Exit castle
0201	Drawbridge raised
0300	Return to castle

CHARACTERS

Characters are essential to a story-based game. Indeed, there are very few narratives without characters of some sort, whether they be people, creatures, or objects. The creation of characters should be an organized and well-thought-out process, as one-dimensional lead characters can shatter the whole game experience.

Types of Characters

Within any story there are several types of characters that have different functions. These character types have parallels to character types in games.

Protagonist (Player Character)

The protagonist is the character with whom we should sympathize, as this is our hero—the character or group of characters (a group is often called a party of characters) who the player will control. A number of different archetypes exist for the protagonist [Jak04]:

The classic hero: A physically strong, good-looking character with charm and charisma—basically, the typical image most people would picture as a hero.

The everyman hero: An ordinary person thrown into extraordinary situations. We tend to empathize more with these characters, as they could be one of us.

The underdog: A hero who at first appears weak or has some disadvantage compared to those around him. As the story progresses, we discover his strength, and he becomes the champion.

The anti-hero: A character whose morals may be a little questionable but still has the charisma that makes him a lovable rogue. He may turn around to the cause of good or may revel in his questionable morals. Tommy Vercetti of *Grand Theft Auto* fame is a prime example of an anti-hero protagonist.

Superhero: A hero with strength or superpowers that makes him more powerful than a mortal man. Using superheroes can be dangerous, as they tend to have few weaknesses. Villains must be at least as powerful, which turns battles into a clash of gods.

Protagonists in computer games are often completely silent. This is often because it can feel odd to the player to have his avatar perform any action without his input. In *Half-Life* the protagonist's silence was a defining part of believing that the player was taking on the role of the character. If the character was speaking all the time it would break this belief [Carless03]. In *Half-Life 2* the fact that the hero never speaks is mentioned by other characters in the game, thus becoming a satirical comment on the phenomenon. Avatars that do speak have to be careful not to go overboard and speak so much as to irritate the player. Simple one-liners at opportune moments tend to work best. Often characters will only speak during cutscenes, when they are out of the player's control.

Antagonists (Enemies)

There are generally multiple antagonists in a story, but there is usually one main antagonist on which much of the plot hangs. The main antagonist usually follows one of the following archetypes:

The tyrant: A person in power, or seeking to be in power, who abuses his position, thereby causing the suffering of others.

The just man: A person who believes he is fighting a just cause, when in fact he is doing harm. Often a just man can be shown the error of his ways and be made to repent.

The traitor: Perhaps the lowest of the low. The traitor seemingly sides with the protagonist, but is later revealed to have been deceiving him all along.

The petulant child: The jealous or disowned character whose resentment builds to the point of lashing out to take revenge or to grab what he can. His ways may at first be hidden behind a façade of charm that hides the hatred bubbling away underneath.

The mastermind: A character of superior intelligence who plots and schemes for his own greedy needs. Masterminds often play games with their enemies to taunt them and to show off their superior minds.

The sadist: A character so evil that taking pleasure in the misery of others is his main goal. Sadists use violence or psychological games to intimidate their prey.

As well as the main antagonist there may be any number of other lesser antagonists—bosses or general enemies the player will encounter:

The minion: Employed by the main boss as the hired help—the general stock and trade of the enemies the player will encounter. Often they are nameless, faceless characters that are there just to be disposed of.

The right-hand man: The trusted, loyal companion of the main boss, who will gladly do his bidding. The right-hand man often features as a boss encounter before the final boss fight with the main antagonist, or as the main antagonist's chief protector. There may be more than one right-hand man.

The self-serving henchman: A comrade of the main antagonist who is not so loyal and is merely serving his own needs in working for his chief. Often he meets a sticky end at either the hero's or even the main antagonist's hand.

The bumbling idiot: A clumsy or idiotic companion of the main antagonist who can never get anything right, but for some reason the boss just has to keep him around. Often used as the comic relief.

The defector: Like the traitor, at first on the side of good (or at least appears to be). The defector will switch to the opposing side for reasons of greed. Sometimes he may be a reluctant defector, changing sides only because the villain has a stranglehold on him.

Supporting Characters (Allies)

Supporting characters have smaller roles to play in the story than the main characters. These are characters who will help the protagonist in their quest. There are several supporting character archetypes:

The sidekick: Often a joke-cracking wise guy who provides comic relief or moments of irritation (such as being clumsy) but is ultimately a loyal friend to the main protagonist. Initially the sidekick and the hero may not get on but will grow to depend on each other. Sidekicks have a very real danger of becoming extremely annoying if they are not handled well.

The vulnerable ward: A character the player must protect. Ashley in *Resident Evil 4* is an example of a character who needs protecting, but she also helped solve puzzles and aided progression.

The loyal companion: An extremely trustworthy companion who will do whatever he can to help out the main protagonist. He can be trusted to get the job done (though sometimes a loyal companion can turn out to be the traitor, which can be the biggest blow of all).

The mentor: The wise figure who guides the hero on his quest and teaches him the necessary skills to achieve his goal. This character often forms the basis of training at the start of a game.

The false villain: A character who at first appears to be on the wrong side, but turns out to be a good guy who has actually been helping all along.

The herald: The character who initiates the hero's quest. This may be a character who issues orders that must be followed (such as a commanding officer) or a character who pleads for the hero's help.

The advisor: A character who is on hand to issue help and advice as it is needed. These are often used in games to help out players who get stuck.

Extras (Nonplayer Characters)

Nonplayer characters (NPCs) serve several purposes:

- To provide information
- To provide items or trade
- To provide challenges or quests
- To add depth to the world
- To participate in the story

There are potentially any number of archetypes that could be used for these characters, but they tend to be less well rounded than the other characters in the game simply because they don't feature as prominently.

Appearance

Appearance plays a vital role in our perception of a character. We can tell much about people by the way they dress and hold themselves. The way we react to them is influenced by their attractiveness to us. Getting the appearance right is therefore an absolutely vital task. A lot of concept work should go into sketching out a number of ideas and refining them until a finished character emerges. Such a process may take several months of constant revision and review.

Physical Appearance

The physical appearance of characters greatly influences how we perceive them. Psychological studies have shown that more attractive people will make us more receptive to their ideas and make us more likely to trust and believe them and more likely to like them. This is a fact recognized by advertisers who use models or celebrities to endorse their products, even if there is a very tenuous connection [Malim98].

It stands to reason, therefore, that the protagonist should be an attractive character, so that we are immediately more inclined to like him. Conversely, making the antagonist ugly will make us more ready to hate him. More subtly making the antagonist attractive will make his insidious actions seem all the more potent.

One trap that many people fall into is objectifying their protagonists (particularly females), so that they are only seen for their attractiveness. This detracts from the depth of the character and ultimately disrupts the players' connection to their avatars.

Characters in animations, comics, and so on are exaggerated, stylized interpretations of the subjects they reflect. Games often try to reflect reality with their characters, and as approximations get closer, the Uncanny Valley effect hits home. This is the phenomenon where the closer graphics get to reality, the more the slightest error will shatter belief in the illusion. Creating a more stylized character can concentrate and channel the desired impact that the character has on its audience. As well as being more attainable, it will ultimately satisfy the audience more than a subperfect rendition of reality.

Costume

Costume also has a very large impact on the perception of a character. It will impart information about the character's status, profession, and self-image. Again it is an important visual aspect of the character that needs to be just right for that character to work and is almost more important than physical appearance. Several factors should be kept in mind:

The character's role: The costume should match the role that the character plays in the game. The clothing must be practical for the task that is to be performed (if the character had time to consciously choose it).

The character's backstory: The profession of the character and his position in society will have an impact on his costume. A down-and-out tramp will have radically different attire than a rich businessman.

The character's identity: Much of a character's personality will be imbued in the way he presents himself. He may be a control freak who requires everything just so or a laid-back, confident character who wears his clothing with style.

The setting: One major influence on a character's costume will be the setting. The time period, the culture, and so on will determine what kind of clothing the character might wear.

If the character is part of a team, his appearance can be used to unify that team. Members of the team can wear similar costumes or have very clear differences that mark them out, but with a common theme that links them together.

Personality

Imbuing a character with personality will help form his depth of character. Generally, main characters will receive much more attention in fleshing out their personalities than incidental characters, as they are more important to the story. NPCs are often fleshed out by using stock characters—stereotyped characters that have been used many times before and whom the audience will instantly recognize (mad scientist, redneck farmer, etc.). Using stock characters can lead to falling into cliché, so it is advisable not to take them to extremes but to use them more subtly. There is also always the potential for stereotypes to offend.

Backstory

Creating a backstory for a character is the best method of beginning the process of fleshing out a character. Giving him a history will enable you to see clearly where he has come from.

A backstory may include a number of items:

Upbringing: The kind of childhood the character had, how he was raised, and what he might have occupied his time with. A lot of our personality is formed though our childhood experiences.

Social background: The area where the character lived; the kind of cultures to which he was exposed. The social background will determine much about a character's attitude toward life and aspirations.

Major events: Traumatic or spectacular events that might have happened in the past. Such large events will have life-changing repercussions on the character's personality.

Manner

A character's manner determines how he holds himself in front of others—the way he speaks and the way he acts. *Lara Croft* creator Toby Gard strongly suggests that the general pose of a character sends a lot of messages [Gard00]. This pose should give out the right message about that character. A character's manner is based on a number of factors:

Self-image: A character's self-image has a very large impact on the way he holds himself. A confident character tends to have a good self-image (though it may be a façade), whereas a shy character may be self-loathing.

Social background and upbringing: A character's social background will impose what is taboo and what is generally accepted. Upbringing will determine how readily he conforms to the rules of social etiquette.

Motivation

Motivation is what drives a character. First, there are the story-based goals for each main character, but there are also a number of other motivations that can be applied:

Help or harm others: A character may wish to help other people or harm them, depending on his disposition and opinion of the other character.

Voice an opinion: A character will often want to make his point of view known and wish to express his opinion on a subject.

Win: Many characters are devoted to the idea of winning, whether it be winning an argument, a race, a bet, or other competition.

Needs: Every character has physical needs such as hunger, thirst, comfort, and so on and may be working out of desire to fulfill those needs.

Greed: Greed may motivate a character may be motivated to perform an action.

Disposition

A character's disposition is his temperament and outlook on life. Characters with sunny dispositions are likely to approach everyone with a smile, whereas other characters may be grumpy and bad tempered. Some people may be naturally good tempered no matter what struggles they may have had in the past, while others may have many luxuries but are still ill tempered.

Characters as Symbols

Characters might symbolize movements and ideals or oppressive aggressors. They might represent specific groups of people such as the poor or the very rich. They might reference historical figures in a respectful or satirical manner. They might pay homage to characters in other works of fiction. Often characters reflect real-world people known by the writer.

The use of these references allows the building of subtle subplots and meta-references that can be used to draw the audience in. They might be used to add depth and weight to the story and provide hidden meaning and context. Alternatively, they might be used to share a joke with the audience. All in all, character can play a major role in storytelling beyond the direct communication of the story itself.

Movement

The way a character moves is extremely important. The weight, balance, and inertia of that character's movement will impact on how a player perceives him. Animation is the key skill in getting characters to move in a convincing manner. Often motion capture of real actors is used, but hand animation can convey a much greater feeling of character if used well. Motion capture is also completely dependent on the performance abilities of the actor.

SUMMARY

Earlier in the book we defined a character-based game as having a narrative that draws the player through the game. Therefore, when building such a game, it is vital that we give the narrative suitable consideration to improve the experience for the player.

We covered several aspects of narrative in this chapter:

Game versus story: Ludologists and narratologists have bickered over the importance of story, but in reality it is fairly immaterial. There are two forms of narrative—embedded and emergent. In addition to this, we must consider three important aspects of narrative:

- **Suspension of disbelief:** The ability of the audience to involve themselves in the illusion (the fourth wall). Breaking the fourth wall can be seen as bad or can be purposely done to remind the players that they are playing a game.
- **Verisimilitude:** The strength of the illusion created by the game world. Generally we want the player to believe the world is real.
- **Continuity:** The consistency of plot, characters, objects, places, and events.

Setting: Many aspects of setting allow us to create a believable world. Building in backstory will increase the verisimilitude of our narrative. There are several aspects of a setting:

- **Geography:** The physical space that the player will explore, from cities to forests and mountains.
- **Culture:** Many different facets of culture can be explored such as time period, technology, fashion, beliefs and customs, language and dialect, and morals and laws.
- **History:** The creation of a rich backstory for the game world will enhance the experience and the believability for the player.

Story: Story is generally perceived to be the basis of the narrative. Story has been studied for centuries: broken down, dissected, and analyzed by academics and scholars. We have examined some of these elements in this chapter:

- **Narrative elements:** Studies have broken story down into mimesis and diegesis. Barthes broke narrative down into five codes—the hermeneutic code, the proairetic code, the semantic code, the symbolic code, and the cultural code.
- **Narrative structures:** Different methods for structuring a story have been investigated over the years and have resulted in many different structures such as the three-act structure, the five-act structure, the monomyth, and branching narratives.
- **Plot:** Plot determines the events that occur within the story. There are several plot themes that might be explored. Events occur in a particular order—a chronology. Several plot devices might also be used to help structure a story.

- **Interactive storytelling issues:** Three issues are encountered when telling a story interactively—internal consistency, amnesia, and narrative flow.
- **Storytelling devices:** Several devices may be used in games to relay a story—sequences, narration and text display, diegetic story elements, and conversations.
- **Story time line:** The tagging of elements in a story so that specific events can be monitored.

Characters: An essential element of a story-based game. There are several aspects to character creation:

- **Types of character:** Many types of character make up a story—the protagonists, antagonists, supporting characters, and extras.
- **Appearance:** Plays a vital role in the perception of a character, from physical appearance to costume.
- **Personality:** The backstory, manner, motivation, and disposition of a character.
- **Characters as symbols:** Characters can be used to represent aspects of the story.
- **Movement:** The manner in which characters move can be used to define them.

Narrative is an aspect of game design that currently faces much criticism. It is an area that needs a lot of attention from designers and writers, first to understand the medium itself and second to explore new avenues and trigger emotions in the player. Good narrative will add an additional dimension to games and will eventually see them become a medium as well respected as film or literature.

GAME STRUCTURE

In This Chapter

- Logical Structure
- Physical Structure

Every system needs some form of structure, and a game is no different. The organization of content and systems within a game will determine a number of aspects of the game. Certain types of game require particular types of structure; others can be much more free-form in their approach. However, almost all systems will be composed of similar elements but organized in different ways. Essentially, the organization of its elements is like the organization of a string of DNA: similar components strung together in different ways to create different final products.

We will study two main types of structure in this chapter:

- Logical structure
- Physical structure

LOGICAL STRUCTURE

The logical structure of a game determines much of its character and dictates the required technology or may be constricted by available technology. Structure can be used to create a feeling for the game, the order of its elements presenting the game content in different ways to the player. Structure can even determine much of the content itself.

There are two major areas of a game's logical structure:

- Game modes
- Content structure

The two are interrelated, so that particular game modes go with a certain content structure and vice versa.

Game Modes

Game modes are essentially the core divisions of game mechanics within a game. Games may have one or more game modes; some may even have a broad selection. Multiple game modes tend to increase the amount of content required and boost the amount of testing needed to make the game stable and balanced, but with good sets of mechanics they can significantly increase the longevity of a game.

Typically game modes are categorized according to the number of players who can participate, with single-player modes and multiplayer modes.

Single-Player Modes

Almost every game features a single-player mode of some sort, even if it is an AI-driven version of a multiplayer mode. This is mostly due to the history of computer games being a typically solitary pursuit.

Single-player games have a number of potential modes:

- Arcade
- Narrative/story

- Career
- Mini game
- Match
- Training

Arcade

Arcade modes are designed to get the players into the game quickly and allow them to play in short bursts. Narrative within an arcade mode tends to be fairly minimal; the emphasis is on action. This mode is most suited to games that provide adrenaline gaming in succinct levels.

Arcade modes may feature a number of submodes in which a new goal is assigned in addition to completing a level. For instance, a typical arcade mode may ask the player to try to achieve the highest score. Time attack pits the players against the clock, as they aim for the fastest time. Survival asks them to complete as many levels or arenas as possible with limited health.

The content of arcade mode tends to be organized either very linearly or completely free-form in the choice of level to play. This means a system of unlocking is highly likely to be used to contain player progression if level selection is used to structure the game mode.

Narrative

A narrative mode is often the main mode or possibly even the only mode of a game. Here the player follows a narrative through to its conclusion.

The structure of a narrative mode can vary greatly. Many games follow a very linear path, as it is much easier to fit to a traditional narrative structure. Branching allows a little more choice for the player as to how a narrative will unfold. Free-form environments are the new rising star of modern gaming structure, with champions such as *Grand Theft Auto* having much success. It offers sandbox play with narrative structure that appeals to a wide-ranging audience.

Narratives are not well suited to free-form level-select structures without some form of limits being placed upon them (such as unlocking); otherwise, the flow of the narrative is destroyed.

Career

This is a slightly more unusual mode, as it tends to signify a much more free-form gaming experience, where the player sets his own goals and the narrative is driven by the player's actions. This is a mainstay of some sports games and might also form the basis for an RPG (though multiplayer experiences in this field are much more popular these days). The classic *Elite* is a prime example of a career mode in an action–adventure game.

This type of game mode is not suited to linear structures, as they restrict the player's freedom of choice. Free-form worlds with plenty of choice (or sports titles) are really the only option.

Mini Game/Challenge

Mini game or challenge modes encapsulate simple mechanics or elements of the main game into small bite-sized portions. Mini games are designed to be simple, very often using only one game mechanic. They are usually unlocked by playing through the main game mode, but a large group of them could constitute the entire game.

A free-form level-select structure is a must, as each game is likely to be a separate entity and not connected in any real way with the other games.

Match

A match in a single-player mode is a single-player version of a multiplayer match. Other players are replaced by AI bots (computer-controlled adversaries that mimic human opponents), so for all intent and purposes it is the same structure as a multiplayer match.

Training

Training mode is an opportunity for the players to familiarize themselves with controls, try out new moves, and improve their skills. Training modes may also be used as a way of boosting a character's attributes for the main game mode.

Training modes are usually a very cut-down structure based on the main game mode, perhaps allowing a few different sections of a level to be played or to act as backdrops for the training gameplay.

Multiplayer Modes

Having some aspect of multiplayer gameplay is now a common request of most publishers, but it shouldn't just be shoehorned into a game just for the sake of it. Some games are well suited to multiplayer modes (shooters, fighting games, and the like) and some aren't (detective adventures, for example).

There are several potential multiplayer modes:

- Match
- Multiplayer arcade/narrative
- Party games
- Career

Match

A multiplayer match is a collection of players meeting on a map to compete against each other. The structure is very free-form, allowing any map to be chosen to compete within. Some kind of grading system may be applied to separate players according to skill, but this is usually only done with online matches.

Tournaments might also be constructed by players, taking account of performance over a number of matches. This could take the form of a league or a knock-out cup. This may be a feature of the multiplayer mode itself but is just as likely to have been set up by the players themselves.

Multiplayer Arcade/Narrative

Multiplayer narrative or arcade mode is usually a cooperative or competitive romp through the standard single-player modes. Cooperative modes require players to work together. There may be specially augmented content to provide extra gameplay for cooperative mode or it may even be the main game mode of the entire game (though the game will have to be designed around this whole mechanic). Competitive games are usually a race for the highest score or the fastest time.

The classic arcade game *Gauntlet*® was a mix of cooperative play, to progress through the levels, and competitive play, to achieve the highest score.

Party Games

Party games are multiplayer mini games. The players compete in a variety of different mini games to determine a winner. Party games are usually an addition to the main game, such as those featured in *Super Monkey Ball*™, where players can play versions of tennis, bowling, pool, and so on. However, the entire game may be based around playing a series of party games, as is seen in titles such as *Fusion Frenzy*®, the *Mario Party*® series, the *Wario Ware*™ series, and *Bishi Bashi*.

Career

Multiplayer career mode is most likely to be a massively multiplayer online (MMO) world. These games are growing in popularity and have only just started to appear on consoles. The task of designing of an MMO game is vast and beyond the scope of this particular book!

Content Structure

Content is structured in different ways in different games, depending on genre, target audience, and the feel the game is aiming to achieve. Content structure can be broken down into two types that define the way the game is constructed and even how it is delivered:

- Narrative flow
- Environment structure

Narrative Flow

Games that contain a narrative are structured in one of three ways:

- Linear
- Branching
- Episodic

Linear

Linear games have a very traditionally structured narrative—a narrative that follows a set course, having a beginning, a middle, and an end (though not necessarily in that order). The story unfolds, and the players have no real effect on the narrative; they are along for the ride, so to speak. Linear narrative is often criticized by the gaming cognoscenti, but some of the best games have been linear: *Half-Life*, *Resident Evil*, and *Final Fantasy*, to name just a few. A good plot and good atmosphere can easily overcome the lack of choice, plus it is a lot easier to develop and maintain. Offering the player choice in lower-level mechanics and having a strictly linear narrative can create a very solid game experience.

Branching

Branching narrative offers the player a choice of how a narrative unfolds and often even the ability to choose the conclusion of a narrative. We give the player choice by offering a selection of several set paths. These branching paths may break away and reconnect to form a single conclusion. There may be a single main story thread with a number of side missions and choices as to which levels or mission are tackled first (this is the narrative structure used in *Grand Theft Auto*). See Figure 4.1 for an example of a linear story with branching.

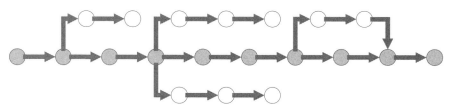

FIGURE 4.1 A linear structure with branching side missions.

A narrative might offer a number of branches that lead to different conclusions (see Figure 4.2).

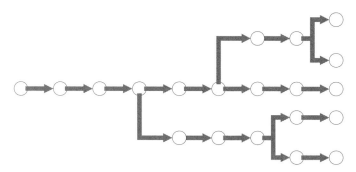

FIGURE 4.2 A branching structure with multiple conclusions.

The biggest disadvantage of a branching narrative is the sheer amount of content that must be created that isn't seen. This offers great opportunities for exploration and replayability but is unlikely to be seen by most players of the game, so it could be considered to be wasted work. If time is a factor (as it often is), branching can be very expensive, as it requires more bug testing as well as extra content.

With a branching structure that allows multiple missions to be engaged at once, there needs to be a method of tracking the player's progress. A handy system for this task is a quest/mission log. This registers all the possible missions and all the objectives required to complete those quests or missions, along with their current status (see Table 4.1).

TABLE 4.1   An Example Quest/Mission Log

MISSION	STATUS
Rescue the sailor	Not started
Find the row boat	Not complete
Find oars	Not Complete
Row to island	Not Complete
Save the whale	In progress
Find large hammock	Completed
Find giant winch	Completed
Winch whale to safety	Not complete
Catch a big fish	Complete
Find fishing rod	Complete
Find bait	Complete
Catch the big one!	Complete

Having a log of mission objectives allows their current status to be tested and makes it easier to produce a save game; otherwise, you end up having random variables here, there, and everywhere.

Episodic

Episodic structures deliver narrative in sections of either self-contained story or smaller parts of a greater whole—much like a TV series. This is a model for game structure that is likely to grow in the future as the Internet allows easier distribution of data and greater connectivity. The longevity of a game can be greatly increased with the prospect of further episodes to download, and further possible revenue can be generated by charging for new episodes.

Environment Structure

An environment is structured in particular ways, as technology limits the amount of information that can be loaded at once. As such, a world is broken into a number of sections that are either loaded or streamed into memory as needed. The structure of an environment often reflects this underlying technology, but a particular structure might also demand a specific technology. Streaming seems to be the better option, but it does have issues such as the amount of time needed to stream separate sections and how detailed each section can be. Streamed worlds often need doglegs—areas of little action to allow the next section to be loaded in.

Several environment structures can be used:

- Distinct levels
- Continuous environment
- Domains

Distinct Levels

By far the simplest structure is to have distinct, hermetic levels. Each level is a self-enclosed space that does not need to connect or even relate to any of the others. Mission-based games often use this structure, so that one minute you could be in Siberia, and the next in Egypt. For a linear narrative they can work well. The spaces between the levels act as gaps in time, so each level could be considered a chapter in the story. Distinct levels mean that loading is the more likely choice, although if levels are particularly large, then streaming might be employed within the level. Distinct levels also suit more-fractured narrative structures, perhaps linked by one hub level to jump to each of the other levels.

Continuous Environment

A continuous environment has one level connected with the next, never teleporting the player in time or space (unless via a physical teleportation device). Each area must flow into the next, but they can still have different styles (*Half-Life* is a great example of a continuous environment).

If pure loading is to be used, then the point at which levels are switched, a holding section needs to be created, where a copy of this section is included in both levels. A streaming world needs a dogleg area where little action occurs so the next level can be streamed in. This can be unrealistic in games that have large amounts of data for each level, as the doglegs will have to be very long or have to occur regularly if level parts are made smaller to accommodate this. Multiple processors on the very latest game consoles may offer solutions to streaming that allow data to be loaded with lots of action still on screen.

Domains

Domain-based worlds are those that are interlinked like a network, so that there are multiple routes to each. Each domain can be a self-contained level linked to one or more other levels by doglegs. The effect is a large world that the player is free to explore. Such worlds may feature loading, or more commonly these days, they will be streamed. Doglegs do not necessarily have to be tunnels or restricted sections. In *Grand Theft Auto: San Andreas* a large free-form world is created by streaming sections beyond the range of visibility as they are needed.

PHYSICAL STRUCTURE

The physical structure, or architecture, of a game will often vary from project to project. These systems are separate parts of the game code that perform specific tasks and are generally created by individual or small groups of coders as the game is built. Often these systems can be middleware—licensed code that forms a particular part or parts of the system.

Most of these systems will have an impact on the designer's limitations and affect the way many of the core game features can be implemented. Thus, it is important that the designer familiarizes himself with how each system works, but he does not need to have in-depth knowledge of the code itself. A typical system is shown in Figure 4.3.

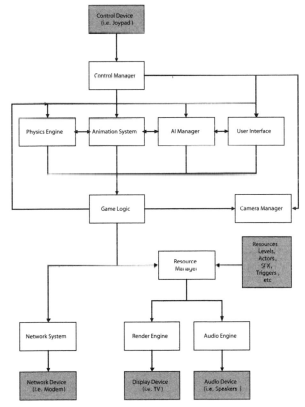

FIGURE 4.3   The potential physical structure of a game.

Many of the game systems are heavily interwoven, impacting upon their connecting systems and determining their structure.

Obviously, not every game is built in exactly the same way. There may be many more systems than those listed here, but the following systems will have a direct impact on what a designer can do with the game.

System Components

Every game is composed of a number of vital components. There may be many more peripheral components that describe specific aspects, or many different ways to break down each component.

Control Manager

A character is controlled via a set of rules that govern which animation is linked to a particular movement. These rules are called movement controllers. In the case of the player, the inputs of the control pad are mapped to different animations according to the context of the current situation. An AI-controlled character might mimic this system by sending dummy control pad inputs to a movement controller. This is a sensible system to use, as it offers the potential for any character to be controlled by the player.

Physics Engine

Physics is a burgeoning area of game development. Originally physics was just composed of basic collision and response systems to determine the boundaries of the world and prevent characters from walking though walls or falling though the floor. Now, however, physics engines are running ever more complex simulations that can accurately represent movement in a procedural manner. Physics is discussed in more detail in a later chapter.

Animation System

Animations are what makes elements in the world move. Several forms of animation might be used in game:

Procedural: An object is moved by altering parameters in code. Procedural animation is generally basic, such as a door sliding open or a lift moving. The benefit of procedural animation is that it is easy to apply to an object and easy to control and manipulate. Physics systems now handle a lot of dynamic movement of objects within the world. Research is being done into more advanced procedural animation, such as moving entire characters and is improving all the time.

Simple animation: Subobjects within the hierarchy are rotated or transformed to create basic animations. This is useful for fairly simple elements that could also be done procedurally. However, animating them places the control in the hands of an animator rather than a coder, which can allow for more interesting movement. Doing this causes problems with dynamic interactions, which are more easily done procedurally.

Deformation: Objects are squashed or stretched by manipulating vertices.

Rigging: A series of linked bones form a structure onto which a skin is placed. Moving the bones in the structure deforms the skin surrounding it according to weighting applied to it. Different joints can be applied to create complex rigs. This is the system by which characters are animated. Render engines have a limited number of bones that they can support per object. A typical skeleton is shown in Figure 4.4.

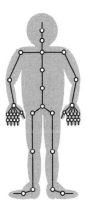

FIGURE 4.4   A typical skeleton for a character.

An animation system might support different methods of manipulating the skeletons of rigged characters, such as inverse kinematics (IK), which allows the extremities of a skeleton to be manipulated to affect all the connecting joints. A foot can be pulled forward and the calf and thigh bones will follow. IK also allows particular elements to be overridden and manipulated separately from the rest of the skeleton.

AI System

The AI system controls every character not under direct control of the player. This includes all enemies, allies, and NPCs. It might also be used to control other systems such as a camera, so that it can move intelligently around the world.

A later chapter is dedicated to the wonderful world of AI in games.

User Interface

The user interface displays information to the player via a heads up display or a series of menus. The user interface may vary in complexity from overlaying 2D sprites to more complex 3D rendering of the user interface elements. The user interface is discussed in a later section of the book.

Camera System

In a third-person game the camera is a very important element that needs to be given a lot of attention. In a first-person game it is much simpler, as there is only one camera. There are all sorts of ways of implementing the camera, from a standard chase camera to fixed splines. A camera system needs to be designed with flexibility in mind and should be easy to tweak. Cameras are discussed in further depth in a later chapter.

Game Logic

Game logic is what determines the functionality of the game and how elements interrelate with one another.

Game Relationships

The relationships between all the different elements can be fairly complex, as shown in Figure 4.5.

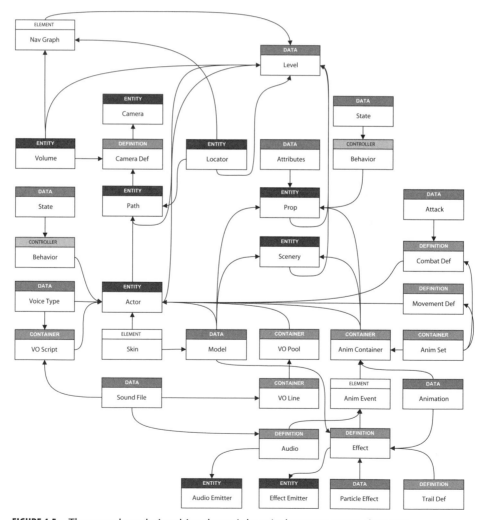

FIGURE 4.5   The complex relationships that might exist between game elements.

Game Entities

Every game world is constructed out of entities. Each varies in type, having a number of parameters that describe it. All of these entities work together to create the final result—a working game world.

All sorts of naming conventions are used to describe these entities, but the metaphor of a movie or play is the most suitable for character-based games.

The physical entities in a game all fit within this metaphor, so that we have:

Actors: The performers or characters in our game world

Props: Objects that the actors can interact with and use

Scenery: The backdrop for our performance

Cameras: The mechanism we use for viewing the action and what creates the images our audience will see

Effects: Particles and special effects that wow the audience

Lights: The source of illumination that enables us to add atmosphere

However, a game has a number of other less tangible mechanisms that go toward making the system work:

Volumes: Sections of world space that are assigned to various triggers, sector loading, cameras, and so on

Locators: Points in world space

Paths: Collections of locators that describe a line through world space to be traversed by physical entities

These entities are studied in further depth in Part 3, "World Building."

Data

Underlying the entities themselves is the physical data that make up various parts of the system. There are several forms of data:

Containers: Data organized into sets for easy reference. For example, an animation container will contain any number of animations so that they can be referenced by entities or script.

Raw data: The raw files that contain sound, geometry, material data, and so on.

Attributes: Data that describe particular parameters of the game entities.

Elements: Specific game data used to describe the world or an element within it. For example, navigation graphs are used to give the AI a representation of world space, whereas anim events are used to describe the point at which an event can occur during an animation.

Resource Manager

The resource manager is a vital part of the game engine that controls access to all the various resources. Its job is to load only what is needed at any given point rather than wasting memory on information that is not presently required.

The manager will do the job of ferrying information from the disc to memory and leaving what is not needed. As such, all sorts of information may be divided up into manageable pieces. Part of a level designer's job is likely to be dividing up level data so that information can be loaded for the current area in which the player is playing without wasting huge sections of memory with level data that is not needed. Another way to save a large area of space is by only loading the animations or textures for a particular sequence when it is needed. The resource manager will also allow audio to be streamed from the disc.

Network System

The network system allows the game to communicate with software running on other devices. This might be through a direct linkup, a wireless link, or the Internet. The actual methods of communication (protocols, packets, etc.) are fairly immaterial to the game designer. All you really need to know are the technical limitations of the system (what amount of data can be transferred, latency, maximum connections, etc.). Other than that, if you really want to dig into networking systems you might want to pick up a book devoted to the subject.

Render Engine

The render engine is often considered the most important part of a game. Famous render engine coders such as John Carmack are revered throughout the industry for their coding prowess. The render engine draws all the graphics to the screen. The more efficient it is at performing this function, the better the graphics can be.

Nearly every modern console game uses a 3D render engine. Previously, in the 16-bit era of the SEGA Genesis® and Super Nintendo Entertainment System, graphics were mostly 2D—sprites drawn over backgrounds. These days a scene is created by performing a lot of complex calculations to work out what can be seen through the camera currently being used.

A render engine is often brought in as middleware so the developers can concentrate on creating assets rather than having to rebuild the wheel each time they make a new game. There are many choices of render engine out there, some of the most popular being Renderware, the Quake Engine, Source, and Unreal. These often cost a large amount to license for a commercial project, but the mod community (maps and modifications made to existing games by hobbyist game developers) around Quake, Source, and Unreal allows enthusiasts to build their own games without the need for a license, as long as they are not to be used for commercial purposes. Modding is a great way for designers to build up a portfolio of work to break into the industry as a professional, and many game studios like to hire from the mod community.

Often too much emphasis is placed on the importance of graphics. Technology advances extremely quickly, and render engines tend to be upgraded with a "me too" philosophy—if someone else does it then it must be copied.

Render engines are often tailored for specific purposes. For them to be efficient, many compromises must be made. A render engine should be built to fit the design, but all too often a design is shoehorned into a render engine without proper thought for how levels are to be constructed. The results can be disastrous. A general rule of thumb is:

- Very high-detail engines generally need to have fairly short draw distances, so levels tend to be interiors or confined spaces.
- Large expanses of scenery or open cityscapes mean high detail is difficult to achieve (not only from a rendering point of view, but also because of the sheer amount of work involved). Where a large vista is required, visual fidelity may have to be sacrificed.

If you are creating a linear, confined experience, then the former renderer will likely fit the bill. However, if you are constructing a large free-roaming city or an open expanse, then the latter kind of renderer will be required.

Audio Engine

Audio is an essential part of a game system that is often overlooked. Audio engines are often programmed as an afterthought and not given the full attention that they deserve. A lot of available technologies use sound in ever more impressive ways. 3D sound has come into its own in recent years and allows for the use of sound in new and exciting ways. However, few people have the necessary setup at home for most of these technologies that require five or more speakers to be set up around the audience for maximum effect.

Audio is discussed in more depth in a later chapter.

System Types

The underlying methods of linking the entities together, which allow them to communicate with each other, can differ from game to game.

Event Message System

In our opinion, the ideal game system is an event message system. This encapsulates information and behavior within each entity so that it knows how to function. An event messaging system is used to send information between entities. These messages then cause the entities to perform specific actions or behaviors.

An event can be triggered in many ways. It may occur when an entity enters a specific volume or leaves one. It may be caused by the enemy being hit or killed. Multitudes of events might be assigned to the various entities in the game world.

When an event occurs, a message is sent to a receiver, which has behaviors built into it that detail how to handle the type of message that is received. An event can be broken down to the following:

Event: The action performed to trigger the event, such as `OnEnter` or `OnExit` for a trigger volume.

Activator: The entity that triggers the event. Events often only occur when a certain activator performs them, such as the Player.

Message: The message that is sent to the receiver such as Activate, Open, Close, and so on.

Message Data: Any extra data that might be sent with a message. For example, if a Change Color message were sent to a light, this might be the RGB values of the desired color.

Receiver: The entity or list of entities that is to receive the message.

Each message attached to an event might also have a delay before trigger, a maximum number of times it can be triggered, and a count of trigger times before the message is sent.

The event message system facilitates much faster and more productive level design, as we shall see later. It is also an easy concept to understand and visualize. One problem with the event system is that the receiver must know how to handle the event. Events can be lost if they are not correctly handled, and entities become reliant on input from other entities in the system. If a message is not handled, but the entity is reliant on receiving it to continue, then the entity will be stuck waiting for a message that might never be sent again. This is potentially game breaking. However, it just requires careful handling of any important events to prevent such a situation from occurring.

Polling System

Another method of linking entities is to cycle through entities requesting information every x number of cycles. This is a proactive system that means that information will eventually be acquired even if the first instance of an occurrence is missed. Also, it makes entities self-sufficient rather than relying on inputs from other entities in the system.

Such a system is generally extremely inefficient, as it means that a lot of unnecessary communication is occurring, which can severely slow down the game. A polling system is rarely used for game logic in large games, as the amount of data that must be processed becomes restrictive. Some game systems may still use polling systems, such as sensory AI.

SUMMARY

The structure of a game is a vital element of development. Both the physical structure of the game systems and the logical structure of the game content will have a major impact on the game itself.

Logical structure: The organization and dissemination of content is defined by two elements of the logical structure:

- **Game modes:** The various modes of play such as arcade, narrative/story, career, mini game, match, or training. Each game mode has its own unique feel and may have different game mechanics than other game modes.
- **Content structure:** The organization of the content: first, to create narrative flow, which may be linear, episodic, or branching, and second, to create environment structures such as distinct levels, continuous environments, or domains.

Physical structure: The systems and elements that allow the game to exist. These systems are a vital part of creating a working game engine. We looked at several aspects of the physical structure in this chapter.

- **System components:** The basic components that are required to make a game including control manager, physics engine, animation system, AI system, user interface, camera system, game logic, resource manager, network system, render engine, and audio engine.
- **System types:** The methods of connecting systems and enabling communication. There are two basic types—event message or polling. Event message is generally the best choice for most systems since it is the least processor intensive, but some systems will require polling elements.

The logical and physical structures of games are likely to change as the language of games changes and new systems evolve to deal with new problems and requirements. Physical structures in particular are likely to get ever more complex as the requirements for content in games increases. A quickly booming aspect of the games industry is middleware for particular systems. It is conceivable that in the future developers will pick and choose various components from which to build their game.

PART

2

GAME MECHANICS

Game mechanics are the basis of various aspects of gameplay. Getting the core mechanics of a game right is an essential skill of the designer. Much of the first stage of development should be spent refining these core mechanics. With these in place, it will be much easier to apply the content—the meat of the game—to these mechanics—the skeleton of the game.

This being a character-based console game, the core mechanics will be very different from a driving or strategy-based game. Very specific systems have to be built and balanced to create the core of a character-based game.

The first chapter in this part of the book explores character control. This is the interface between the players and their on-screen avatars, and it is vital to the success of the gameplay. Get this part of the game wrong and you can forget about anyone truly enjoying the game, as they will have to battle with frustration from the very beginning.

The second chapter covers viewpoints and cameras. This describes the visual representation of action on screen. Again this is a vital aspect of gameplay, as the players must be able to see what they are doing.

The next four chapters explore various aspects of combat—a game mechanic that is more than likely to be part of character-based game in some form or another. Being such a ubiquitous game mechanic, it is deserving of in-depth exploration.

Finally this part of the book takes a look at game economies. There are many more economies than you first may think when looking at games. Besides the obvious economy of wealth, there are character attributes, ratings, time, lives, and more that will be explored in this chapter.

CHARACTER CONTROL

In This Chapter

- Control Input
- Standard Movement
- Advanced Movement
- Object Interaction
- Quick Time Events

Interaction is a key element of computer games. It defines the medium. One of the most vital tasks for any designer is getting the control system right. It is where most of initial focus should be concentrated. Build a prototype and get the character control just right. If there is any problem with controlling the character, then the player is going to have a worse experience, no matter how good the content may be. This goes for all elements of control, from the basic movement of the character to the amount of control the player has over the camera.

We will cover several aspects of character control in this chapter:

- Control input
- Standard movement
- Advanced movement
- Object interaction
- Quick time events

CONTROL INPUT

In a character-based game the relationship between character movement and control system is inseparable. Bad controls will make a game unplayable, as control is the translation of player input into on-screen action. Even if the right controls are available, unless the default settings are good for the majority of players, they will be instantly put off from playing the game.

Control Devices

Many styles of control device have been invented over the years. Some have stood the test of time, and some leave us wondering, "What were they thinking?"

The Joypad

The de facto standard for game control on a console these days has to be the joypad. Sure, you can get joysticks, keyboards, and mice, but the only control device you can be sure the potential player of a console owns is a joypad (until some new device replaces it).

Joypads have come on a long way since the one-button digital pad or paddle controllers of the very first consoles. Now we have dual analog sticks and buttons coming out of every orifice. However, while having all this control is a good thing, it can lead to some bad design. There are several considerations the designer should keep in mind when designing control layout.

Ergonomics

The überjoypad below shown in Figure 5.1 is purely fictitious but describes a typical pad design that has become commonplace on today's consoles.

One problem with such a pad is the sheer overwhelming impression it leaves on many nonhardcore gamers. For many people this type of control device is a barrier to playing games.

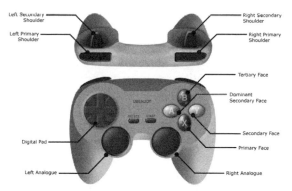

FIGURE 5.1   A typical console pad layout.

Analog Sticks: The use of dual analog sticks is becoming a standard for joy-pads. It enables the player to have analog control using both thumbs, which allows for full 3D movement in game space. The left stick is usually used for movement. The right stick can be used for any number of other things, though it is usually assigned the task of controlling the movement of the camera. Some joypads also have click-down functionality on the sticks themselves, which is generally used as some kind of toggle function (as it feels very awkward to hold the stick down and move it).

Digital Pad: The digital pad is often overlooked as a relic of a bygone era, but it still has its use on a control layout. Its distinct on/off digital nature can be used for situations where the analog controller can be unforgiving. Menu navigation and additional commands are a popular use for the digital pad, but many players may also prefer digital control of their character, so it should never be overlooked or dismissed off-hand.

Face Buttons: Face buttons are the buttons on the front of the joypad that gen-erally lie underneath the player's right thumb. These buttons act as the main control buttons in most games but are difficult to use effectively in first-person games that use both sticks, as they require the player to release his thumb from the right stick or form a strange claw shape with the right hand—not a comfortable playing position. To differentiate between all the face buttons, they can be broken down in order of importance:

- **Primary:** The function that is used most
- **Dominant secondary:** The second-most-used function
- **Secondary:** The third-most-used function, often as important as the dominant secondary
- **Tertiary:** The least-used function on the face buttons

Sometimes a joypad will have more face buttons. These generally take less precedence than the main four buttons that appear on most joypads. Note that the layout of the uberjoypad is based on a Western gaming model. Eastern control layouts may have different primary and dominant secondary button layouts.

Shoulder Buttons and Triggers: Shoulder triggers are generally for more periphery functions in most games. The main functions are generally placed on the face buttons. In first-person games shoulder triggers come into their own, as they allow the players to keep their thumbs on the right stick and use their fingers to perform the actions.

Functional Buttons: Most joypads have two functional buttons: Start and Select (or Back in the case of the Xbox®). These are assigned mainly to user interface functionality, offering pause menus, inventory screens, and the like. Their positioning is usually out of immediate reach, meaning that they should only ever be used for these purposes and should not be mapped to prime functions.

Feel

Feel is vital. You can have the most perfect-sounding control configuration on paper, but if it doesn't work well in practice, it is going to severely hinder your game.

One of the most important things to get right from the very beginning of designing a game is the fluidity of the controls. Once you have that, you have crossed the biggest barrier to player immersion. Design a control system that they can master with ease, and they will be navigating their way around your world like seasoned pros. Get it wrong, and the joypad will feel the brunt of your mistakes as it is hurled against the TV set.

Silly mistakes are often made because the designer hasn't properly thought about ergonomics when planning the control layout. As noted earlier, if the players have to use both sticks to control movement, they would find it difficult to use the face buttons at the same time unless they develop claw-like hands.

The best way to plan a control method is to hold the pad in your hands. Envision yourself playing the game and get a feel for how those controls will work. Having the controller right there will allow you to instantly tell if something works, even if you do look a bit silly while doing it.

Additional Features

As well as these primary buttons, controllers may have a number of other features that read input or provide feedback.

Vibration: Vibration is an interesting addition to the control scheme and can provide important feedback to the player. Using vibration in the right way can enhance a gaming experience. Using vibration in the wrong way can leave a player hurting—really hurting. Vibration should be fairly subtle. Make sparing use of it and use it in appropriate ways. Good examples of this are notifying the players when they are hit or when they hit an enemy. It could be used to build tension. Imagine the controller acting as the avatar's heartbeat. As a scary situation unfolds the heartbeat increases, or maybe it can even be used to indicate that the player character is nearing death. The essential thing to remember is not to go crazy. Having large or prolonged shocks over a period of time will literally hurt the player. Remember that subtle is more effective. Many console manufacturers won't allow vibration above a certain level anyway, so you could find your game failing their requirements for such an apparently minor thing.

Force Feedback: Force feedback is different than vibration. This is designed to make control more difficult under certain circumstances—to force against the player's movement. This is generally confined to racing games at present and is unlikely to be found in any control device but a steering wheel. However, we may see more joypad force feedback in the future.

Motion Sensing: The latest controller craze is for motion sensing. After Nintendo announced its revolutionary new controller for its Wii™ console, Sony followed suit with an announcement that rumble in the PS3 controller was to be replaced by motion sensing in six axes. The applications for these will potentially revolutionize the way we interact with games, so there are some exciting times ahead.

Keyboard and Mouse

The keyboard and humble mouse are the rulers of the PC world. There has not yet been invented a better pairing of input devices (that isn't a stupendously expensive prototype) for everyday computer tasks.

The mouse and keyboard lend themselves well to certain genres of game, such as the point and click adventure and of course the FPS. The suitability of the mouse and keyboard to the FPS genre is the main factor in their popularity in the PC market. On paper the mouse and keyboard aren't really the ideal input device for the FPS, but in practice the precision and speed of the mouse makes it invaluable and far more effective to use than the joypad.

Keyboards and mice are available for most consoles, but they tend to be fairly obscure and are highly unlikely to be the primary control scheme for the majority of players.

Alternative Control Devices

Joypads are the most popular choice for game control, but there are plenty of other types of controller available.

Light Gun

Light gun games were popular in the arcades and migrated to the consoles and enjoyed a mild success in the 16-bit era. They don't really find success on home consoles these days, mainly because they are so utterly limited in comparison to the fluidity and freedom of the FPS.

Dancemat

The dancemat is a fairly new craze that began when rhythm games or "Bemani" became hugely successful. The dancemat introduced gaming to millions of teenage girls who previously thought computer gaming was only for the geeky boys. It's a sign of the times that games can now appeal to such wide-ranging audiences.

Cameras

Using cameras in game control is a relatively new concept. At the time of writing, Sony's EyeToy® has made a fairly large impact on the gaming scene, bringing a new style of gameplay into the home. The players themselves become the game characters. There really is no greater immersion than being inside the TV yourself. The full body movements required to control games with this device make them very tiring to play. Currently the control techniques are mainly limited to movement detection, which has a number of drawbacks, not least of which is fidelity and the ease of being able to cheat the system. However, there are plans to have depth detection built into the camera, which will enable much more complex interaction with the game world.

Touch Screens

While touch screen technology is far from new, it has not been a major feature of gaming until Nintendo introduced its DS™ handheld system. The touch screen offers a more visceral interaction with the game world, allowing more direct manipulation of objects, as well as providing a changeable user interface for a different variety of functions to be laid on the screen at any point. The screen can also be used as a substitute for the analog controller, allowing the user analog movement input by dragging across the screen.

The Pointing Wand

At the time of writing, the Nintendo Wii is making a splash with a new form of controller. This is based on the concept of a TV remote with a few basic buttons. The clever part is the motion sensors and infrared that enable it to act like a light gun or be tilted to move in multiple directions. Now the players can "feel" the actions they are performing. It remains to be seen whether this will end up causing serious arm ache or whether it will be a truly revolutionary way of interacting with game worlds.

Bespoke Devices

Bespoke devices are those tailored to a particular game mechanic: Sega® *Bass Fishing's*™ fishing rod, *Samba de Amigo's* maracas, *Donkey Konga's*™ bongos, *Guitar Hero's*™ guitar and many more. Bespoke devices are the most specialized of game control devices and thus will usually not translate to any other types of game, but the sense of immersion they can induce is unparalleled.

Control Schemes

When designing a control scheme, it is imperative that you do your research. Play as many similar games as possible. Learn what works in control schemes and look for what doesn't work so that you can avoid falling into the same traps.

A few golden rules apply to any control scheme:

Ergonomics: The first concern is how the player is to physically interact with the device in a comfortable manner. A good control system must not encourage or require uncomfortable positions.

Intuitiveness: A control system should be easy to learn and should feel connected to the actions that are to be performed. A lot of games of the same genre share similar control schemes. This is for a good reason, as natural selection has occurred over time, with some truly unworkable systems going the way of the dinosaur. These schemes are familiar, which allows the player to interact immediately. Evolution allows the designer to take a good control system and refine it. However, never be afraid to be wildly experimental. Sometimes it takes a leap of faith to create a control system better than the rest. Just make sure it is thoroughly tested, and if it isn't working, don't be afraid to ditch it.

Simplicity: Overly complex control systems will confuse the player. Having to remember whole sequences of button presses to perform an action will distract from the player's sense of immersion. Use context sensitivity to map similar functions onto one button. Also, don't feel that you have to use every button on the joypad. If your game doesn't need the button, then don't use it.

Responsiveness: It is essential that the controls be responsive. Any delay between a button press and the action being carried out will result in the controls feeling very sluggish. Blending between a standing to a walk or run should be almost instantaneous; otherwise, the players will feel like they are wading through molasses. The players only feel like they have issued a command when they see an immediate response on screen. Keep everything responsive, and the game will feel fluid.

Flexibility: Not everyone is going to find the same control scheme perfect for their style of play. It always pays to offer players the opportunity to configure their control layout to the style they would like, and is fairly cheap to do.

What follows is a selection of different control schemes that might be used on a particular type of game. These have been used in one form or another on many of these types of games. That does not mean they are gospel, but it does show they are schemes that work.

Platformer

Things are always fairly simple with platform games (or at least they should be). The primary action is jump, as this is the action the player will be performing the most through the game. Attack is then assigned to the dominant secondary. The other buttons may be assigned to any number of different skills that the player character may have. The platformer layout is shown in Figure 5.2.

FIGURE 5.2 A typical platformer layout.

First-Person Shooter

The fairly essential element of the FPS is the use of the two thumbsticks to control their character's movement. This means that the face buttons are no longer as useful as they might be in other games. All reaction-based actions such as jumping and firing weapons, the primary functions, are therefore mapped onto the shoulder buttons.

The face buttons can then be used on less action-orientated functions such as changing weapons, reloading a weapon, or using items. Figure 5.3 shows a typical FPS layout.

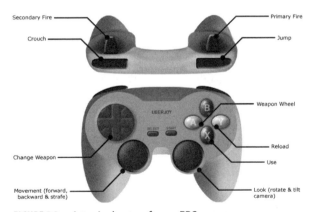

FIGURE 5.3 A typical setup for an FPS game.

Third-Person Action Adventure

The action adventure tends to place less emphasis on dexterous movement and more on interaction with the environment. A very basic example of this genre would have a simple control layout. The key ingredients in any action adventure are usually:

Use: Interact with a context-sensitive object such as a switch.
Jump: Jump up onto higher ledges or other objects.
Attack: Perform an attack against an opponent.
Inventory: Open up inventory to review objects.
Lock On: Many third-person games that contain ranged combat may have a
lock-on feature to improve aiming.

The buttons listed above are for an adventure-orientated game. Should a different function form the core of the gameplay, then that function should be mapped to
the primary button. If combat is the main focus of the game, then there may be another button dedicated to a second attack, whereas if acrobatics is the main drive of
the action, then there may be other buttons mapped to specific acrobatic functions.
A typical layout is shown in Figure 5.4.

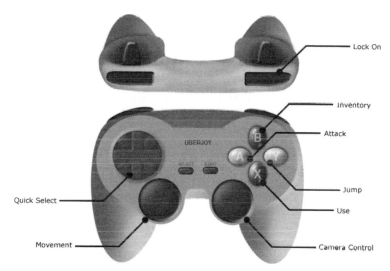

FIGURE 5.4   A typical third-person action–adventure joypad layout.

The quick select is a device often used in adventure games, whereby items or
weapons can be assigned to the pad, and a simple direction press uses or selects them.

Combat Action

If a game is heavily oriented around combat, then the control functionality will be
mapped accordingly. Many or all of the face buttons will be mapped to various types
of attack. Also, the shoulder buttons may contain other styles of attack, usually
throws and grappling moves. A typical layout is shown in Figure 5.5.

The layout shown in Figure 5.5 is only an example of a possible combat layout.
There are many different ways a combat scheme could be mapped to a controller,
depending on how your combat system is designed to work. *Tekken*, for example,
mapped every limb to a face button on the controller.

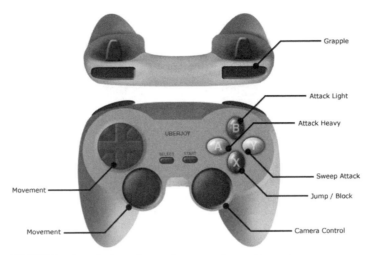

Grapple

Attack Light

Attack Heavy

Sweep Attack

Jump / Block

Camera Control

Movement

Movement

FIGURE 5.5   A typical combat action game joypad layout.

STANDARD MOVEMENT

Standard movement of a character describes the act of moving the character around the world via inputs from the control pad. This is very basic movement such as creep, walk, and run.

Movement Styles

The two basic styles of movement are screen-relative movement and character-relative movement.

Screen-Relative Movement

This is perhaps the more common style of movement. Essentially the direction of the stick is directly related to the movement of the character on screen. Thus, if the player moves the stick upward, the character will move up into the screen. Should the player move the stick left, the character will move to the left on screen.

Sometimes the camera is turned when any direction other than forward is pressed to bring the new direction of heading into view. This will require the player to steadily move the controller around to the up position to retain a straight heading, but this tends to be a natural behavior as the camera turns.

Advantages of screen-relative movement are:

- It is a simple control mechanism to grasp.
- It is fast and fluid—allows rapid changes of direction.

Disadvantages are:

- It can be difficult to aim ranged projectiles.
- The character cannot walk backward without adding a further layer of control.

Character-Relative Movement

Character-relative movement is less popular than it used to be at the advent of 3D gaming but still has a place in today's gaming world. With character-relative movement the stick is divided into four main action areas: forward, back, left, and right. Forward causes the character to move forward, back makes him walk backward, and left and right rotate the character respectively.

When the camera is locked behind the character, this control system is fairly simple to use, but it starts to fail when the action is viewed from a different angle, as it requires a good deal of spatial awareness on the player's part to work out the required direction. Also, the method of rotating the player tends to be fairly sluggish. Often some form of quick 180° turn is incorporated.

This method is suited to aiming ranged weapons, as the method of rotation allows the players to aim like they would in a first-person game.

Advantages of character-relative movement are:

- Aim is fairly accurate.
- It allows easy backward movement.

Disadvantages are:

- It can be difficult to change direction quickly.
- It can be very difficult for players to grasp if the camera is not locked behind character.

Range of Movement

Analog controllers have allowed player control to become a much more tactile experience than in the days of digital-pad-only gaming. It allows the player to move the controller to different ranges along a single direction, allowing different speeds of movement. With no direction held, the avatar remains fairly motionless. This is known as the idle pose.

Typically three ranges of movement can be employed across the analog stick (creep, walk, and run), but there can be as many as the designer wants (within reason, of course). These three are a good basic set, however, as they allow pretty much all the movement speed a player would want. When designing the ranges for movement, it is important to get a good-feeling threshold for each. Allow enough space in a range to be able to hold the stick steady without flicking between two different states. The states can be blended to get a smooth range of movement across the stick. Obviously ranges of movement should start slow and move to the fastest movement speeds with the extremities of stick movement.

ADVANCED MOVEMENT

The advanced movement available to a player will vary vastly from game to game. Only a limited amount can or indeed should be crammed into a game, so all of the following information should not be stuffed into a game design. Instead, the following topics are meant to be food for thought: ideas for the sort of abilities you might furnish your hero with.

Jumping

Jumping is a mainstay of gaming. Nearly all character-based console games have jumping. It allows the players to navigate the environment in a more interesting manner, allows them to dodge low attacks in combat, and offers interesting puzzle design possibilities to the designer.

Getting jumping right is important. If it's done wrong it can look very odd. However, there is a lot of flexibility with how jumping can be done depending on the feel of the game:

Realistic jumping: The player jumps only a limited height and falls under normal gravity with no air control (the ability to guide the player as he falls).

Arcade jumping: The player can jump very high and floats to earth under reduced gravity with air control.

Platformer jumping: The player is able to jump high and perform another jump in the air (a double jump). He might also fall under low gravity with a high level of air control.

It is important to work out the metrics of all jumps and any other advanced movement skill before building levels. Otherwise, changing mechanics will require the levels to be drastically rebuilt or altered to suit the new metrics.

Jump Up

Jumping straight up is performed when the player presses the jump button from a standing pose. The character jumps straight up into the air and then drops back down to earth.

Jump Forward

Jumping forward is a little more complex—or can be depending on how you want the jump to feel. A basic method is to have a standard jump length no matter what level of movement is occurring at the time. This makes it easy for the player to judge how far the character is going to move with each press of the button and thus allows for more precise jumping. This is often used on platform games to make the mechanics of jumping simple.

A more-complex and more-natural-feeling system will take into account the speed of movement of the player character. This can be done in a couple of ways:

- Direct correlation of speed to jump length
- Grades of jump according to grades of speed

Direct correlation of jump speed to jump length is driven straight from the user's input. This can make jumping slightly tricky because of its highly analog nature. It might also require animation of several poses to make the jump look more natural.

A slightly more rigid method is to have a couple of grades of jump according to grades of speed. Thus, a creep will produce a small jump, walking a medium jump, and running the longest jump length. These lengths are all set distances, however. Figure 5.6 shows a jump produced from low movement speeds, while Figure 5.7 shows a jump from larger movement speeds.

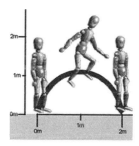

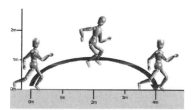

FIGURE 5.7   A jump from running movement produces a large jump.

FIGURE 5.6   A jump from standing or creep movement rate produces a small jump.

Momentum

To add a feeling of weight to a jump, the landing pose also needs to be considered. Matching the pose when landing will help this, particularly if a slight run-on were to be added from a large jump.

If you're making a game with precise jumping sections, don't overdo this, or players might overshoot tight jumps, resulting in much frustration.

Double Jump

A very arcade-like addition to a game is to utilize a double jump. This allows the player to jump once in the air in addition to the initial jump from the ground. To get maximum height from the jump, the player needs to press the jump button at the apex of the first jump (see Figure 5.8).

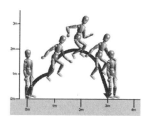

FIGURE 5.8   A double jump.

Often a window of opportunity will be incorporated into the jump, so that the second jump can only be made for a limited period of the first jump. This is usually around the apex of the first jump.

The animation for this second jump could be something fanciful such as a somersault—as long as the character can still land in the correct pose.

Air Control

Air control allows the player to guide the character as they drop back down to earth. This generally comes in three types:

No air control: The jump is forced in a particular direction.
Direction control: The arc of the jump is set, but the direction of the character's facing can be changed.
Full control: The character's heading as well as direction can be changed or guided to some degree.

Air control is usually engaged once the apex of the jump has been reached and the character starts to drop back down to earth.

Wall Bouncing

A fun extension of the double jump mechanism is the wall bounce, where the player uses a vertical surface as a springboard to jump even higher. When colliding with a vertical surface, the player has a limited window in which to press the jump button to allow the character to bounce off the wall and farther up into the air (see Figure 5.9).

For even more impressive wall bouncing, two vertical surfaces placed opposite each other within jumping distance could allow the player to bounce from wall to wall all the way up (see Figure 5.10).

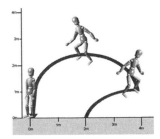

FIGURE 5.9   Wall bouncing in action.

FIGURE 5.10   A multiple wall bounce.

Dropping and Falling

Dropping is when the character drops under gravity through a normal move or down a short distance. Falling occurs when the player character passes beyond controlled dropping. Falling in game can be approached in several ways, again depending on the style of game you want to create. Typical ways of dealing with falling include:

Unlimited falling: The character simply drops under gravity. This is usually combined with air control in an arcade-style game.

Limited falling: The player character can drop a certain distance before starting to receive injury.

Death falling: Once a player reaches a certain level of dropping, he enters the fall state, which results in death upon hitting the ground or disappearing into a ravine, gorge, canyon, whale's mouth, or any other sufficiently large orifice.

With limited falling, a scale of damage can be used that will increment damage for larger falls. For example, 10 points of damage could be incurred each meter. This scale is completely controllable by the designer. Just create something that feels right. Ultimately using this method will naturally produce an instant death height.

Charging and Evasion

Fast movement allows the player to move out of harm's way quickly or position himself better in combat or to approach an obstacle.

Charge Forward

Charge forward moves the player character forward faster than standard running to get to an enemy quicker or to move quickly underneath a moving obstacle (for example, rolling under a closing door).

Evade Left and Right

Evading left and right allows the player to sidestep incoming attacks, projectiles, or obstacles. This could be a side step, side roll, cartwheel, or something similar.

Evade Back

Evading back moves the player character away from an incoming attack or obstacle that cannot reach the character's new location. This could be a simple run backward but could look much more impressive as a backflip or something similar.

Sprinting

Often an option to sprint is placed onto a specific button. When held, this button allows the player to move much more quickly with standard directional movement. Sometimes this is limited by a maximum sprint time. This is a gauge that decreases until depleted as the player character sprints. Once the gauge is depleted, the player character cannot sprint until the gauge has begun to recharge. When the character is not sprinting, this gauge will recharge up to its maximum value.

Noncombat Stances

There are three useful noncombat stances: standing, crouching, and prone. Standing is the standard stance in which most of the game is likely to be played. Crouching and prone are not necessary, but either could be added at the designer's behest; it depends on what you would like to achieve in the game. They are most likely to be used for stealth gameplay or for accessing tight areas. If they don't serve any purpose, then there is no reason to include them.

Advanced actions can be performed in all stances, but this will require animations for each stance. Alternatively, actions can be restricted in certain stances, or different actions can be substituted; for example, when the character is crouched the attack could be a neck snap rather than the standard punch when approaching from behind.

Crouching

Crouching allows the player to duck behind obstacles to provide cover or move undetected. It also allows him to enter areas he couldn't while standing. Often when crouched, the player character will move at a reduced speed, but this can be an advantage in stealth scenarios; with reduced speed would come reduced noise.

Crouching can be a toggle button or a held button to keep the crouch pose. Toggle tends to be more useful, particularly if it is assigned to the click down function of an analog stick (it's hard to keep it pressed and move it).

Lying Prone and Crawling

Lying prone involves lying flat on the ground. This makes the player character less visible when behind cover and allows him to crawl into tight spaces such as the ubiquitous air vent. Cameras can be difficult in such spaces. It is often a good idea to switch into first-person perspective when crawling through such tight spaces.

Switching Stances

Depending on whether you decide to give your hero the ability to both crouch and lie prone, you need some mechanism of switching between the three states: standing, crouching, and prone. The ideal solution would be to have a button assigned to Crouch and one to Prone. Then the player can quickly move from one to the other and back to standing. However, this set-up requires the use of two buttons that could be put to better use. Instead, the player could toggle between the various stances with a click of the button. The order could realistically be one of two methods:

Cyclical: Stand -> Crouch -> Prone -> Stand
Ping-pong: Stand -> Crouch -> Prone -> Crouch -> Stand

Swimming

A movement set often seen in games is the ability to swim. There are issues with this, as water is often used as a world boundary. Ignoring this use of water for the moment, let's look at how swimming might be implemented.

On entering a water volume, the player will enter a swim mode of movement. Often this is separated into two further subsets: surface and underwater swimming. Surface movement allows the character to move across the surface of the water in a method similar to normal movement except that the animations are adjusted to suit movement across the surface rather than walking movement. A button is then pressed to perform a dive.

Underwater movement is more tricky, as the player can now move in all three dimensions. Two buttons are usually assigned to perform climbing and diving. A button press might also be required to perform the act of actually swimming, and then the stick is used to control the direction of movement. The swim button might require the player to press the button repeatedly to move or may simply let him hold it down for continued movement. While underwater, it is likely that the character will have limited air and will have to return to the surface at some point to replenish his air supply. On contact with the surface plane, he will switch from underwater movement to surface movement.

Sneaking

Stealth games have become increasingly popular in recent years, and the ability to move around unseen seems to attract a lot of would-be assassins. We have already discussed a number of player actions that could be used as stealth actions. Creeping, crouching, and lying prone all offer either silent movement or the ability to conceal the player character from view. Besides these actions, we could add the following actions to improve the range of tools available to the players.

Wall Press

Pressing the player character flat against a wall enables him to shuffle along the wall and remain out of view—so long as an enemy is not looking directly at him of course. By pressing up against a wall, you could also allow the player to shuffle along a narrow ledge that he would not be able to walk along normally. In fact, you could have this functionality without the stealth element.

The character could also crouch while pressed against a wall or could use crouched wall press to hide behind low cover. Wall press could be implemented either as a toggle or performed for the duration of a button press.

Peer Around Corner

Often done from a wall press, this movement allows the character to take a look around a corner without moving his whole body into the enemy's line of sight.

Quiet Landing

The stealth-based third-person action game *Splinter Cell* features a button that, when pressed while the character is about the hit the floor, cushions his landing by making the body flex more when landing. This makes less sound when the player character hits the floor.

Acrobatics

The actions you can give your character are almost limitless. If you are producing a particularly athletic hero, then you may want to give him a lot of acrobatic abilities.

Climbing, Swinging, and Spinning

Ladders, ledges, ropes, and poles are often found in a game that allows interaction of a particular kind: object-relative control. Object-relative control means that when the objects are being interacted with, the control method is switched so that different directions correspond to different interactions with the object. Each object may have radically different controls.

Ladders

Ladders might be very simplistic and simply require the player to press a button to start running up or down the ladder, and the action is automatically performed. Alternatively, they may require the player to press the action button to latch onto the ladder or may automatically cause the player to attach when they run against it (the latter can be frustrating if the intent was to run past it). Once on a ladder, up will move the character up the ladder and down will move him down. Often the down animation can be implemented as a slide to make it faster and more impressive.

A complex freestanding ladder could allow the player to flip around to the other side with the left and right stick, but this is not an essential feature. Ladders might also allow the player to perform attacks in particular directions as they climb.

Ledges

Ledges are usually jumped up to. When a jump is performed near a ledge, the character will automatically stretch his arms out to grab the ledge. The player character also might be able to catch ledges as he is falling through the air. A good safety net mechanic for a player walking off a ledge is to automatically turn the character to grab the ledge as he falls (if it is above safe drop height). This prevents player frustration in tricky narrow-ledge areas. However, an auto-grab may have limited hold time, so that if the player does not pull the character up after a short time the character will lose his grip.

Once a ledge has been gripped, control is changed so that the character can shimmy left and right along the ledge with left and right movement, respectively, drop off the ledge by pressing down, or pull himself up by pushing up. He could also jump upward with a press of the jump button or jump backward using the wall of the ledge as a springboard. These actions could be assigned to other buttons while the character is attached to the ledge, but the directional stick tends to feel the most natural.

Rigid Ropes and Vertical Poles

Rigid ropes and vertical poles are very similar to ladders in that they allow the player character to climb up and down with the corresponding vertical movement of the analog stick. However, since they are not flat interactions, the player is able to spin around in the left and right directions to change his facing.

Horizontal Poles

Poles can be used to spin around, to shimmy along, or simply to hang from to avoid a momentary danger. Shimmying would work the same way as on a ledge, though up could be used to swap the character's direction of facing if necessary. A moving pole would make this shimmying action more interesting, so the player had to avoid obstacles as he traveled. Swinging could replace shimmying, with swinging on left and right motion, down could drop the player character off the pole, and up could be used to switch direction.

Both shimmying and swinging might be facilitated by using the four compass-point directions in relation to the player character on screen.

Swinging Ropes

Swinging ropes offer a variety of possibilities. The possibility of swinging across the environment like Tarzan is fairly appealing. Up and down could be used to move up and down the rope, leaving left and right for swinging.

The ability to build up momentum makes ropes fairly interesting, as does the physics of swinging at the top of the rope rather than the bottom. It also enables a number of exciting environment design possibilities.

Balancing

Balancing can be a nice mechanic to use for objects that require the player to negotiate a thin space such as a tight rope or to slide along a rail. The Tony Hawk series of skating games uses a balance meter when the character is performing rail-based or grind-based tricks.

A similar concept can be used for balancing in general. Basically a player must keep a bar at the center of a meter. As the player character moves, the bar has a tendency to move to one of the extremities. The closer it gets to the edge, the more tendency it has to move in that direction. Should it reach the edge, then the player character will over-balance in that direction.

Wall Runs

The wall run allows the player to defy gravity for a brief time as he runs along and up walls. The two types of wall runs are:

Set-limit wall runs: Used in *Prince of Persia: The Sands Of Time*, these are limited animations that have set metrics.

Dynamic wall runs: *Ninja Gaiden*® uses a more dynamic system where the player can move on the wall almost like it was the floor for a limited time or for as long as the player can keep the character there.

For a set-limit wall run there are two basic styles: vertical and horizontal, depending on the angle from which the player approaches the wall. Parallel movement will produce the horizontal run, and perpendicular movement will allow a vertical run. The set-limit run is a rigid system that will have clearly defined mechanics, but this can often be an advantage, as the player learns that a set action will have a set consequence. A rigid wall run is shown in Figure 5.11.

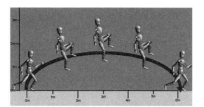

FIGURE 5.11   A rigid wall run.

Ninja Gaiden's wall run only allows horizontal movement once in a wall run, but you could design a dynamic system however you want. These kinds of systems can be fairly tricky to perform. While they are more free-form, they do not offer the tight structure of design created by having set metrics.

Gliding

Gliding is a fairly old-school platformer mechanic. When a jump is performed, a glide allows the player to guide the character to a destination, though characters are restricted from gliding upward. Vertical movement is a steady drop.

The usual method is similar to double jump, but in this instance the button is held to allow the glide. A window of opportunity to press and hold the button is offered at the apex of the original jump. Should the player let go of the glide button, then the character will drop as normal.

OBJECT INTERACTION

Object interaction is an important aspect of any game, as it allows the player to feel as if he is actually having an effect on the world around him.

Context-Sensitive Action/Use

Context sensitivity allows one button to perform a range of functions. This button should stand alone. Lots of context-sensitive buttons can become exceedingly confusing. A catch-all Use or Action button keeps things simple. The Action or Use button usually performs fairly basic interactions with world objects. It either simply triggers the behavior of the targeted object or switches the player into a new control mode, for example, getting into a car or grabbing hold of a ladder.

Action buttons can also perform a range of set moves in an Action Hotspot. An Action Hotspot would be a specific function to that area. While in the area at the right time, pressing the Action button will perform that function, for example, a set piece of a pillar being pushed over to cave the roof in on an approaching enemy. These unique actions tend to be heavily scripted, that is, have special technical implementations, as they need a tightly controlled environment to work well.

Interaction Mechanisms

In a third-person game where the player character can be seen, interaction with an object needs to be aligned to the character, and their animations need to be synchronized (though some games cheat and move into a different view to perform the action and therefore do not have to show the character).

With static environment objects the player character needs to be moved into position by either popping (which can be obvious if the object activation radius is too large but can be hidden by a camera cut) or by blending the position of the character to the right location (which will cause the character to slide if the activation radius is too big).

Object Controls

Some objects may have altered control schemes. For example, interacting with the object may require the player to button-mash the action button or rotate the analog stick to match a rotation in the game world. These objects may give feedback to the player as they are interacted with—through vibration of the controller or in the movements they must perform on the control pad. For example, a heavy lever might require the player to match a particular frequency for button mashing. If this frequency is not matched, the lever will move back to its resting position. The frequency required to raise the lever may increase as it reaches its activation point.

Object controls increase the level of interactivity the player has with the game world beyond a simple button press to perform an action.

QUICK TIME EVENTS

Quick time event (QTE) sequences can add interactivity to a cutscene or allow extremely complex actions to be performed. They stem from the gameplay of interactive movies that were all the rage for a brief period. *Dragon's Lair* and *Space Ace* required the player to press buttons or move in a specific direction at various points during what was essentially one massive cutscene.

These early examples were graphically astounding at the time, but the gameplay proved to be shallow to the point of being almost nonexistent. The biggest problem was that little indication of what action was required was given, and failure meant instant death. The result was a movie where you had to watch the same sequence over and over till you got the right action at the right time.

The idea remained fairly limited until it resurfaced in a Dreamcast™ title called *Shenmue*™. Often the player would be presented with a sudden cutscene where he was in danger, and button presses were flashed on screen. Failure to press the right buttons didn't mean death. This elevated the gameplay from something with little depth to a much more useable and fair system. It's a technique that is finding more favor. QTEs can be found in such titles as *Fahrenheit*, *Resident Evil 4*, and *God of War*.

One development benefit of using QTEs is that they put the emphasis and risk onto the art department rather than code. This can be a benefit, as art and animation are quantifiable and tangible, whereas code and technology can be much higher risk factors. However, the amount of work involved in creating compelling QTE sequences can be surprisingly large and may actually be considerably more work than a form of implementation in gameplay.

The anatomy of a QTE can differ from game to game, and the language of button presses and outcomes will dictate how successful these are. QTEs are made up of a series of actions. At each point before an action, a button press will be required. In order for the action to play, the required input needs to be received within the window of opportunity. If it is received, the action is considered a success and the sequence continues. If not, then the action is considered a failure.

QTE Usage

Where would you use a QTE sequence? There are plenty of possibilities. As *Dragon's Lair* showed, a whole game can be built around them, but in most games they are used for fairly specific purposes:

Powerful attacks: A QTE is ideal anywhere a highly elaborate attack against an enemy is wanted.

Environment interaction: For particularly spectacular environment interaction, a whole canned sequence can be created. This takes the player character beyond the realms of his normal movement set.

Surprises: This includes sequences where the player is surprised by an event such as a collapsing bridge, where only quick reactions will save him.

Defense: QTEs can be used when the player character is defending against a vicious attack by a boss or other powerful enemy.

Player Input

There are a huge variety of button presses that can be used. For the simplest input, single button presses could suffice. These are flashed on screen, and the player has a window of opportunity to press the button before that action is deemed to have failed. This could be expanded with simple directional movement such as left, right, up, or down.

Taking this further, we could add motions with the controller such as performing a half or full circle in a certain direction. At the top end of the scale, button combinations mixed with direction and movements can be built into complex patterns, but there is a limit to human reactions. Don't make QTEs too complicated, as most people will fail.

One important feature is the ability to provide instant feedback for a successful action, so that the action is immediately performed or a head up display (HUD) item acknowledges that the press has been made. Otherwise, the player might continue hammering the buttons, not realizing that he has already successfully completed the action.

The decision also has to be made whether a wrong button press is considered a fail or whether it is simply ignored. Registering input during a window requires some sort of penalty for inputting the wrong pattern, or else a player would simply be able to button-mash through a whole sequence.

There are two valid methods for penalizing the player:

Time based: The input is locked for a period of time. During this time the input display is grayed out to show that the player has inputted the wrong value. A good time system to use is a percentage of the remaining window. This ensures that mistakes made early in the window still offer plenty of opportunity for correction.

Chance based: This offers a number of chances to get the input right. The player may have two, three, or more chances to perform the right input before the window is deemed to have been failed.

Once the correct input has been registered, this should immediately be shown to the player so that he knows he has succeeded—perhaps by a tick icon on screen. A failure is only shown at the end of a window, unless a chance system is being used and all chances have been wasted.

Where a button must be mashed, success is also shown at the end of the window. This input is read by reaching a target frequency (often in hertz). This should be read as the number of times the button is pressed in the window rather than having to match the value for the whole duration; otherwise, it becomes too easy to fail by missing one beat.

Analog results of button mashing frequency often require special movement mechanisms. For example, in *God of War* there are sections where the button must be mashed to overpower an opponent. The animation system matches button input to progress through an animation. This is like a tug of war between the player and time. The player must exceed a certain frequency to drive the animation forward to a succeed point, but if they fail to match this frequency, the animation plays back to an eventual failure point.

Outcomes

The outcome of a QTE is either success or failure. What that success or failure is will depend on the context in which a QTE sequence is used.

Player Threat

Much of *Resident Evil 4*'s QTEs are used as threats to the player. In this case success is survival and failure is death. This could be considered overly harsh; failure could cause damage rather than instant death. Whatever the result, however, failure during a player-threatening QTE should cause a negative result. Otherwise, there is no threat in the first place.

Enemy Threat

The alternative use is as a threat to the enemy. *God Of War* uses QTE sequences throughout for attacks on enemies. When the enemy is damaged to a certain point, a button icon appears over his head. At this point the QTE will be activated when the player presses the button within range of that character. This allows much more specialized action on a per-character or environment basis. Success means causing damage or killing an enemy. Failure simply drops the player back into normal gameplay.

Branching

One method of furthering the interactivity of QTE sequences is adding the ability for branching, that is, offering a choice of input to alter the course of a sequence. The result is that a sequence becomes a tree of actions or short sequences that can be traversed. This branching could also be done through the failure of action so that the player has several layers of possible action as a safety net before the ultimate failure occurs.

QTE Interfaces

Presenting QTE information to the player can be a fairly tricky proposition. There are two major conflicting concerns: getting the message across to the player as to what control input is required and displaying the input in a way that doesn't detract from the action.

Many games tuck the QTE display in the corner or edge of the screen, which ensures that the display doesn't obscure the action. However, moving the focus on screen causes the player to miss most of the action, as his eye is trained on empty screen space, waiting for something to happen.

Alternatively, icons can be placed within world space—on the items that need action or in the top middle of the screen where the eye can still see the action. The complaint here, though, is that having icons in the game world breaks a lot of the suspension of disbelief. The icons could be disguised in some manner—made to look more like part of their environment—but this runs the risk of making them ambiguous and hard to spot. In making this decision, you should bear in mind that gameplay is generally the most important part of making a good game, and communication of the player's objectives is a key element in promoting good gameplay. Sometimes it is too easy to forget that a game is made for entertainment, not as a work of art.

SUMMARY

This chapter focused on character control methods and examined several aspects of control that might be employed in a game.

Control input: Control input is a vital part of a game. Without it there is no interaction. Several aspects must be considered when looking at the control input:

- **Control devices:** There are many kinds of device that might be used to interface with a game console, though the ubiquitous joypad has currently taken pride of place. Other systems include keyboard and mouse, alternative devices such as light guns, dancemats, cameras, pointing wands, and bespoke devices that are tailored to particular games.
- **Control schemes:** Several elements of a control scheme must be considered, namely the ergonomics, intuitiveness, simplicity, responsiveness, and flexibility. We explored a number of standard control schemes that offer a starting point to control scheme layout.

Standard movement: The basic movement of a character can be described fairly simply, but there are some important aspects that require consideration:

- **Movement styles:** Movement of a character is either screen relative or character relative. Screen-relative movement is generally more intuitive but will change as the camera moves. Character-relative movement remains the same no matter what the camera angle but may require some spatial awareness on the part of the player unless the view of the character is locked behind him.
- **Range of movement:** The basic movement is spread across several ranges, depending on the movement of the analog stick. This movement is generally split into idle, creep, walk, and run.

Advanced movement: More complex character movement can be performed with different control systems or combinations of buttons and movements. We explored several advanced movements in this chapter:

- **Jumping:** Generally either realistic, arcade, or platformer styles of jumping are used. Jumps can consist of jump up, jump forward, and double jump and may also have air control or even wall bouncing.
- **Dropping and falling:** A drop or a fall system will either be unlimited, limited so that damage is inflicted at certain heights, or will produce instant death.
- **Charging and evasion:** A charge gets the player nearer to an enemy or out of the way of danger. An evade sidesteps or moves the player backward from an oncoming attack or a trap.

- **Sprinting:** The sprint allows the player to move more quickly by holding a button, though this will often be limited by endurance.
- **Noncombat stances:** Several stances may be used outside of combat (though they may also form part of a ranged combat system)— standing, crouched, and prone.
- **Swimming:** May be a feature of games where water plays a large role. There are generally two slightly different control methods while in water— diving and surface movement.
- **Sneaking:** Where stealth is a feature of the gameplay, there may be movements that encourage the player to be more cautious such as the wall press, peering around a corner, or the quiet landing.
- **Acrobatics:** All manner of acrobatics may be included in a game, such as climbing, swinging, and spinning, balancing, wall runs, and using ladders, ledges, rigid ropes, vertical poles, horizontal poles, and swinging ropes.
- **Gliding:** Certain characters, typically in a platformer style of game, might be able to jump and hold to perform a glide.

Object interaction: Being able to interact with the environment makes for a much more interesting and believable world. We examined several aspects of object interaction in this chapter:

- **Context sensitive action/use:** The use of context sensitivity makes it much easier for the player to quickly interact with elements in the environment.
- **Interaction mechanisms:** The act of interacting with an object may require animation synchronization and the ability to move a character into position without any visible glitching.
- **Object controls:** While interacting with an object there may be an altered control scheme, such as the use of button mashing to use the object.

Quick time events: QTEs are a method of making more impressive object interactions and interactive sequences for particular parts of the game. They are labor intensive, but they can create some pretty spectacular scenes if used correctly. When creating QTEs, there are several considerations to be made:

- **QTE usage:** A QTE may be used for a variety of purposes such as a powerful attack, environment interaction, surprises, or defense from an enemy attacker.
- **Player input:** The types of input required might vary from simple button presses to button mashing or more complex movement such as circular stick movements or combined button presses.
- **Outcomes:** The outcome of a sequence depends on its type. Player threat scenes may cause damage or death to the player on failure. Enemy threat scenes will cause damage or death to the enemy with success.
- **Branching:** A QTE may have branching to offer the player more choice.

- **Interfaces:** The feedback of the required input to the players is vital. They must know what button to press each time and be informed of a correct or failed input. This must be done without distracting them from the on-screen action.

As games continue to increase in complexity, they also continue to offer new kinds of control to the player. Ultimately everything in a game comes down to player control, as without any form of interaction, it is no longer a game. It will be interesting to see how the new motion-sensing methods of control will impact on the current methods employed in controlling the game. While they have the potential to revolutionize certain types of gameplay, they may also prove to be too tiring to use for long periods of time or not accurate enough for certain aspects of play. However, these are very exciting times in control input design, and we are sure to see large leaps forward in the coming years.

VIEWPOINTS AND CAMERAS

In This Chapter

- Viewpoints
- Camera Basics
- Game Cameras
- Animated Cameras
- Multiplayer Game Cameras

We examined the control of game characters in the previous chapter, and now we must look at how the action is displayed on screen. All our interaction with our on-screen character depends on the viewpoint we choose to view the action with, as well as the way our cameras are set up within the game world. Several aspects of this will be covered in this chapter:

- Viewpoints
- Camera basics
- Game Cameras
- Animated cameras
- Multiplayer game cameras

VIEWPOINTS

The choice of viewpoint is an important consideration in game design, as it has a number of implications for development. Once, a seemingly long time ago, isometric, side-on, or top-down views were the prevailing methods of viewing the action. As the move has been made into 3D, traditional viewpoints have fallen by the wayside (certainly in the console game arena).

3D technology has made two viewpoints the most popular: first person and third person. Most console games are one of these two, or as is happening more and more often, a combination of the two.

First Person

First-person games are viewed from the perspective of the avatar, as though the player were actually looking through the eyes of the player character. An example is shown in Figure 6.1.

This viewpoint offers a number of advantages:

Eradication of camera problems: The forced viewpoint is very easy to implement and does not require complex camera code to navigate the environment.
Freedom of view: The players are free to look wherever they wish. This allows them to examine the environment more thoroughly, enabling them to view the world as if they were really there.
Ease of aiming projectile weapons: Aiming a projectile weapon in first-person mode is very easy. A cursor on screen points to the target and the player fires.

It also has a number of disadvantages:

Disconnection from the character: It can become much more difficult to portray the avatar as a character. This is a particular problem in licensed games, where the character is perhaps the most important visual aspect of the game.
Confusion: Many people find the first-person viewpoint tricky to navigate in, as it is constantly moving.
Joypad control: Related to the above problem is that many people find the first-person viewpoint difficult to control with a joypad, as they must con-

FIGURE 6.1   An example of a first-person viewpoint. *Tom Clancy's Rainbow Six Vegas.* © Ubisoft Entertainment. All Rights Reserved.

trol two spatial elements at once: direction of movement and direction of facing. Also, many people who are used to keyboard and mouse first-person games may find the joypad clunky and unresponsive in comparison.

Motion sickness: In addition to confusion, many people may experience more extreme reactions to the first-person viewpoint, in that all the constantly moving imagery will provoke motion sickness—something that cannot really be compensated for completely in this viewpoint.

Difficulty of melee combat: While projectile combat is made much easier in first person, it becomes very difficult to make melee combat work effectively, as you cannot see where attacks are coming from or what moves the avatar is performing.

Difficulty of spatial puzzles: Trying to keep track of a spatial puzzle becomes rather difficult when you do not have a full picture of everything around you. Jumping can be tricky when you are not entirely sure where your feet are.

Games designers often say that first person offers a greater sense of immersion, but as James Newman suggests in his article "The Myth of the Ergodic Videogame" [Newman02], there is no lesser sense of immersion for the player with any one viewpoint.

Third Person

Third-person games are viewed from a camera that follows the player through the world or offers different cameras as the player moves through the world. An example of a third-person viewpoint is shown in Figure 6.2.

This provides a number of advantages over first-person games:

Connection with the player character: Being able to see the player character is a strong storytelling device and helps the player connect with the avatar.

FIGURE 6.2   An example of a third-person viewpoint. *Heavenly Sword* for PlayStation® 3. © Ninja Theory Ltd. 2006.

Joypad control: The third-person viewpoint lends itself much more readily to the joypad method of control. Only one level of spatial movement need be thought about at a time.

Navigation of environment: Because the whole environment isn't constantly tilting and rotating around the players, it makes it much easier for them to get their bearings. It also allows the player to see more of the environment and allows the designer to tailor the camera to the specific area.

Cinematics: The viewpoint is much more conducive to switching to cutscenes or to allowing the designers to craft dynamic cinematics, as the player is much more likely to actually see them, particularly if forced cameras are used.

Easier melee combat: Third person makes melee combat much more viable. The players can see what moves they are performing and where enemy attacks are coming from.

Easier solving of spatial puzzles: Spatial puzzles are much easier to visualize in third person, as the players have an overall view of the space and are able to see exactly where their avatars fit into that space.

The third-person viewpoint does have a number of serious disadvantages:

Camera difficulties: Complex camera mechanics will be needed to allow the camera to successfully navigate an environment unless static cameras are used.

Constricted view: The players are limited in where they can actually look. They cannot move the camera to the exact position they may require to get a look at a higher platform, for example. However, the view does offer some side benefits such as being able to see round corners or over objects, for example.

Difficulty aiming projectile weapons: While it is possible to make projectile combat work well in third person, it does not have the same immediacy or skill level that is almost automatically imbued with aiming projectile weaponry in first person.

Using Both First and Third Person

Most third-person games these days offer a first person view of some kind to counter the issue of constricted view and to offer improved projectile aiming. There are several ways that first person can be incorporated into a third-person game:

Fixed look-around: The player manually switches to first person to look around. When in first person, the player is locked still and is not allowed to move. Usually the same stick that is used for direction will also be used to look in this mode. Sometimes the players may also be able to aim their weapons while in this mode.

First-person aiming: Whenever the players switch to a projectile weapon, they are moved into this view. This allows them to move around while firing their weapons. The camera control stick is usually used to allow the player to look around while in this view.

Hybrid: This is fairly rare in games at present, for no apparent reason other than the extra work required to make sure the game performs well in both viewpoints. This allows the players to freely switch between the two viewpoints whenever they wish. They could play the whole game in whichever mode they choose or switch to the best view for a particular situation.

Over-the-shoulder: This is not so much a separate style as a different interpretation of the first-person viewpoint. A camera sits slightly behind the avatar, placing the avatar's head and shoulder in the bottom left (or maybe right) of the frame. The player has a similar view to a first-person viewpoint but also has the benefit of still seeing the character. This is best used when aiming projectile weapons, as it would tend to get in the way when the player is simply looking around.

Isometric

In the days before home computers and consoles could display anything more than wireframe in 3D, isometric was the view of choice for someone wanting to create a 3D feel.

The isometric viewpoint displays all three dimensions equally, forming a diamond-shaped view on screen (though the viewport may only display a window of the whole scene). An example of an isometric viewpoint is shown in Figure 6.3.

While not as widespread as it once was, the isometric viewpoint does still have a home. Sim and strategy games are particularly suited to this style of view, which allows the user an overview of large sections, with the ability to view several angles of the scene.

The isometric viewpoint should not be ruled out for console style games, however. There is always a market for a quirky game that draws on retro gameplay or mechanics and could even become appealing to many players.

FIGURE 6.3   An example of an isometric viewpoint.

Side-On

Side-on view was hugely popular in the 8-bit and 16-bit eras, when 3D was simply too technically demanding for home machines. Side-on is like looking at a cross section, as the avatar is displayed running around this slice of the world. Screens were originally a whole level unto themselves; as the player stepped off one screen, the next was displayed. However, scrolling was soon introduced, allowing a much larger scene to be held in memory as the viewport moved with the character. An example of a side-on view is shown in Figure 6.4.

FIGURE 6.4   An example of a side-on viewpoint. *Alien Hominid HD* for Xbox 360 Live Arcade. © The Behemoth 2006.

This viewpoint was a favorite with platformers, which heavily dominated the scene at the time. Some modern games use this viewpoint as a throwback to the by-gone days of gaming, and one-on-one beat 'em ups still use the viewpoint for most of the gameplay. The view is also very popular with web-based games.

Top-Down

Like side-on, top-down was a firm favorite in the 8- and 16-bit eras. The action is viewed as if looking directly down (or the three-quarter view, where it allows the player to see the characters a little better). An example of a top-down viewpoint is shown in Figure 6.5.

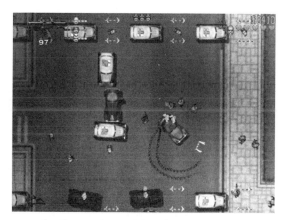

FIGURE 6.5   An example of a top-down viewpoint. ©2006 Rockstar Games. All Rights Reserved.

Top-down was generally the preserve of shoot 'em ups, sports, and racing games, where the action required that the player have a good view of his surroundings.

This viewpoint is still fairly useful today and is often given as an option in sports games. However, in action–adventure games, the view is somewhat redundant, as looking at a floor for the entirety of a game isn't really pushing the boundaries of visual splendor.

CAMERA BASICS

Cameras are very important in 3D games. If they're not pointing in the right direction, the players are not going to be able to see the action and, even worse, are not going to be able to play because they can't see their characters.

Cameras can be split into two main types:

Game cameras: Cameras used to display the action and control the character
Animated cameras: Cameras used to further the story or highlight an important event

The designer must know about a number of basic features of cameras, as it is generally a designer's job to set up game cameras.

Camera Movement

Being able to describe camera movement is a pretty important skill to learn, but is difficult, as confusion often arises as to what particular terms mean. That is because different people often use the same terms to describe different things. As game designers, we need to develop a common terminology so that confusion can be avoided. The basic movement of a camera is shown in Figure 6.6.

Track: Horizontal and vertical movement of the camera perpendicular to the facing of the camera.
Tumble: Rotation of the camera around a focal point
Pan: Horizontal rotation of the camera
Tilt: Vertical rotation of the camera
Roll: Twisting of the camera along its view axis
Dolly: Movement of the camera toward or away from the target
Zoom: Movement of the camera lens to adjust the focal range

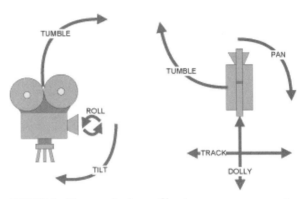

FIGURE 6.6   The terminology of basic camera movement.

The Camera Lens

Often game cameras are designed to mimic real-world cameras, so the properties of a camera lens are modeled.

Field of View

The field of view (FOV) dictates the angle of the view cone, essentially controlling how much information is rendered on screen. Different FOV values are shown in Figure 6.7.

A narrow FOV makes for much less visible area on screen, meaning a claustrophobic feeling can be created. It also makes objects larger on screen but can also flatten any sense of depth in the image. A wider FOV shows more on screen but shrinks everything, making it feel smaller. The lens begins to "fish-eye" when particularly wide.

Depth of Field (Focus)

Depth of field is essentially focal range, dictating what parts of the image are in focus and what will appear blurred. This is a fairly recent development in game graphics,

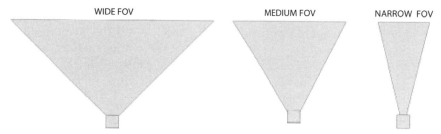

FIGURE 6.7   The effect of FOV on the camera.

as it has been notoriously processor intensive to perform. Now that games consoles pack a lot of processing clout, it is a lot more feasible for this effect to be used. In a game this is often achieved by having two blur planes: near and far. The near plane blurs objects close to the camera and is placed behind the object being focused. The far plane is placed at some point in the distance.

The effect makes the game appear more cinematic, as it can behave much like a real camera, picking out particular objects to focus on. However, it can also be overused, making the game unplayable, as it becomes too difficult to navigate if the player cannot see through the background blur. Subtlety is the designer's watch word when using many effects, and depth of field is no exception. Keep blurring to a minimum in actual gameplay and use the focus controls well, and it can really enhance a game. Excessive amounts of blur on an image can severely reduce performance. If you want to go wild with depth of field, reserve it for cut scenes.

Lens Flare

Lens flare is a side effect often seen in film. Light that enters the lens at a particular angle bounces around the lens in an unintended manner, causing it to reflect off parts of the internal workings, which results in the creation of beads and streaks of light. This usually comes from very bright light sources such as the sun.

This has long been an effect that the film industry has done their best to nullify but is occasionally purposefully left in. Not long ago there was a fad for throwing in lens flare in games at every available opportunity—a fad that is, thankfully, beginning to die out. Lens flare does have its place, but remember that it is a camera-specific effect. To put lens flare in a first-person game is just plain strange, as the human eye does not produce lens flare. It does make sense if we are making the players believe they are actually viewing the action through a camera lens.

The Physical Lens

Game designers also like to splash the screen with water, blood, mud, and so on. This is a technique used very sparingly in film, but, as so often occurs in the game industry, there was a fad for splashing the screen with abandon.

Just like lens flare, this has its place, but again it reminds us that we are viewing the game through a camera lens. It works well if the game suggests that there is a physical barrier between the viewer and the world, such as the visor in first-person shooter/platformer *Metroid Prime*®. Here it seems perfectly acceptable to throw objects up against the screen. As the player walks through fog, the visor fogs up. A nice touch was that when a bright weapon was fired, the player character's face was flashed up as a reflection in the visor. This adds a level of immersion that doesn't break the fourth wall.

Motion Blur

Motion blur is an effect used in cinema to emphasize movement. Effectively, the image is smeared in the direction of movement to prolong its placement on screen. Motion blur can be an effective tool to use in games but must be used with care.

As with many techniques, subtlety is key. With motion blur, the whole image can be obscured when an object moves in front of the camera and the target if the blurring is particularly heavy.

GAME CAMERAS

Two main categories of camera are based on the chosen viewpoint:

> **First-person cameras:** Any first-person viewpoint will utilize a first-person camera.
> **Third-person cameras:** All other forms of viewpoint utilize third-person cameras.

First-Person Cameras

First-person cameras are the easiest to set up and implement, simply because they don't need any complex actions associated with them.

The first-person camera does have a number of important considerations that must be made when it is created. However, the great thing about using a first-person camera is that once you have it done, it is highly unlikely that you will need to ever touch it again. The only area that may need refinement is the controls.

Player Height

The height of the player determines how he fits within the scale of the world. Assuming the world uses meters as the base unit, then the player height is best set at around 1.75 to 2 m (if the character is a human). This gives the right sense of height between the ground and camera location (assuming the FOV is set between 50 and 60°).

Field of View

The FOV is particularly important in the first-person perspective, as it will not be changed throughout the course of the game. Standard FOV for a human is set between

50 and 60°, but may well move a little way in either direction. For non-human characters a starkly different FOV such as a fish-eye effect might be used to create a more alien feeling. For certain sections of gameplay you might wish to adjust the FOV. For example, in *The Chronicles of Riddick*™ on the Xbox the FOV was widened when the player entered a secondary vision mode known as "night-shine." This creates a slight fish-eye effect, making it appear distinctly different to standard view.

Look Control

The mechanics of a first-person camera's look control are particularly important. With poor controls the player may struggle to control the game at all. Console games using the joypad for FPS control are notoriously difficult for novices.

The look control of a first-person camera is generally tied to the right analog stick so that left and right movement control the rotation (pan angle) of the camera and up and down control the vertical motion (tilt angle). Generally, the stick controls speed of rotation, but the vertical movement could also be directly proportional to directional movement of the stick. This means that the stick must be held at a level vertical position in order to target; otherwise, it returns to center.

The option for players to invert vertical movement if they wish is essential. Some people prefer the flight control method used in planes, where up moves the view down and vice versa.

A number of factors affect the look control that can be tweaked by the designers in an effort to produce the best control system.

Sensitivity

Analog sticks allow different values of an input to be received, which allows more control over a camera. By moving the stick a little, we can rotate the camera slowly, or by moving the stick a long way, we can rotate the camera at much higher speeds.

We could interpret these stick values in different ways, as there is no direct correlation in stick movement to camera speed. This interpretation is essentially the look sensitivity, but just how much is a little and how much is a lot? It is a very good idea to allow the player to be able to tweak these values, as not everyone likes the same level of sensitivity. Some people like a very responsive system that allows them to make very fast movements. Others may find this far too sensitive and prefer to make much larger gestures with the analog stick. The default sensitivity needs to lie somewhere between these values—not too sensitive or too slow to respond.

Dead Zones

An important part of the control sensitivity is the inclusion of dead zones. A dead zone prevents unwanted movement of the camera by ignoring tiny movements of the stick. The stick must be moved a set distance before the input value is large enough to move the camera.

Why is this useful? Imagine pushing left on the stick but having a tiny amount of upward input as you do this. Because it is analog, it is difficult to push precisely in one direction. The result would be a gradual movement upward as well as the desired left rotation. The dead zone eradicates this, but dead zones that are too large will make the control system seem sluggish.

Sensitivity Scale

The simplest method of receiving input is to linearly scale the value for movement across the stick, but this can mean that it is far too sensitive for smaller movements and far too slow for larger movements. An alternative is to use a curve to describe the input value across the length of the stick movement. This means movement can be slower for small movements of the stick but can be much faster when moved to the extremity. The two types of movement are shown in Figure 6.8.

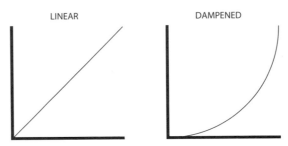

FIGURE 6.8 Sensitivity scaling as linear and curved graphs.

Acceleration

When the stick is pushed to the far left or right for a longer period, or if the look stick is double-tapped, it can be useful to allow it to accelerate quickly to maximum speed. You can see this technique at work in Bungee's *Halo*. Push left or right and hold for a second or two, and you will see the camera suddenly scale up to maximum speed.

Auto Center

One problem many novices face is moving the look too far in one direction and then becoming disorientated. They need some way of quickly returning to the central position. Auto center can be employed in many different ways, two of which are especially useful.

The first way is a button press such as clicking down on the look control stick if the ability to do this is available. This, of course, means that that button is now unavailable for any other functionality, which may not be desirable. The second way is to auto center when the player moves without any look movement being applied. When movement is received from a standing position, the look can gradually be interpolated back to the central position until further look movement is applied. Auto center will not be applied during movement, as it would cancel out any player control of the look movement.

Constraints

Having complete freedom of movement in a first-person camera is usually undesirable. In a flight simulator or a game set in weightless space it might be fine to allow complete rotation in the vertical direction, but if you are suggesting that a character could rotate his head all the way round without moving his body, then the player might start to question the laws of the game. Also, it can become very disorientating for players if they accidentally rotate the camera upside down.

Thus, vertical camera movement is constrained so that the camera will not rotate too far in a vertical direction and flip over. Some games constrain this to straight up or straight down, but even this might be too much. A slightly smaller angle might seem more realistic.

One problem with looking straight down is the realization that the camera is disembodied, as more often than not there is no player model, so no feet are seen when looking down. This is becoming less acceptable, and it is more believable to include legs and feet.

Third-Person Cameras

Third-person cameras are much more complex than first-person cameras but offer a number of advantages. They show the character at all times, which gives the player a stronger sense of the identity of that character. It also gives the designer tighter control of what the player sees.

The added complexity can cause problems, though. If the camera doesn't work, then the game falls at the first hurdle. It almost doesn't matter how good the underlying gameplay is; if the game camera is bad, then the game will be almost impossible to play. Unfortunately a third-person camera system is difficult to get right, so it will need a good deal of time and attention spent on it. The camera is bound to be a source of headaches and late nights through the game's development.

Several approaches can be taken when designing a camera system, though most third-person cameras fall into one of two categories:

Chase camera: The camera is attached to the character and will follow him as he moves about the environment. The camera is free to move around the player within a set of rules. The player is highly likely to have some level of control of this camera.

Environment cameras: The camera is tied to the environment, either fixed to a specific point or attached to rails that it can drag along. The player is likely to have only limited control of the camera.

Games may be limited to one of these categories or may use a combination of the two types of third-person camera. This is more likely with a chase camera system that may use environment cameras in areas where space is at a premium.

Camera Target

A third-person camera must have a target. This is the subject the camera is focused upon—the point of interest. In most cases cameras focus directly on the player character, but this need not be the case. Often a camera may want to provide a target that is offset from the player character to give the player a better view of the action.

This can be done by implementing an importance system and a range of influence. Each object and actor has an importance value between 0 and 1—the player character being 1. The other objects and actors have different levels of importance that never reach 1. The player character has a circle of influence around him. Outside this circle all objects have an importance of 0. When they enter the circle, their importance will scale up to the maximum value they get closer to the player character.

The target for the camera is calculated as a point between the center of each object or actor's importance root (this may be offset from the actual root of the object or actor), being biased to the higher importance values. This means that the higher another object's importance becomes, the more the camera will move to look in its direction. This movement is smoothed to prevent erratic behavior and jerkiness.

Simple Chase-Camera System

Chase cameras require less setup than a series of environment cameras. However, chase cameras rely upon AI to get the best shot, and there are more things that can go wrong when the camera isn't tailor-made to fit into a space.

A chase camera has a number of advantages and disadvantages compared to an environment camera setup:

Advantages:

- Having the camera attached to the player is much more conducive to ranged combat and aiming.
- The set-up of the camera is much simpler and much less time consuming.
- It is easy to give the player full control of the camera.

Disadvantages:

- The camera is prone to error and can get stuck behind objects.
- It often doesn't give the best view of the environment or the action.
- It offers no scope for cinematic camera work.

The construction of a chase camera involves several elements:

Position: The placement of a chase camera
Movement: The response of the camera to player movement
Player control: The extent to which the player can control the camera
Camera AI: How the camera responds to various problems (discussed further later in this chapter, as it can be applied to all third-person camera systems)

Position

A chase camera is essentially attached to the player. You could imagine it as being attached via a beam, with the camera lens pointing toward the player character.

This beam could be pointed anywhere in world space, for example, pointing directly into the sky so that the camera looks straight down at the player. Obviously we need to find a sensible position to place the camera so that it gives us a good view of the player and the action around him. This position tends to be angled slightly upward so that the camera is pointing down toward the character; we see the horizon but still have a good sense of the immediate surroundings. A chase camera rig is shown in Figure 6.9.

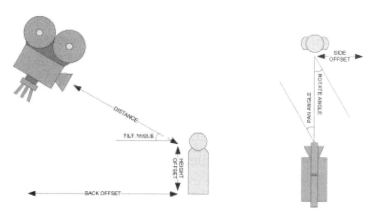

FIGURE 6.9   A typical chase camera rig.

We can describe the camera position with a number of variables:

Height offset (y): The offset of the camera's target from the character's root (the root is usually placed right at the base of a character)

Back offset (z): The offset opposite to the character's facing

Side offset (x): The offset to the left or right of the camera target that angles the camera to allow more of the side of a character to be seen

Tilt angle: The rotation of the camera from the target that elevates the camera

Pan angle: The rotation of the camera from the target that moves the character to the left or right in shot

Rotate angle: The rotation of the camera around the character (in the y axis), determining what part of the character the player sees: the side, back or front

Roll angle: An unlikely angle to be used, which rotates the camera along its own axis, resulting in a skewed image of the world

Distance: The length of the imaginary beam between the character and the camera

Movement

Moving a chase camera introduces complexity, as there are many different ways in which the camera can be moved and many subtle techniques for creating good-looking movement.

Movement controlled by the camera system rather than the player can be fairly simple or may have added layers of depth with large amounts of camera AI trying to get the best shot. It can be a fine balance between creating a very complicated system that works most of the time but may frustrate the player by not always having the right angle or allowing full player control and keeping the AI camera movement very simple. Chase camera movement can be broken down into several types:

Rigid: A rigid camera does not allow the distance or tilt angle to alter as the character moves around. It may also lock the rotation angle so that the camera remains behind the character at all times. This system is simple but is likely to suffer from jerkiness as the player moves around. There is no smoothness to the camera, and this will be obvious to the player. A small amount of smoothing will drastically improve the results of such a camera.

Elasticated: An elasticated system allows the distance and tilt angle to change with a smooth acceleration and deceleration of the camera as it moves around. A number of extra variables will be employed for this:

- **Min/max distance:** The minimum and maximum values to which the distance can scale
- **Min/max tilt angle:** The minimum and maximum value to which the tilt angle can be adjusted (directly linked to distance, so only one or the other is needed)
- **Acceleration:** The rate at which the camera accelerates, creating a lag time before it reaches full speed
- **Deceleration:** The rate at which the camera decelerates, creating a lag time before it becomes stationary
- **Lag offset:** The distance at which the camera will start to move, allowing small movements of the player character without the camera moving to catch up (though it will still rotate to face the character)

Elasticated systems are employed in a lot of games. There are often many more variables applied to a camera system to perform damping and smoothing besides those shown above. However, it is best not to overcomplicate the system.

Tracking

A tracking system of movement attempts to return to position behind the player character when the player starts to move. This system uses elasticity in the distance and couples this with automatic rotation back to the ideal camera position after the player has been in motion for a second or two.

A few parameters are used to describe a tracking camera in addition to those used for an elasticated camera:

Rotate acceleration: The rate at which the camera moves to top rotation speed
Rotate deceleration: The rate at which the camera slows to the ideal camera position
Rotate speed: The top speed of rotation

Auto Look

Some games may call for auto look, where the camera automatically moves to impart specific information to the player. There are several purposes this might serve:

- Show the player a point of interest
- Show the player an incoming enemy
- Form part of the lock-on system
- Allow the player to aim a projectile weapon

The system automatically rotates the camera around the player to face the target. This may be a subtle movement just intended to indicate a direction to move in or, more likely, a move to face something directly.

What player-movement implications this has are dependent on what effect you want to achieve. With a split-body animation system, you could rotate the top half of the body to face the target while keeping the body moving in the original direction (within the realms of the character's physical limits of course). This allows a player to shoot one way while running another. Alternatively, the character could change direction as the camera rotates, keeping the camera behind the character. The problem with this is that it might be unwanted movement for the player and could become very frustrating. Finally, the direction of the movement could be retained while the stick is held, but the camera is rotated—movement only being reset when the stick is released. If the camera then rotates back to the ideal position once the target is lost, the movement will return to normal without the player having to release the stick.

Many more parameters can be applied to a chase camera:

Auto-look rotate speed: The top speed at which the camera will rotate to look at the target.
Target priority: The importance of a target if more than one is in range.
Auto-look rotate acceleration: The rate of acceleration to top speed.
Auto-look rotate deceleration: The rate of deceleration to target facing.
Target range: The area in which a target is considered. The range could be linked to the rotation angle so that the camera rotates only as the target gets nearer.
Maximum rotate angle: A constriction that limits how far the camera can rotate from the ideal position.

Auto look is most useful for turning to face objects or enemies that have been specifically locked on to. Here the player has specified that he wants to lock on, so it makes sense that the camera would move to show this. In these instances there might be no delay or lag in shifting the camera, and either it will have very fast movement or the camera could simply pop to the ideal position for the locked-on target.

Player Control

Many games allow the player to control the camera to some degree. This can be both a blessing and a curse. Giving the player control means that when a bad angle does occur, the player will always be able to change the view to see the action properly. In addition, and perhaps more importantly, it enables the player to look around his surroundings.

It can be a curse if the camera controls are not set up well. People have many different preferences. Which way should a camera rotate with left and right movement? Do they like up and down movement to be inverted? How sensitive should the movement be? These should all be set up as adjustable options, but the defaults need to be right for the majority of people. A further problem is that while player control allows the players to get good shots, it also allows them to be stuck in bad ones. Another big problem is that the player could be looking in the wrong direction when a major event occurs.

With a chase camera the player should be able to control some or all of the following, though they may be restricted in some manner:

Rotation (tumble): Moving around the character. This is the standard player control and is unlikely to be constrained, but it might be limited to a certain angle from the ideal position.

Tilt: Adjusting the tilt angle allows the player to see more of the horizon or more of the floor. This is nearly always constrained, often to a fairly narrow angle, as looking straight down or going through the floor is pretty much useless for navigation.

Dolly in and out: Adjusting the distance allows the camera to move closer or farther away from the player character. Dolly in and out will be constrained to a minimum and maximum distance.

Typically camera movement is mapped to the right analog stick. However, there is a problem trying to fit all three camera movements onto one stick. Left and right immediately lend themselves to rotate, but up and down could be used for either tilt or dolly in and out. Usually it is a case of choosing one or the other, but you might consider mapping the other function elsewhere if you can.

Simple Environment Cameras

Environment-based cameras can easily be implemented with a few basic cameras, without the need to get overly complex.

Fixed Cameras

The simplest cameras to implement are fixed-position and fixed-direction cameras. These are cameras that do not move at all. Instead, they are cut between as the player runs around the environment activating their triggers.

The *Resident Evil* series on the PlayStation used this technique. Because the cameras didn't move, the designers could prerender the environment, allowing the graphical quality to exceed what would have been possible with a true 3D world at the time. A prerendered image was then overlaid with a 3D collision mesh. Any foreground objects in the image were assigned a Z buffer value so that the object could be drawn over the player if the player walked behind them. Any object the player had to interact with wasn't prerendered, which made it stand out from the backdrop, as it didn't look quite as stunning as its surroundings. This technique was great for the time but is likely to look a little antiquated now, as players expect to be able to fully move around the environment in a cinematic manner.

Tracking Cameras

The next step up from fixed cameras is tracking cameras, those that are set in a fixed position but are free to follow a target (the player). Like with fixed cameras, transitions are probably made by cutting, but because the world cannot be prerendered, more elaborate transitions are possible. The two positions can be interpolated between in a straight line, but this poses the risk of moving through objects that might be placed between the cameras. This can be solved by very specific placement of the cameras. Cameras can be placed without restrictions if splines are used to guide the transitions between cameras.

Tracking cameras are useful but are more likely to be used as part of a larger system of cameras in a modern game.

Spline Cameras

Spline cameras move along a predefined path. This keeps the camera in the best position for the action and alleviates any problems with bad camera angles. However, it means the designers have to lay out splines throughout the entire level, which can be quite a mammoth task.

How a camera is moved along a spline is a fairly complex issue, as there are lots of factors that can be taken into consideration. Like with the chase camera, a set distance can be used to drag the camera along the spline. This could be rigid or will more likely use the elasticated system to allow smoother movement. While pulling the camera along the spline is fairly easy, the situation gets more complicated when the player moves in the opposite direction—toward the camera. One option is to let the camera remain still until the maximum distance is reached in the opposite direction, where the camera will begin to pull again. The problem with this is that the player can reach a position where he is directly under the camera, which is a serious problem for screen-relative movement (discussed later in the camera transitions section). This problem can be solved by placing the spline over areas under which the player character cannot walk.

Alternatively, the camera can have a push effect so that it is kept at a minimum distance from the player character. This will move the camera backward along the spline. The only problem with this system is that it can result in the player having to move into the camera and thus not seeing which direction he is walking. Figure 6.10 shows a spline camera using the push–pull system.

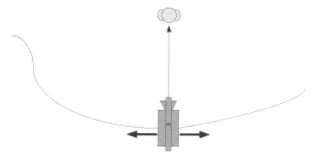

FIGURE 6.10   A push–pull spline camera.

Component-Based Camera System[1]

The component-based camera system allows designers to construct complex systems from smaller constituent parts. These parts work together in different ways to allow all of the above cameras systems as well as more complex cameras. The basis of the system lies with three controllers that determine the behavior of the camera:

> **Movement controller:** Determines how the camera is moved in world space
> **Look-at controller:** Determines what the camera is aimed at
> **Lens controller:** Determines the function of the lens, such as FOV or depth of field

With the controller system, it may be desirable to allow each controller to have a different camera target. They will likely all use the same target, but a movement controller might rigidly follow the player character while the look-at controller tracks a position between important scene elements. Meanwhile, the lens controller may use a separate target to focus on a specific object or actor.

There are also support components that are used to describe limitations or improve the functionality of the camera:

> **Volumes:** Used to activate the camera or bind the camera to world space
> **Smoothers:** Used to smooth camera movement and eliminate jerkiness or erratic behavior
> **Tweakers:** Allow the player to exert control over the camera in a limited fashion

Movement Controllers

The movement controller is responsible for translating the position of the camera in world space. Several different types of movement controller can be used:

> **Fixed position:** The camera is anchored to a specific point in world space and cannot be moved around.

- **World position:** The position of the camera.
- **Boom:** The camera is attached to an imaginary beam, which has a pivot point. This means the camera moves in the opposite direction to the target's movement around a fixed world position (see Figure 6.11).
- **Boom pivot:** The position of the pivot in world space or as an offset in one axis from the target's position so that the camera can track the player into and out of the screen. The y axis value of the pivot will also dictate the tilt angle of the camera.
- **Boom length:** The distance from the camera to the pivot point. This could be made to scale dynamically according to the target's distance from the pivot point.
- **Bounding volume:** A volume that limits movement of the camera to specific bounds.

---

[1]The author thanks Wil Driver for allowing him to use the basis of his idea for a component-based camera system in this book.

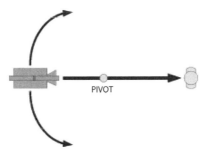

FIGURE 6.11   A boom camera.

Target relative chase: The chase camera is based on the same movement as a simple chase camera, where an imaginary beam can be drawn between the target and the camera. The same values used to describe a standard chase cam also apply:

- **Distance:** The length of the imaginary beam
- **Tilt angle:** The angle of tilt of the imaginary beam
- **Rotation angle:** The starting point or ideal rotation angle of the camera relative to the target's root
- **Min/max distance:** The maximum and minimum length the distance can stretch and squash
- **Min/max tilt:** The constraints of the tilt angle
- **Min/max rotation:** The constraints of the rotation should they be used
- **Acceleration:** The rate at which the camera moves to full speed
- **Deceleration:** The rate at which the camera slows to a standstill
- **Max rotate speed:** The maximum speed at which the camera can move
- **Ideal camera position:** An offset that specifies the ideal position for the camera to take
- **Camera return:** The camera's return to the ideal position
- **Bounding volume:** A volume that limits movement of the camera to specific bounds

Spline locked: A spline-locked camera, as its name suggests, is attached to the spline. This is the same system as the spline cameras discussed earlier. The camera can be pulled or pushed along the spline as the target reaches a specific distance from the camera. A number of variables control the camera:

- **Min/max distance:** The minimum distance is used if the camera is to push as well as pull; otherwise, only the maximum distance is required.
- **Acceleration:** The rate at which the camera moves up to full speed.
- **Deceleration:** The rate at which the camera slows to a standstill.
- **Max speed:** The maximum speed at which the camera can move.
- **Lag distance:** The amount of distance the target has to move before the camera will begin to move.

- **Bounding volume:** A volume that limits movement of the camera to specific bounds should any adjustments be made to its basic movement.

Spline guided: A spline-guided system requires two splines to be placed into the world. One spline locks the camera movement to a specific path. The second spline is used to proportionately map the target position to the camera movement on the locked spline. The target is mapped to the nearest point on the guide spline, so when the target is one-third of the way along a position on the guide spline, the camera has moved one-third of the way along the locked camera movement spline.

Look-At Controllers

Look-at controllers are used to control rotation of the game camera and face the camera toward a look-at target. Several types of look-at controllers may be implemented:

Fixed direction: The camera is set to face in a locked direction and will not rotate in any way to track a target. Direction specifies the direction vector that the camera faces.

Standard tracking: The camera rotates to face the look-at target in the standard manner. This is the most widely used look-at controller. The look-at controller may have a number of variables:

- **Max pan speed:** The maximum speed at which the camera can pan
- **Max tilt speed:** The maximum speed at which the camera can tilt
- **Max pan angle:** The maximum angle to which the camera can pan
- **Max tilt angle:** The maximum angle to which the camera can tilt
- **Tracking lag:** A time or degree measurement that the target can move before the camera will begin to track.
- **Track acceleration:** The rate at which the camera moves up to full pan or tilt speed (might be a separate acceleration for pan and tilt)
- **Track deceleration:** The rate at which the camera slows to a standstill (might be a separate deceleration for pan and tilt)
- **Target offset:** An offset from the look-at target (can be used to frame in a particular manner)

Spline guided: A spline-guided look-at system controls the look-at target of the camera as the target moves along a guide spline. The target is mapped to a point on the spline in line with the camera position and the target itself. This system can be used to look at a particular point. Imagine walking past a cathedral. The camera could be made to angle up at the belfry as the player character walks past by curving the spline upward at this point.

Lens Controller

The lens controller is a standard type that has a number of different options. However, you might want to create preset lens controllers as if they were a series of interchangeable real lenses. You might have a highly zoomed telephoto lens, a wide-angled lens, a standard lens, and so on.

A lens controller has several attributes:

Zoom: The level of zoom applied to the camera lens.
Dynamic dolly: Allows the camera to dolly in and out to keep a target proportionately the same size on screen.
FOV: The field of view of the lens.
Depth of field: The amount of blurring applied to unfocused images. Often assigned as near and far blur plane distances.

Smoothers

A camera set to rigidly track a target without acceleration or deceleration values may produce erratic movement or jerkiness. This can be solved by applying smoothers to the controllers. A smoother takes a number of samples of movement over time and takes an average of these values that is then used for the final movement or rotation values. This lessens any erratic movement but if heavily smoothed may cause too much lag.

Tweakers

Tweakers allow the designer to determine the amount of control the player can exert over a particular camera. Two forms of control can be applied: character relative or camera relative.

Character-relative control rotates and tilts the camera around the character. Camera-relative movement pans and tilts the camera to adjust the view, meaning the player character will be moved in screen space. This is usually confined so that the player cannot move it too far from the focus of the player character. This allows the player to look a little way ahead.

Using the Component Camera System

With the component camera system in place, the designer must select the right bits and pieces to create a camera. Let's look at a couple of examples of fairly complex cameras using the component system.

Example 1: A Simple Room

Let's imagine we have a room where we want the camera to remain low and move along a spline to the center of the room but track the player as he runs to the sides. We want to be able to see as much of the room as possible—not just the back wall. However, when the player gets to the near wall, we want the camera to lift up. The layout of the camera rig is shown in Figure 6.12.

To create this system, we use two cameras. One covers the majority of the room, and the second covers the wall the camera is mounted on. We use two camera volumes to cover the room and two cameras: near camera and far camera.

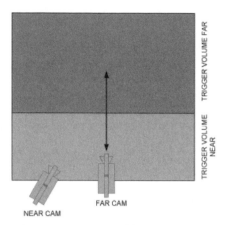

FIGURE 6.12   A near and far camera rig in a square room.

Near camera: This is fairly simple. It uses a fixed-position movement controller to keep the camera rooted into a ledge built into the wall. A standard look-at controller allows the camera to track the player, and a basic lens controller gives a FOV of 60°. This is transitioned to the far camera via a 1-second linear interpolation to the far camera (transitions are covered in a moment).

Far camera: The far camera is slightly more complex. It uses a spline-guided camera for the movement controller. The guide spline reaches a little way out from the wall to three-fourths of the way into the room. The camera lock spline reaches from the wall to about halfway into the room, so the camera will slide into the room as the player moves away from the camera. A standard look-at controller is used to track the player. This means the camera will rotate to face the player as he moves out to the sides of the room, but the camera remains attached to the spline. The lens controller uses a standard setup with the same FOV as the near camera. Dynamic dolly could be added to allow the camera to move sideways as well, effectively creating a volume in the center in which the camera moves. A camera transition of a 1-second linear interpolation is used to seamlessly blend into the near camera.

Example 2: A Path with a View

Let's go back to the cathedral example we used for the spline-guided look-at controller and extend it. Let's add a path around the outside of the cathedral and create a camera that follows the player character around the path, then looks up at the belfry as he moves past. This can all be done with one carefully planned camera (see Figure 6.13).

First, for the movement controller we will use a spline-guided movement controller to provide motion. We place the guide spline along the path, following the corner. Next we place the lock spline around the outer edge. When we get to the point where we want to make the camera look up, we place a dip. This will move the camera down at this point to create a low angle.

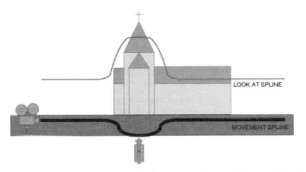

FIGURE 6.13   A camera with a look-at guide rail that will look up at the belfry as the player moves along the path.

Next we use a spline-guided look at controller to create the line the camera look-at target will follow. The guide spline follows the path of the movement guide spline, except that we create a peak at the point where we want the camera to look up. We also place a point of interest on the belfry so the camera AI knows we want to frame this point as well as the player.

Finally we use a standard lens with dynamic dolly to ensure that the player character stays in the shot when the camera moves to show the belfry.

Camera Transitions

There are two basic approaches to transitioning environment cameras. The first is to place trigger volumes around the level that transitions between one camera and the next. This means having to lay volumes at each of the crossover points.

Alternatively, a default chase cam can be active whenever the player is not inside a camera volume. The camera volumes will then need to cover the whole area where the intended camera is to be used. Camera volumes overlap to allow transitions when the player leaves one volume and enters another. Exclusion volumes can also be applied to specific cameras to make complex shapes easy to create.

When moving between cameras, there must be some kind of transition. Transitions link one camera to another and specify how the camera will behave at the point where the next camera takes over.

Transition Types

Several types of transition can be employed:

Cut: The simplest and default transition is a cut. The camera simply jumps from one camera position to the next.

Fade: The image from the two cameras is blended over a specified time. This presents a number of problems such as potentially doubling the render load, as two scenes must be rendered to fade from one to the other, and this transition may not necessarily be obvious to the player. Alternatively the view may fade to a particular color, make a cut while nothing can be seen, and then fade back up into the next camera. This avoids the rendering of two different scenes.

Interpolation: The camera uses linear or spherical interpolation (LERP and SLERP) to move smoothly from one camera position to the next over a specified period of time. When interpolating movement, the look-at controller should be free to keep focused on the look-at target. With interpolation, all sorts of extra variables can be added for acceleration, deceleration, and speed, but generally time is the only needed variable, and the time period should be kept at around 1 or 2 seconds. If it is too fast, it will appear to be just like a cut. If it is too slow, it will cause too much lag.

Spline: Cameras could be linked by splines that determine the exact path of the camera transition. These transition splines would have a set period of time to travel the length of the spline. Depending on length, this time is likely to be similar to an interpolation. The advantage of a spline is that it can navigate complex environments that might otherwise result in clipping with the standard interpolation method. The disadvantage is the large amount of time required to set these up.

Control Issues

Cameras can have problems when transitioning during gameplay if using screen-relative movement (character-relative movement will not have these problems). These control issues occur in two instances: when running directly underneath a camera and when cameras are switched to an opposing angle.

Snap control map: Usually the new control map is immediately applied to the new screen image, meaning the character switches directions when opposing angles are displayed. This ultimately means the character gets stuck flicking between the two cameras or remains stuck constantly changing direction while directly underneath a camera (a scenario known as gimbal lock).

Retain control map: One solution is to keep the controls mapped to the original camera while they are still moving and then switch to the new control map once the movement has stopped. However, this also creates problems in that control can start to feel very strange if the movement is held across several camera transitions.

Interpolate control maps: A more complex solution is to interpolate between the control maps, so that the player must gently compensate for the change in direction. Getting the timing right for this is important; too short a time will make it will feel just like the snapping control mechanism and too long will be back to the retained control method.

Cameras and Level Design

Cameras can have a lot of difficulty when placed in a tight area, as there is not enough space for them to move around freely. Chase cameras are particularly troublesome, as they are not designed specifically for a particular area. Several factors can be taken into account to make camera placement easier when building a level.

Don't build tight spaces: The simplest solution is to not build tight spaces. In an outdoor setting this is a fairly easy task, but in interiors this can be a little trickier.

Build high ceilings: High ceilings give the camera room to move around and not cut through actors or objects.

Build camera grooves: Build ledges and grooves for the cameras to move in. These allow the camera to sit back out of the way of any object and prevent any problems with objects moving directly underneath a camera.

Avoid tall narrow spaces: Spiral staircases are always difficult for camera movement when enclosed by walls. Think differently and a spiral staircase can still work. For example, the staircase could wind around the outside of a tower.

Camera AI

When a camera is not specifically tailored to fit an environment, a degree of camera AI will need to be implemented to allow it to position itself sensibly. Even with a well-designed environment camera, there are points where the camera may be obscured by a dynamic object being in an awkward place or a character standing between the camera and the player character. Camera AI allows the camera system to interpret a situation and take action to rectify the problem to ensure that the view is maintained.

Steering

There are two situations where camera will need AI steering: collisions and obstructions. Collisions occur when the camera collides with the environment or a bounding volume. A camera is considered to be obstructed when an object is placed between the camera and the player character, completely obscuring the view of the player character. It is perfectly acceptable for objects to pass in front of the camera, as long as they do not block the view completely or are gone within a short time.

Steering moves the camera to a new position that still gives a good view of the action. To do this the camera AI must work out the best result from all the possible options and extrapolate the consequences of any movements it might make. There are generally four actions a camera is likely to perform on collision with a surface: shorten distance, tilt up, rotate left, or rotate right. It is unlikely that the camera will tilt down, as this will not give it a good view of its surroundings.

In order to determine the best choice of action, the camera needs to gather information on the situation. Generally the first action to occur would be a shortening of distance or tilting of the camera. Upon reaching the threshold for these actions, it is then left with the rotation options. Often a specific direction is preferred, so any calculations will be made initially on this direction, and should any problems occur, then calculations on other directions will be made as needed.

The calculation takes a specified length of predicted camera path and checks for any further collisions. If none occur, it is said to be a safe bet. However, if a collision occurs, other directions should be tested. Should these also result in collision, the best direction to take is probably the direction with the furthest collision.

This system can still have problems in certain situations, such as in the corner of a room where all three directions will be blocked. In such a situation it may be necessary to cut the camera to a safe position or transition to a different camera system should one be available.

Transparency

An easy way out of the camera steering problems is to simply not have environment collision and use transparency when a camera moves outside the bounds or is obscured. The wall or object will become translucent, allowing the player to see through to the action beyond.

This only works well with interior locations so that an empty backdrop (usually black) can represent the void—nothing space. Exterior locations would show the skybox behind when the camera clips out of the environment. Also, this kind of rendering technique can be fairly expensive in processing terms.

Camera Framing

A camera can be set up to automatically move and control the lens to frame a shot in the best manner possible. Characters are assigned a radius describing a sphere that needs to be kept on screen by the camera, according to their importance levels. An importance level of 1 means the sphere must be kept on screen. This is generally reserved for the player only.

With the player character, the size of the framing sphere is very important. If dynamic dolly is to be used, then the camera will attempt to keep this sphere at a continual proportion of the screen space. This means a small sphere will result in a close-up image, whereas a larger sphere will be dollied out further (see Figure 6.14). The sphere can be offset from the root of the character so that exact positioning is possible.

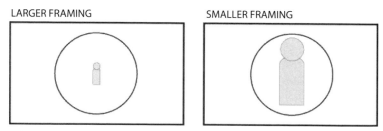

LARGER FRAMING   SMALLER FRAMING

FIGURE 6.14   The camera sphere size controls the size of the character on screen.

The importance of other characters is likely to be less, which means the camera system will only keep a portion of their spheres on screen. A target distance from the main target is also used so that other characters are only considered for framing when within a certain distance of the player.

Other characters are likely to have smaller spheres than the main character, depending on how much movement of the camera is desired. Larger spheres will produce larger movement to keep the targets framed.

Camera Rigs

Several different game mechanics will probably be employed in a game, which are likely to demand different functionalities from the camera system. The solution is to have a number of camera rigs that alter or completely change the camera according to the situation. By adjusting the basic camera in a number of ways, the ideal view of the action can be found:

Tilt: Locked to a maximum tilt angle and ideal tilt range and moves with a defined speed.

Rotate: Tumble around a subject. Does not need to have a maximum rotate angle, but it might be desired. Also moves with a defined speed.

Zoom: Move the camera away or toward a target with a maximum distance and a defined speed. The camera should still conform to any bounds such as a camera volume.

All of these values require damping and smoothing to prevent sudden motion.

Exploration Cameras

An exploration camera rig is essentially the standard camera rig that is designed to show off the environment to maximum potential while keeping player controls as the primary concern. The exploration rig must meet several goals:

Ease of navigation: Give a good view of the player and allow him to see where he is going. The camera system should avoid the player having to run toward the camera without being able to see what is ahead.

Spatial awareness: Give a sense of scale and perspective and make the player aware of his surroundings and allow him to get a lay of the land.

Aesthetics: Give the best camera angle possible to show off the environment and the character. This is likely to be a fairly low angle, which tends to conflict with the above goals. The key is to strike a balance that works.

An important point to note when designing the level is that all the environment work will go to waste if it is never seen by the camera. Planning out cameras beforehand enables the artists to build the levels so that the best artwork is seen and shown to its maximum potential.

Exploration cameras will more than likely need to allow some degree of player control over the camera so that players can assess their surroundings and get a better sense of their positions within that environment. This control may allow full or limited adjustment of the camera.

Combat Cameras

Combat demands a different view of the action from the standard exploration for a number of reasons. The emphasis moves away from a need for spatial awareness of the environment to the more immediate threat the player faces.

Typically exploration cameras are able to frame the environment from an equal level, giving the best view of the world around the player character. In combat the concern is no longer providing a beautiful vista, but giving the player the best information possible. This information varies between the two main types of combat: melee and ranged, as each has its own unique requirements:

Melee combat cameras: In melee combat the threat must get close, but the enemies may still be spread around the character in a circle. Generally the camera will have to adjust to accommodate the action.

- **Number of enemies:** The type of camera required will change with the number of enemies the player faces. In one-on-one combat it might be desirable to get as close as possible to a traditional beat 'em up side-on view. With a large number of enemies the camera should move back a fair way to accommodate them without moving so far as to make the action too small to see.
- **Camera tilt:** With the camera so low and enemies close at hand, it is highly likely that the camera will be obscured or will intersect an enemy. Therefore, it is necessary to tilt the camera to move it above the enemies' heads. This presents another problem in that the camera sees more floor than surrounding scenery, which can be a very dull view. The key here is to pick an optimum tilt angle that shows the enemy without filling the whole screen space with floor. A technique that could be used is an auto-tilting camera, so that the camera remains low until it becomes obscured, at which point it tilts upward until the obstruction is gone (there should be a hold time before returning to a low angle to prevent constant camera jerking, and the tilt will need to be smoothed to prevent erratic movement).
- **Point of interest:** Having the player central on screen offers pretty poor framing for a shot. By using points of interest between the player and one or more threats, a better view of the action can be maintained. A threat level can be assigned to the enemy that dynamically changes the importance of a character in the point of interest calculation. This enables the camera to focus on the action as needed. For an attacking character to be given higher importance, as he is a greater threat than a nearer, nonattacking character, the camera would lean more toward his direction. This needs to have a level of damping and smoothing to prevent constant jolts as characters move back and forth. There should also be a maximum distance from the player for this to occur.

Ranged combat cameras: The best cameras for ranged combat are first-person or over-the-shoulder views. When aiming in third person, the camera needs to be as low as possible to show the horizon as much as is feasible. The same kind of problems apply here as with melee combat in that characters may obstruct the view when the camera is this low. However, the camera should not rotate away from the player character's direction of facing.

When using cameras around the environment instead of chase cameras, there is a real danger of not being able to see anything. The solution might be to shift the character to one side of the frame to open up space in the direction he is facing. The key is to provide as much distant information as possible without dollying the camera back ridiculous amounts.

Separate Exploration and Combat Modes

Many Japanese RPGs such as the *Final Fantasy* series approach the issue in a different manner, by completely separating combat and exploration. The lavish environments in exploration mode give way to simple combat arenas that display the action in the best and clearest way possible. This does cause a strange feeling of detachment from the area being explored and the area that is being fought in.

This technique will probably be seen less and less as the drive for realism and cinematic experiences continues. After all, a lot of abstractions were made for technical reasons that no longer exist, but convention keeps those abstractions in use. Of course, that is not a reason to avoid them, as conventions do have their place.

Overview Rigs

For more sedate and cerebral stages of the game such as puzzles, an entirely different kind of camera rig may be required. An overview rig has a different set of goals than exploration or combat rigs, with the emphasis on giving the player as much relevant information as possible. Aesthetics should not be important here but should always be considered. Also, the player still needs to be able to navigate easily.

Prince of Persia: Warrior Within™ has a system that allows the player to switch between the standard exploration camera rig and a pulled-back overview camera that gives a much better view of the surroundings. Since this is a game where environment traversal is a large part of the gameplay, the overview camera proves invaluable.

The overview camera might be achieved by making tweaks to the exploration camera, but this can be imprecise and may easily collide and intersect with other characters and the environment, or it may be difficult to get the optimum angle. Another alternative is to have another network of cameras around the environment designed to give the optimum view. These can be transitioned between when the player wants to switch to the overview. Keep in mind, however, that this is a lot of extra work in camera placement and testing.

Boss Battle Camera Rigs

While standard combat cameras have a number of requirements, a different set of requirements may be needed with a boss character. Often these will be specially designed camera rigs. The difference from normal combat and the changed requirements are:

Size of the enemy: Bosses are often much larger than standard enemies and are often impossibly large. A camera will need to display as much of the boss as possible.

Foreshadowing attacks: Boss attacks are often elaborate and require the player to be forewarned. The camera may need to move to show the incoming attack.

Player feedback: The player needs to be kept abreast of his progress. This can mean seeing reactions from a character who is possibly too large to fully fit on screen. It may require adjustments to a camera to see this.

A boss rig is heavily tailored to work with the character and its behavior, which can mean using a combination of different cameras and adjustments to provide information to the player and to show the boss character in all its glory.

ANIMATED CAMERAS

Animated cameras can have much more sophisticated movement than the standard game camera—especially if what they are showing is not interactive. Unless you have an editor that has extensive camera controls, you're best off doing camera animation in a professional package such as Maya®. With the right tools, you can have a film-quality level of control over cameras, and therein lies another problem. This absolute control means that to get high-quality cameras you need to know how to animate a camera properly. Many designers aren't taught these kind of skills, and without this training, they shouldn't be doing animated camera work in games.

Qualified and trained camera animators would be much better at getting the angles and timing right and creating a better story with what is already there. That's why films have cinematographers and cameramen—to ensure that every shot is as close to perfect as possible. You wouldn't hire a script writer to hold a camera, so don't expect an untrained designer to be able to do perfect animated cameras.

MULTIPLAYER GAME CAMERAS

Problems result from having multiple players instead of one. The most problematic issue is displaying these characters on the same screen. Online or system links provide a nice solution, in that each player has his own screen and thus can view the action as normal. When playing on the same screen, there are only two real options: split screen or zooming the camera to fit all players on screen.

Split Screen

Split screen divides the screen into a number of sections so that each player has his own smaller viewing window. The maximum is usually four; otherwise, the window becomes too small to see the action, and it is too confusing to decipher who is who.

Another issue is that two or more scenes have to be rendered at once. This results in an increased load on the render engine that can have a serious impact on framerate unless the quality of each scene is diminished to account for this.

Zooming Camera

Allowing the camera to zoom resolves the problem of having more than one scene rendering but introduces several other issues. The levels have to be quite small to keep all characters on screen unless the camera zooms out really far. If it zooms out too far, it can cause problems with having to draw all of an expansive level, plus the players will be unlikely to be able to read what is happening on screen. This system cannot really be used in enclosed spaces, as it will clip through geometry.

To prevent the camera from zooming too far, some mechanism can be introduced to keep players together. In *Final Fantasy Crystal Chronicles* this was a crystal that had a radius of influence within which the players had to try to remain. Players may actually be physically prevented from moving beyond the screen limits, so in cooperative games the characters have to move in the same direction to progress.

SUMMARY

In this chapter we have looked at how the world is visualized on screen and learned the importance of the game camera in displaying the action to the player. We have covered a number of topics during this discussion:

Viewpoints: Several types of viewpoint have been used over the years, though two now form the majority of current console game releases.

- **First person:** The advantage of a first-person view is that we eradicate tricky camera problems, we offer the player freedom of view, and we make projectile aiming much easier. However, there are a number of disadvantages: a disconnection from the player character, possible confusion for the player, tricky joypad control, the possibility of motion sickness for some players, and difficulty performing melee combat as well as spatial puzzles.
- **Third person:** A third-person viewpoint offers advantages over the first person, namely connection with the player character, easier joypad control, easier navigation of the environment, cinematics, easier melee combat, and easier solving of spatial puzzles. However, there are also a number of disadvantages. There are severe camera difficulties posed, there is often a constraint on what the player can see, and it can be difficult to use projectile weapons in this viewpoint.
- **Using both third and first person:** Some games seek to solve the weak points of one viewpoint by allowing elements of the other. Games may use a fixed first-person lookaround, first-person aiming, and hybrid systems so they can switch between the two, or offer an over-the-shoulder aiming viewpoint.
- **Isometric:** A fairly old method of viewing a scene that is being used less and less these days as real 3D spaces can be rendered in a similar manner.
- **Side scrolling:** A classic platformer or beat 'em up viewpoint that is still used in one-on-one beat 'em ups or used to create a retro feel.

- **Top-down:** Another retro favorite that is rarely used outside of strategy games these days.

Camera basics: Two main types of camera are used in games—game cameras and animated cameras. We also learned about other basic aspects of cameras in this section:

- **Camera movement:** The terminology for camera movement, namely track, tumble, pan, tilt, roll, dolly, and zoom.
- **The camera lens:** We learned the definitions of field of view and depth of field, as well as exploring techniques to mimic the physical lens.

Game cameras: Game cameras are cameras that are moved procedurally by the game engine to monitor the on-screen action and are usually set up by the design team. We learned several important elements about game cameras:

- **First person:** The easiest types of camera to set up, as they only require player height, field of view, and look control.
- **Third person:** Two main types of third-person camera might be used— chase or environment cameras. We examined a simple chase camera system, then looked at simple environment cameras—fixed, tracking, and spline. We then looked at an idea for a more complex component-based camera system that uses movement controllers, look-at controllers, and lens controllers alongside volumes, smoothers, and tweakers to allow the designer to set up all kinds of different cameras.
- **Camera transitions:** Several types of transition might be made between cameras—cut, fade, interpolation, or spline. During a transition we may need to alter the controls via the use of control snap, by retaining the control map, or by blending the control map.
- **Cameras and level design:** A level should be built with some idea of the use of cameras in mind. When building a level, don't build tight spaces. Try to build high ceilings or provide grooves for the camera rails to run in. Also try to avoid tall narrow spaces, as they can be a nightmare for the camera.
- **Camera AI:** Chase cameras in particular need camera AI to prevent them from performing actions that render the scene unusable for the player. They require steering to avoid obstacles or obstructions, though they could cheat and use transparency on a object that passes between the player and the camera. Camera AI is also used on all types of camera to provide good framing of the scene.
- **Camera rigs:** Different camera setups may be needed in different gameplay situations. Often these rigs adjust the base camera properties such as tile, rotate, and zoom. Typically a game might have exploration camera rigs, combat rigs, overview rigs, and boss battle rigs.

Animated cameras: More complex camera movements for noninteractive moments (other than basic tweaks) may be done with an animated camera rather than the standard game cameras. This enables much more impressive camera motions to be animated and played out.

Multiplayer game cameras: For multiplayer games where there is more than one player sharing a screen, there will generally be two methods of displaying the action—either split screen or by zooming the camera to encapsulate the action.

The use of cameras is an important area of research, as it is an area that can still benefit from improvement, particularly in the field of camera AI. Certainly third-person cameras are the hardest to implement and will require a good deal of time and attention throughout a project. There are no easy answers to these problems, but with careful thought they can be solved either by improving the AI of the camera if using chase cameras or by very careful placement and rigorous testing if using environment cameras.

COMBAT FUNDAMENTALS

In This Chapter

- The Basics of Combat
- The Combat Procedure
- Basic Combat Dynamics
- Aiming and Targeting

I t's a cliché to say that games are violent, but it is true that the vast majority of games feature violence of some sort or another, whether it be comedy slapstick or full-on gore.

Combat is such a popular aspect of game design that it is worthy of an in-depth investigation of the mechanics that describe and define it. It is a large and complex subject that will depend on the type of game you are trying to create. What follows is an investigation into many different types of combat and the myriad of possibilities that are open to a designer. This list is not exhaustive. New combat mechanics are being designed and refined all the time.

This chapter focuses on the following aspects of combat:

- The basics of combat
- The combat procedure
- Basic combat dynamics
- Aiming and targeting

THE BASICS OF COMBAT

While combat is a vast and complex subject, many aspects of combat apply to all games. These basic elements that are required of all combat systems will be the first port of call for any designer who is beginning to plan out core game mechanics.

Combat Entities

A combat entity is anything in the game world that can be interacted with and affected using the combat system:

- Player character(s)
- Allies and NPCs
- Enemies
- Breakable objects

Health

Every combat entity has a set level of health. When this health reaches zero, the entity is considered to be dead. Death can mean different things for different entities.

Player Health

Player health is a measure of how close the player character is to death. The way in which a health bar is replenished can significantly affect the way a player plays the game. There are several standard methods of replenishing player health that will have drastic effects on the gameplay:

No replenishment: The most harsh method is to offer the player only the health he has at the start of a level. This encourages players to be extremely cautious and will likely make them less prone to perform running attacks and so on. However, it can also be extremely frustrating if the player makes mistakes early in the level.

Health pickups: Health is replenished by collecting objects in the environment. This form of replenishment encourages players to search for all extra health items to keep themselves topped up. If pickups can be carried and used later, this behavior is further encouraged.

Recharge points: Specific points in the level might be used to replenish lost health. These are fixed locations that therefore promote gameplay bursts. When the player is close to one of these recharge points, he is likely to be fairly blasé. The further away from one of these points the player is, the more cautious he is likely to become.

Recharging health: Some games have recharging health schemas in which health automatically recharges over a period of time. These schemas are quite problematic, as they encourage the players to hang back from fighting to allow their health to recharge. At the end of a battle the player may as well go make a snack and wait a few minutes for his health to recharge. A quick recharge after a delay of a fairly short period of time is the best way to implement this and avoid the danger of the player just hanging around. Therefore, the players will only really die if they receive a large number of hits in a small amount of time.

Player health can be visualized in a number of different ways. The following ways are some of the more popular:

Numbers: The player's health may be simply displayed as a number. This makes it very quick to see exactly how much health the player character has left but does not fit within the context of the game world.

Health blocks: Health blocks are defined portions of health. Every hit will reduce the number of blocks by a set amount (usually 1). This produces a clear and defined damage system but produces little subtlety. This is generally used for platform games or games with simple combat mechanics.

Health bar: The health bar is a more ambiguous gauge for judging health. Each hit can be of any size and will simply scale the bar accordingly. One hundred is always a good number for health, as it makes it easy to think in percentages. The bar is generally used in more combat-orientated games where combat scope is favored over presentation.

Shield: A more exotic health method can be seen in *Halo*. Essentially, a rechargeable health bar protects a series of health blocks—a combination of the above two methods. The health blocks will not be lost until the shield has been depleted. The shield will recharge after a few seconds, during which time the player's health is left open and vulnerable.

Vital object(s): The classic platformer *Sonic the Hedgehog* required the players to collect gold rings that acted as their health. While they had gold rings in their possession, they could take a hit without dying. When the player was hit, the rings would scatter across the screen. The player then had a limited amount of time during which he was invulnerable to collect the rings before they would disappear for good.

Power stages: Sonic's longtime commercial rival Mario used a slightly different health mechanism, which is similar to health blocks but tied into other game mechanics. As Mario ate mushrooms, he became more powerful in set stages. When he took a hit, he would drop back down a stage. Only in his base stage would he actually die.

Buddy health: Third-person adventure game *Ico* used a very unusual health system in which the main character was all but invincible (unless he fell to his death) but was escorting a vulnerable "buddy." Should Yorda, the buddy, get dragged into a shadow pool, then all was lost.

Enemy Health

Enemy health is generally a hidden number within the combat system. However, the game might expose this information in some way to the player. With simple combat systems this may equate to a health value that requires x number of hits to kill the enemy creature. The health of a creature could be displayed using sound or color when hit. A changing pitch of sound gives the combat an interesting rhythm and reinforces the sense of impact (see *Sphinx and the Cursed Mummy*™ or *The Legend of Zelda: The Windwaker*™ for examples of this).

More elaborate combat systems could use a health bar. The simplest way of displaying their health would be to have the bar displayed on screen, above the enemy character's head for example. A more advanced system that requires more work would be to have different animations for various health stages and apply injuries to the character models. This looks great but has implications for memory, performance, and the time required to build the system.

More complicated enemies could have all sorts of convoluted health methods, such as being invulnerable until another creature is killed or having a shield system like the one described in the Player Health section above.

Breakable Object Health

Breakable objects tend not to have health bars but may have subtler systems such as levels of damage that can be switched back and forth. These at least give a visual clue to the player that these actions are having a discernable effect.

THE COMBAT PROCEDURE

The combat procedure is wholly dependent on the style of game you are producing and how complex you want to make the combat system. One of the most important distinctions in a combat system is the structure of combat itself. Is it turn based or real time?

Turn-Based Combat

Turn-based combat is like playing a board game. Each sides' actions are calculated in turn—one side attacking, then the other. Turn-based combat is used often in RPGs, particularly Japanese RPGs such as the *Final Fantasy* series.

Turn-based combat tends to be more strategic and stat heavy than real-time combat. Often it requires a lot of user interface with menus and icons for all the various actions the player can perform.

Turn Style

Several styles of turn might be used:

- Turn-by-turn
- Time-based turns
- Real-time turns

Turn-by-Turn

The simplest style of turn-based combat is turn-by-turn. Like a game of chess each side (in this case the player and the AI) takes it in turns to make their move. The first turn is dictated by who initiated the combat. Usually the emphasis is placed on the player going first, so he will always have the first turn unless he is ambushed. Once everyone has finished their turns, the cycle starts again. Each one of these cycles is known as a round.

Time-Based Turns

A slightly more sophisticated system is time-based turns. Here each character has a unique turn speed. This is how quickly they can cycle though turns. Time will advance until a character is ready for his turn. At this point the game freezes so the player can make his attack choices. Once these are made, time begins to pass again until another character is ready for his turn. Should two characters be ready at the same moment, it is usually the player's turn that takes precedence. A time-based turn is shown in Figure 7.1.

This means that one character could have two or three turns before an opponent even has one. Status effects could also be applied to characters to slow down their turn speed, skip their next turn, and so on.

Real-Time Turns

Does this sound like a hybrid system? In a way it is, though it adheres more rigidly to the turn-based paradigm than to fully real-time combat. Essentially, the time line is broken into blocks of turns. When combat begins, time is frozen—ready for the player to input his first move. The characters then maneuver into combat positions, and the character that strikes first has the first turn.

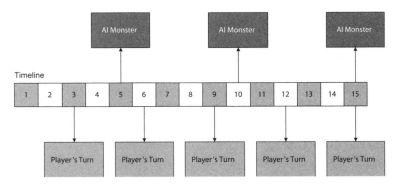

FIGURE 7.1   An example of a time-based turn.

The player character(s) are controlled by AI unless the player makes an input. This AI may be controlled from a set of predefined styles. When the player makes an input, it will be queued up ready to be executed on the next available turn. A real-time turn is shown in Figure 7.2, which shows the following events occurring:

1. Game is frozen. Waiting for player's input on first move. Player selects attack and real time begins.
2. Monster's turn.
3. No input has been received from the player. Auto action is performed.
4. Monster's turn. Receive input from player to perform a special attack. This action is queued ready for the player's next turn.
5. Queued action from turn 4 is played. Character performs special attack.
6. Monster's turn.
7. Player's turn. An input to defend is received, but since the turn has already begun, it must be queued ready for the next available turn. An automatic action is performed.
8. Monster's turn.
9. Queued action from turn 7 is played and the player defends.

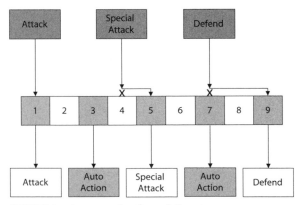

FIGURE 7.2   An example of a real-time turn.

Turn Procedure

Turn procedure determines what happens in each turn. This procedure will be heavily dependent on how complex you want to make the combat system. Most turns will follow the basic procedure shown in Figure 7.3.

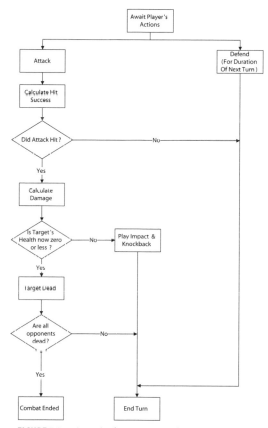

FIGURE 7.3   A typical turn procedure.

Real-Time Combat

Real-time combat is utterly dependent on input from the user and the AI of the opponents. Figure 7.4 shows a basic combat procedure—the type that would be perfectly adequate for a platformer.

Every time an attack is issued, a procedure begins—starting with checking that the attack has hit anything. Next it will check whether the target itself is vulnerable (i.e., it's not blocking or the hit location is not invulnerable). Then it will calculate damage. This will vary greatly depending on numerous variables that could be set in place (damage is discussed in depth in a later chapter). The appropriate impact reaction will also be applied. Finally a check is made to see if the target is dead. If so, then it is turned to a ragdoll or removed from the world. Otherwise, the target will eventually recover.

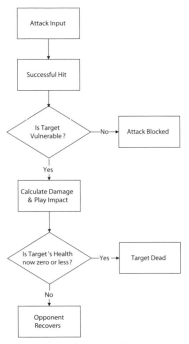

FIGURE 7.4 A basic combat procedure.

More complex procedures build on this basic framework, adding different damage zones, hit reactions, and so on.

BASIC COMBAT DYNAMICS

Once we have described the basic structure of our combat, we need to start considering the finer details. Dynamics describes the elements that will define and enhance various aspects of the combat system. We will discuss the dynamics of the two main types of combat, melee and ranged, in the next chapters. Here we will discuss elements that are common to both of them.

Engaging Combat Mode

For many games that have combat as the central gameplay premise, engaging combat mode will not be an issue, as the player's weapon will always be at the ready. However, many games have lots of other mechanics besides combat, and having the weapon drawn at all times might not be desirable.

In these instances it is sensible to differentiate between normal exploration and combat modes. Many aspects of the game's systems are fundamentally affected by this. Places where combat can be initiated are often restricted in games for many reasons. For example, some games might require flat ground during combat, as the AI and animation systems don't support multilevel or angled environments during combat.

There are three basic ways of handling combat mode:

Always in combat: The character is always in combat mode (for combat intensive games).

Automatic: The game automatically places the player in combat mode when the situation suits.

User controlled: The player presses a button to switch into combat mode by unsheathing his weapon.

With automatic combat situations it is likely that there will be some kind of lock-down or similar system used to perform the fights. Classic Japanese RPGs such as *Final Fantasy* tend to have entirely separate environments in which to fight battles. The exploration screen switches to a combat screen when battle begins—as though the world has zoomed in to the new location. *Final Fantasy* does this purely randomly, whereas other RPGs (such as *Skies of Arcadia*™) might show enemies on the exploration map, which allows them to be avoided.

A commonly used system defines combat zones as distinct locations where barriers prevent the player from wandering outside the zone while combat is in progress. These doors are closed as combat is initiated and opened when the last enemy is defeated.

Turns versus Real Time

Turn-based combat uses many of the same dynamics as real-time combat. The difference in dynamics lies in control. Turn-based games tend to use menu systems for the player to input his action for the turn, so the player chooses to attack with a particular move or spell or defend for that turn. Real-time games require specific input from the player throughout the duration of combat.

Another major difference is that the interactions are generally much simpler in turn-based games than they are in real-time games, since there is only a set amount of action happening at any one time.

Combat Cinematics

Combat cinematics are events that dramatize the on-screen action. With judicious use they can enhance a combat system and create some very stylish and spectacular moments. Adding these elements may seen superfluous, but it will make the difference between a good combat system and a truly great one [Song05].

Cameras

Cameras are a useful tool in improving the feel of combat. It is important to not overdo cinematic cameras, however. While they are great the first time they are seen, it can get tiring very quickly to sit through the same sequences again and again. Always include an option to turn cinematic cameras off, use them sparingly, and keep them as short and sweet as possible.

Highlight Cameras

A good method of highlighting particularly impressive melee moves is to use a different camera angle to get in close. These cameras can also be animated so that they swoop around the action for *Matrix*-like effects.

Cinematic Combat Cameras

With even more showmanship, some really cinematic sequences can be put together. These can even be done dynamically. Imagine cutting to a shot of the gun barrel, then following the bullet through the air and watching it enter the victim's body, and then cutting to the reaction on the victim's face.

Creating dynamic sequences like this can be tricky, as cameras have to interact with the world without clipping through objects and breaking the illusion of solidity. Often volumes will have to be established that determine safe positions for a cinematic camera to occur within so that it does not clip through walls and so on.

Camera Effects

Two camera effects work well for emphasizing impacts:

Camera shake: Camera shake does exactly as it says on the tin and shakes the camera. This shake should be fairly subtle and not too regular. The oscillations of camera shake used in movies is great reference for getting the right effect.

Camera shift: Shifting the camera slightly in the direction of an incoming attack subtly emphasizes the attack by adding motion. This must be a subtle effect, however, or the player may end up suffering severe motion sickness.

Playing with Time

Altering time is another way of highlighting action and can even become part of the game mechanics themselves. Bear in mind that playing with time in multiplayer games is impossible, as different players cannot be in different time spaces in the same game. The alternative is to slow everyone to the slowest speed, but this will most likely cause severe frustration for other players, as the game will slow down at unexpected times.

Freeze Framing

Freezing frames at moments of impact can be used to emphasize a hit, especially in conjunction with other techniques such as screen flash. Doing this gives the player a chance to see the impact and really makes the player aware of the moves he is performing. This should only be applied to the player's hits and only used in single-player games, or else it might become frustrating. It should also be limited to powerful moves, as overusing it can make the combat feel sluggish.

Replays

Performing replays allows the players to experience truly great moments again and see action they might have missed before. It also gives the players the feeling of having achieved something if replays are set to play automatically.

Replays require a fair bit of memory, as the game state for a section of time must be kept in memory, that is, every button press, AI command, and physics interaction. With this information the game can replay segments of action, but obviously this is going to become a lot of information after long periods of play. The solution is to only store a fairly small segment of time—say the past 10 seconds or so.

Slow Motion

Another extremely useful mechanic for highlighting action is the ability to slow the game down and use slow motion. This allows the player to get a good grasp of the action. This can be performed automatically at certain points, such as when the player pulls off a particularly impressive move. There are three types of slow motion that might be used:

Automatic: The action is slowed during particularly powerful or impressive moments of action to emphasize them. This can be frustrating if overused.

User-controlled slow motion: This can also be incorporated into the mechanics of the game so that the player can purposely activate slow-motion when it's needed. This allows the player time to think in fast action situations and gives him a better idea of what is going on around him.

Time distortion: Time distortion is an advanced version of slow-motion, in that the world around the character slows down while the character stays at normal speed. This means the character could inflict blows upon many opponents before they have a chance to retaliate. This requires the game to be able to run different systems at different speeds or slow down animation speeds on particular groups of objects and enemies.

Screen Effects

Screen effects are another method of emphasizing impact or heightening the importance of an attack.

Screen Flash

Flashing the screen white (or another bright color) for a very brief time can embellish a successful hit, but should be used sparingly. One consideration when using screen flashes is that epilepsy sufferers can have a seizure when exposed to repetitively flashing lights. Try to be considerate to all gamers.

Screen Darken

The environment around the attacker and defender can be darkened to highlight the move being performed. This works really well for special moves performed by the player, but it is likely to become annoying if the enemy also causes this effect when attacking the player, though in a boss battle it might be pertinent to use the effect to illustrate just how powerful the enemy is.

Background Replace

Instead of just darkening the background, you could replace it altogether. A super special move in *Street Fighter Alpha 3* is marked by the background being replaced with a brightly colored scrolling background, but this could be anything (though it should of course make sense unless you are being purposely surreal).

Interactive Cinematics

Interactive cinematics are more involved versions of the screen effects discussed above that can also become part of the game mechanics themselves.

Camera Control

Giving camera control to the players during a replay allows them to direct their own mini-movie. The players could alter the facing of the camera or even switch between a variety of different cameras.

Skill Attacks

Skill attacks are unique attacks such as spells or feats. These are separate in many ways from the main combat systems but may use some of their basic mechanics. Common skill attacks are:

Set attack skills: Set attacks are predefined animations that are triggered by the players as they need them. They will then perform a set attack against the chosen target. Set attacks might have some kind of aiming mechanism that allows the player to line up the attack before it is unleashed. To do this, the player might guide an attack area by rotating the character or even via a separate targeting reticule. The area could be a circle, an arc, a straight line, or anything else that suits.

Interactive skills: Interactive skills are more involved skill attacks that can slow down time, distort time, and allow target painting or lock-on. These require the player to actually perform the action or select targets in order to actually carry out the attack.

Aiming and Targeting

Aiming and targeting may seem like the same thing, but there are subtle differences:

Aiming: The act of lining a weapon up with a target to make the shot or blow hit the opponent

Targeting: The act of selecting a specific target for the shot or blow to be inflicted upon

Aiming

Aiming is generally the domain of ranged weaponry. It is unlikely that a melee weapon or physical attack will need to be aimed, other than facing in the right direction.

Manual Aiming

Manual aiming requires the player to accurately position some device (usually an aiming reticule such as a crosshair) over the target and account for any factors such as trajectory or movement of the target when firing the shot.

First-Person Aiming

First-person aiming is relatively simple. The standard convention is to have some kind of aiming reticule, known as the crosshair, to indicate where the weapon is being pointed. The player then aims the crosshair at the target and pulls the trigger. Obviously he has to take into account movement of the target or possibly more complex issues such as the trajectory of the weapon.

Over-the-Shoulder View

Some games use an over-the-shoulder view, which is the same as first-person aiming. The camera is simply mounted on the character's shoulder. This allows the character to be on screen but still affords the benefits of accurate first-person aiming.

Third-Person Aiming

Third-person mode often uses targeting rather than manual aiming, particularly when a screen-relative control system is used. The reason is that the players can't see much ahead of them in most third-person views, and the precision required to line an enemy up in third person can prove tricky to master without some form of targeting being used (even if it is transparent to the player).

Games that do have screen-relative control and use manual aiming tend to lock the camera behind the character and place a crosshair on screen. This is the same kind of dynamic as first person. The left stick controls movement (forward, backward, and strafe), and the right stick controls the aiming (moving the camera around the avatar as it does so). Wild West shooter *Red Dead Revolver*™ uses this method to good effect, as well as several other great targeting features that will be covered later.

Character-relative movement offers a different way of approaching aiming. Since it offers pretty accurate movement of the avatar, it is easy to translate that to the ability to aim. The original *Resident Evil* games used character-relative movement with manual aiming to good effect. (Though many people found it unwieldy, others liked the system.) The ability to rotate and move the weapon up and down offered the player the opportunity to aim at varying heights. The rather slow speed of movement in these games became part of their atmosphere, as slow lumbering zombies were difficult enemies to induce panic if the player could move like lightning. Interestingly, the improved movement controls in *Resident Evil 4*, which uses a locked-behind-the-character camera, mean enemies no longer shuffle along but now lunge with some speed at the player.

Pinpoint Aiming

Pinpoint aiming allows the player to move the aim independently of the look or camera movement. This is generally a second mode or an extension of a targeting system.

Second Mode: Free Radical's *Timesplitters* series and Rare's *Goldeneye* (incidentally, developed by a lot of the same people) allowed the user to hold down a button to enter Pinpoint Aiming mode. In this mode the look no longer rotates the camera but instead moves the weapon around the screen (to rotate look in this mode, the weapon is pushed to the extremities of the screen). This allows for some skillful positioning of the crosshair but still allows basic movement.

Targeting Extension: EA's *James Bond: Everything or Nothing*™ uses a very different system. The player is able to hard-lock on an enemy and perform pinpoint aiming via a small dot that is moved with the right stick. This is recentered when a new target is acquired. The dot moves only in relation to the targeting reticule, meaning that no matter how much the player moves about, the dot remains fixed on the same point of the target.

Aiming Guidance (Auto Aim)

Aiming guidance is not another form of aiming but is a guiding system for manual aiming. This is something generally only used on console games, as a mouse offers far more accurate aiming control than a standard joypad.

Crosshair Proximity

One method of auto aim is crosshair proximity, where an imaginary circle (though it could also be presented to the player if you want) exists around the crosshair. Anything within this circle is considered a viable target to lock on to. The amount of auto aim can be increased or decreased by altering the radius of this auto aim circle.

If more than one target exists in the circle, you are most likely to want to pick the nearest target to the avatar. However, with this system you could add more complex relationships that could be set by the player. For example, the system could adjust aim to the strongest, weakest, furthest, most damaged, or least damaged enemy. This is the method we used in *Serious Sam*™*: Next Encounter*, and it works well to provide a very fluid and fast method of auto aim that doesn't interrupt the speed of the game.

Sticky Aiming

Sticky aiming adjusts the character movement to that of the enemy in order to provide a mild lock-on (a targeting system). Essentially, this is a hybrid system, but we have placed it under aiming because of the more refined player control involved.

When the crosshair moves over an enemy, it becomes locked while the enemy remains inside the crosshair's radius. This affects the players' movements, so that they turn at a slow rate toward the target as they strafe, but larger movements that move the cursor off the target will release the lock. This turn speed while locked determines just how sticky the aiming is. A high turn speed will have extremely sticky consequences, whereas a low turn speed will produce a much more subtle effect.

The hugely popular FPS *Halo* uses this sticky system (they coined the term *sticky targeting* for this system), and it works perfectly with the slower pace of gameplay, where the adjustments in control aren't noticeable. *Halo* is often regarded highly for the feel of its control scheme.

Targeting

Targeting is the act of selecting a target and guiding the attack in the direction of that target. This generally moves the avatar in the direction of the victim so that they are lined up properly for attack. Targeting works equally well for melee or ranged combat.

Hard Lock (Lock-On)

Hard lock is what most people would consider targeting to be. This is certainly the most visceral and immediate method of providing lock-on. To hard-lock, you need a Lock-On button and a method of cycling between targets.

Lock Target

As soon as the lock-on button is pressed, an enemy will be selected and highlighted in some manner. The button may be held down to hold the lock or might toggle lock-on or -off. The advantage of holding the button down is more precise control, but it suffers in that it removes the player's finger from other uses. The lock-on button is generally best placed on one of the shoulder buttons.

Cycling Targets

Cycling targets allows the player to switch between targets in some way. This could be done in a few different ways.

> **Toggle Tapping—One-Way Cycling:** One method that could be used in conjunction with a toggled lock-on button is a tap to target the next available enemy. Each tap would move to the next target until all have been accounted for. Another tap of the button at this point would start the cycle of targets again from the beginning. This system would only be useful if there were only ever a few targets to choose from. A large number of targets would become cumbersome very quickly.
> **Simple Dual-Way Cycling:** A better method is to provide the ability to move back and forth through the available targets. You will need two buttons to do this, which could utilize the D-pad face buttons but is probably best

suited to the shoulder buttons or right analog stick (which generally also controls the camera). The player can then cycle through the list of available targets in turn.

View Cone Selection: A better method of dual cycling is to cycle to the next-nearest target within the current cone of view. Outside this cone you might want to select targets in order of nearest angle to character facing.

Automatic Switching: You could automatically switch targets based on proximity or nearest attacker, but we would advise against this in a hard-lock system for the simple reason that you want the players to always feel in control of what they are doing. Avoiding player frustration should always be a top priority of interface design.

Movement While Locked On

When targeting an enemy, either the player character will turn to face the target, or, if you have a split-body animation system, the top half of the character will move to face the target.

Changed Movement: Movement can be changed to be relative to the target (see Figure 7.5). When locked onto a target, the player remains facing the target at all times. Movement becomes target-centric. Thus, moving up and down moves the player toward and away from the target, respectively. Left and right move the player character counterclockwise and clockwise, respectively, around the target.

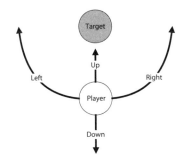

FIGURE 7.5   Locked-on, target-relative movement system.

Split-Body System: Core Design's classic platform adventure game *Tomb Raider* made use of a split body system so that the top half of the character could move independently of the bottom half. This was limited so that she couldn't perform *Exorcist*-style body movement, but allowed her to face toward a target while running in a slightly different direction. The arms would also bend around the body so that the target was held for as long as possible while facing away from the enemy. Once this reached the limit of its bounds she would hold the guns up in front of her to indicate that she could no longer fire them at the currently selected target.

Soft Lock (Auto Targeting)

Using an automatic soft-lock targeting system that remains transparent to the players allows them to remain immersed in the game world and feel that they have ultimate control. There is no need to lock onto individuals or switch between selected targets. Instead, the targeting system automatically decides which target is locked with the targeting device.

The targeting device is not usually shown to the player but is set up with two areas that dictate what enemy is locked and thus which way the attacks will be directed. This system is used in many games, but because it is transparent, many people don't even realize it is there.

The Targeting Device

The targeting device can be done in many ways, but the simple design shown in Figure 7.6 is perhaps the most basic and the most useful.

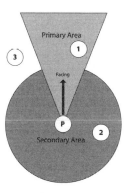

FIGURE 7.6   A basic targeting device.

The targeting device is split into two areas: a primary cone and a secondary circle.

Primary cone: Any enemy in the primary area will be targeted first. When the button is pressed without a corresponding direction, the facing direction of the player character is the facing of the primary cone. The cone is of a fixed length. Enemy 1 will be targeted in Figure 7.6.

Secondary circle: The secondary circle is centered on the player character for a set radius. Any enemy in the circular area will be targeted if there is not an enemy in the primary cone. When locked onto a target, the player character's facing will turn at the player's combat turn speed toward the target while performing the attack move. In the example in Figure 7.6 Enemy 2 would be targeted if there were no Enemy 1 in the primary cone.

Out of bounds: Any enemies out of these areas will simply be ignored, and the attacks will be made in the player's current direction of facing. Enemy 3 does not fall into either area and thus is ignored by the automatic targeting system.

The device will have a number of variables that can be set by the designer in order to tweak the system to create the best feel when playing (see Table 7.1).

TABLE 7.1 Targeting Device Variables

VARIABLE	DESCRIPTION
Cone angle	The view angle of the primary cone
Cone length	The length of the primary cone
Circle radius	The radius of the secondary circle

Player Targeting Control

In order to advance the system we can add player control to the primary cone. In the example shown in Figure 7.7 the primary cone is not rigidly set to the player character's facing. The player can point the cone in any direction with the left stick. This enables the player to quickly change direction during an attack to fight enemies behind and to the sides.

The cone exactly follows the movement of the directional stick, even if character facing takes a little while to catch up.

The enemy lock decision is made the moment an attack button is pressed. At that moment the state of the targeting device determines where the attack will be placed. If this position is to the rear, then the player will turn to face at the avatar's maximum turn speed.

Enemy Proximity

With each of the target reticule areas, the proximity of the enemy is also taken into account. If more than one enemy occupies an area, a check is made to find the closest (see Figure 7.8).

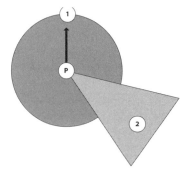

FIGURE 7.7 Player control over the primary cone.

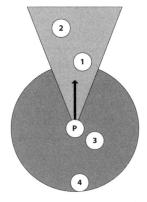

FIGURE 7.8 Determining the closest character to the player.

In Figure 7.8 Enemy 1 is closer than Enemy 2 in the primary cone and is thus the primary candidate. Enemy 3 is closest of all, but lying outside of the primary cone means he will not be selected before Enemy 2. Enemy 4 would be the final candidate in this example, as he is furthest away in the secondary circle.

Multiple Targeting Cones

Where several grades of attack range are used for lock-on attacks, more than one targeting cone may be useful. A cone for each range grade will allow each range to be adjusted individually. The likely set up for these attack cones is to narrow the cone angle over longer distances, so that there is not too wide a range that will result in selecting the wrong targets. A wider target cone close up will result in a more forgiving system. The closer targeting cones are likely to warrant a much higher priority than longer-ranged ones. A multiple-cone system is shown in Figure 7.9.

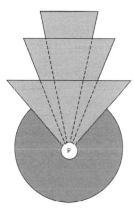

FIGURE 7.9   A more complex multiple-cone system.

Distance- and Angle-Weighting Bias

With a targeting system, the ability to determine a preference between distance and angle is useful. By enabling weighting between these two values, the system can be tweaked so that it feels just right.

This weighting could also be dynamic, so that preference changes in different situations. A preference for angle will pick targets that are directly in front of the player over those closer but at a wider angle. A distance preference will do the exact opposite, selecting the closest target no matter what the angle. A balanced system will select closer targets within a certain angle.

Threat-Priority Weighting

A threat-priority weighting system assigns a higher targeting weighting to characters in specific situations, so that they are more likely to be selected as a target if they are of a higher threat. In combination with distance and angle weighting, this creates a comprehensive description of a situation.

Threat weighting is likely to be based on a number of factors:

Current combat state: Different weighting multipliers are applied to each stage of an attack: Not attacking (e.g., 0), buildup (e.g., 1), strike (e.g., 1.5), recovery (e.g., 0.5). By adjusting the recovery multiplier, you could make a character more attractive for lock-on while recovering.

Character threat: This is a static value based on the character and how dangerous it is. More dangerous characters will be given a higher threat rating.

Health: This is a measure of how near to death the character is. It is likely that a player will want to knock all enemies to as low a health as soon as possible. However, this could be tweaked upward as an enemy nears death to make it a more attractive target. This could even be set up as a game option.

Status effects: If an enemy is currently subject to an impediment, it is likely that the player will want to target other healthy enemies. Alternatively, this could be scaled upward when a status effect is applied to make them more attractive targets. Again this could be set up as a game option. Different status effects could have different effects on the threat weighting. For example, being blinded could be considered more of an impediment than being poisoned.

Debug Targeting Information

When adjusting and balancing a targeting system, it is imperative that the designer have a visual representation of every aspect of the system. Displaying the targeting cone and circle should be the first step. Having the active targeting area highlighted will show the designer which device is operative. The active target should be displayed by highlighting the character in some manner, making him glow red, for example.

To be able to get a sense of the weighting system at work, the overall weight of an enemy should be placed over his head.

Sweep Selection

Sweep selection is an analog method of selecting multiple targets by using the joystick to point at the target(s). Generally these kinds of systems are used for special skills or for combat games that are designed to be able to fight more than one character at once.

Sweeping Bar

The melee combat–based game *Mark of Kri* utilizes a sweeping bar to select opponents. Once these opponents are selected, a different attack button is applied to each of the enemies. The bar is controlled with the right analog stick. By using circular motions, the player could spin the bar around the avatar, thus moving over available targets and selecting them.

Target Painting

Like sticky aiming, target painting is essentially a hybrid of aiming and targeting. It is included here as a targeting feature because the outcome is to select a number of targets rather than to assist aiming. Target painting is best used as a skill—a mode that the player can enter to perform a special interactive ability. *Red Dead Revolver* uses two forms of target painting that both work excellently in the context of the game.

The first is called the dead-eye skill. This allows the player to move the crosshair across the screen. Any potential targets under the crosshair are locked onto with targeting reticules. When time is restored, these locked-on targets are hit with a blast from the avatar's gun.

The second is the draw. The player pushes a cursor that has a good deal of momentum and has six button presses to lock onto various parts of an enemy. The player must perform these button presses within a specific time limit. Once that expires, the six shots will be unleashed to kill the recipient before he lands a shot on the player.

These are great examples of using targeting systems in imaginative ways.

SUMMARY

In this chapter we looked at the fundamental elements of a combat system. These elements form the basis of any complex system we want to create:

The basics of combat: We looked at the basic elements of any combat system:

- **Combat entities:** The entities that are considered when performing combat actions, namely the player character, allies and NPCs, enemies, and breakable objects.
- **Health:** The system of player health has been used for a long time in games but may take a variety of forms—no replenishment, health pickups, recharge points, recharging health that can be visualized as numbers, health blocks, bars, shields, vital objects, power stages, or buddy health. Enemy health may be displayed in fewer ways, usually as blocks, numbers, or a health bar.

The combat procedure: Combat is either turn-based or real-time.

- **Turn-based:** Turns can occur turn by turn, be based on time and character speeds, or occur in real time. Each turn will follow a set combat procedure where the attacker makes an attack and then the opponent's defense is calculated.
- **Real-time:** All combat events occur in real-time, so the combat procedure is performed every time an attack is made.

Basic combat dynamics: Having determined whether a combat system is turn based or occurs in real time, we can investigate other aspects of the combat dynamic.

- **Engaging combat mode:** Combat might be the default mechanic and thus be available at all times. Otherwise, activation of combat mode may occur automatically when combat starts or require the player to perform an action to enter combat mode.
- **Turns versus real time:** The interaction of the player in a turn-based system is generally driven by menu selection or events occurring during the lull between turns (except for real-time turns). Real-time combat is driven purely from actions made by the player or the AI-controlled characters.
- **Combat cinematics:** Elements of the combat can be made more cinematic through the use of highlight cameras, combat cameras, and camera effects such as shake and shift.
- **Playing with time:** Time can be altered using freeze framing, replays, and slow motion.
- **Screen effects:** Screen effects such as flash, darken, and background replace can be used to highlight the action.
- **Interactive cinematics:** The player can be given control of the cinematics with camera control during these moments or via the use of interactive cinematic elements such as skill attacks.

Aiming and targeting: Aiming and targeting are used to allow the player to accurately hit a target with a melee or ranged attack.

- **Aiming:** The act of lining up a weapon with a target to make the shot or blow hit the opponent. This may be manual aiming, where the player is in full control, or may have an element of aiming guidance, such as crosshair proximity or sticky aiming to help the player hit the target.
- **Targeting:** The act of selecting a specific target for the shot or blow to be inflicted upon. Targeting may use a hard-lock to lock the aim onto a particular target. Alternatively, a more transparent soft-lock system will work under the hood to help the player select the desired target. A sweep selection system could even be used to select multiple targets.

Over the course of the next three chapters we will look in depth at more advanced aspects of a combat system.

MELEE COMBAT DYNAMICS

In This Chapter

- Combat Control Systems
- Melee Combat Balance
- Melee Weapons
- Attack Parameters
- Attack Windows
- Types of Moves
- Changing Attack Sets
- Combos
- Defensive Moves
- Weapon Trails

In the previous chapter we looked at the basic elements of combat. In this chapter we shall refine our view of one particular type of combat: melee combat. Melee combat features a lot of physical interaction between characters. It requires a good deal of control mechanics to be fine-tuned and polished to perfection. Specialized systems are required to make melee combat a possibility in a game.

In this chapter we will look at the following topics:

- Combat control systems
- Melee combat balance
- Melee weapons
- Attack parameters
- Attack windows
- Types of moves
- Changing attack sets
- Combos
- Defensive moves
- Weapon trails

COMBAT CONTROL SYSTEMS

The choice of a system of control is entirely dependent on what type of game you are making and how complex a system you wish to create. As a guide to what kind of system you might use, think about how central combat is to your game. How many other mechanics other than combat do you want in your game? If combat is essential to your game, then think about making it fairly complex, while still remembering that you might need room on the joypad for other functions.

The likely combat systems for various genres are:

Platformers: Most platformers are perfectly served with a simple one-button system but may benefit from a more general system.
Action–adventure: These will usually need a general combat system.
Beat 'em up: Most likely, these will need an advanced system.

Simple One-Button System

The one-button system is used for the most basic of combat models, where you might want one or two different styles of attack, depending on the context in which the button is used. The simple attack button might perform a spin attack, for example, but if the character is in the midst of performing a jump, this spin might become a dive. If a direction is held while the button is pressed, a dash may be performed instead.

This context sensitivity allows a lot of use from a single button. Any defensive moves are performed with a jump or the player's own skill of avoidance.

General Combat Systems

For most games a little more complexity is required than the simple one-button system. Instead, it is often necessary to have at least one offensive and one defensive button or stretch to two attack buttons. There are all sorts of different set-ups you might require for the game. It is important to think about your exact needs before you start designing.

Defense

The addition of a defensive button adds a whole new dimension to combat. It is more than likely that this defensive maneuver is some kind of block—a move that will stop all attacks except block breakers. Now the players can use a little more strategy when planning their attacks.

Light and Heavy Attacks

Using two attacks allows for a good deal more strategy. The light and heavy attacks offer a new system based on timing. A light attack is faster and can therefore be used to hit an opponent before he hits you, but it does a small amount of damage. The heavy attack is slower and leaves the opponent vulnerable for a longer time, but, should it hit, will cause more damage.

Sweep and Focused Attacks

As well as the timing of attacks, the direction of the attack can be used to differentiate types of attack. Sweeping attacks are horizontal sweeps that can hit many enemies at once. Focused attacks are attacks that attack the area directly in front of the avatar and cause more damage to a single target. Focused attacks could also be used to pop an enemy up into the air, where the player character could then "juggle" the opponent.

High and Low Attacks

If you have attack data that can detect different regions of a character, it might be useful to have high and low attacks. With this system it becomes necessary to have some way of defending against the attack. In a fairly simple combat model this would be as simple as having to jump to avoid low attacks and block to stop high attacks.

Advanced Systems

Games in which combat is an essential element—or even the only element—need a much more rigid and focused set of combat controls. However, you might want to incorporate certain elements of an advanced system in a less convoluted fashion than might be found in a complex beat 'em up.

Limb Model

The *Tekken* series uses one button for each limb approach, so the player can independently control arms and legs and thus know roughly what kind of move will be performed before a button is pressed. Pressing two limb buttons at once performs throws and double-limbed kicks or punches. This system is very intuitive for hand-to-hand combat games but doesn't work well for weapon-based combat.

Attack-Type Model

Beat 'em ups *Soul Calibur*™ and *Dead or Alive* use a control system based on the type of attack. Each of the four buttons corresponds to a different attack, so you might have focused, sweep, kick, and throw, for example. The advantage of such a system is that it can fit any model of fighting, but it can be a little confusing as to what move will be performed next with the general attack buttons.

Strength Model

The strength model is based on different strengths of attack being inflicted on the enemy. Generally the heavier blows take a little longer to hit but do more damage. The arcade version of *Street Fighter* uses heavy, medium, and light strength of punch and kick attacks. *The King of Fighters*™ series uses two punch strengths and two kick strengths. This could even be done using the analog function of the buttons, so that a harder button press will result in a heavier attack (though this can be wearing on the joypad).

Other Models

Plenty of other models can and have been used. *Mark of Kri*™ uses a novel system where each button on the pad represents a strike toward a different enemy. There are going to be many different combat systems in the future, and as they continue to evolve and new ideas come to the fore, who knows what kind of controls will be driving combat in the future.

Defensive Moves

Most advanced fighting games include all of the following defensive moves: evasion, blocking, counterattacks, and floor evasion. These may be mapped onto the controller in many different ways (see the Defensive Moves section).

MELEE COMBAT BALANCE

All attack systems must have an internal balance that dictates which actions win over other actions. There should always be some method of defense for an incoming attack (for a player character at least). Thus, a network needs to be built up. Often the model of rock, paper, scissors is used (see Figure 8.1).

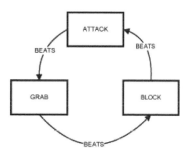

FIGURE 8.1   The rock, paper, scissors balance model applied to combat.

However, combat systems tend to have a much more complex system of balance. In a real-time system the majority of this is based upon timing—the right attack used at the right time. Each form of attack has an appropriate defense, so that timing must also be used in defending, as well as attacking.

In a turn-based system these definitions are much more stringent and are unlikely to be based on timing. Thus, the right choice of action during a turn is more important than reflex or dexterity.

MELEE WEAPONS

Melee weaponry includes any implement that can be used up close. That could be anything from a fist to a sword or even the butt of a gun.

Types of Melee Weapons

Melee weapons can be classed into several types, often according to their range or the type of damage they inflict.

Unarmed

Unarmed weaponry is what you were born with—the various parts of your body, whether this be foot, fist, knee, elbow, or head. Unarmed combat tends to do limited damage unless it is the only form of weapon used in the game. It will nearly always cause impact damage if damage types are being used in the combat system (see later chapter on damage).

Blades

Blades cover all sharp-edged objects: axes, knives, swords, even broken bottles. Blades are perfect for causing plenty of damage. They will cause cut damage when swung or piercing damage when thrust into an enemy.

Bludgeons

Anything heavy, solid, and not sharp edged is a bludgeon. This could cover anything from morning stars, clubs, and baseball bats to a lead pipe. Bludgeoning instruments cause a good deal of impact damage.

Spears

Spears are pointed objects designed to pierce the flesh of an opponent. These would include all manner of spears, bayonets, or stabbing devices. Spears cause piercing damage when thrust and, if they are fairly long, might also be used as an improvised bludgeoning weapon to cause impact damage when swung (though this damage wouldn't be nearly as much as when they are used properly).

Weapon Parameters

Melee weapons are fairly simple instruments and are likely to have only a few parameters associated with them, as shown in Table 8.1.

TABLE 8.1   Melee Weapon Parameters

Weapon strength	How much damage the weapon will do to a target
Damage type	What kind of damage the weapon inflicts
Status effect	What status may be applied on a successful hit (status effects are discussed in a later chapter)

ATTACK PARAMETERS

Each attack has a number of parameters that define it. Each of these parameters describes a particular aspect of the attack.

Direction

An attack can be made in several directions, which will have different effects on the strength of the hit and how many targets it might possibly hit.

Sweep Attacks

Sweep attacks have the possibility of hitting many opponents in one strike. They may move in all manner of arcs, but most likely will perform a roughly 90°, 180°, or 360° arc. Such an arc is shown in Figure 8.2.

Sweep attacks tend to cause less damage than focused attacks, as they can hit more enemies.

FIGURE 8.2   A sweep attack arc.

Focused Attacks

Focused attacks concentrate directly in front of the player character's facing, thus hitting only one opponent at a time. As such, they tend to do more damage than a sweep attack.

Uppercuts

Uppercut attacks are designed to pop the target up into the air so that the character player can juggle him by hitting him repeatedly back up into the air as he falls from the previous hit. Juggling is a very valuable tactic in some fighting games, though it does remove the game from the realms of realism somewhat.

Speed

Slower attacks tend to do more damage than faster ones, but a quick attack leaves the player far less vulnerable during execution. Attacks have two windows of times in the action when the character is particularly vulnerable:

Buildup: The period of time the attacker must charge before the attack can be unleashed

Recovery: The period of time the attacker must recover before another move can be performed

These two periods can also be used by AI to determine if a character can get an attack in at a specific time.

Attackers may also be vulnerable during an attack if a complex body zone system or high/low attack system is being used, as they might receive a low hit while they miss with their high attack.

Height

The height of an attack might be included in a system to offer the player a range of tactical decisions. There are several heights that might be used in a combat system. Using them all would make for a pretty advanced combat model.

Ground: Attacks made on opponents on the floor
Low: Attacks aimed below the waist
Mid: Attacks aimed at the upper body
High: Attacks aimed at the head
Air: Attacks made while in the air

Attack height is also used by the AI to establish what kind of action to perform in a particular situation.

Strength

Strength equates to the force of the attack. This is used to determine the hit reaction strength of an attack and possibly the amount of damage it causes.

Damage

This is the base damage of an attack before any kind of modifier is applied to it. If more than one type of damage is used in a combat system, the type of damage will also need to be specified (damage is discussed in a later chapter).

Having set damage for each attack is the simplest method of modeling combat but doesn't allow for character progression. Damage might not be based on the attack, but rather on some character and/or weapon attribute such as strength. Some attacks don't cause damage but have different effects, such as the block breaker, which will knock an opponent out of a block and leave him vulnerable for a short period.

Attack Range and Distance Scaling

Animated attacks are generally performed in areas close to the character and are animated to set distances. This means that often attacks will fall short or will look fairly rigid in action. A trick that can be used to fix this is distance scaling, where the distance traveled by the attacking character is scaled by minimum and maximum amounts. The animation needs to be scalable, which means it needs to disguise as much of the travel as possible. Leaps are the most effective for this, as the lack of contact with the ground removes any foot sliding that may occur, and it looks very dynamic. Over short distances this is less of a concern.

Another way to increase the dynamism of combat is to allow the player and AI to attack from greater distances. A number of different attacks could be initiated based on the attacker's distance from the target, So moves could be broken down into close, medium, and long range. This should not be done over too great a distance. Anything more than 8 meters is likely to get too confusing and cause too much movement. The long-distance attacks would have a long buildup time and a long distance to travel before a strike occurs. Distance scaling would work alongside ranges, as shown in Table 8.2.

TABLE 8.2   Distance Scaling

ATTACK TYPE	DISTANCE
Short	0–3 m
Medium	4–6 m
Long	7–8 m

Hit Class

To implement a degree of strategy, each successful attack hit can be of a certain class that dictates the type of reaction elicited from a struck opponent. This may be a static, guaranteed reaction for every opponent, may differ between the various types of enemy, or can even be based on the vulnerability of an enemy at a certain point.

Several classes of hit can be employed:

Damage only: The hit only causes damage to a vulnerable opponent but does not cause any hit reaction. The hit may be indicated via a special effect or by flashing the character red (or any other suitable color), as without any feedback the players will be unsure of their successful strikes.

Standard hit: The hit causes damage and a hit reaction under normal game rules. The standard hit will not break a block or cause damage when an opponent is blocking.

Block damage: A hit will cause standard damage and a hit reaction to a vulnerable character but can also damage a blocking character by a reduced amount. This may cause a block hit reaction but will not break the block.

Block breaker: A block-breaking hit is designed to smash through an opponent's defense, leaving him exposed and vulnerable. Therefore, a block-breaking attack is likely to provoke a large hit reaction but little, if any, damage.

Special/guaranteed: The attack is absolutely guaranteed to break through a block and cause damage to the opponent but usually costs some kind of game resource (such as magic points) to perform in order to limit its use.

ATTACK WINDOWS

The attack windows describe the various parts of attack. Each of these windows is represented by an animation from the attacker, and several of the windows will result in reaction animations being forced onto the opponent.

Getting the timing of these windows right is crucial for melee combat, as it forms the whole structure for an attack. Careful balance of these timings will result in an expressive and responsive combat system that feels right, but it will take a lot of playtesting and refinement to find the perfect balance.

Window Types

There are four types of attack window:

- Animation
- Registry
- Interrupt
- Response

These windows occur at different stages of an attack. Figure 8.3 shows some of the windows that might be used.

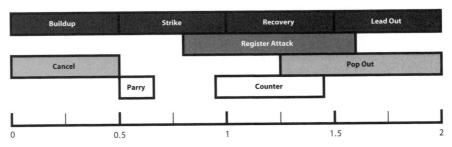

FIGURE 8.3 A potential attack window layout.

Animation Windows

Animation windows describe the attacker's movement stages of the attack. If no other button is pressed by an attacker or defender, this sequence will play out in its entirety. These movements can be scaled in time by playing the animation at different speeds. There are obvious limits to the amount an animation can be sped up or slowed down.

The attack is broken down into several parts:

Buildup: Generally the attacker is vulnerable during buildup (except perhaps special moves that cost a great deal to execute such as magic spells). The weapon is moved into place ready to strike or a spell or weapon is charged. Quick attacks have a very short buildup time, and long slow attacks have a long buildup to offer the opponent an opportunity to attack before the strike occurs.

Strike: The attack is being made and damage is applied should a successful hit occur. This may be a fixed damage amount, random damage, or variable damage, depending on a number of factors, or have a damage curve applied across the length of the window.

Recovery: The recovery period is when the attacker is immobile and recovering from the attack. Attackers are most likely to be vulnerable at this point. The attacker cannot move until this period has elapsed, but there may be an opportunity to perform another move in a combo chain if a pop-out window is provided in the interrupt windows for the move. The recovery period should be kept as short as possible while still looking and feeling right; otherwise, a control system can seem sluggish and unresponsive.

Lead out: The lead out phase follows the recovery phase and returns an attacker to his standard idle stance. Unlike the recovery phase, the attacker is perfectly free to move before the end of the window, so the animation does not have to fully complete. This phase is used to make the move feel solid and keep animation looking smooth.

Registry Windows

Registry windows are used to register information. The only thing we would want to register is a button press for the next attack in a combo.

A register attack is a window that registers presses of buttons and buffers the move ready to be activated when the pop-out window arrives. These windows are seperate, as it is often desirable to predetermine attacks to allow whole strings to be initiated or a button mashed. Having a small time difference between register attack and pop out makes for a very responsive system that requires precision, whereas large time differences make for a less responsive but much more forgiving system.

Interrupt Windows

These are used by the attacker to control an attack or to chain moves together to form a combo. There are two types of interrupt window:

Cancel: Enables an attacker to perform a direction or button press to cancel the queued move or combo. This should generally only be allowed during an attack buildup. This allows the attacker to feign an attack to promote a defensive response, which he can then use a different tactic against. For example, the attacker could feign a standard strike and then use a grab against the blocking character.

Pop out: Allows the next move to be initialized. Once the window starts and a button has been registered in the Register Attack window, the next move in the combo is executed.

Response Windows

The response windows give the defender time to react. There are natural windows that occur during an attack when there is an opportunity for the defender to be offensive—during buildup, recovery, or lead out. However, a slow defender against a swift attacker is unlikely to be able to pull off an attack before the strike window of the faster attacker causes him to receive a hit.

There are two response windows that can affect this:

Parry Window: A parry occurs when the two combatants' weapons clash together. The parry window is not really an effective defense, as it is unlikely to be a large window of opportunity. Otherwise there would be hardly any strikes occurring. Parrying is not used often in games but can be a nice visual effect and adds an element of strategy when similar-speed attackers are pitched against each other. When two combatants perform an attack at the same time, their parry windows might overlap. Should this happen, a parry is said to have occurred and the weapons bounce off each other. This returns both characters via a stumble to a position of stalemate. However, if a parry occurs between two different-strength attacks, it might be conducive to have the weaker attacker knocked back more by the blow, giving the heavier but generally slower attacker the advantage.

Counter window: A much more common situation is the counter. This is a period of opportunity when the defender can return the attack to the attacker. It generally occurs in a short time frame just after the attacker's strike occurs while the defender enters a blocking state. The attacker is then either repelled, leaving him vulnerable or attacked by the defender immediately.

Using Attack Windows

The whole move must be considered and balanced within the context of the whole system when implementing attack windows. This balancing task can be very tricky. A quick strike is likely to have short windows in all areas—short buildup, strike, recovery, and lead out. It follows that all heavy strikes have much larger windows. However, for balancing fights where one opponent faces a multitude of enemies, these would be played around with. The buildup for an enemy's attack is likely to be much longer on all attacks, allowing time for the enemy to announce his move so that the player has a chance to react. The key to getting combat feeling right is to allow enough time at each stage to react and respond to an attack but keep the combat feeling fast and fluid.

Attacks might have multiple windows. Imagine an attack that has two slashes in quick succession. This could be done as a combo move but might also be done as a single animation that is always executed. There will be two buildup and strike windows. This could of course become even more complex with many parts to a single attack. There is, however, a point at which moves should be separated into a combo rather than being a single move, as this offers more flexibility.

A designer might also want to have multiple interrupt windows, offering branching combos based on timing of a button press. An attack with several distinct phases would be needed for such a system in order for a player to clearly understand any distinctions.

TYPES OF MOVES

Several different types of move can be employed in a melee combat system.

Basic Attacks

Basic attacks are the most primitive attacks. These are made when the button is pressed once and simply play out the standard move.

Command Attacks

Command attacks require combinations of a direction and button presses to perform a single move. For most games this is an extension of the basic attack, so should the player push toward the character and press the attack button, a different move will occur. Fighting games may have some incredibly tricky combinations of direction and button presses to execute a move.

Combinations can get quite complex, particularly in beat 'em ups that use side-on views. A normal 3D action game might make use of up, down, left, and right. In screen-relative terms this will adjust the direction needed on the joypad according to the facing of the avatar.

A side-on view allows more directions to be easily incorporated such as diagonals and quarter turns. Other popular combinations of direction and button are double-taps—a swift move in a direction, then release, then the same direction again along with the button presses. Many of these command attacks can be tricky to pull off and are often classed as special moves.

Lock-On Attacks

Lock-on attacks allow the player to ignore near targets and specifically attack a selected target. This will be activated when a direction is pushed and a target lies within the targeting cone range when used with a soft-locking targeting system. When the button is pressed with this target acquired, any targeting information aside from the locked-on target is ignored.

Multiple-Button Attacks

When two or even three buttons are pressed at the same time, different attacks can be created. These might be stronger versions of the existing attacks, a combined style of the two buttons, or some other function such as a throw or grapple.

Tekken made good use of two or more button attacks. Double punch performed a double-fisted attack, and double kick did a double-feet attack. Combinations of punch and kick were used to perform throws, and three or four buttons together performed particularly dazzling moves. This is often a method used to perform a special move.

Jump Attacks

Jump attacks allow the character to have a different repertoire of moves while in the air. Often these attacks perform overhead slams, where the character uses his height to slam to the ground in a more forceful manner. Whilst in the air, juggling combos can also be performed. This will require some kind of synchronized animations for aerial attacks and juggle knockbacks.

Jumping in combat can be problematic, as it allows the player to easily avoid being attacked by constantly jumping. This can be solved by giving enemies attacks that can deal with a jumping opponent, so that the player will no longer be able to use constant jumping as a valid avoidance tactic.

Context-Sensitive Attacks

Some systems incorporate complex interactions into a basic button system. In this case you might want to use case-sensitive attacks to allow one button to perform more than one action. How the case sensitivity is used depends entirely on the needs of the game. For example, an attack could differ when launched from the front or rear of a character. From the front the attack might be a simple punch, but from the rear the same attack might club the victim into unconsciousness. This offers rewards for playing the game in a particular way.

Special Moves

Getting a handle on special moves is pretty difficult, as they are performed many different ways in many different systems. However, they are usually a move that causes a good deal of damage or are unblockable.

Standard Special Move

The standard special move is based purely on skill—using it at precisely the right time or being able to pull off the right combination of button presses. Often the move will leave the player vulnerable to attack. The move becomes balanced, as the opponent has the opportunity to interrupt the attack.

Gauge-Based Special Moves

Gauge-based moves require the player to fill a bar to either increase the potency of the attack or allow the attack to be performed.

Enhanced: The bar is able to be used at any point. The value of the bar at the point of use dictates the potency of the attack.

Restricted: The bar must be filled to specific levels before the special move can be unleashed.

Negative: The bar is reduced each time the special move is used. This might even be the health bar, so that each time a special move is used, health is lost.

The bar might remain depleted or might be replenished in one of a few ways:

Overdrive: The bar increases when the character makes successful attacks. Special moves might fill this bar more quickly.

Rage: The bar increases as the character receives damage.

Time: The bar fills up slowly over time.

Ground Attacks

Ground attacks are made on a character that has been knocked to the floor. It is best to make the attacks context sensitive to this scenario, so that the player will be able to intuitively attack the grounded opponent, rather than sending attacks wildly over the grounded body. Many action games use the ground attack to dish out a killing blow, such as thrusting a sword through the victim's chest.

Rising Attacks

Rising attacks are those made as the knocked-out character rises from the floor. They give a vulnerable character a chance at attacking an oncoming assailant by performing a move from the ground that may catch the assailant unawares.

The first knock to the ground is likely to have a long delay before a rising attack is allowed, but multiple floorings in succession could reduce this time and prevent an assailant from not letting the victim get a chance to retaliate. Frenzied button mashing might also speed this up to add a feeling of panic.

Throws and Grappling

Throws and grappling moves are designed to break a block, thus making even a blocking character vulnerable to some form of attack. Throws are set animations that play when a successful throw move is initiated. Bear in mind that these moves require close interaction between two characters. This will only work if the animation is specifically designed for the skeleton of the opponent. Different skeletons will require new sets of animations. Combos may be possible from a throw that allow additional hits to be chained to the end of the throw move.

Grappling is a more complex situation, where one character has a hold on the other in some manner. From this hold the character can perform a number of attacks or even move around and drag the enemy with him. Such moves require very complex interaction between characters, and as such only specific rigs can be employed without having to completely change all data for each character. The level of interaction means that you can't just use set animations but will need a good deal of specific code written to handle the grappling situation. Care must be taken with these interactions to make sure that body parts do not clip through the other character as the moves are made.

Charge-Up Attacks

Charge-up melee attacks allow the players to choose how much power they want to put into an attack. To charge an attack, the player must hold the button for a period of time as the attack gains in strength. The attacker can either release the button at any point, as he will be vulnerable while performing the charge or will be purposely left vulnerable during the charge to increase the risk associated with attempting the move. Feedback is given when the charged attack is full to let the player know that he can now dish out full damage, perhaps through a particle effect.

Attacks During Actions

To increase the repertoire of moves, attacks might also be made while the player is performing another action such as holding onto a ladder, performing a wall run, and so on. The number of attacks from this is potentially limitless, but obviously there is a limit as to the number you would put in any one game. For example, you might be able to swing your sword behind you while climbing a ladder or holding onto a ledge, or you might be able to perform a diving lunge by back-springing off the wall. Choosing the right repertoire of moves can seriously increase the tactical opportunities that the game offers.

Skill Attacks

Skill attacks are particularly impressive moves that have a different dynamic than the standard attack system. Essentially the attack moves the combat into a different mode, which generally plays a set animation of some kind. More interactivity can be added to this by having an aiming system for the attack, such as a targeting cone projected in front of the player, or it may have more complex targeting systems applied, such as the ability to select a number of targets.

CHANGING ATTACK SETS

Having a number of different attack sets provides layers of depth for the combat system.

Combat Stances

Combat stances are different poses and sets of attacks used in melee fighting. Having a number of stances that a character can switch between allows a new repertoire of moves to replace the previous set. One of the particularly good features of this system is that switching stances could completely change the behavior of the character. This may be a simple change such as changing moves from being punch centric to kick centric. It may also be much more elaborate, such as changing from fast agile attacks to slow but hugely powerful attacks.

While this is great from a combat depth point of view, a designer must realize that there is a lot of work involved in such an increased move set. A whole new set of animations must be created, requiring that each move be set up, balanced, and thoroughly tested. The balancing work will need to balance the new set of moves against all the other moves in the game to ensure that it is not overly powerful or completely underpowered. For every extra move a character has, the workload increases almost exponentially.

Switching between stances is done in one of two basic ways:

Toggle: Toggle switching requires a button press to change stance. The character will remain in that stance until another stance is activated. This might be a single button assigned to change stance, but it is unlikely that this would warrant a dedicated button with limited space on a control pad. An alternative is to map it to a button combination like a special move. For example, for the character Gen in *Street Fighter Alpha 3* the player selects a punch-based stance by pressing all three punch buttons simultaneously or a kick-based stance by pressing all three kick buttons simultaneously.

Hold: Hold switching requires a button to be held for the character to remain in a particular stance. This means there is a dominant stance and a number of lesser stances. With such a scheme the buttons would need to be dedicated and would be best mapped to shoulder buttons to allow comfort and ease of use.

Weapon-Based Attack Sets

Some fighters might change an attack set based on the weapon being carried at that moment. Like stances, this may require a lot of animation, but animations are likely to be reusable across a number of different characters.

Having this system would mean different animations would be used when an axe is being wielded than when a sword is being used. This also means a character could pick up and use any weapon that he finds lying around. This makes logical sense and creates a more believable world but can mean a lot more work.

Progression-Based Attack Sets

A strong visual method of progression is to change characters' animations as they get more adept at fighting. The players will then see that their characters are becoming physically stronger and more skillful. For example, the character may begin with a repertoire of rough street moves. Over time these would be refined, and new animations would replace the old ones until eventually the character's moves look like they are being performed by Bruce Lee.

The resulting hit reactions could also be beefed up so that they have more visual impact. Again this means a lot more work, but the reward of such a system is worth the effort, as it emphasizes a character's progression. It also gives the players goals to attain and provides feedback for their efforts.

COMBOS

Combos are moves that are designed to be strung together so that they play one after another. Generally they are used to inflict maximum damage on an opponent, either by not allowing the opponent to block once the moves have started or by increasing the amount of damage done further down the combat string. They were originally created purely by accident by the developers of *Street Fighter 2* who saw the possibilities of the system and expanded upon it.

Buffering

The key to allowing one move to flow into another is to register the press of one or more buttons in the current combo move. This is known as buffering and can be done in several ways:

Whole-string buffer: A whole string can be read into the buffer at once.
Timed buffering: Only one button or string is buffered per animation.

One-button buffer: Only one button is buffered at a time, but it can be changed before the move is executed.

Whole-String Buffering

Once a combo move is begun, the entirety of the string can be entered. This system has its advantages and disadvantages:

- It is a simple system that allows easy input of combo strings
- Often this leads to button mashing (or bashing), where complex combos can be entered just by pressing any of the buttons at random.
- It cannot be cancelled once the combo string has been entered unless some kind of cancel feature is implemented. This problem is exacerbated during particularly long combos.

Timed Buffering

Single button presses or strings can be entered at specific phases during the animation. This phase is known as the register attack window. Should a valid button or combo be pressed during this phase, the combo will initiate the next move when it reaches the pop-out window.

To make the system more rigid you could add fail events in case the buttons are entered outside the register attack window, which would either stop the combo entirely or play a failed combo animation. To make the system more forgiving you can reset the buffer if an invalid string or button is entered. This gives the player an opportunity to enter the correct string or button if there is enough time.

The timed buffering system has its advantages and disadvantages.

- Combos are unlikely to be button-mashed as in the whole-string buffer system (unless a reset option is used).
- There is opportunity to stop performing a combo halfway through a chain, though a single time block cannot be cancelled once entered.
- The lack of button mashing can slow the pace of combat down.
- Some people find the rhythmic nature of this system difficult to grasp.

One-Button Buffering

Single button presses are stored in the buffer and are activated when the pop-out window occurs. Before the move is activated, this buffer can be swapped with a new button press. Its advantages and disadvantages are that:

- It allows the player to correct any action or change before the move is executed.
- It doesn't allow complex string entry at each time slot.
- People might not understand that the buffer is being overwritten, so some indication of button presses might be required.
- It increases the chances of button mashing even more than whole-string buffering.

Combo Length

The length of a combo is determined by how many animations are played within the combo string.

Set-Length Combos

Set-length combos have a particular number of moves in the combo. A player might only perform a certain part of the string, however, so essentially the combo length is a maximum that can be achieved for that particular string. A three-move combo will therefore have a maximum of three attacks in the string.

Chaining

Chaining is the ability to continually link moves together indefinitely—to make your own combos on the fly. Not all moves will necessarily be chainable, but by making all basic moves chain into each other, a system can become very fluid and powerful.

Combo Animation Flow

For animations to move smoothly from one to the next, some form of animation flow must be established.

Combat Animation Types

Several types of animation are used in combat to determine how the character behaves and are linked together in a particular manner. This may be through animation linking, blending, or a combination of the two.

- **Combat aware:** Used when combat is initialized or the character hasn't performed a move for some time. This could be blended between a noncombat idle over distance so that the closer the enemy gets, the more the character is in combat-aware pose.
- **Combat idle:** Used between moves or when locked on to an enemy.
- **Combat idle incidental:** Used during long periods of quiet or in reaction to an event. Could be a laugh, cheer, spinning of sword, or something similar.
- **Attack:** The character is performing an attack.
- **Hit reaction:** The character is in the midst of being hit by an attack.
- **KO:** The character has been knocked to the floor.
- **Rise:** The character is getting up from the floor.
- **Combat moving:** The character is moving around while still engaged in combat.
- **Lock-on move:** The character is locked onto a target and is moving in relation to the target. This is generally slower and more threatening than a standard combat movement.

Animation Linking

Single-weapon combat is perhaps the most difficult to create an animation flow for, since the weapon will finish at different points around the body after each move. Hand-to-hand or dual-weapon combat are a little easier, as they are succinct parts and can thus generally end at the point at which they started. The simplest form of animation linking is a non-branching structure in which one move flows only into one other.

Linear Flow

With this system each animation starts from the previous animation end pose. Any failed or cancelled combos will either blend back into combat-idle pose or an animation from the last move to idle. Using blending requires far fewer animations to be created and uses less memory to store the animations but requires a more sophisticated animation system.

Branching Flow

A more complex system would allow branching combos. This is a case of creating a number of different animations for each part of the chain. Again the pose of the next move should match the end pose of the previous move.

Unlimited Branching

A more complex system can be created to allow unlimited branching and allow infinite combo strings. Let's create an example to illustrate how different animations might blend together. We want to create a system in which the avatar will draw his sword and is then able to chain together a series of attacks. In this case we will be able to get from any one attack to another.

We need the following combat poses:

Normal pose (N): From the normal pose the character must move into the combat pose by unsheathing his sword.

Combat pose (C): The combat pose is used when the sword is drawn and an attack is not being performed.

Left combat pose (L): The left pose is always the even-numbered attack in a chain.

Right combat pose (R): The right combat poses are always the odd-numbered attack in a chain.

Charge combat (CC): This moves from armed run animation into an attack. Always finish in left combat pose.

These poses are the start and end points we must reach with an animation, so that the animation begins at the point set by the pose and ends at the point where the new animation begins. This will produce smooth flow to the sequence, which can be seen in Figure 8.4.

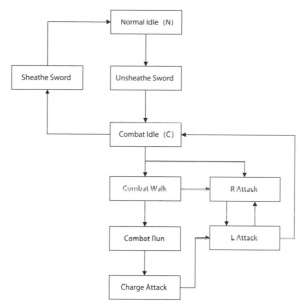

FIGURE 8.4   An example combat animation flow.

Of course, this is only one of many animation flows that we could create for our combat model. This is a particularly useful one, as it allows us to chain any one move into another. It is always important for the designers and animators to sit down together when sketching out the animation flow, so that both groups get input and spot any potential problems.

Animation Blending

An alternative method to the somewhat complex animation linking method is to rely on animation blending to move between two or more animations. Animation blending places the burden on the animation system and thus has a fairly small associated performance hit, but the rewards can far outweigh the costs.

Essentially it calculates how the bones will move from one pose to another to interpolate between animations. The danger is that this can cause physically impossible movements or cause the character to intersect with itself. These issues can be avoided with constraints added to the skeleton.

The interpolation needs to happen over a large enough time period such that there is no longer a visible pop. This will need to be longer for much larger differences in pose. This time period can be automatic or be specified by the designers. Relying on animation blending to do the linking between moves results in less concern about getting animations linking, although, because of the time needed to blend between large differences, it is often sensible to have a rudimentary level of animation linking to ensure that poses are fairly similar between animations to keep the system feeling fluid.

Interrupts

Interrupts are events that interrupt the combo flow, such as performing a counter. In these instances the animation will pop if it is in the wrong pose, so some kind of method needs to be employed to stop this popping. There are two basic methods of doing this:

Patch animations: Without the ability to blend between animations in code, patch animations are used to fill in the gaps.

Animation blending: An extremely useful tool here is the ability to blend animations, as it allows smooth movement between animations without having to create unique patch animations.

Some animations might require immediate interruption, such as hit reaction animations. It is useful to build a system that allows you to tweak all of these components: add patch animations where they are needed and fine-tune blend times so that it looks just right without being too slow.

Combo Damage Multiplying

Combo multipliers increase damage as the sequence gets longer. This can be done in one of two ways:

Individual multipliers: Each move has a specific damage multiplier applied to it. The move is only likely to be performed mid-sequence and cannot be performed outside the combo structure.

Increasing tally: Using an increasing multiplier with each successful hit of the combo encourages the player to use combos more. Interruptions to a continuous chain result in the multipliers being reset.

Attack Movement and Hit Reaction Synchronization

The forward motion of an attack needs to be synchronized to the hit reaction of the enemy in order for the next move in a combo chain to hit the intended target. For this to occur the forward movement needs to match or exceed the backward movement of the victim. If it is less, the next attack will fall short. This may prove tricky in a dynamic hit reaction system, as situations can occur where attack strength is very high and the victim is weak and thus receives full hit reaction. It is perhaps best to choose an average so that the combo will work in all but the most severe of cases. Hit reactions are discussed in a later chapter.

DEFENSIVE MOVES

Defensive moves in combat add a good deal of strategy to the system. There are plenty of different ways the designer can incorporate defense into the combat system.

Blocking

Blocking is a way of deflecting incoming blows, giving the player time to think and, in turn, the opportunity to retaliate.

Block Control

Blocking can be controlled in a number of ways:

Button controlled: The block is assigned to a specific button.

Direction controlled: The block is activated by pulling away from the attacker when an attack is being made. If no attack is being made, then the character simply moves back as normal. This works best for side-on beat 'em ups rather than the standard third-person view.

Automatic: The character automatically blocks unless performing another action.

Blocking should be as responsive as possible, as it can cause severe frustration if players are not able to block incoming attacks in time.

Block Coverage

The area covered by the block is an important consideration, as it will affect the usefulness of the block itself or will transform how the block is used.

Front block: The front block covers the front hemisphere of the character but leaves their rear vulnerable. This can mean difficulty if the character becomes surrounded. Some form of visualization is required for the shield.

All around block: The character is blocked from all directions. This allows the character time to think when surrounded, though it can look odd if the animation or effect does not suit (you might get around this by turning the character to face an incoming attack, but this can upset player control).

Movable: The player has control over a limited shield. Essentially the player can now control which area he is blocking from, but this could still cause problems if the character becomes surrounded.

High block: The character blocks high- or mid-level attacks but is vulnerable to low attacks.

Low block: The character blocks low attacks, and high attacks will not connect, but he is vulnerable to mid-level attacks.

Block Restrictions

Restricting the block can give the player a greater sense of urgency than having a block that makes him utterly invulnerable. Types of block restrictions include:

Reduced damage: If damage is greatly reduced but still occurs, it will encourage the player to keep moving and use blocking as a fail-safe. A protected block could be used to give full protection if it is activated within a set time of the attack being made—in effect rewarding good reactions.

Block meter: A block meter restricts how long a block can be maintained before it is broken. This time is reduced with each hit or over time. The meter could replenish fairly quickly while the character is not blocking.

Evasion

Evasion allows a character to move out of the way of an incoming blow. There are plenty of ways the character could visually move out of the way, such as side-step, roll, flip, or teleport—whatever suits the character. Evasion can be mapped in several ways:

Direction: A press of the D-pad or the use of the right analog stick might be employed for evasion.

Button and direction: A combination of button (perhaps the block button) and direction could be used.

Double-tap: A quick double-tap of a direction could move the character out of harm's way.

Jump: Using jump is a great way of avoiding low attacks or any attack if the jump is high enough.

Floor evasion: Pressing directions while lying on the floor might allow the character to roll about and avoid any incoming ground or pursuit attacks.

Counterattacking

Counterattacks are moves that can be performed by using quick reactions to reverse an incoming blow. If the character presses the counterattack button within a small time frame as an attack is about to hit (the counterattack window of the incoming attack), then a successful counter is achieved.

The outcome of a counter might be to simply knock the opponent off-guard and leave him vulnerable for a second or so. Alternatively, the counter might be an attack in itself, reversing the opponent's attack and using the leverage for the player character to perform a move. These can be quite spectacular.

Parrying

Parrying is the collision of two weapons during a move. If two attack areas collide or two parry windows coincide, it can be said that a parry has occurred. At this point a couple of things could occur:

Separation: Both parties are knocked back and recover.

Dominance: The heavier of the two weapons knocks the other character back, leaving him vulnerable for a short time.

Conjunction: The characters become stuck together for a moment. This may result in them having to wrestle to unlock or win an attack. The winner could be the person who hammers the button as many times as possible or wiggles the stick as fast as possible in a set time.

WEAPON TRAILS

Melee attacks can be very fast, some moving over as little as 10 frames or possibly even fewer. With low frame rates it can be difficult to discern an attack moving at this speed from the animation alone—even with a silky smooth 60 frames per second it can be difficult to interpret fast attacks.

A method of reinforcing the movement of an attack is to utilize weapon trails. A weapon trail is an effect that follows the motion of an attack. This trail can be composed of particle effects, geometry with alpha textures, or any other suitable rendering method. For a realistic game these would be fairly subtle, but for a more fantastical game they may be over the top with large glows and bright colors. Weapon trails could be personalized for each character or even for particular weapons.

SUMMARY

Melee combat is a very visceral system that provides plenty of reward for the player if it is done well. Unfortunately it is also a very difficult system to get right and requires a massive investment of time and resources.

We looked at several aspects of melee combat in this chapter:

Combat control systems: The control of a combat system should take on a suitable level of complexity for the game.

- **Simple one-button system:** Very basic combat games are likely to only use one attack button.
- **General combat systems:** More advanced systems might be based on light and heavy attacks, sweep and focused attacks, or high and low attacks.
- **Advanced systems:** Games in which combat is the main focus are likely to have much more complex systems, such as a limb-based model, an attack-type model, a strength model, or some other unique system. They are also likely to have some form of defensive moves.

Melee combat balance: Melee combat is often structured around a simple rock, paper, scissors balance, where one type of move beats another. This ensures that there is no one move that will defeat all others. There is always a counterstrategy.

Melee weapons: We examined several aspects of melee weapons:

- **Types of weapon:** There are several types of melee weapon, namely unarmed, blades, bludgeons, and spears.
- **Weapon parameters:** Each weapon can be described by a number of parameters—weapon strength, damage type, and the status effect that the weapon might inflict.

Attack parameters: Every melee attack can be described with a number of parameters:

- **Direction:** The angle of attack, which may be a sweep attack, a focused attack, or an uppercut.
- **Speed:** The speed of the attack.
- **Height:** The height at which the attack is being made, differentiating between ground, low, mid, high, and air attacks.
- **Strength:** The force of the attack will determine hit reaction produced on a successful strike.
- **Damage:** The amount of damage the attack will inflict upon the opponent should it land.

Attack windows: Attacks are deconstructed into attack windows that describe the components of the attack and how button presses are handled.

- **Window types:** There are four basic types of window—animation, registry, interrupt, and response.
- **Using windows:** Longer windows will naturally produce slower moves, which are generally used to describe powerful attacks. Multiple windows might be used for several strikes in a single animation.

Types of moves: A number of different types of moves might be employed in a melee combat system:

- **Basic attacks:** Single button presses.
- **Command attacks:** Button presses combined with directions.
- **Lock-on attacks:** Locking onto a specific target to direct attacks in the target's direction.
- **Multiple button attacks:** Require multiple buttons to be pressed at once.
- **Jump attacks:** Different attacks are performed while jumping.
- **Context-sensitive attacks:** Attacks are changed according to the current situation.
- **Special moves:** Particularly impressive attacks that might work in much the same way as a standard attack or be gauge-based to limit their use.
- **Ground attacks:** Moves performed while lying on the floor.
- **Rising attacks:** Moves performed while getting up off the floor.
- **Throws and grappling:** Synchronized animations to perform particularly complex character interactions.
- **Charge-up attacks:** Holding down the attack button to increase the damage dealt by the attack.
- **Attacks during actions:** Attacks made during changed control methods, such as being on a ladder, a ledge, and so on.
- **Skill attacks:** Different movement modes that allow complex movement to be performed.

Changing attack sets: More complex combat systems may want to change the repertoire of moves available to a character at certain points. There are several ways of doing this:

- **Combat stances:** Switching between different combat stances that have different move sets.
- **Weapon-based attack sets:** Different move sets activated by using different weaponry.
- **Progression-based attack sets:** Different move sets that are unlocked as the player progresses through the game.

Combos: Combos are strings of attacks that are performed together to create a much more formidable attack than single attacks alone. We examined several aspects of combos in this chapter:

- **Buffering:** The method of storing the next move in the sequence, which might use a whole-string, timed, or one-button system.
- **Combo length:** A combo may be of a set-length or may allow chaining to let the players build their own combos.
- **Combo animation flow:** We examined the types of animations used to create a flow, the linking between these animations (linear, branching, or unlimited), and animation blending to smooth the transitions between animations.
- **Interrupts:** Should an animation be interrupted, then a patch or blend can be used to prevent popping.
- **Combo damage multiplying:** As the length of a combo increases, the amount of damage can be scaled either with individual multipliers or by a tally.

Defensive moves: Most combat systems have at least one form of defense available. More complex systems may have several.

- **Blocking:** The act of preventing an incoming attack from landing by adopting a defensive position. This defense may be button based, direction based, or may be performed automatically if no other action is being performed. A block might cover just the front of the character, all around the character, be movable, block high attacks, or block low attacks. Restrictions may be applied to the block so that it only reduces damage or has a block meter.
- **Evasion:** The act of quickly moving out of the path of oncoming danger. This may be direction based; require the use of a button and a direction, a double tap, or a jump; or may include evasion while grounded.
- **Counterattacking:** The act of turning an attack around on the attacker to attack him instead.
- **Parrying:** The act of two attacks being performed at the same time to produce stalemate or to stagger the weaker attacker.
- **Weapon trails:** Trails can highlight fast moves and improve the visual impact of an attack.

Melee combat is a complex game system to set up but can yield fantastic results. New technologies will add further depth to a melee combat system in the years to come. Developers are already experimenting with procedural animation systems that will allow much more complex interactions and believable reactions between characters. It remains to be seen whether it will be capable of producing animations as impressive as those created by an animator. It is likely that such systems will be worked in with current technologies to create a hybrid of standard and procedural animation to get the best of both worlds. Movement-sensing control methods may also have a large impact on the way melee combat systems work in the future.

9

RANGED COMBAT DYNAMICS

In This Chapter

- Projectile Weapons
- Beam Weapons
- Mine Weapons
- Defense Against Ranged Attacks
- Ranged Combat Animation

The second form of combat is ranged combat. Owing to the remote nature of ranged combat, its dynamics are based much more around the action of a projectile reaching the enemy than the interaction between the characters themselves. We shall explore several aspects of ranged combat in this chapter:

- Projectile weapons
- Beam weapons
- Mine weapons
- Defense against ranged attacks
- Ranged combat animation

PROJECTILE WEAPONS

Projectile weapons can attack at range by firing a projectile of some kind. There are different methods of firing a projectile and different types of projectile that can be fired. Projectile weapons can cover everything from a gun to a bow and arrow or even a magical thunderbolt.

Firing Methods

A projectile can be fired several ways. Different methods create very different feels for the weapon in question.

Single shot

The weapon fires once every time the fire button is pressed. This is best used for sniper rifles or similar styles of weaponry, where each shot should be carefully considered or where you want the player to have maximum control over firing.

Automatic

Automatic weaponry fires at the weapon's fire rate while the fire button is held. This is a good system to use for most weaponry. With pistols or any other weapon where there is a fairly slow rate of fire, you might also want to add a semi-automatic functionality. The player can then keep it held for automatic firing or pump the fire button for faster firing rates.

Charge

A charge weapon requires the fire button to be held to charge up the power of the weapon. This generally means that the players can charge as little or as long as they like (up to a maximum point) before releasing the button to fire the projectile. This might also be based on analog properties of the button rather than a charge time, so the further the action button is depressed, the greater the charge.

Firing Modes

Many weapons have several fire modes—different ways of firing the weapon or switching the ammunition used.

Primary Fire

Primary fire is the main firing mode of the weapon. This will be the most basic functionality, the weapon mode that the player is most likely to want to use.

Secondary Fire

Having a secondary fire allows the player to very quickly fire a weapon in a different mode. This mode could be very different from the primary fire mode. For example, secondary fire on a machine gun could fire an under-slung grenade launcher or perhaps fire one barrel only of a double-barreled shotgun.

Switching Fire Modes

If a weapon has more than two firing modes, it might be useful to have a switch that toggles between the modes rather than independent firing buttons for each mode.

Ammunition

Ammunition is vital to a projectile-based weapon. The acquisition of ammunition can often be an important game mechanic.

Ammunition Functionality

Each projectile needs to come from somewhere. Exactly how this projectile is generated depends on the weapon itself.

Distinct Projectiles

Distinct projectiles are physical objects that are fired from the barrel. These physical objects must be acquired before they can be used and will be diminished as they are fired. Most projectile weaponry is likely to be of this type. You might want to have some form of infinite ammunition weapon as a back up if you have no other form of attack for the player to adopt (such as a melee attack). Otherwise, players may enter a game situation where they are defenseless.

Distinct projectiles might be only usable with a particular weapon or might be capable of being used with a variety of weapons. You might, for example, have different calibers of ammunition available. You can then only fire a particular caliber of bullet with a particular weapon, but the ammunition could be used across a range of weaponry. You might have different styles of bullet in each caliber, so that you'd have standard bullets or explosive bullets able to be fired from the same weapon.

Power Drain Projectiles

Power drain projectiles require a power source to generate the projectile within the weapon. This power source might be a battery, gas canister, or power cell. Every projectile fired will drain a certain amount of this power source. The projectile itself might be chargeable, so this drain may vary depending on how much power the players put in each projectile they fire.

Recharging Weaponry

Recharging weaponry doesn't need ammunition but does require time to recharge. Recharge might vary according to how much charge was released in the first instance or might dip a set amount with each shot. A weapon might recharge instantly after each shot, or recharge might not occur until the weapon charge reaches zero.

Fire Rate

Fire rate describes how quickly a weapon can fire the next projectile once the last projectile has fired. High fire rates mean a weapon can spew out projectiles in quick succession.

Balancing fire rate against damage is the best way to control a weapon's potential damage per second (accuracy of a weapon is another good balancing tactic). Weapons with high-damage projectiles generally should have a fairly low fire rate, whereas projectiles with low damage are more likely to have a higher fire rate.

Magazine Size

Magazine size refers to the amount of ammunition held within a magazine, or container for the projectiles. Each magazine will need to be reloaded once empty but often can be switched before it is completely empty. When switching a clip, it is often just topped off from a pool of ammunition, but if you are aiming for ultra-realism, you might want any spare bullets to be discarded when a nonempty magazine is switched.

More arcade-styled games do away with the idea of using clips and reloading to keep the pace fast.

Reload Time

The reload time refers to the amount of time required to insert a new magazine once the old one is spent. This can be another balancing factor in ranged weaponry, where short reload times allow faster turnaround than long ones. You might want to balance this against magazine size, so a large-capacity weapon can fire for long periods of time but then has a much longer reload than a weapon that fires for short periods of time and requires regular reloading.

Fire Effects

Fire effects are applied to the weapon or ammunition to enhance the feel of the weapon. These effects cover two main areas:

Muzzle flash: This effect is played as the projectile leaves the weapon. It could be anything from a standard muzzle flash on a gun to the dissipation of magical energy from a staff.

Projectile trails: This is the effect as the projectile moves through the air—perhaps a smoke trail or tracer bullet trail.

Flight Type

The flight type of a projectile describes the manner in which it moves through worldspace.

Straight Line

The simplest method of firing a projectile is simply in a straight line. This direct line is usually suitable for bullets or beam weaponry.

Scatter

Scatter is performed by firing a number of projectiles at once. As they leave the gun, they scatter in many directions following straight line paths. The number of projectiles and the angle at which they leave the gun dictates the scatter area. They could scatter all along the same plane or in a large conical area. When a large number of projectiles are being scattered (such as from a shotgun), it might be more efficient to model it as a beam weapon rather than a standard projectile weapon. Essentially a conical attack area replaces the mass of projectiles.

Trajectory

A trajectory projectile moves in an arc as the projectile drops because of gravity as it travels. This could be applied to ballistic weaponry as well as thrown objects or heavy projectiles. Using trajectories adds an element of skill, as the player has to get the trajectory right in order to hit the target. It also means the player must have accurate control over the weapon's elevation. Otherwise, trajectories could be automatically calculated to hit the target if in range and thus they would only be a visual feature rather than a functional one.

Homing

Homing weapons are able to track a target in a particular way. The degree of homing can be adjusted to suit. A projectile might relentlessly follow a target until it crashes into a wall or may only be slightly adjusted to the target's change of position.

Cone-of-Vision Homing

A powerful method of homing is to use a cone-of-vision, which will have a view angle and a view range. If the projectile spots a target within this cone, it will turn at its maximum turn speed to face this target. The speed of the turn determines how much the projectile will be able to home in. A fast turn speed will make a highly maneuverable projectile; a slow turn speed will reduce its homing capabilities. The intelligence of the projectile can be determined by what the projectile considers to be a target within its view cone. A simple heat-seeking missile would target any potential combat entity, either friend or foe. If you are making more exotic weaponry, you might want to make it only target enemies, thus making it more intelligent.

Locked On

Alternatively, the targeting process may select a particular target to attack. The missile could then theoretically stay locked to this target and either move directly toward the locked target or attempt to path-find its way around obstacles. The level of sophistication is determined by just how deadly you want the homing projectiles to be. Again the degree of homing is determined by the speed at which a projectile can turn to face a target.

Player Guided

Player-guided projectiles can be controlled or affected by the player while in flight. There are two methods of doing this: aftertouch and switched view.

Aftertouch

Half-Life's rocket launcher used the aftertouch method. The players retain control of their characters when the projectile is fired, but any movement they make will affect the flight of the projectile. In the case of *Half-Life* the look movement was used to control the rocket. On a joypad it might be sensible to use the right analog stick to control this aftertouch. The only problem with this method is a lack of direct control and the possibility of not being able to see the path of the projectile properly. However, the method works well for short ranges.

Switched View

Unreal Tournament's Redeemer weapon uses the switched-view approach. Here the player is transferred to control of the projectile itself, usually with a first-person view from inside the projectile. The player can then guide the flight of the projectile directly with movement input. The switched view has the advantage of allowing perfect user control over the flight of the projectile, but it has two very problematic downsides.

First, control is taken away from the players' avatars. What happens to them while they are controlling the projectiles? What happens if they get attacked? One solution is to switch back to the avatar if they get damaged, but this will waste the projectile currently in flight. Alternatively, the players could have a button for the projectile that allows them to switch back when they receive damage, but they will need to be notified of damage while flying the projectile.

Second, and more problematically, the projectile will be able to fly anywhere, and in many cases (generally outdoor maps) that might mean out of the map itself.

This is obviously undesirable. Even if the projectile isn't out of the map, it might be in a position where holes can be seen. In addition projectiles might be able to get to positions where they can view large sections of the map at once. The engine might not be built to cope with this and thus the frame rate will drop. The solution to this problem is to only use the switched view when you know the game can handle it and to stop it going out of bounds by defining safe volumes, where control is relinquished when the projectile enters them.

Projectile Velocity

The velocity of a projectile specifies how quickly it travels and is determined by what type of projectile it is. A bullet is an extremely fast projectile that cannot be seen by the naked eye, whereas a grenade is a lot slower moving and can easily be seen in flight. However, while in the real world we might not see an incoming projectile, for the purposes of a game and good gameplay this might need to be abstracted a little. Slowing bullets to a speed at which the player can see them and possibly adding trails and other highlighting effects allows the player to see the danger and have the opportunity to evade. This is not essential, but it can make it easier for the player to interpret an attack situation.

Accuracy

Weapon accuracy can be interpreted in many ways and can be handled differently for different styles of gameplay.

Player Skill–Based Accuracy

When accuracy is purely based on the character's skill, it is not likely that you will want to make characters wildly inaccurate, or it will lead to player frustration. Generally if the player is pointing the crosshair at a target, or is locked to a particular target, he expects to hit that target.

However, there are legitimate situations where accuracy could be affected and shots may scatter wide of the mark. This is usually indicated to the player in some way, such as widening the crosshair to show that accuracy is diminished.

Movement

When running or moving you are unlikely to be as accurate as when you are standing still. Furthermore, you can improve accuracy by steadying the gun to prevent your hands from shaking, so if you were to crouch or lie prone, you could steady the gun even further. Placing it on a low wall or sandbags or any other solid surface would also improve your accuracy owing to lack of hand shake. All of this can easily be applied to a game world if you want to include this kind of detail.

Recoil

Recoil is the action of the gun moving backward as a bullet is fired. In automatic weapons this causes the gun to "walk" upward with continued firing. This is counteracted by burst-firing the weapon—pressing the trigger for small intervals then releasing for a moment before firing again.

Object Interaction

When using another object that requires the use of one hand, less steadiness can be applied to using a weapon. This will result in reduced accuracy.

Hit Reaction

When being hit by an incoming attack, it is likely that a character's accuracy will be severely affected.

Stat-Based Accuracy

Stat-based accuracy is more likely to be used in turn-based games or for AI-controlled units, where the character is more likely to be choosing specific targets rather than manually aiming.

Simple Accuracy Calculation

Stat-based accuracy uses some type of calculation to determine whether the attacker hits his target. This calculation could be based on several factors, depending on how deep you want the simulation to become. A simple turn-based calculation is

$$H = \frac{C + W}{2} \tag{9.1}$$

where:

H = hit chance
C = character accuracy
W = weapon accuracy

Assuming that these accuracy values are out of 100, this will give us a hit chance between 0 and 100, zero being no chance of hitting and 100 being a guaranteed hit. Next we create a random number to determine whether the attack hits home:

$$A = H - R \tag{9.2}$$

where:

A = shot accuracy
H = hit chance
R = A random number between 1 and 100

If this number is positive, then the shot hits; if it is negative, then the shot misses. Negative values can then translate as how much the shot has missed by.

Increasing the Complexity

We could make this calculation much more complex to improve our simulation. Imagine that we could improve character accuracy in several stances or affect their accuracy if they were performing a particular action. We apply a modifier to the character accuracy stat based on the character's present action or stance, as shown in Table 9.1.

TABLE 9.1   Determining the Accuracy Modifier

ACTION OR STANCE	ACCURACY MODIFIER
Running	0.25
Walking	0.35
Creeping	0.5
Standing	0.75
Crouching	0.85
Prone	1
On ladder	0.2
Being hit	0.1

Now our hit chance calculation can be expressed as

$$H = \frac{(AC)+W}{2} \tag{9.3}$$

where:

H = hit chance
C = character accuracy
W = weapon accuracy
A = accuracy modifier

We could also add critical hits and fumbles when extreme numbers are produced. Thus, if the random number is 100, it automatically produces a fumble, no matter what the hit chance is, or if it is zero, it causes a critical hit no matter what the hit chance result is. Alternatively, these could be done with threshold values; for example, +50 is a critical hit and −50 is a fumble.

With certain projectiles such as arrows we might want to add a wind factor. The player has to take this into consideration while aiming and thus adjust the angle he aims at to account for the wind. Alternatively, we might simply add another modifier to the hit chance based on the strength of the wind.

Applying to Real Time

While it seems most suited to turn-based combat, the accuracy stat could be applied to a real-time system by making the variation in the scatter less as the accuracy stat increases. Thus, you could move and shoot as the character gets more proficient.

You can convey this information to the player by having a reticule based on the accuracy stat. When the reticule is wide, it shows that the weapon is not accurate. When the reticule is reduced in size, it shows that accuracy has improved. As character accuracy improves, the size of this reticule and the variation when moving or stationary will be reduced.

However, care is advised when affecting a skill-based game dynamic with random events. It is very easy to make the players frustrated, as they do not have as much control as they otherwise might have. Simulation should take a backseat where gameplay is concerned.

Impact Methods

Projectiles have several different reactions on colliding with a surface.

Standard Impact

A standard impact will simply terminate the projectile on contact with any object or surface and inflict damage if it has collided with a combat entity. On terminating the projectile, a hit effect is likely to play based on the hit-effect matrix (see later chapter for more on the hit-effect matrix).

Impact Attack Area

An impact attack area creates an area attack volume at the point of impact. This would represent an explosion or similar effect.

Bounce

Bounce is used most often on trajectory-based projectiles that use an impact attack area (such as grenades). These generally bounce with a smaller trajectory each time. The dampening of a bouncing projectile is important to consider, as it greatly affects the behavior of the projectile. Once the projectile comes to a stop, a secondary impact area attack may be instigated. It may also be wise to make the projectile detonate when it hits a combat entity to make it easier for the player to hit a target.

Bouncing applied to a straight-line flight results in a projectile that will ricochet around a room. These projectiles will continue moving until they hit a combat entity or until a certain number of bounces have occurred, at which time they will either terminate or a secondary impact area attack may be performed.

When using such projectiles, it is important to have a sensible limit on the number of bounces to prevent projectiles from remaining in the world for too long. If this happens, a buildup of projectile numbers will require a lot of calculations, and this will eventually reach the point where it has a serious effect on frame rate.

Penetrating

Penetrating projectiles are capable of going through a combat entity (possibly even the environment as well) and causing damage on their way through. This enables the player to line up enemies and damage many at once. Commonly this type of weapon is known as a rail gun.

You may want to restrict the depth of penetration a weapon can achieve. Thus, you might place a restriction on what materials, depth of wall, or number of objects the projectile can penetrate.

Projectile Weapon Parameters

There are many potential types of projectile weapons that will have many different attributes and abilities, from ancient long bows to modern day assault rifles. However, a number of parameters can be used to describe generic attributes of projectile weaponry. These are shown in Table 9.2.

TABLE 9.2   Projectile Weapon Parameters

PARAMETER	DESCRIPTION
Weapon strength	How much damage the weapon will do to a target
Damage type	What kind of damage the weapon inflicts
Rate of fire	How quickly shots can be fired
Reload time	How long it takes to reload a weapon
Ammo clip size	How much ammo or charge one ammo clip holds
Blast radius	How large the area of effect is for a projectile if it has a secondary attack area on hitting
Fuse time	How long before a thrown projectile will activate after being thrown
Accuracy	How accurate the weapon is (may be modified if held down longer, for example)
Status effect	What status may be applied on a successful hit

BEAM WEAPONS

Beam weapons are similar to projectile weapons in that they can be targeted at range, but they differ in their functionality. They do not fire projectiles, but rather a continuous attack area protrudes from the end of the weapon. In essence they could be considered to be a combination of a projectile weapon and a melee weapon. A beam weapon could be a flamethrower, laser beam gun, or any similar style of weapon where the beam has a certain range.

Beam Weapon Functionality

Beam weapons fire a beam or cone from the end of the weapon. Anything caught in this beam or cone will be inflicted with the appropriate damage. The beam may take time to scale up or may switch on and off instantly. The skill in using a beam weapon is to keep the opponent in the attack area for as long as possible. While opponents remain in the beam, they will continue to receive damage.

Beam weapons are likely to use a power drain method of ammunition, which requires a power source such as a battery, gas canister, or power cell. The power source is drained a certain amount for each unit of time the button is held. A power source might also be able to slowly recharge over time, so that the beam weapon is effectively infinite. Obviously this only makes sense with a battery or fuel cell rather than a gas canister power source.

A shotgun might also be considered a beam weapon that only fires when the button is pressed rather than being continuously on. Rather than firing all the various projectiles and calculating them individually, the fire effect can be played as one special effect and a conical attack used to determine the attack area. This is far more efficient than calculating every projectile.

Advanced Use of Beam Weaponry

Beam weapons can be used for some very creative purposes, because of the skill involved in keeping the target in the beam. This time-based skill opens up a number of opportunities. The things you could do are limited only by your imagination, but there are a number of functions that have been done well before.

Repel and Attract

The beam could be used to push or pull an enemy around the environment. The repel beam could be used to push the enemy over a large drop or into the path of some deadly trap. The attract beam could be used to bring the enemy in closer for a melee attack.

Inflict Status

All sorts of statuses could be inflicted by a beam weapon. If the effect is analog, it could continually affect the opponent while in the beam. For example, a shrink ray would continually shrink the opponent. Alternatively, if the status is more binary— simply on or off—there would need to be a threshold amount of time to keep opponents in the beam. This binary effect could be igniting them in flame, freezing them with liquid nitrogen, or any other crazy idea you can conceive (such as turning enemies to chickens like the Morph-O Ray in *Ratchet and Clank*™).

Beam Weapon Parameters

Beam weapons can all be based around the same base parameters, as shown in Table 9.3.

TABLE 9.3   Beam Weapon Parameters

PARAMETER	DESCRIPTION
Weapon strength	How much damage the weapon will do to a target
Damage type	What kind of damage is inflicted by the weapon
Power use	How fast the weapon uses its power source
Reload time	How long a weapon takes to reload
Power source size	How much charge one power source holds
Range	How far the beam or cone stretches from a fire point on the weapon
Status effect	What status may be applied on a successful hit

MINE WEAPONS

Mine weapons are dropped or stuck in place and then armed. They can come in various shapes and sizes and have different methods of triggering.

Mine Functionality

Mines have a variety of ways in which various aspects of their makeup can function.

Laying Technique

There are different ways that mines can be laid and interacted with once placed.

Thrown

The simplest mines are simply thrown to the ground, where they wait until their triggers are activated to detonate them. They could be picked up again once dropped.

Limpet

The limpet mine can be placed on any surface, allowing the player to hide the mine away from prying eyes or place it tactically to set a trap. Bear in mind that this could cause some unforeseen issues. First-person shooter/RPG *Deus Ex* has limpet mines that have collision. It is possible for the player to use them to create a ladder. Players throw one mine, jump onto it, then throw another, and thus eventually break the map by getting to places they shouldn't.

Remote Controlled

Remote-controlled mines have some form of locomotion that allows them to be moved by the player once thrown down. The viewpoint then switches to that of the mine. This means the player is left vulnerable while controlling the mine, so it might be useful to switch back to the player if he is receiving damage. The remote control could take all sorts of forms such as a remote-controlled vehicle or even a spider mine that can climb walls. Be careful if you allow a mine to crawl on any surface, as it is possible to create situations where the player will be able to break the map by getting to unforeseen locations.

Trigger

Mines are differentiated mainly by the type of trigger they use to activate.

Proximity Mines

Proximity mines are activated by a target coming into their activation radius or detection beam. A radius is the simplest of the two systems, so that if any enemy walks into the detection sphere, the mine will detonate. A beam detection system will cast a beam out from the mine so that when the beam is broken the mine will detonate.

Timed Mines

Timed mines are set to detonate after a specific period of time. This suits placed explosives such as C4, where the player would plant the bomb and then retreat to a safe distance.

Remote Detonation Mines

Remote detonation mines require the player to manually trigger the explosive by pressing a button. This will generally mean that players need to be able to see the target area in order to successfully time their button press to detonate the mine.

Mine Weapon Parameters

Each mine weapon may have a number of attributes that describe its behavior. These parameters are shown in Table 9.4.

TABLE 9.4   Mine Weapon Parameters

PARAMETER	DESCRIPTION
Weapon strength	How much damage the weapon will do to a target
Damage type	What kind of damage the weapon inflicts
Detection radius	The area of detection for a proximity mine weapon
Blast radius	How large the area of effect is once the fuse time has expired
Fuse time	How long a timed mine's fuse is
Status effect	What status may be applied on a successful hit

DEFENSE AGAINST RANGED ATTACKS

Defending against ranged attacks is a very important skill. The danger from ranged attackers tends to be more prominent than close-range attackers, as they are effective from a distance.

Avoidance

The simplest method of defending against a ranged attack is to not get hit, and to not get hit the best tactic is to move out of the way.

Strafing

Strafing is a common method of avoidance. It is the act of side stepping—facing in one direction while moving in another. This allows the player to keep firing at an enemy while avoiding incoming attacks.

One particular tactic that tends to get used in 3D shooting games is circle strafing. This is a tactic where the player continues to face the enemy while strafing continuously around the target. This is a perfectly valid tactic but can become a little boring for the player, so it might be useful to add attacks that attempt to minimize too much circle strafing. Enemies could fire ahead of the player's movement vector or charge toward the character to encourage him to back away (more enemy tactics are discussed in the chapter on AI).

Evasion

Evasion is a quick dash out of the path of an incoming projectile. This could be a roll, flip, or jump to the side. It could be performed in the same manner as melee evasion, with a double tap or a button combined with the desired direction.

Blocking

Another method of defense is to block or deflect the incoming projectile, though this might not make sense for every ranged weapon. It is pretty difficult to block a bullet. Blocking works much like melee blocking, allowing just the front or the whole character to be protected. Manual blocking is more useful in a ranged combat scenario than automatic blocking, as long as the projectiles don't move too fast for the character to react to them.

RANGED COMBAT ANIMATION

Ranged combat animation has a very different set of criteria than melee combat. Incorporating both styles into a game can be a fairly demanding task. There are many ways that ranged combat can be approached, which will have different effects on the requirements of the system.

First Person

First person gives an intimate view of what the character can see, but in order to immerse the player in the world, it is good to have the weapon on screen. Weapons generally sit in the bottom left or right corners (usually right, but some games allow left-handed models as an option). They should not obscure too much of the view, or the player will have trouble being able to see anything.

Animation Requirements

Several animations are necessary for the weapons to function correctly:

Idle: The weapon would generally remain rigid when idle.

Walk: When the character is walking, the weapon is often made to bob a little; otherwise, it can look very rigid.

Fire weapon: Firing the weapon will need some kind of animation, such as recoil and the chamber retracting, the string of a bow being pulled back, and so on.

Reload: Reload will require some kind of animation, such as pumping new shells into a shotgun or placing another arrow into a bow.

Optional extra animations could be used to add character:

Amusing idle: Should the avatar remain idle for too long, then he will start to perform some kind of action to alleviate boredom, such as blowing down the end of a gun.

Turning: This could be done in code, so that the weapon turns slightly as the character turns.

No Hands

There is a way to remove a lot of the fuss from the required animations for first person—remove the hands. Either the weapon can be dropped low so that the hands can't be seen, or, as in Free Radical's *Timesplitters* series, the hands need not be there at all. Instead the guns seem to float there magically.

This affords several advantages:

Animations removed: The need for many animations is removed and can now be applied as translations in code. The only issue is the reload animation, but this is easily bypassed by dropping the weapon off the screen for the reload time. Firing the weapon is still likely to need a specific animation.

Applies to multiple characters: Having different characters in a game means you will have to have models or skins for the hands for every character. Without hands you remove the need to have this first-person rig for every single character. You can now use the same rig for everyone.

Reduced polys: The reduced number of polys required is a side benefit, but one that will matter less and less as technology improves. Of course, as we strive to immerse the player further in a game world, the lack of hands might start to become a distraction and break the sense of immersion.

No Feet

One problem of a first-person viewpoint is that so far, few developers have bothered to really immerse the player in the eyes of the character—they have no feet. While this is not really a problem, it can be a little odd to look down and see nothing there.

Simple Third Person

The most basic third person method is to have a system that simply fires the weapon in the direction in which the character is facing. This requires no new systems to be set up to perform combat. Instead, a standard animation system can be used.

Animation Requirements

Several animations are necessary for the weapons to function correctly:

Idle: The combat idle shows the character holding the weapon.
Move (creep, walk, run): Separate animations are required from unarmed movement animations, as the character will now be holding a weapon.
Fire weapon: The arms will need to move into position quickly for the weapon to be fired. This will need to be as responsive as possible.
Reload: A reload animation shows the character placing a new clip into the weapon.

Optional extra animations could be used to add character, such as an amusing idle. Should the avatar remain idle for too long, then he will start to perform some kind of action to alleviate boredom, such as spinning a gun in his hand Clint Eastwood style.

Split Body/Partial Animation System

The split body system allows for much more comprehensive third-person aiming to be performed. This splits the upper and lower body at the waist. The legs can be animated separately from the upper body, so the two can do separate things at the same time. The upper body is restricted in its movement but can rotate around the hip and bend the spine back and forth. This allows the character to aim accurately, as the movement of the torso is completely independent.

A split body system would also be needed for first-person games where you would show other characters aiming accurately. If you did not have the split body system, it would not effectively show where characters are currently aiming but would instead show them rigidly pointing ahead.

Partial animation systems would also allow the character to be animated by using combinations of animation, but the partial animation could be applied to one specific part of the body.

Summary

Ranged combat is a feature of many games and has been refined over the years into the "ultimate" ranged genre: the first-person shooter. While ranged combat is perfectly feasible in third person, it is a lot more complex and much more difficult to get right. We covered a number of different topics in this chapter:

Projectile weapons: The basis of most ranged combat is the projectile weapon. This requires the weapon to fire an object toward the target for damage to be caused. We explored many aspects of projectile weaponry:

- **Firing methods:** A projectile weapon is either single shot, automatic, or charge based.
- **Firing modes:** The weapon can be fired in primary fire mode or possibly secondary fire mode. If more than one mode exists, we need a way to switch between the two modes.
- **Ammunition:** There are several aspects of ammunition to consider—the functionality (distinct projectiles, power drain, or recharging), the fire rate, the magazine size, and the reload time.
- **Fire effects:** There are two basic methods to enhance the feel of a projectile weapon—muzzle flash and projectile trails.
- **Flight type:** A projectile will either move in a straight line, scatter, have a trajectory, home in on a target, or be guided by the player.
- **Projectile velocity:** The speed of the projectile is important. Extremely fast projectiles might need to be modeled with a beam weapon system rather than as a standard projectile weapon, or else the collision might pass through the target in a single frame.
- **Accuracy:** A weapon can either have the natural accuracy of the player or be modified during particular actions such as while moving, recoiling, or interacting with an object. Stat-based accuracy may be used to make the accuracy of characters better as they progress through the game or to model AI behavior.
- **Impact methods:** Once a projectile hits a target, it may perform one of several behaviors. It may simply expire, cause an impact area attack, bounce, or even penetrate the surface and come out the other side.
- **Projectile weapon parameters:** A projectile weapon can be described with a number of parameters—weapon strength, damage types, rate of fire, reload time, ammo magazine size, blast radius, fuse time, accuracy, and the status effect applied on hit.

Beam weapons: Beam weapons fire a ray for a certain range from the barrel of the weapon. This ray may also have a radius (which can differ along its length) to determine the width of the beam. It can be used to model laser beams or even flame throwers. Very fast projectiles such as bullets might use a beam system instead of a projectile.

- **Functionality:** While opponents remain in the beam, they will receive damage.

- **Advanced use:** The beam might be used purely for more esoteric functions such as repel and attract or for inflicting a status.
- **Beam weapon parameters:** A beam weapon is described with a number of parameters—weapon strength, damage type, power use, reload time, power source size, range, and status effect that might be inflicted.

Mine weapons: Mine weapons drop an object at a point in the world, which will then cause damage when a trigger is fired.

- **Functionality:** A mine will have a laying technique (thrown, limpet, remote controlled) and have different triggers (proximity, time, or remote detonation).
- **Parameters:** A mine weapon can be described by several parameters—weapon strength, damage type, detection radius, blast radius, fuse time, and status effect that might be inflicted.

Defense against ranged attacks: To build a fair system it is important that there are strategies to defend against ranged attacks. We explored some of these in this chapter:

- **Avoidance:** The simplest defense is to avoid the incoming projectile. This can be achieved easily if the characters are able to strafe. Alternatively, they could evade an incoming projectile.
- **Blocking:** For certain projectiles it may be possible to block the attack, causing the projectile to expire or ricochet out of danger.

Ranged combat animation: A ranged combat system has certain animation requirements to make sure that everything on screen looks and feels right:

- **First person:** A first-person system may require animations if hands and feet are visible. They would need idle, walk, fire weapon, and reload and might benefit from an amusing idle and from turns.
- **Simple third person:** A simple third-person system would require the standard movement set to be mirrored with animations for movement with the weapon.
- **Split body/partial animation system:** A split body system allows different animations to be played on the upper body and the lower body. Partial animations perform a similar function but can be applied to very specific parts of the body.

Ranged combat has reached a point where it is already fairly polished. Certainly, first-person shooters have refined the mechanic to a very high degree. However, there is always room for improvement. Third-person ranged combat has always been tricky, and many implementations have been very hit and miss. We are likely to see more games that blend first-person and third-person elements to get the best of both worlds. New motion-sensing control inputs also have the potential to revolutionize the way ranged combat is performed and may bring whole new levels of interaction to the player.

DAMAGE AND IMPACT

In This Chapter

- The Hit Test
- Damage
- Impacts and Hit Reactions

D
amage is a vital aspect of any game that features combat or trap avoidance. The concept of health in video games is engrained and is a mechanic that every game player will recognize. However, the methods of showing damage and impact in games is constantly evolving and being improved as new techniques are tried.

We will look at several elements of damage and impact in this chapter:

- The hit tcst
- Damage
- Impacts and hit reactions

THE HIT TEST

The hit test determines whether an attack makes contact with a combat entity.

Hit Detection Method

There are several ways to test for hits, depending upon the type of attack being made. Melee combat and ranged combat tend to use different systems, depending upon the speed of a projectile. Fast projectiles would not reliably produce hits using a collision-volume-based system. They require a more finite collision position such as ray casting.

There are two reliable methods of determining an attack hit: attack volumes and deterministic.

Attack Volumes

The attack has an attack volume and uses the collision system to determine if the attack volume has collided with the collision volumes of the target object. Slow projectiles can use this system, but anything of the speed of a bullet would be problematic.

Advantages of this system are:

- Doesn't require a specialized system
- Doesn't require obstruction tests
- Allows interaction with the environment without adding any extra layers to the system
- Describes any type of attack

The disadvantages are:

- Fast attacks may miss because of collision frame issues (the attack moves so fast that it moves through the whole object in a frame).
- It can cause unwanted hits to enemies surrounding the attack (where the collision volume just touches an enemy on the backswing for example).

The attack volumes describe the shape that the attack forms. Two main parameters describe the volume and its behavior:

Hit frequency: The frequency at which a hit message is issued after the first hit has been registered. This could be used to hit multiple times during one move but is generally set to only hit once.

Volume type: The shape of the volume. This will generally be one of the following: sphere, cylinder, cone, cube, or torus.

Attacks can be split into several types:

- Melee attacks
- Projectile attacks
- Area attacks

Melee Attacks

Melee attacks are any combat where the physical weapon must collide with the target in order to cause a hit. They are generally the physical weapon itself. In these instances the attack volume will be formed from the weapon or from a simplified outline of the weapon. When using an outline of the collision, the weapon can be attached to a locator to enable it to move with the animation, or it could be physically built into the model.

If collision was turned on permanently, it would look very odd for the character to walk into an opponent with a sword, only for the opponent to get knocked back several feet. The timing of attack volumes needs to be controlled so that characters are only actually attacking when an attack animation is being played. This is achieved by setting up the strike windows for the attack. These windows might be based on time values set in data or might be embedded within the animation time line and exported as specific events. Having the events in the animation allows for accuracy, but for flexibility it is much quicker to have the timing separate and designer adjustable (otherwise the animation will more than likely have to go through a build or export process each time a change is made).

Projectile Attacks

Projectile attacks are used with any weapon that is used at range, where the projectile must hit the target to cause damage. The volume is best kept to spheres to keep collision calculations to a minimum, but cylinders are also useful shapes for projectiles.

Projectiles send an object with a certain collision volume toward the target. Its flight could be done in any number of ways such as a direct line, a trajectory, or homing (see the previous chapter for a more in-depth look at flight paths).

Area Attacks

Area attacks are not necessarily attached to a weapon but can be placed anywhere in the environment. They can be used for explosions, which might be started as the result of a projectile hitting an object (e.g., a rocket hitting a wall and exploding) or beam weaponry such as flamethrowers or a beam laser. Alternatively, they could represent steam blasts or any other environmental hazard.

The volume could take on any shape the designer wanted: cylinder, cube, torus, sphere, and so on. For example, imagine the player could cast a wall of fire around himself. This could be done with a torus primitive.

An area attack will have several parameters:

Scaling: The ability to scale a volume allows the designer to produce a variety of different effects, such as using a scaling cone to represent a flamethrower.

Fall-off: With an area attack it is feasible to have fall-off to make damage at range less than damage for a character caught in the middle. Fall-off would create different damage away from the center of the volume, which could be controlled in many ways—linear, curve, inversely squared, or whatever else fits.

Secondary area: A more simplistic method of achieving fall-off is to use two attack volumes for an attack. The inner volume is the main damage, and the outer volume is the fall-off damage.

Deterministic

The attack hit is calculated by testing with ray casting and/or positions within a volume. Projectile or beam attacks can use a single ray to detect the hit. Melee attacks would use a more complex system to test whether the character is in range during an attack.

Advantages of this method are that:

- It provides guaranteed connection of a hit.
- It allows strikes to be timed perfectly with the animation.
- Ray casting can allow for accurate hit location information.
- Attack will only hit the desired enemies.

The disadvantages are that:

- Being separate from the general collision means that the weapon cannot easily interact with environment (e.g., smashing objects in the environment).
- It requires extra calculations and a tailor-made system that is separate from the basic collision system.

Instead of using the collision system alone to detect a hit, the deterministic method uses more accurate and reliable methods of determining a hit. The exact methods used depend on the desired type of attack.

Ranged Attacks

The simplest method is used for fast ranged attacks. This is the only reliable method of performing ballistic attacks where the projectile hits the target almost instantaneously. Essentially the system casts a ray toward the direction of fire. If this ray hits anything in the environment or hits an object, then that ray is terminated. If the hit is against a combat entity, damage is applied (hitting the environment might produce other effects such as decals and an audio effect).

Melee Attacks

Melee attacks are slightly more complex, as enemies must be tested against a volume to see if they are in range. A cone projected from the facing of the player determines where this range is. If an enemy is inside this volume when an attack strike is made then he is said to be hit by the attack. Each attack would have its own range volume, so that a sweeping attack might have a much wider angle than a vertical slash attack.

The system must also check that there are no obstructions between the target and the attacker. Thus, a ray must be cast to ensure that no obstruction exists before the attack is determined a success.

Hybrid

A combination of methods might be used to simulate different weapons, so a sword might use an attack volume system, whereas a gun might use deterministic ray casting. To get round the problem of environment interaction for a deterministic system, the two systems can be used in parallel for melee attacks, so that a collision volume on the weapons allows environment interaction, and a deterministic system is used to calculate the hit on an enemy.

Target Collision Types

Collision can be a very complex part of the gaming system, and getting it right is imperative. While designers do not need to know the intricacies of collision algorithms, they do need to know what the resultant collision's limitations are. Each entity will have some sort of collision volume, or possibly a whole host of different collision volumes that are used for different aspects of the system. Different attacks will require different levels of fidelity.

There are several main types of collision volume:

Collision sphere: The simplest and lowest fidelity
Hemispheres: A higher fidelity version of the collision sphere, which breaks the sphere into separate areas
Collision trees: A collection of spheres or other shapes at a much higher level of fidelity
Collision mesh: A complex mesh that is usually only used on static elements in the environment but could be used for dynamic object collision as computing power increases

Melee attacks do not require as high a level of precision as ranged attacks and thus do not need to use more complex systems. Most melee systems can get away with using a few hemispheres.

The Collision Sphere

Because of the processing time required to calculate collisions, the collision sphere is often used as the most basic collision mesh, generally for collision between the entity and the environment. A sphere only has one required value: the radius.

A slightly improved version of this is an ellipsoid—a stretched sphere that has two values of measurement. Alternatively, a capsule can be created, which is two smaller spheres linked by a cylinder whose radius matches the spheres at either end. The three methods are shown in Figure 10.1.

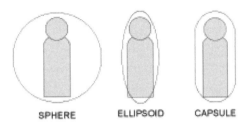

SPHERE   ELLIPSOID   CAPSULE

FIGURE 10.1 Different basic collision modeling methods for a character.

This kind of collision is very basic, as it often includes a lot of null space. If you were to shoot between the legs of a character that used a sphere for attack collision, it will still be classed as a hit. This problem is much more noticeable on larger creatures or during projectile-based combat (particularly in the first-person viewpoint where weapons can be accurately aimed).

Simple sphere collision is used mainly for melee combat, where the fidelity of attack required is far less that that of projectile combat.

Hemispheres

The sphere (or similar object) can also be split into hemispheres to allow a finer level of hit detection:

Front and back hemispheres: Front and back are perhaps the most useful distinctions, since they allow the system to play different animations for receiving a blow to the front and to the back. Assigning different vulnerabilities to hemispheres allows for some interesting combat strategies. For example, if a monster was only vulnerable in the back hemisphere, the player would have to maneuver himself behind the creature to attack.

Upper and lower hemispheres: Upper and lower are useful distinctions if you have high and low attacks. Separating between the two allows you to have low attack moves or high attacks. Low attacks could knock the opponent to the floor, for example.

Left and right hemispheres: Perhaps the least immediately useful of the categories, this would allow you to determine whether a sideways blow had been dealt and thus perform a side-hit animation. By combining all of these hemispheres into an attack's reaction, you can create a fairly detailed picture of where the attack struck, for example, front upper left. This allows a more detailed level of hit reaction to be produced from a successful attack.

Collision Trees

Collision trees can be used for more complex interactions that require higher fidelity, such as determining if a small ranged projectile attack (e.g., a bullet) hit a character. These are a network of volumes connected to the model's skeleton that roughly describe the shape of that object. They obviously require more calculations than single volumes but boast useful benefits:

- The body can be separated into different parts.
- Collisions with null space are much less of a problem.

Sphere Trees

Using a collection of spheres is the most efficient solution. However, it is difficult to describe square or long thin shapes easily.

Bounding Boxes

Boxes can be used to define a shape in much the same manner as sphere trees. They are particularly useful for defining angular, long, and thin shapes, but they require a good deal more calculation to determine a collision.

Mixed-Volume Trees

To get the most efficient yet accurate collision tree it may be helpful to use a mixture of collision shapes. This allows a good description of a shape and maximizes the fidelity without compromising speed.

Body Zones

Body zones separate the collision mesh into sections that can have different reactions to hits. This allows specific animations to be played when hits in particular areas occur.

The body zoning of a human might include:

- Head
- Torso
- Left arm
- Right arm
- Left leg
- Right leg

Each of these body parts could have a separate hit reaction animation to be played when hit in that area. Such a system requires a lot of animation if there are many different types of enemy, unless they all share the same base skeleton for their animation.

Complex Collision Meshes

It is highly likely that in the future more and more complex collisions will begin to be calculated as the power of the technology increases the amount of raw processing that can be done each frame. This will allow for far better modeling of complex collision interactions between objects in the world. However, at present, complex collision mesh collision on dynamic objects is extremely expensive and is therefore not used for determining attack hits.

Vulnerability

When a character is hit, it must be determined whether that character is vulnerable at that particular moment in time. Each animation can have different vulnerabilities for each character. By assigning a vulnerability to a specific volume during an animation or part of an animation, a complex system is very quickly created.

When a successful collision is detected, that volume needs to be tested to see what state of vulnerability is currently applied. There are many states that a designer could apply here. The following are some examples of vulnerability types that could be applied to each collision volume:

Vulnerable: The character will be susceptible to all forms of attack and will be knocked back for the full hit strength of the attack.

Invulnerable: The character is immune to all forms of attack in this volume.

Damage only: The character is immune to being knocked back altogether. The hit could be displayed by flashing the character red if you want to show that a hit is actually causing damage, even if the character does not seem to react to that hit.

Hit reaction only: The character is immune to all damage but performs hit reactions as normal. This would make the character invulnerable in this zone but could be used to slow the character's progress or knock him back away from the player for a moment.

Blocking: The character is immune to all standard attacks in blocking mode, though he may receive guard damage (blocking sound and particle effects will be applied). Block-breaking attacks will break a defender out of this state.

Melee invulnerable: The character is immune to all melee attacks but still vulnerable to projectile attacks.

Projectile invulnerable: The character is immune to all projectile attacks but is still vulnerable to melee attacks.

Melee no-hit reaction: The character will not be knocked back by melee attacks but will still receive damage. Projectile attacks are as normal. Again you might want to flash the character red or emphasize the hit effects to show the player that a hit has occurred.

Projectile no-hit reaction: The character will not be knocked back by projectile attacks but will still receive damage. Melee attacks are as normal. Again you might want to flash the character red or emphasize the hit effects to show the player that a hit has occurred.

Weak spots: The collision mesh itself can be used to determine vulnerability. Every individual sphere could theoretically be assigned a different vulnerability value. Perhaps more useful is the fact that particular spheres can be flagged as vulnerable, allowing the designer more design possibilities. When creating weak spots, it is important to visually reinforce that these sections are vulnerable. Design them to look particularly distinctive. If a giant dragon is only vulnerable on its underbelly, then make that underbelly look particularly soft and squishy in comparison to the armor-plated scales that cover the rest of it.

DAMAGE

Damage is an essential part of the combat system and can be a fairly complex system to design. It is essential that you get the system right to make a good combat system feel great.

Damage Calculation

The damage calculation can be pretty much whatever you want it to be, but there are a number of solid methods already used that can be applied to your combat system.

Damage Methods

There are several methods of attributing damage to characters or objects.

Set Damage

Damage can produce a set amount with every hit. This can be very basic and be one value for every successful hit. Alternatively, each different type of attack could have a set damage value. This simple damage system is generally used in games in which the combat is fairly simple, such as a platformer. Here the cause and effect of every collision is clearly defined and thus is obvious to the player.

Variable Damage

More complex damage systems vary the amount of damage with every hit. There are many ways of approaching this, but the following are good examples of existing systems.

Melee Move Damage: Melee move damage is calculated from the weapon strength, the strength of the attacking character, and the current damage multiplier for the move performed. The damage multiplier allows damage to be increased for later moves in a combo. This can be expressed as:

$$D = d(W + S)$$

(10.1)

where:

D = damage inflicted
W = weapon strength
S = character strength
d = damage multiplier

Melee Damage Curve: Damage can vary according to the time that a button is pressed during the strike window, so that pressing the attack button to make the collision occur at precisely the right time will cause maximum damage. To make this system work, a curve is used to describe the damage over the course of the strike window (see Figure 10.2).

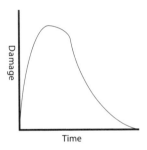

FIGURE 10.2   An example melee damage curve.

Critical Hit: A critical hit is a chance that a blow will inflict a multiplied amount of damage to a target. It is generally the preserve of the RPG. A critical hit has a certain probability of occurrence, which is based on a number of factors:

- **Character attributes:** Chance of critical hit increases with luck, strength, or dexterity.
- **Weapon:** The current weapon the character is wielding may have different critical hit chances.
- **Status effects:** Magic or status effects the character is currently afflicted by can affect the chance of a critical hit.
- **Apparel:** This includes additional items the character is holding such as an amulet that specifically boosts critical hit or a relevant character skill.

The result of a critical hit is a multiplied damage score. This multiplier could also be manipulated by certain factors but is generally best kept uniform to avoid confusion. A good multiplier to use is double the standard hit damage.

Projectile Damage: Projectile damage is generally calculated purely from the strength of the weapon.

Random Damage: Random damage is added to the standard melee or projectile damage after all other damage calculations have been made. A random damage value in a certain range is calculated on a per-weapon or per-move basis. This is often useful in RPGs to add an element of luck. Luck or skill could be used to increase this random range to show that the character is becoming luckier or more skillful.

Reducing Health by Damage

A simple calculation is performed to reduce the health by the amount of damage that has been inflicted:

$$H = h - D \qquad (10.2)$$

where:

H = new health
h = old health
D = damage inflicted

Two outcomes are possible from this calculation:

Health > 0: Character has been damaged but has health remaining. The victim is then checked for hit reaction.
Health ≤ 0: Character is dead.

Types of Damage

Damage can be separated into many different types. This allows the designer to introduce more complex rules to determine what kind of attack will be successful against an opponent. There is no limit to the different types of damage a designer could create, but there are well-used types of damage that can be employed.

Physical Damage

Physical damage is any kind of damage caused when one object hits another. This could be split further into subgroups:

Slice: Any sharp-edged weapon such as a sword causes slicing damage when used in its intended fashion. This cuts through clothing and flesh with ease but would struggle with tougher materials.
Impact: This is simple bashing damage. Any quick impact attack causes this damage. This bruises and cracks bones and dents and buckles weak armor.
Pierce: Thrusting sharp pointed objects at a target causes piercing damage. Piercing attacks affect a small area but puncture through any material not designed to defend against this form of attack. Bullets are a form of piercing attack.
Crush: Sustained pressure on an object would be considered crush damage. This causes severe damage to any object not strong enough to stop the crushing effect. This would usually be some kind of environment feature such as closing walls rather than a type of weapon.

Explosion: This is essentially an extreme form of impact damage, though it might include fire-based damage also. This would be kept separate from impact damage so that a different hit effect could be used.

Elemental Damage

Elemental damage refers to any attack that causes damage without two objects colliding. Instead, damage is cause by burning, freezing, or any number of other methods. This kind of damage might be standard environmental or magical damage depending on what kind of game you are creating.

Environmental Damage

Environmental damage is based on naturally occurring hazards in the environment. These hazards can cause various afflictions to the player and may require specific protection to be circumvented.

Flame: Any flame will cause burning on unfortunate characters who are not resistant to it. A video game convention is for the character to be ignited and continue receiving damage for a period of time after the initial hit. This may even be indefinite ignition until the player can find a source of water to douse the flames.

Electricity: This shocking hazard will zap any unfortunate person without adequate protection. Electricity also tends to make a deadly combination with water.

Toxics: Poisonous or toxic hazards such as the ubiquitous glowing green goop must be avoided with some kind of protection. Poison usually causes the player character to continue taking damage after being hit. This may continue for a set time or may require a specific antidote to be remedied.

Steam: Steam has the ability to nastily scald a character. Often damage is fairly minor where steam occurs, and there's usually a handy valve somewhere nearby to shut off the flow.

Lava: Lava is a bit of a gaming cliché (along with ice levels) but can make an interesting environmental hazard. It might induce burning like the standard flame attack or maybe even instant death.

Magical Damage

Magical damage is a stalwart of the RPG genre. These magical attacks often take on elemental damage—manifestations of real-world phenomena in magical form. Often these elements have interactive relationships, for example, fire beats ice, ice beats water, water beats fire, and so on. You could use any element that you wanted here, but there are some popular choices you might use:

Fire: Burns victims like standard flame

Ice: Freezes victims with intense cold

Water: Uses the power of water to cause damage

Wind and Air: Uses the power of wind or the air to cause damage
Lightning: Uses powerful blasts of electricity to damage a foe
Spirit: Uses ethereal energy to drain the life from a victim

Status Effects

Status effects don't cause damage directly but instead afflict the victim in some manner. This may have a positive or a negative effect on the victim. It is a good idea to limit the duration of a status and provide objects or spells that can cure status effects, so that the effects can be reversed.

Positive Statuses

A positive status has beneficial effects on the affected character. This could be almost anything you like, from health regeneration to increased visibility. Some examples of popular positive statuses are:

Boost: Increases the damage the affected can deal
Haste: Increases the speed of the affected
Protect: Decreases the damage the affected receives
Regenerate: Adds a portion of health every few seconds or so
Lighten: Increases the affected character's visibility

Negative Statuses

Negative statuses have detrimental effects on the affected character and could again be anything you like. It makes sense to have a negative for every positive. Some effectively opposite statuses are:

Weaken: Reduces the damage the affected character can deal
Slow: Reduces the speed of the affected character
Curse: Increases the damage the affected character receives
Poison: Removes a portion of health every few seconds or so
Darken: Decreases the affected character's visibility.

Temporal Statuses

Temporal statuses are ephemeral statuses that last a short time but have a severe effect. Most statuses tend to apply to RPG-style games, but temporal statuses could apply to any action game.

Blinded: The character cannot see for a time because of a blinding light (e.g., Flashbang Grenade). Usually the screen is turned completely white for a period of time to indicate this.
Deafened: The character is deafened for a short time because of loud noise (e.g., Flashbang Grenade). A high-pitch whistle and the removal of other sound is a great way to relay this information to the player.

Stunned: The character is vulnerable for a short period and cannot move. Could be shown with stars around the character's head for comedic effect.

Petrified or Frozen: The character is turned to stone or frozen and cannot move until unpetrified or unfrozen or the effect wears off.

Damage Zones

Damage zones split a character into different areas. These areas can take different amounts of damage and react to hits in different ways. The body could be split up in any manner the designer wanted, but there are several standard methods:

- Head and body
- Head, upper body, and lower body
- Head, torso, left arm, right arm, left leg, and right leg
- Head, torso, upper-left arm, upper-right arm, lower-left arm, lower-right arm, upper-left leg, upper-right leg, lower-left leg, and lower-right leg

What is done with all these zones? Well, the lesser parts could mainly be used to create different reactions to being hit. Being hit in the arm would produce a different animation and reaction than getting hit in the head. As technology improves, more and more body parts could be split into zones, but animations and reactions are going to have to be made for all these new zones, so the amount of time and work required to do this will increase significantly. Hit reactions could be done procedurally on a single body zone, so this extra work may be less of an issue.

The amount of damage inflicted can be adjusted according to where the blow lands. For instance, head shots could be particularly devastating. Each body part would have a damage modifier.

Damage zones are best utilized in shooting games, where individual parts of the body can be targeted easily. In many games this level of detail is unnecessary and can often cloud the game mechanics, so only use a damage zone system where needed.

Damage Modifiers

Damage modifiers alter the amount of damage received by a target. These modifiers are based on factors involving either the attack or the target.

Resistance and Armor

Natural resistance or armor can restrict the amount of damage a target receives.

General Resistance and Armor

The simplest method is for armor or resistance to reduce all damage by a set amount. This will be a simple modifier between 0 and 1, 0 being complete resistance and 1 being none at all. The effect on damage can be calculated as

$$D = A(d(W + S))$$ (10.3)

where:

D = damage inflicted
W = weapon strength
S = character strength
d = damage multiplier
C = critical hit modifier
A = target's armor or resistance modifier

Type-Specific Resistance and Armor

Resistance to certain types of damage means that more complex combat situations can be set up. Armor could have different resistance values for each type of damage or be restricted to one, depending on how complex a designer wants to make the combat system (RPGs would suit this level of depth, but an action game might not). Resistance and armor could be spilt into different styles:

Resistant: Has modifier to damage type between 0 and 1.
Immune: Is immune to damage type; modifier equals 0.
Engorging: Is empowered by damage type; modifier less than 0.

Let's say, for example, that we have a suit of armor called Dragon's Bane. It is resistant to physical attacks, susceptible to lightning, and gains strength from fire attacks (see Table 10.1).

TABLE 10.1   Dragon's Bane Damage Modifiers

DAMAGE TYPE	MODIFIER
Pierce	0.5
Cut	0.5
Impact	0.5
Crush	0.5
Lightning	1
Fire	−1

The resulting damage calculation looks like this:

$$D_f = A_f(d(W + S))$$ (10.4)

where:

D_f = fire damage inflicted
W = weapon strength

S = character strength
d = damage multiplier
A_f = target's armor modifier for fire damage

Attack Damage

As discussed earlier, the damage inflicted by an attack may vary from a set figure according to a number of factors. These can be factored into the damage calculation.

Random Damage

We might want each attack to cause a random amount of extra damage. We can achieve this by giving damage a range from which a random number is generated rather than a fixed value. This could be added on top of the standard damage amount for the chosen weapon.

Critical Hits

These are hits that are assumed to hit harder and deeper than normal. For this system we would need to implement two variables:

Critical hit chance: The chance of a critical hit happening, probably best implemented as a percentage or value between 0 and 1.

Critical damage modifier: The multiplier to apply to the damage when a critical hit occurs. A fumble could also be added to this, so that a weaker attack is made. A fumble chance and modifier would be needed.

Our damage calculation is now getting quite complex:

$$D = A\{C[d(W + S) + R]\} \tag{10.5}$$

where:

D = damage inflicted
W = weapon strength
S = character strength
R = random number (for variable damage)
d = damage multiplier
C = critical hit multiplier
A = target's armor or resistance modifier

Body Zones

A body zone, as described above, may affect the amount of damage a target receives. Arms and legs receive significantly less damage than the head.

Status Effects

Some status effects could affect the damage calculation. We use the following set of terms for these modifiers, but they could be anything else that makes sense. Two modifiers affect the attacker's damage:

Boost: Increases the attacker's damage amount: modifier greater than 1
Weaken: Decreases the attacker's damage amount: modifier less than 1 (negative modifiers would heal the opponent rather than harm)

The other two modifiers affect the target's resistance:

Protect: Decreases the damage received by the target: modifier less than 1
Curse: Increases the amount of damage received by the target: modifier greater than 1

Our melee damage calculation is even more complex now:

$$D = r(A(M(C(d(W + S) + R))))$$ (10.6)

where:

D = damage inflicted
W = weapon strength
S = character strength
R = random number (for variable damage)
d = damage multiplier
C = critical hit multiplier
A = target's armor or resistance modifier
M = attacker's damage modifier (for status effect)
r = target's resistance

This complex combat damage calculation is probably way more than is needed for the average game. Keep it simple. If you don't need this kind of detail, then don't use it.

IMPACTS AND HIT REACTIONS

It is important to feed information back to the player whenever a hit is made—to give audio and visual feedback about the actions happening in the game world.

Hit Effects

Every attack made against an enemy, or any blow that hits another object in the environment, will produce a hit effect of some kind. This hit effect takes the form of audio and a visual special effect. It might also include a decal—an effect pasted onto a surface to represent a hit, such as a bullet hole in a wall.

Impact Effects

When an attack or defense is made, it is a good idea to give visual feedback to the player about what is occurring. Visual feedback is provided by playing an attack-type hit effect at the point of impact. Giving different looks to each of these types allows the player to distinguish exactly what has occurred. For example, we might use:

Red: Successful hit (can look like blood, which some audiences may be sensitive to)
Blue: Blocked hit
Green: Counter
Yellow: Grab
White: Parry

Another way of emphasizing an impact is to use a weak dynamic light. This uses a point light placed at the point of collision, which will subtly illuminate the characters.

Material Hit-Effect Matrix

The material hit-effect matrix is a table of data that determines what hit effect will play when an attack collision occurs between two surfaces. Every surface and entity in the game world is assigned a material, so that when it is collided with, the appropriate effect can be produced. Many different types of material may be used in the game, and each of these needs to be assigned to the surface of a level or object via some world-editing tool or the modeling package in which it was created.

Cross-referencing each material against the hit-effect matrix results in a particular combination of effects being played, an example of which is shown in Table 10.2.

TABLE 10.2 Example Hit-Effect Matrix

	FLESH	STONE	WOOD	METAL
Flesh	Dull thud	Fleshy thud	Dull thud	Blood spray
Stone	Fleshy thud	Dust	Splinters	Sparks
Wood	Dull thud	Splinters	Clack	Splinters
Metal	Blood spray	Sparks	Splinters	Sparks

In addition, different types of damage will produce different hit effects on contact with various materials, so there may be a different hit-effect matrix for each type of attack.

Hit Reactions

Hit reactions are animations that show the impact of a blow. These animations are played as soon as the character is hit. This interrupts the player's current action. Hit-reaction systems are great for use in melee-based combat.

Hit-Reaction Strength

The strength of a hit reaction determines how far the character will be flung when hit. This is shown in Table 10.3.

TABLE 10.3   Hit-Reaction Strength

HIT-REACTION STRENGTH	DESCRIPTION
Weak	Character flinches
Medium	Character buckles back a little
Strong	Character moves back a good distance
KO	Character is knocked to the floor
Mega	Character is knocked to the floor a long way back
Up	Character pops up into the air

Hit-Reaction Direction

The hemisphere system for collision allows us to detect whether a hit is coming from the front or back of a character. Thus, we can make a hit look appropriate to the attack by playing a front hit reaction or a rear hit reaction. Each character will therefore have a front and rear animation for each hit-reaction strength:

- Hit Front Weak, Hit Rear Weak
- Hit Front Medium, Hit Rear Medium
- Hit Front Strong, Hit Rear Strong
- Hit Front Over, Hit Rear Over
- Hit Front Mega, Hit Rear Mega
- Hit Front Up, Hit Rear Up

This system could be extended further to include hits from the side, but front and back tend to be adequate for most hit reaction systems.

Low Hit Reactions

If a character is hit with a low attack, we can play different animations than for a high attack. These low attacks could also be given different strengths, though it is unlikely you'd want to have the same level of detail as a standard knock back. A low hit would probably also require front and rear animations:

- Hit Front Low Weak, Hit Rear Low Weak
- Hit Front Low Over, Hit Low Over

Air Hit Reactions

A hit with an uppercut is likely to cause a character to be knocked into the air. When in the air, air hit reactions could be used. These could allow juggling moves to be performed by repeatedly hitting an opponent up into the air (as shown in Table 10.4).

TABLE 10.4   Air Hit-Reaction Strengths

KNOCK-UP STRENGTH	DESCRIPTION
Weak	Knocks up only slightly (usually breaks a juggle)
Medium	Knocks up standard amount
Strong	Knocks up a large amount
Level	Knocks away rather than up (usually breaks a juggle)

Thus, for air hit reactions we would have:

- Hit Front Air Weak, Hit Rear Air Weak
- Hit Front Air Medium, Hit Rear Air Medium
- Hit Front Air Strong, Hit Rear Air Strong
- Hit Front Air Level, Hit Rear Air Level

Block Hit Reactions

A block hit reaction is a visual extra to reinforce that a hit has been made but blocked by the opponent. It would allow different animations to be played according to the strength of the hit. It could be done in a simpler manner by simply moving the character back a little when hit.

A block would probably only be made from the front, leaving the rear vulnerable (though you might want to do all-around blocking for ease of play). Thus for block hit reactions we would have:

- Hit Front Block Weak
- Hit Front Block Medium
- Hit Front Block Strong

Melee Attacks and Hit Reaction Synchronization

An important consideration in a melee fighting game in which you intend to use combo moves is to ensure that hit reactions are synchronized with attacks. The distance and timing for each attack needs to lead into the next move. There are two important points to consider here:

Distance: The weapon must be able to reach the target. The forward motion of the attack animation must match the backward motion of the hit reaction.

Time: The target must still be in the hit reaction animation when the second attack hits, or else the target may be able to hit the attacker before he can finish his attack (though this may be deliberate if the opponent is supposed to be a very fast and agile character).

This synchronization allows combos to be performed without the player character being knocked out of the sequence or missing the enemy, which can be extremely frustrating.

Advanced Hit-Reaction System

Our standard hit-reaction system would apply a hit reaction to each individual attack, meaning that no matter what size or type of enemy you were to hit, it would produce the same amount of hit reaction. This might look a little strange if we were to hit a creature twice the size as another and get the same results.

To add more depth to this system, we could affect the amount of hit reaction based on the mass of the character. To do this we need two new variables:

Attack strength: This is a measure of how powerful an attack might be. Each attack would be assigned an attack strength. A useful range for this would be 1–10.

Mass group: We could try to incorporate a very accurate mass scale here, but the simplest solution is to split all characters into a number of mass groups. A useful range for this would be 1–5.

With these variables we can produce a look-up table for each type of hit reaction, so now the same attack can produce different amounts of knock back. An example of this is shown in Table 10.5.

TABLE 10.5 Example of an Advanced, Mass-Based Hit-Reaction System

	MASS(1)	MASS(2)	MASS(3)	MASS(4)	MASS(5)
Attack(1)	Weak	Weak	None	None	None
Attack(2)	Weak	Weak	Weak	None	None
Attack(3)	Weak	Weak	Weak	Weak	None
Attack(4)	Medium	Weak	Weak	Weak	Weak
Attack(5)	Medium	Medium	Weak	Weak	Weak
Attack(6)	Strong	Medium	Medium	Weak	Weak
Attack(7)	Strong	Strong	Medium	Medium	Weak
Attack(8)	Over	Strong	Strong	Medium	Medium
Attack(9)	Over	Over	Strong	Strong	Medium
Attack(10)	Mega	Over	Over	Strong	Strong

We could also play with this system further and make attack strength dynamic. For example, we could have a critical hit affect the attack strength as well as inflict damage.

Hit Reaction Issues

There is one major problem with the described hit reaction system, in that the animations are designed with a flat surface in mind. To make it easy to implement the system, it is therefore best if all combat occurs on a flat surface. This is obviously going to have major implications on how levels are designed. How do you contain combat in specific areas? Do you lock the player in or do you simply not let enemies move into uneven ground? There are ways around this.

One solution is to simply rotate a grounded character to face the surface normal, but on uneven territory this could make the character clip through the floor or appear to half float in the air. Alternatively, separate landing poses and animations could be constructed for a range of likely positions, and the character could be blended into these poses when the situation is met. For example, if the player were to hit a wall during a hit reaction, he could be switched to a wall-hit animation and slump to the ground. Matching situations accurately can be a difficult task, and this may cause as many problems as it solves.

Hit Recovery

When hit and knocked into a hit reaction, the player is left with no control. However, a combat system can be imbued with an element of player control by allowing hit recovery.

Wriggle

Wriggle is the art of hitting buttons or wiggling the direction stick to allow the character to exit a hit reaction more quickly. The faster the wriggle, the shorter the hit reaction play time, up to a certain threshold. This will cut short a stagger hit reaction but would not make sense for a KO reaction. In this instance wriggle will allow the character to spend less time on the floor and rise faster.

Instant Recovery

During a KO a small window for hitting a specific button press may allow the player to instantly recover and immediately rise. This may warrant a more impressive rise animation, indicating to the player that his skilful timing paid off. Imagine, for example, characters flipping themselves up with their legs instead of a normal rise using their hands.

Body-Zone Animations

Body zones allow the use of specific animations in relation to a hit on a particular area.

Impacts

An alternative to the hit reaction, and one that would generally only be used in FPSs, is an animation according to body zone, where the body-zone hit will influence the animation that plays. Thus, we could divide a simple zombie character up into zones as shown in Table 10.6.

TABLE 10.6   Animations for Body Zones on a Zombie Character

BODY ZONE	ANIMATION
Head	Head removed and death
Torso	Knocked back a touch
Arms	Arm flinches
Legs	Stumbles on hit leg

A human might have some longer animations such as grabbing the wounded area for a moment before continuing. The animations used are only limited by your imagination.

We could split the body further and have some really detailed animations for a hit, but we need to be careful that these body hit animations are not overused. Generally only high-damage hits should register, and a cooldown period should be executed before another animation is played to avoid characters jerking around from repeated playing of the same animation over and over when they are hit.

Gore

We could go further with body zones and become quite gruesome. By implementing the ability to remove parts of the body, we can have some truly disturbing violence. Generally it is best to only remove body parts when a character will actually be killed. Arms are the easiest to remove and still have the character moving about with no problems, but when you remove the legs, you are going to need a whole new system of movement. This is, of course, perfectly possible, but needs to be remembered when implementing a gore system.

Ragdoll Physics

Ragdoll characters have been a bit of a buzzword in recent years. However, until recently they have been very limited in what they can do. Most ragdolls in games are only switched on when the characters die because if they were still alive they would have to get back up. A ragdoll is unpredictable, meaning the body can land in almost any position. This means there is no easy way for the characters to move themselves in a natural-looking manner to get back up. More than likely, in attempting to move a limb from under himself, the character would intersect with his own body or perform a movement that is physically impossible for a human.

Recent strides in physics middleware are coming up with solutions to these problems. Now ragdolls can be used for hit reactions, as the models move under physics but with a number of constraints that move the body into target poses that allow the playing of animations that look right to get back up. Another technique is to ragdoll only a small section of the body, such as an arm. This means it can be incorporated into a standard hit animation but will look far more dynamic, as it is controlled by physics.

The technology keeps improving, and we will probably see more and more exciting ways of expressing physics-based hits in the years to come.

SUMMARY

Combat relies on detecting a hit on an opponent and applying damage. However, we must give feedback to the players of any impact made in the game. Otherwise, they will not know that a hit has occurred. We examined several aspects of damage and impact in of this chapter:

The hit test: One vital aspect of showing impact is determining the hit in the first place.

- **Hit detection:** There are two methods of testing for a hit—collision-based attack volumes and the deterministic method. Attack volumes don't require a specialized system or obstruction tests and allow interaction with the environment without any extra functionality. They can also describe any type of attack. However, they have a collision problem where the attack might go through a target in a single frame, and they may also produce unwanted hits on nearby entities. The deterministic method guarantees connection of a hit and allows the strike to be perfectly timed with the animation. Ray casts can allow accurate hit location information, and the attack will only hit the desired characters. This is a separate system from collisions and requires an extra system to be built. However, a hybrid system might be used to harness the advantages of both.
- **Target collision types:** The target's collision may be formed from a collision sphere, a number of hemispheres, collision trees, or possibly even collision meshes.
- **Vulnerability:** A target's level of vulnerability can be set to one of several values.

Damage: The process of inflicting damage can be very simple or can be made pretty complex, depending on the scope of the combat system and the type of game you want to create. RPGs tend to have fairly complex damage systems, whereas basic arcade games are very simple.

- **Damage calculation:** Damage may be calculated as either set or variable.

- **Types of damage:** Several types of damage might be used—physical damage (slice, impact, pierce, crush, explosion), elemental (environment or magical), or status effects.
- **Damage zones:** The character may be split into a number of different zones that will receive different amounts of damage.
- **Damage modifiers:** A number of modifiers may be applied to increase or decrease damage, such as resistance and armor, attack damage (random or critical hits), body zones, or status effects that modify damage.

Impacts and hit reactions: Once a hit has been made and damage applied, we need to provide some feedback to the player. This is performed through impacts and hit reactions. We explored several aspects in this chapter:

- **Hit effects:** Several hit effects might be applied—impact effects or material-type effects based on a hit-effect matrix.
- **Hit reactions:** Hit reactions have a certain strength and a direction and may be a standard, low, air, or block reactions. Melee attacks and hit reactions need to be synchronized to make combos possible. We also looked at a slightly more advanced hit-reaction system based on mass.
- **Hit recovery:** There are ways to recover from a hit—via wriggle or instant recovery, which require the player to press buttons at the correct moment.
- **Body zone animation:** Hit reactions can be localized to particular body zones and animations played specific to those impacts. We may even include gore, where a body part can be damaged or removed.
- **Ragdoll physics:** Ragdolls are often used to make reactions look more impressive, but they do have potential proplems.

Damage and impact are key to successful combat systems, as good feedback to the player will ensure that the combat system as a whole feels much more believable. More impressive effects and new technology will only serve to improve the visceral element of combat and make the combat in games even more believable in the future.

ECONOMIES

In This Chapter

- Character Economies
- Progression
- Wealth
- Inventory
- Rating
- Time
- Lives and Saves

Economies are to be found in many places in a game, even though at first glance it may be difficult to recognize them. Economic conflict will take some form within the game world, whether it is as simple as health during combat or as complex as an intricately modeled supply and demand economy.

Adding economic elements to a game can add a great deal of extra gameplay or interest for a player, with relatively little extra cost other than balancing and playtesting. Therefore, it might be wise to look at your game design and see where suitable economic elements might fit in without changing the entire feel of the game or detracting from its core functionality.

The following aspects of game economies will be explored in this chapter:

- Character economies
- Progression
- Wealth
- Inventory
- Rating
- Time
- Lives and saves

CHARACTER ECONOMIES

A character in a game is defined by certain attributes and skills. These can be predefined by the designers, or may be created by the player.

Attributes

Attributes, or "stats", are a measure of a character's abilities in a number of fields. These attributes can be radically different from game to game. A simple action game might need as little as character strength and health. Complex RPGs are more likely to have a lot more attributes.

There are two basic classes of attributes: static and dynamic. Static attributes remain fixed (unless affected by a modifier or permanently increased). Dynamic attributes have a fixed maximum value, but the actual value of the attribute fluctuates regularly.

Some typical attributes used in games (though they may appear under different guises according to the game's setting) are:

Strength (static): How physically powerful an actor is.
Health (dynamic): How much damage an actor can stand.
Armor (static/dynamic): How much resistance an actor has to damage.
Speed (static): How fast an actor can move.
Agility (static): How nimble an actor is.
Dexterity (static): How well the actor performs intricate tasks such as lockpicking.
Accuracy (static): How good the actor is at aiming.
Charisma (static): How charming an actor is and how he performs socially.

Magic (dynamic): How much magic is available to the actor.

Wisdom (static): A measure of how powerful an actor's magic is.

Special (dynamic): How close an actor is to being able to perform a special. This is an attribute that starts off empty and can be built up.

Luck (static/dynamic): An actor's good fortune.

Courage (static): The resolve of an actor in the face of danger.

Awareness (static): How aware of his surroundings an actor is.

Strength

Strength is mainly used by the combat system for melee attacks to determine the amount of damage caused by an attack. It might also be used to determine whether a character is able to perform particular feats of strength, such as lifting a heavy object. Strength might be modified by a status effect. Possible alternative names are power, brawn, force, and muscle.

Health

Health is perhaps the most important attribute in any game and is probably used in one form or another in every action–adventure title. It is a measure of how much damage the actor can take before dying. There are many different ways that health might be expressed, which are discussed in the combat section. It is nearly always a pot that can be taken away from and usually also added to. The decision to use health pickups or not is dependent on the game type being created and the desired atmosphere. One striving for realism might choose not to include them. If they are to be included, the second consideration is whether they are picked up and used immediately or whether they can be stored in an inventory and used later. Health is also often applied to objects such as props and scenery as well as the actors. Possible alternative names are constitution, damage, stamina, energy, and vigor.

Armor

Armor is a protective attribute that can behave in several ways: reduce damage, act as a buffer, or a combination of the two. If it is simply reducing damage, it may remain forever. If it is being used as a buffer or for both purposes, it will most likely eventually run out. The actor will then have to seek out more armor to regain resistance. Possible alternative names are resistance, defense, guard, protection, ward, and shield.

Speed

Speed can influence many aspects of gameplay. It can affect the speed of attacks, the speed of movement, and more. Generally speed is a factor of physical size. Large characters are likely to be inherently slower but more powerful (have much more strength). Faster characters are likely to be more lithe, but their attacks are generally weaker than their larger brethren.

Speed might often be modified to make the character faster or slower temporarily. This has a very large impact on the actor's effectiveness with even a little change. Possible alternative names are pace, quickness, and swiftness.

Agility

Often agility would be classed within speed or dexterity, but it makes sense to have it as a separate attribute. Agility can be used to describe the gracefulness or clumsiness of an actor. The lower an actor's agility, the more likely he is to fumble. Conversely, the more agile he is, the more likely he is to pull off a stylish move. Fumbles and stylish moves could be applied to various situations. Combat moves are likely to be the most obvious use, but acrobatic movement would also be a good candidate for such a system.

Like any other static attribute, agility might be temporarily modified to make a character supremely clumsy or incredibly graceful for a short period. Possible alternative names are grace, athleticism, balance, poise, and style.

Dexterity

Accuracy and agility might be lumped in with dexterity as an attribute, but it might be applied only to a smaller set of character movement—how skilled actors are with their hands. This can be useful for many skills such as lock picking, bomb disposal, and so on. It might reduce the time it takes for a character to reload a weapon.

Dexterity might temporarily be modified, perhaps by injury. There might be methods of boosting dexterity, perhaps with magic or with nerve-calming drugs. Possible alternative names are skill, proficiency, and aptness.

Accuracy

Normally this would be included as part of dexterity, but it is such an essential part of most games that it often deserves its own attribute. Accuracy basically describes an actor's ability to aim a ranged weapon. What this translates to in game terms is how much less wobbly a targeting cursor is or how improved the auto aim becomes. It might also make auto aim target more deadly areas, such as the head instead of the torso.

Accuracy might be increased or decreased in various ways. Maybe a nerve-calming drug is taken to reduce wobble. Conversely, the wobble may become worse when the actor is in a stressful situation. Possible alternative names are aim and marksmanship.

Charisma

Charisma is a much more abstract attribute that describes an actor's ability to charm and persuade others. This is often a very difficult concept to realize in a game world, where little is left to the imagination. In order to communicate this to the player, actors must speak and act according to their level of charisma. Other options might also be available for the player, such as offering more branches in the conversation tree. Possible alternative names are charm, persuasion, and flair.

Magic

Magic is the preserve of the fantasy RPG, but small elements might emerge in other genres (such as telekinesis or perhaps Jedi powers). In order to balance the amount of magic actors can use, they are often attributed a certain amount of magic points that they can spend. Each spell might cost a different amount of magic points to cast. Thus, an actor can cast many more weaker spells than stronger ones. There are also other ways of limiting magic, such as requiring magical reagents to cast a spell.

Magic might also be disguised as special skills or moves that the actor can perform, such as Dead Eye in *Red Dead Revolver*. Possible alternative names are mana, aura, skill points, and nerve.

Wisdom

While magic points might be used to measure the number of spells that can be cast, wisdom is used to measure the power of these spells. Wisdom might also be used as a measure of an actor's intelligence, such as being able to understand a foreign language or finding hidden meanings. Possible alternative names are essence, intelligence, and IQ.

Luck

Luck is a strange concept to model. Can we really measure someone's luck? Well, in game worlds we can do whatever we please (within reason of course). Luck can be a very useful attribute to apply. There are the obvious applications for luck, such as making actors more likely to win in a gambling situation, effectively reducing the odds of them losing. However, luck might be used in less obvious situations.

Luck might be viewed as having a lucky escape from bad fortune. Consider a combat situation where a character is about to be dealt a killer blow. We might want to test against his luck to stop this from being a killer blow. Should the luck test be a win, then the blow would not cause enough damage to kill.

Luck can either be static or dynamic, depending on whether you view luck as a system that some people either have or they don't or as a reservoir of luck that people have. If dynamic, then luck is diminished each time a luck test is made. Luck might be bolstered by collecting lucky horseshoes, rabbit's feet, or four-leaf clovers. Possible alternative names are fortune, karma, and kismet.

Special

Special is a measure of how close a character is to being able to perform a special move. Special bars are built up from the character performing well, badly, or both. There are benefits and disadvantages to each. Rewards for playing well are good for a competent player but mean novice players are unlikely to be able to use them and are further disadvantaged in a versus situation. Specials built from playing badly are fairer but offer opportunity to play badly on purpose and offer no reward to the good player. Possible alternative names are rage and overdrive.

Courage

Courage is an actor's ability to resist fear and to perform brave actions. It is not likely to be applied to a player character unless the whole game is based around fear as a game mechanic. It is usually only applied to AI characters. Possible alternative names are braveness, boldness, daring, heroism, and fearlessness.

Awareness

Awareness is the actors' ability to spot things around them. This can mean different things for different types of character. For player characters it might mean extra attention being given to things in their surroundings so that a bright effect is applied to an object of interest or an extra announcement is applied to a forthcoming action so that they have more time to react. It might also open up opportunities to view a section of the level ahead if their awareness is high enough.

For AI characters this means having heightened senses, so they will be able to see farther or in a wider angle. They might also be able to hear sounds at much more sensitive levels. Possible alternative names are alertness, attention, perception, and sentience.

Character Creation

Many games, particularly RPGs, allow the players to create their own characters. This allows them a much greater sense of identification with their avatars and a much stronger sense of ownership.

The creation of a character generally involves several stages:

Name: Give the character an identity.
Character type: Define the class, race, gender, and profession of the character.
Appearance: Define their looks.
Attributes: Assign values to their abilities.
Skills: Choose a selection of skills for the character.
Inventory: Select or purchase items and equipment for the character.

Assigning a Name

A large part of a character's identity is in its name. Allowing players to personalize their characters enables them to feel much more connected to them. However, there are problems with allowing players to name their characters:

- The chosen name might not fit within the context of the world. Many players give their characters ridiculous names such as "Jack Ass" or "Poop Breath" (or much ruder), which aren't really in keeping with the game world.

- The name cannot be spoken by characters. Because the name can be customized, it is impossible to create speech for. Therefore, the player's name shouldn't be referred to in the script (unless it is completely based on text). Use "you," "his," or "hers" instead.

Choosing a Character Type

Character types are based on one or more of three factors:

Race: The ethnicity of the character
Class/profession: The role of the character (often the same thing as profession)
Gender: The gender of the character

Race

Race is only really used in RPGs when we talk about groups of humanoid characters such as elves, dwarves, humans, hobbits, and so on. It doesn't usually apply to human ethnicity for reasons of political correctness.

Race has a direct influence on the appearance of a character. Dwarves are generally short and stocky, whereas elves are tall and lithe. Each will restrict any appearance settings that are available to the player.

Race also has an impact on the class/profession a player chooses. For example, many games might refuse the opportunity for the player to create a dwarven wizard. Alternatively, it might be feasible to create such characters, but they will be severely impaired in comparison to more suitable races.

Class/Profession

The class/profession of a character may have an effect on the appearance of a character. Warriors tend to be more stocky and muscular than an intellectual-looking wizard. The biggest impact of class/profession is upon skills, attributes, and equipment. They will have very specific limitations and benefits for each class/profession.

Gender

Gender is often a purely cosmetic feature, but it may have an impact on attributes. Be careful not to be too stereotypical or sexist if affecting attributes in this way.

Defining Appearance

Most character creation systems allow the users to define the physical appearance of their characters. There are several ways in which this can be done:

Choice of presets: The most limiting method is to allow the player to choose from a set of predefined characters.
Body elements: The player can combine elements of appearance like an identikit. The depth of the system depends on the number of elements made available to the player.

> **Analog manipulation:** The player can tweak various characteristics of the model on an analog scale.

Preset Characters

Offering the player a choice from several presets is the simplest method of choosing a character's appearance and allows the artists to get each character looking just how they want. Bioware®'s *Jade Empire*™ uses a preset choice of characters, each of which has their own distinct personality.

Presets may be made to look great, but they don't offer much freedom to the player, so players are likely to feel less of a connection to a preset character than to one that is created in a system with more freedom of expression.

Body Elements

The most common method of creating unique characters is to allow the players to mix and match features from a set of predefined body elements. This system requires the players to select a specific element for every part of the body, so they might choose from:

> **Head shapes:** Heart, oval, square, long, round, and so on
> **Body shapes:** Will be based on weight and the race or gender of a character and will affect stature and muscle tone.
> **Facial features:** Players choose predefined heads or have a more refined choice such as mouth, eyes, nose, and so on.
> **Hair:** The styling and color of a character's hair; possibly beards and other facial hair as well.
> **Skin color:** Where race does not predetermine a skin color, the shade of a character's skin might be tweakable.

Additional body elements could be broken down so that the players could even precisely choose what kind of feet they want. The complexity and uniqueness of a character is purely dependent on the number of elements that have been created. However, body element systems are far less controllable than preset characters, and it can result in some very odd looking characters. Incidentally, this kind of system is often used to generate a multitude of NPCs that can look different from each other if there are enough choices of element.

Analog Manipulation

The ultimate character appearance creation allows the player to directly manipulate and tweak various parts of the mesh. Sliders, or some similar mechanism, allow the player to stretch and squish various parts of the character's anatomy. This can be simply making a character taller or fatter (and is often combined with a body element system for facial features). However, it can be taken to further extremes, allowing the player to bend and stretch facial features, for example.

Usually this is too complex a system to use. First, the interface needs to be fairly elaborate, and the technology to allow this system to be used in games is complex. Second, the system will often produce some fairly hideous results, and it is difficult to produce nice-looking models that will have as much detail and charm as a predefined model. Third, the constraints to allow the model to work with the animation sets will be too limiting, unless a variety of animation sets are produced. Larger people do not move in the same manner as lithe, athletic people.

Assigning Attributes and Skills

While appearance is the visual aspect of character creation, it is the skills and attributes applied to a character that affect gameplay. Generally a player is given a number of points to spend on improving attributes and purchasing skills, but a number of restricting factors may be applied.

Maximum values: Limits are often placed on what can initially be invested in attributes and skills.

Character race: Affects the starting values and limits what points can be spent on. For example, a dwarf might be naturally stronger than an elf, who would have far greater natural awareness and dexterity.

Character profession/class: Has a substantial impact on the skills and attributes that points can be spent on. For example, a wizard would start with more wisdom and magic than a warrior, who would be blessed with more strength.

Inventory

A new character needs equipment such as clothing and weapons. Usually a basic set of equipment is given to the character to begin with, often with a limited amount of cash to go shopping with. This initial equipment is likely to be based on a character's profession/class or possibly even race. Hence, a warrior might receive armor and a sword, while a wizard receives a staff, robes, and a spell book.

PROGRESSION

Progression is the advancement of characters in skill, power, and ability or by improvements in the equipment they carry. Many grades of progression are used in games, from the very simple (gaining newer and better equipment), to the complex (RPG-style levels and experience). The depth of progression used in a game depends entirely on the types of experience the designer wants to promote. However, it is unlikely that a very action-oriented arcade-style game would have a complex progression system, just as an RPG would seem less in keeping with its genre if its progression was limited.

Item Progression

The most basic and immediate method of progressing is to acquire new and more powerful items. This is a simple system to implement. As the game progresses, the player finds items such as weapons that do more damage, reload more quickly, and so on. These improvements are generally in tune with an increase in the level of difficulty.

In addition to simply finding items, a system where the player can choose to enhance a particular item might be employed. There are two basic ways to handle item upgrades:

Point system: Add points to improve various stats
Augmentations: Add bits to improve or give certain features

Point-Based Upgrades

Every item will have a number of parameters. For example, a gun might have damage, reload, time, capacity, accuracy, and fire rate. These parameters might have a number of different stages. Points can be spent on purchasing the next improvement stage. Each successive stage costs more points to purchase.

In most cases the points used to purchase item upgrades will be money, but there might be situations in which other units are used, such as using magic to enchant an item. Limits might be set on the structure of upgrades so that they are evenly balanced. For example, in *Resident Evil 4* all of a particular upgrade level for each parameter are required before the next level of upgrades is available.

Upgrades are also limited by where they can be performed. Usually a special character must be interacted with such as a blacksmith or a weapons expert.

Augmentations

Augmentations are extra bits and pieces that are attached to an item to improve parameters or to offer new functionality. They can come in many guises. For example, they might be scopes attached to sniper rifles, runes inscribed into a sword, or stocks added to machine guns. An augmentation has to make sense in relation to the item it applies to, so they are generally tailored to one specific type of item.

Augmentations may be bought from a particular character or found during the course of exploration as an inventory item that can then be combined with the suitable item of equipment. The effects they have may be radically different, such as adding thermal or night vision to a rifle scope. Magic runes might offer all sorts of benefits to the weapon's standard behavior such as extra damage, sucking health from the victim, or more.

Character Progression

A major feature of many games, particularly RPGs, is the ability to improve your character or party of characters. There are many approaches to this. The approach should suit the type of game you are creating. A complex leveling-up character progression system isn't really the best choice for an arcade-style "pick up and play" action game. Some character progression systems can be very intricate and may require a lot of the player's attention. However, even the most basic of action games may incorporate a limited amount of player progression beyond the player's own skill improvement.

Unlocking Content

A simple method of progression is to lock away much of the content and slowly allow access to new gameplay features as the game progresses.

Content Types

Generally this unlockable content is either skills, moves, or attacks.

- **Skills:** Skills are abilities that enable the character to perform new functions, such as learning how to pick locks. A new skill opens up gameplay possibilities that weren't open to the player before. It might also mean that the player can replay a part of the game to gain access to an area that was previously inaccessible.
- **Moves:** New moves are generally athletic feats that were not possible previously, such as double jump or wall run. Like a new skill, a new move will more than likely make any area previously inaccessible now reachable.
- **Attacks:** Attacks are often gradually unlocked, not only to allow progression, but also to ease the player into the gameplay. Often combo patterns that are initially locked become available as the player progresses. This improves a player's combat performance over time.

Locking Methods

To drip-feed content, some unlocking mechanism must be used. There are a number of potential mechanisms.

- **Predefined Unlocking:** At specific points during the game the features are unlocked. This might be triggered by defeating a particular boss or by speaking to a particular NPC. It is important to tie the unlocking to the context of the game so that it makes logical sense and doesn't seem arbitrary.
- **Item-Based Unlocking:** The player must collect specific objects or artifacts to unlock another level of progression. These objects are related in some way to the feature they are unlocking, such as collecting a lock-picking tool to unlock the lock-picking skill.
- **Training:** Another method of unlocking is to require the player to complete a specific challenge in order to receive the prize. This challenge is something related to the prize—hence the term training. For example, to learn the swimming skill, the player might have to go through a series of swimming challenges. Training missions are often used as tutorials to introduce the new gameplay feature.

Basic Point Progression

Unlocking tends to be a fairly transparent mechanism of player progression. However, as character progression gets more complex, more of the detail of the system needs to be exposed to the player. A step up from unlocking in its basic form is the application of points to spend on improving abilities or buying new gameplay features.

Points are awarded for performing certain actions (often called experience, though this might be called style or something similar in a more action-oriented game). At certain points within the game, perhaps at the end of the level or when a certain NPC has been visited, these accumulated points can be spent on character improvements. An improvement will cost increasing amounts of points as it reaches higher levels or particularly powerful new features.

Experience Points and Levels

The most recognized RPG method of character progression is the ubiquitous experience points/levels system that has many slight variations. All these systems have a common theme. The nucleus of the system is the acquisition of experience points. These are accumulated whenever particular actions occur. Most often experience points are awarded for killing an enemy. Usually an enemy has a set experience point value given on its death. However, there are other actions that experience might be attributed to, such as:

- Inflicting damage
- Casting spells
- Outwitting an opponent
- Completing a puzzle
- Helping an NPC
- Completing a quest or mission

Experience points accumulate over time until eventually the player will have a large amount. However, experience points don't mean much to anyone until they are applied to some kind of scale. This scale is known as a character's level. A level is a measure of how experienced a character is. A level is attained by accumulating a set number of experience points. Each level has a threshold value of experience points that must be attained.

Usually this experience point scale will increase in an almost exponential manner, so that it becomes harder and harder to attain a new level (see Table 11.1).

TABLE 11.1 Experience Required to Achieve Levels

LEVEL	EXPERIENCE REQUIRED
1	100
2	250

$\rightarrow$

LEVEL	EXPERIENCE REQUIRED
3	500
4	1,000
5	2,000
6	5,000
7	8,000
8	12,500
9	25,000
10	50,000

Many games place a restriction on the number of levels that can be obtained.

Event-Based Progression

Rather than accumulate experience points by performing lots of micro actions over time, progression may be based on much more unique events. Such a system would allow characters to progress when they have achieved something specific, such as completing a certain quest, defeating a certain enemy, or visiting a certain NPC.

One problem with such a system is that it offers little choice to the player. Also, progression may occur too infrequently, unless there are plenty of events available.

Complex Unlocking

With more advanced character progression, the methods of unlocking new skills, moves, and attacks are often much more elaborate.

   Point Spending: By far the most common of these methods is point spending. Each time characters gain a level they are awarded a number of points to spend in a variety of ways. These points might be called knowledge, take the form of orbs, or form any other sensible system that suits the game setting. The number of points given is generally a fixed amount for each level acquired (see Table 11.2).

TABLE 11.2   Knowledge Awarded for Particular Levels

LEVEL	KNOWLEDGE AWARDED
1	2
2	2
3	4
4	4

$\rightarrow$

LEVEL	KNOWLEDGE AWARDED
5	6
6	6
7	8
8	8
9	10
10	10

Points can be spent on:

- Upgrading attributes
- Purchasing new skills, moves, or attacks
- Upgrading existing skills, moves, or attacks

Upgrading Attributes: This is likely to be the most common form of spending, as it boosts the character's performance in a specific area. Generally one knowledge point equates to adding one point to that attribute. However, a designer might build in different career paths for a class of character so that certain attributes are more expensive for certain classes or are limited at a smaller maximum value. Restrictions on the choice of upgrade might also be applied in a career path, so that the choice of upgrade offered is limited at each character level.

Purchasing New Skills, Moves, or Attacks: Giving the player a choice of which skills, moves, or attacks a character can have allows the player to finely craft the avatar. Skills, moves, or attacks will often have different cost levels to indicate their power. Alternatively, certain skills, moves, or attacks may be locked until a certain level is reached or may even be locked until a certain attribute reaches a particular value.

Upgrading Skills, Moves, or Attacks: Often skills are divided into a series of levels to indicate proficiency in that field. Moves and attacks might also have a number of levels. This might improve the distance of a jump or damage of an attack, for example. Again, like initial purchase, the upgrade of skills, moves, or attacks is limited in some way—by greater cost for higher levels of ability, by character level, or by attribute requirements.

Inventory Experience

The method of skill, move, or attack upgrade used in *Final Fantasy VII* was somewhat unusual. Players could collect orbs known as Materia. Materia was of a specific type that offered new skills and attacks, and these could be placed on slots in weapons and armor. Once equipped, the skills and attacks offered by the Materia became available to the character. The interesting bit is that Materia also gained experience when equipped. Like the character, they also had levels. Each time a new level was reached, a new skill or attack was unlocked.

This is an inventory experience method of progression, allowing items to improve with use, and these items in turn provide skills to the player.

Coded Pathways

The *Final Fantasy* series has a reputation for creating new upgrade methods, and *Final Fantasy X* is no exception, as it offers a very convoluted coded pathway. Essentially a coded pathway is a predefined tree in which slots must be filled with specific elements in order to progress. Elements are specific types of move, skill, attack, or attribute, for example, Magic, Melee Combat, Ranged Combat, Physical Prowess, and Mental Prowess. Each element might yield a different result within these fields, so one magic element might boost by 10, while another might provide another spell.

This produces an easy way to balance progression, but the tree needs to have enough branches to allow interesting player decisions. When the player looks at the *Final Fantasy X* Sphere Grid for the first time, it is really quite daunting with the sheer size and choice available.

Character Augmentations

Character augmentations are similar to item augmentations. They offer a character boosts to their attributes or new gameplay features. Augmentations are generally only used in sci-fi games, where the idea of bionic or genetic enhancements makes sense. However, there might also be some kind of magical augmentations that can be applied in more traditional fantasy genres.

WEALTH

Wealth is the most obvious example of an economy—what we most likely visualize an economy to be. In an action–adventure game wealth serves two purposes: currency with which to buy new items and a rating of a player's progress.

Most games tend to have a very closed, fixed wealth economy. Items are set at specific rates and do not change through the course of the game. However, a game might feature a much more fluid, transient economy, where the prices can move up or down. This enables the player to move about the world between various traders in search of the best price. This can be an entire mechanic in itself, as the players try to make their way financially in the game world.

Wealth comes from three main sources:

Treasure and trade items: Objects in the world that serve no other purpose than to be exchanged for currency

Inventory items: Objects that have a specific purpose but may be sold to provide cash

Raw materials: Items that must be processed in some way before they yield money or may provide more money than the basic value if processed

A few main systems are involved with the accumulation of wealth:

Collection: Finding and acquiring raw materials, valuables, or currency
Manufacture: Turning raw materials into valuable items
Trade: Buying and selling goods to receive currency
Gambling: Testing luck to try to gain wealth

Collection

Money must be acquired by collecting something. That something might be the direct collection of currency or the acquisition of raw materials or valuables to facilitate trade. Collection is discussed in the Player Inventory section.

Manufacture

Many games extend the basic wealth economy to include the ability to manufacture goods. This might be as simple as combining two or more items to produce another or may require a more complex set of rules to be followed.

Basic Combination

At its most basic, a good is worth little or no money, but if it is combined with another item, it can become a valuable object that is worth more than the sum of its parts. For example, a simple diamond is worth a fair amount, but combined with a silver bangle it is worth far more.

Basic combination relationships are predefined; that is, an object can only be matched with specific partners. Often clues are given such as slots in one item that have a missing element. The player then knows that something can be added to this to increase its base worth.

Processing

Processing takes raw materials and creates a product from them. This requires some kind of process to be applied to the raw material(s). For example, gold ore might be worth very little money, but if it is smelted, it is worth far more.

There are two ways a process might be implemented:

Specific location or character: The raw materials must be taken to a place or to a character who will perform the process.
Player fabrication: The player is able to craft an object from raw materials. This might be done through some kind of editor. The great thing about this is that it enables user content to be created, which could then be shared between players in some way. This could also involve a skill level so that fabrication might be fumbled and mistakes made.

Specific amounts of a raw material must be acquired to produce different items. For example, creating a king's crown might require several units of gold, several gems, and even specific animal furs. This cost drives a player to find more resources to feed the manufacturing process.

Advanced Combination

Basic combination only allows predetermined combinations to be made. More advanced combination allows the players to be more experimental and discover new results themselves.

To drive such a system, a set of rules must be laid down about reactions of one item to another. Usually these items are created to serve a specific purpose such as casting spells. Advanced combination is discussed in further depth in the inventory section.

Trade

Trade is the buying and selling of goods in the pursuit of profit. To do this, a player must have first collected or manufactured goods to trade.

Trade is performed via specific characters or locations in the game world. These characters or locations facilitate the purchase and sale of items for prices. A game market is either static or dynamic. A static market has fixed prices each time the player visits a merchant or shop, whereas in a dynamic market prices will fluctuate.

Static Market

In a static market every price is fixed, but that does not mean prices have to be the same from trader to trader. It is perfectly feasible for each trader to have a specialization—a field in which they offer the best prices for sale or purchase. The result of this is that the player can shop around for the best price. There are pitfalls with such a system, such as creating loopholes where a player can buy masses of goods from one trader and sell them to another for profit. Some restrictions must be placed on the amount of goods a player can carry or what goods traders can sell. It is highly likely in a static market that traders will not be able to sell valuables to the player—only useable items.

A static market could include prices that drop for older items when newer and more useful equipment is unlocked.

Dynamic Market

Prices in a dynamic market fluctuate. This means a trader may offer a price at one point that changes upward or downward later in the game, or even from moment to moment. The result is that a player can try to work the market to turn a profit. By buying from a seller when prices are cheap and selling when prices are high, players can turn a tidy profit. Whole game mechanics have been built around the premise Just look at the classic trading–exploration game *Elite*.

A dynamic market fluctuates in certain ways:

Rigged: The whole system is completely predetermined, so that prices are changed at particular times or when particular events can be learned of and the knowledge shared among players.

Random: The whole system is random, so that prices fluctuate by sheer chance. This is slightly dangerous because of its sheer unpredictability. It is essentially gambling.

Event driven: The market prices are random within ranges driven by events occurring in the game. For example, if there is an earthquake, there might suddenly be a huge demand for shovels.

Trade with Other Players

A particularly interesting trading opportunity comes when players can trade with each other. There are two ways this can be done:

In-game context: Gamers can meet up in the game world and trade items (although we are dangerously close to creating an online RPG here, which is beyond the scope of this book).

Out-of-game context: Players can swap items via memory cards or chat rooms. This tends to have less impact within the game context. Often this might simply be for the pleasure of collecting rather than the pursuit of game profit. There might be some kind of subgame where players compete for items, like a "keepsies" game of marbles.

Gambling

Gambling is the pursuit of wealth based purely on luck. Any number of subgames might be implemented, such as poker, slots, or roulette. The player can choose to engage in these games and bet on the outcome.

The odds in games tend to be more in favor of the player than the house (certainly more than real-life gambling), as they are playing to win. A luck attribute might also be used, so that the odds are better with higher luck scores. This might also be a positive feedback loop, where as a character's luck improves, his chances of winning also improve.

INVENTORY

Inventory is the ability of a character to carry and utilize items. The amount and type of items a character is equipped with have a huge impact on their effectiveness.

Player Inventory

A player's inventory is often the key to his success in the game. The items the player acquires will enable him to interact with the environment in meaningful ways. It is possible for a game to have no real inventory to speak of, but this would leave players with only themselves as weapons and the means to traverse the environment.

Acquiring Inventory Items

Items are acquired in two main ways:

> **Purchase:** Items are bought from merchants or shops.
> **Collection:** Items are found in the environment.

Purchase

Items can be bought from NPC merchants or by going to shops in the game world. Each merchant or shop may sell a wide range of goods or may specialize in one particular field.

Collection

Collection of goods may be done in different ways, depending on the good that is being acquired:

> **Finding:** The object is simply lying around, waiting to be collected. The inhabitants of game worlds tend to be extremely careless with their items.
> **Looting:** Searching through people's houses, in chests, or by smashing objects. Strangely, looting seems to be an acceptable practice in video-game worlds. Few NPCs even seem bothered in most games.
> **Bounty:** Enemies drop their loot when they die. Often the reward has seemingly little to do with the dead character. While a human might have been carrying cash or an Amulet of True Wisdom, it seems unlikely that a slobbering beast of doom would be doing the same. Making an enemy drop a sensible item, perhaps its own hide or tooth, would be more in keeping with the game world.
> **Mining:** The act of extracting a valuable item from the environment, such as gold ore. Often these raw materials have to be processed in some way to yield maximum benefit.
> **Quest or mission reward:** The good is given as a reward for completing a quest or task.
> **Payment:** The character is paid for performing specific actions such as killing enemies.

Inventory Scope

The scope of an inventory is the boundaries and limits placed on the number of items that can be carried or utilized. The system of inventory may differ from item to item, so, for example, cash might be unlimited, but all other items are size based.

Several different inventory systems can be used:

Single item: A limited inventory might only allow the player to carry one item at a time.

Unlimited: As many items as collected are placed in the inventory.

Slot based: Items are placed in specific slots so only a certain amount can be carried.

Size based: Items are limited by their physical size.

Weight: The players are limited in what they can carry by their physical weight.

Class based: A character class acts as the limit to the type of items available.

Storage boxes: Players are able to store items at various locations and retrieve them later.

Unlimited

The simplest inventory system is to allow the players to collect as much as they like of any item. Over the course of a game this may result in a massive number of objects being acquired, which means navigating the inventory can become tricky.

Being able to sort through different types of items becomes fairly essential. RPGs often have a shared unlimited inventory for the party, but then have a slot-based system for placing apparel on individual characters.

Slot Based

Slots allow specific numbers of specific item types to be carried. This can be a very simple system, such as *Halo*'s two-weapon slot system. Any two weapons can be carried, but only two. This means the players have to think carefully about what they might require and monitor ammunition levels carefully. *Counter-Strike* limits a player's weapon buying to a machine gun, a pistol, and three grenades.

More complex slot systems allow only certain items to fit into a slot. An RPG favorite, used by the likes of Bioware's *Knights Of The Old Republic*, is to have slots for various parts of the body. A player can assign clothing to the torso and legs, weapons to the hands, necklaces and amulets to the neck, and so on.

Size Based

Size-based systems require the players to manage the layout of their inventory. The inventory is often broken down into a grid (as the attaché case in *Resident Evil 4* is). Each object takes up a certain amount of grid squares, so a pistol might be 1×2 and a machine gun 2×4.

Items might need to be rotated to fit into these spaces or shuffled about (one game required objects to be put into a backpack in a specific order, simulating a real backpack, but this proved frustrating and a little unnecessary). To increase inventory, larger cases or bags would need to be acquired that have more grid space.

Weight Based

A weight-based inventory assigns a set weight to each item. Characters can carry a specific amount of weight. This is often based on their strength, meaning that as their strength improves, so does the amount they can carry.

This weight limit might act as a barrier or more as a guideline. If it is possible to go over this weight limit, then it can have a detrimental effect on characters. Carrying too much weight would make them slower or make them tire much more quickly, affecting how long they can sprint and so on.

Class Based

Inventory based on class is generally used in multiplayer games but might also appear in single-player experiences. Essentially it limits inventory to specific items based on the class of character a player chooses. For example, a sniper class is provided with a sniper rifle, whereas a heavy weapons guy might have a rocket launcher.

There might be an opportunity to have limited choice in the selection of items, so perhaps the players can choose between two or three sniper rifles if they select the sniper class or a variety of rocket or grenade launchers if they choose the heavy weapons class.

Storage Boxes

Storage boxes are usually supplementary to a player's normal inventory. These are places where a player can store extra items —places where the player can put an item so that it is not despawned from the world when the player leaves the current sector. The contents of a storage box are saved when the game is saved.

Boxes might use one of the other inventory systems, though they are often unlimited. Storage boxes might take larger forms such as the garages in *Grand Theft Auto*, where acquired cars can be stored.

Some storage boxes are a little more ubiquitous, such as those used in the first *Resident Evil* game. A storage box's contents could be accessed in every storage box that was encountered, which while great for gameplay, made little logical sense.

Generally storage boxes are good for free-roaming games where the player is likely to want to save lots of items and will be able to return to a specific location.

Item Lifetime

Items discarded from an inventory often just disappear from the game world, never to return. Alternatively, they can be dropped back into the game world at the player's feet. Here they might last a period of time before being despawned, may remain while the current sector is loaded, or possibly (if memory permits) remain there indefinitely.

Item Types

There are several types of item:

Weapons: Any device that allows the player to inflict damage.

Ammunition: Many weapons (usually ranged) need ammunition to operate.

Support items: Any item that is used to benefit the player.

Vehicles or steeds: Any object or character that facilitates faster travel.

Treasure or valuables: Items held for trading purposes.

Money: Currency to buy items.

Quest or mission items: Items used to further story progression or complete side quests or missions.

Apparel: Clothing, armor, and trinkets that a player character wears for style or protection.

Tools: Objects a player uses to facilitate specific gameplay mechanics.

Weapons

Weapons define any item that can inflict damage or status effects on an opponent. The combat section deals with the mechanics of specific weapons in detail. A weapon inventory tends to be structured in a variety of ways:

Unlimited: All weapons found are added to the inventory.

Simple slot: Only a limited number of weapons of any type are allowed (*Halo*'s two-weapon rule for example).

Weapon-based slot: Weapons are broken down into categories, and only one of each kind of weapon is allowed. This may not apply to thrown weapons such as grenades, where a larger number might be allowed. For example, weapons might be broken down into melee, pistols, machine guns, rifles, heavy weapons, and so on.

Size based: The inventory is sized based, so more powerful weapons are likely to take up more room.

Weight based: Similarly to size-based weaponry, more powerful weapons are likely to be larger and heavier.

Class based: Weapons are organized into groups then assigned to an inventory, based on the player's choice of character.

Ammunition

Ammunition is required for many weapons to operate. This becomes a limiting factor for the use of these weapons, meaning they cannot be used until more ammunition is acquired. Thus, players must be aware of their ammunition reserves. In some games such as *Resident Evil* ammunition is particularly scarce, making each shot fired extremely important.

Ammunition varies from weapon to weapon. Guns use magazines, or clips, that contain a certain number of rounds. A clip can be self-contained, meaning that when reloaded, any bullets remaining in a clip are lost. For the sake of fairness, most games simply keep bullets in a store and load in only what is needed rather than having separate magazines each time.

Bows use quivers, which are stores of all available arrows. Generally only one arrow can be loaded into a bow at a time (though some games play with the basic interpretation of a bow and allow repeating bows or multiple shots to be fired at once).

Some weapons might be one-shot deals, where they become useless once the weapon is fired.

How the store is handled depends on the inventory mechanism used. An unlimited inventory would allow a player to collect unlimited amounts of ammunition, but most games place a limit on the amount of each type of ammunition that can be collected. Size-based inventories allow a certain amount of space for a set amount of ammunition. The player may then fill several spaces as the ammunition accumulates (imagine boxes of bullets—each can store a certain amount, and each box takes up an inventory slot). Weight-based inventory is restricted by its weight.

Support Items

Support items are those that provide benefit in some way to the player. Once a support item has been used it is discarded. There are several types of support item:

Health: Items to boost health and recover from damage.
Magic: Replenish lost magic points.
Reagents: Some magic systems need ingredients in order for players to cast spells.
Cures: Items that remove negative status effects.
Charms: Items that provide positive status effects.
Boosts: Items that permanently upgrade an attribute.

Each item has either a value of points that are added to an attribute (generally a dynamic attribute) or provides an effect for a period of time. Often (especially in RPGs) each item has levels, so a health potion might come in the flavors shown in Table 11.3.

TABLE 11.3 Healing Items

ITEM LEVEL	EFFECT
Ointment	Heals 20 damage
Salve	Heals 100 damage
Potion	Heals 1000 damage
Elixir	Heals all damage

Better items are more expensive or harder to find.

Support items are often unlimited, though they are commonly set a maximum total amount, or sometimes a maximum number of each can be held. Support items also fit a size- or weight-based inventory system.

Vehicles and Steeds

Vehicles or steeds are slightly unusual inventory items, as they are not carried by the player, but instead carry the player, allowing them to move around the world more quickly. Only one vehicle or steed can be used at a time.

Often vehicles or steeds have weapons or attacks of their own that the player can utilize. This might be in their direct control or might be handled by another AI character on the vehicle or by the steed itself. Vehicles and steeds can be stored in "storage boxes" such as garages or stables, where the player can return to use the vehicle or steed again.

A vehicle might also be upgradable, so that new parts can be fitted to change its appearance or to improve its performance. Parts such as new engines, trims, and so on could be purchased from an auto shop or mechanic. Vehicles might even act as a base of operations, allowing the player to move about the world but also being a safe place to save or recharge. *Final Fantasy VII* and *Final Fantasy X* both have airships that perform just such a function.

Treasure and Valuables

Treasure can take many forms and is dependent on the game world. Valuable items might take the form of crystals, raw materials, precious items, and so on. Each treasure has a value. This value might be different to different people or even at different times, depending on the marketplace. Generally treasure serves no other purpose than to reward the player, usually in the form of cash. As such, valuables often have an unlimited inventory, or at least a maximum amount for the total number a player is able to carry of each individual item.

Money

The currency in a game tells much about the game world. An "olde worlde" fantasy game might have florins as the base currency, whereas a high-tech society might deal with credits. No matter what the money is called, it has the same purpose—to allow the player to buy items or services.

Generally money has an unlimited capacity, so the players can accumulate as much as they want.

Quest and Mission Items

Quest and mission items are those collected in the game world that are used to progress the story or a subquest in some way. All of these items are essentially keys, even if they may be somewhat disguised. They are all objects that when used with a specific object or character unlock a desired action, such as a door opening or some information being imparted. These could be more abstract and take the form of notes (useful pieces of information the players acquire in their travels) such as the number for a key-coded door.

Some objects might need to be combined before they are useful as a key, for example, having two shards of an emblem to fit into a door panel. It is unusual for more than two elements to be combined unless they obviously fit together; otherwise, it becomes too confusing.

Quest and mission items are usually infinite inventories, as it becomes frustrating to juggle essential items, but they can fit under any system.

Apparel

Apparel is any item the character wears, such as clothing, boots, gloves, rings, bracelets, goggles, and so on. Apparel serves two main purposes:

- To offer some kind of benefit to the character such as increased armor rating
- To allow the players to dress characters to their tastes

The first values the function of an item over its form. The second is purely for player vanity—rating form over function.

> **Function:** When an apparel item is used for its function, it promotes judicious inventory management by the players. They will have to carefully select items in order to get the best benefit out of the available items. There are several types of function that an item of apparel might perform while being worn:
>
> - Increase armor value
> - Increase attribute value
> - Allow a skill to be performed or magic spell to be cast
> - Automatically cast protective spells on the characters
> - Protect the character from certain offensive spells or specific attacks, for example protect from certain elemental attacks

Function-based apparel tends to use very specific slots, usually based on parts of the body, that allow only one type of that apparel to be worn at a time. Often the slots are broken down into:

Head: Helmets, crowns, tiaras
Neck: Necklaces, amulets
Torso: Jackets, shirts, armor plating, Kevlar vests
Arms: Arm protection, elbow pads
Left wrist and right wrist: Bangles, bracelets
Left hand and right hand: Gloves, gauntlets
Fingers: Rings
Legs: Trousers, pads, leg armor
Feet: Boots, shoes, sandals

Some restrictions may be placed on which items can be placed with certain other items, or which types of character can use certain items. For example, gloves and gauntlets might make the use of rings impossible. Elves might not be allowed to wear metallic armor, as it clouds their magical abilities. These restrictions have to make sense within the context of the world and shouldn't feel arbitrary.

Weight might be used on top of a slot system so that there are restrictions on the amount of heavy armor a character can carry, or a character must have a certain strength value to wear it. Some games might use a much simpler system in which sets of apparel can be switched. Each set offers different functions, so if a character is in his mountain climbing suit, he has all the necessary apparel (and tools) to go climbing.

> **Form:**   When dealing purely with form, apparel serves only to give the player aesthetic choices. Generally players will create looks they really like or pick the most outrageous costumes they can.

There are two main ways to do this that make sense: predefined suits and a slot-based body inventory. Predefined suits give the player very little choice but are much easier to implement, as they are a simple skin or model change.

Multipart slot changes are more complex to implement but give much more customizable results, as they allow a player to place different combinations of apparel together. The following choices are often given:

Head: Hats, caps
Torso: Shirts, jackets, hoodies
Legs: Trousers, shorts
Feet: Boots, shoes
Neck: Necklaces, chains
Hands: Gloves, rings
Wrists: Watches, bangles, bracelets

Players might also be able to add decals to the characters' skin such as for tattoos or be able to style their characters' hair into a variety of predefined styles and colors.

Tools

Tools are items used to enable gameplay mechanics, such as a grappling hook, lock picks, or a door decoder. Tools are designed for very specific jobs, and thus much of the level design needs to be created with use of a particular tool in mind. Once acquired, a tool tends not to be disposable, as it often is an essential element in game progression.

Generally because tools are so important, they have an unlimited inventory, as only a few different tools are likely to be used in any one game. Tools that no longer have a use in the game might be automatically discarded to avoid cluttering up the inventory.

Multiplayer Differencing

Differencing is the act of giving each player options in their choice of equipment that will enable them to make tactical choices. Generally this is a choice of weaponry that they use during battle. Different systems tend to be used for different game types, but there are a few basic differencing systems.

Collection

Collection requires characters to find what they need in the level. Designers place objects throughout the level to encourage the flow of gameplay. On the start of the round each player is spawned on an equal footing. From then on they must rush to find any equipment they might want. Often dead enemies will drop all or some of the equipment they were carrying, which acts as an extra reward for the victor. This prize will disappear after a period of time if not collected, to prevent huge amounts of clutter later in the game. Equipment usually respawns after a set time period to ensure a constant supply.

Weapon, ammunition, and power-up placement is organized in two ways: specific placement and weapon sets.

Specific Placement: Every object in the world is placed specifically by the designer for that level and game type. These are set in stone and have to be changed by the designer. This system is good when maps have been specifically tuned and playtested only for those weapons.

Weapons Sets: The designer places equipment nodes in the level that are then filled dynamically with equipment at game time. Weapon sets are choices of weapons that will appear in the level. Each node placed by the designer has a rank, which tallies up to a rank in the weapon set based on the power of the weapon. Weapon sets easily allow for large changes in game dynamics just by changing the available weapons. For example:

- **Melee:** Melee weapons only. This makes for a very scrappy, meet in the open and slug it out, kind of game.
- **Low power:** Low-powered weapons only. This makes for longer games, which tend to require more accuracy.
- **High power:** High-power weapons only. This has the opposite effect of low-powered games and reduces the time it takes to kill an opponent.
- **Spray and pray:** Weapons that don't require much accuracy such as machine guns. This makes for games with more use of cover and the element of surprise.
- **Snipers:** Long-range weapons only. This makes for a much slower-paced game.

Close range: Close-range weapons such as shotguns. This makes for a more frantic, rushing style of gameplay.

Opposites: Having only very close- and very long-range weapons makes for an interesting mix of tactics.

There are plenty more possibilities, but you get the idea.

Collection is used mainly in free-for-all-style games, as territorial and mission-based games define stronger roles for players from the offset.

Player Classes

A popular team-based method of differentiating players is to offer several classes to choose from. These classes define distinct roles for every player on the team.

Classes have a set inventory of equipment or abilities that enable them to perform special functions. There are many types of class, but there are a number of well-used classes:

Infantry: Basic all-rounder who has a variety of weaponry.

Scout: Lightly equipped so they can move fast.

Heavy weapons: Equipped with powerful weaponry for maximum damage, but this often makes them slower.

Medic: Equipped with the ability to heal their teammates. They are a vital support class (though hardly anyone ever wants to play in a support role).

Engineer: Can repair vehicles, place traps, or sabotage enemy equipment. Another important support class.

Anti-vehicle: Where tanks, planes, or helicopters (possibly even dragons) are featured, there needs to be a character able to take them out. This is usually at the expense of infantry-based weaponry.

Classes are a very popular multiplayer mechanic, as they are easier to balance than more complex equipment selection systems. They are also quick to select in the heat of battle.

Equipment Selection

Equipment selection is the act of allowing the players a choice of inventory that they can take into battle. To restrict what players can carry, some kind of limit needs to be placed on what they can select. There are three main methods of limiting selection:

Slots: Only a limited number of slots are available for weaponry.

Cash: Each weapon costs money to buy. Money is earned by scoring points. Cash is often combined with a slot system to prevent the richer team from entering a positive feedback loop and having too big an advantage (positive feedback loops are discussed in the Balancing section).

Weight: Each character is only able to carry a specific amount of weight. The more powerful weapons weigh more and slow the player down.

Weapon selection does have one disadvantage: it can be pretty tricky and time consuming to select weaponry before spawning or once the round has commenced, meaning quicker players get a head start. This can be solved by allowing the players to set up a small number of favorite quick selections.

Opposites

A very different approach to differencing is taken in *Splinter Cell: Pandora Tomorrow*. The two teams have totally different abilities, equipment, and even viewpoints. One team is the Spies, having to rely on stealth to complete their objectives, while the Mercenaries team is armed to the teeth but limited in vision. The result is a game that has a totally different feel for each team, but actually works very well as a mechanic. With well-balanced abilities, this is definitely a method of producing differences between players that can work well, but it does run the risk of people preferring to play one team over the other.

Enemy Inventory

Enemies have two basic inventory elements:

Carried: The items that they use (usually weapons)
Bounty: The items they drop on death

These elements are not usually the same, as we shall see.

Carried Items

Enemies have a much more basic system than the player. They will generally carry some kind of weapon, and they might carry secondary thrown weapons. They might also be equipped with some kind of armor. Special enemies, such as bosses, might have more sophisticated apparel or tools that they can use like a player character. They might also carry support items that they can utilize at certain points.

Bounty

When killed (or sometimes just when hit), an enemy will often leave behind some kind of bounty. This bounty can be one of several things:

Weapons: The weapon they were carrying. If the player already has the weapon, collecting it will give him more ammunition for that weapon if ammo is applicable. With melee weapons, this event is rare. Often the weapon will disappear along with the character. However, it could be dropped and used as a weapon to throw at enemies.
Treasure: The character drops valuable items that the player can use to trade. A steal skill might allow a player to take extra treasures that might not get dropped with the bounty.
Support items: Health, magic potions, or similar items.
Apparel: The character drops an amulet or other trinket that blesses the wearer with new skills or protection. They could drop larger items such as armor.
Money: The character drops cold, hard cash.

Ally Inventory

Ally inventories are likely to be very similar to an enemy's. They will have carried items and quite possibly a bounty as well. However, they might also have a stock inventory. This is a store of items that they can use to aid the player when required. For example, the team following a player has a medic and infantry support. When the player is nearing death, the medic might try to help by healing him. When the player is low on ammunition, the infantry support can supply him with more. These stocks might have an unlimited supply or might have a limited maximum.

NPC Inventory

NPCs may have a stock inventory, but might also have carried and bounty inventories if they are able to attack or be killed. A stock inventory consists of one or more items that the character will sell or give to the player. There are two main types of NPCs that have a stock inventory:

> **Quest and Mission NPCs:** Characters the player needs to interact with to complete the quest.
>
> **Merchants:** Characters that buy and sell goods.

Quest and Mission NPCs

Quest and mission NPCs are those that give rewards in exchange for a quest being fulfilled or those that give items to the player when conversed with. Their stock is generally very limited indeed, consisting of only the quest or mission item and the reward for completion.

Some NPCs act as recharge points, being able to heal the player, for example. These NPCs generally have unlimited capabilities, but the player has to seek them out.

Merchants

Merchants buy and sell items from the player. The merchant system is either persistent or nonpersistent. It might also be a hybrid of the two systems.

Persistent

All goods have a limited number, so the player can only buy as much stock as the merchant has. Any items sold back to the merchant are added to his stock. These can then be bought back (often at a higher price). The merchant may receive more stock between player visits. A merchant might refuse to buy items from the player if he already has enough stock of that item.

Non-persistent

The merchant has an unlimited supply of goods. Any goods sold to the merchant are simply swallowed up and disappear into the ether (they are not added to the merchant's stocks).

Hybrids

Some semi-persistent systems have an unlimited supply of goods but might allow items sold to be added back to the stock.

Environment Inventory

As well as characters having inventory, the game world often holds many items that can be collected. There are several methods of placing pickups in the world:

Simple placement: The item is simply lying around waiting to be collected.

Smashables: The player must break objects in the environment that then spawn items on their destruction.

Lockers: Items are placed inside objects such as chests or cupboards that must be opened to reveal the prize.

Recharge points: By visiting a particular location, the player can recharge various dynamic attributes (such as health or magic). This may be achieved by staying at an inn for example.

RATING

Rating is a measure of a player's skills and abilities and their achievements in the game.

Single Player Rating

Traditionally games encouraged players to compete for high scores. More recent games have shied away from this mechanic and have progressed with a reliance on narrative. However there are still plenty of action–adventure games that use score as a game mechanic—though it may be packaged as "style", "kudos" or something similar. Score can be based on one or more of the following events:

- Performing a stylish attack or move
- Killing an enemy
- Surviving an enemy wave
- Dodging an attack
- Figuring out an alternate solution
- Collecting an item
- Triggering a hidden event (i.e., shooting a rope to drop a crate on a monster's head)

Some games might even use score as a form of currency, allowing the player to buy items or character upgrades with their accumulated points.

Multiplayer Scoring

Scoring is an important part of competitive multiplayer games, as it is a measure of the main motivation for players engaging in competition: the motivation to win.

Free-for-All Game Scoring

Scoring in free-for-all matches is all about being at the top of the table. There are several ways that scoring is achieved, depending on the type of game. There are several base units by which an individual's score is measured:

Kills (aka frags): How many enemies the player has killed or beaten.

Deaths: How many times the player has been killed or beaten. Usually used to define the positions of players tied on kill points.

Time: How long the player has held an objective (large time scores are either good or bad depending on the game type).

Accuracy: Some games might want to measure the accuracy of its players as a measure of their skill. This is defined as the number of shots that have hit an opponent, against how many shots have been fired.

Kill speed: Another unit of skill measurement that might be used is kills per minute. This is a valuc that is defined by averaging the amount of kills over the time played.

Kill/death ratio: Some score schemas might be based on the number of kills minus the number of deaths to reward cautious play. This results in a much slower game pace, as players seek high scores by sniping or camping.

Originally multiplayer gaming used pretty simple scoring systems to keep track of player's achievements—usually this was based around simply the number of kills a player had accrued. This is still a major factor for most games today, however, it does have one flaw that seriously unbalances the system: the better players can target the weaker players to improve their scores. There is no need for expert players to go easy on new players, as those that do would score less than other good players who specifically target weaker players. This makes it hard for new players to enjoy the game when they are so vulnerable. There are ways of working around this problem.

Ladder System

Instead of points everyone is just a position on a table. When a fight occurs, the victor switches position with the victim if the victor's position is lower than the victim's position. This creates a system where everyone wants to kill the guy at the top of the table, but also makes it very arbitrary as to the skill of the players and the justification of their position on the table.

Spread Reward

Another way is to vary the amount of points awarded for a kill based upon both their positions on the board. Thus a top player killing a low-placed player will reap very little reward, but a low-placed player killing a high-placed player will give much greater reward. This creates a system where it is far more rewarding to compete on your own level or try to beat those above you.

Territorial Game Scoring

Territorial scoring focuses much more on the team than the individuals, though there is usually a scoreboard for individuals as well. Team scores are based on two systems: points that drop during a time frame or points that accumulate for each territory held. The length of a time period in the first system changes based on the bias of territories held. Generally when more than 50% of territory is held by one team, then the other team's score starts to drop. As this percentage increases the score drops faster. The second system rewards points for the whole time that the territory is held.

Each territory is worth a certain number of points. The more the value of the territories held, the faster a team's score will accumulate.

Individual scores are based around kills but, since the team objective is to capture territory, more points are usually awarded for achieving this goal than for a simple kill. Points are often deducted for killing teammates to discourage players from maliciously ruining the game for others (often they will be kicked from the game for repeat offenses).

Mission-Based Game Scoring

Mission-based game scoring, like territorial scoring, places an emphasis on the team score. This is based on the number of times the objective has been accomplished. Where money-based player differencing is being used, the teams are awarded different amounts of cash based on their performances.

Again there are still likely to be individual scores. Again this is usually based on the amount of kills a player accumulates but, as the mission objective is of highest priority, the players are encouraged to complete these by being awarded more points (or more cash) to achieve these objectives. Preventative measures might also be rewarded—such as returning a stolen flag dropped by the enemy team during capture the flag. Again points are usually deducted for killing a teammate (see Table 11.4).

TABLE 11.4   Example scores for a capture the flag game.

Capture the Flag	10
Return Stolen Flag	3
Kill Enemy	1
Kill Teammate	−1

Online Rankings and Achievements

As consoles move to being online devices, it makes the creation of online ranking mechanisms—score tables, leagues, etc.—a viable possibility. Each game could easily offer the ability for a player to upload their best score, or form a league with a group of friends or even complete strangers!

With the Xbox 360, Microsoft has introduced a particularly interesting ranking scheme called Game Achievements and Gamerscore. This system encourages developers to assign 1000 achievement points as rewards to be spread across various parts of the game. Players can then try to find all 1000 points in a game. These achievements are shown as a Gamerscore on the player's profile for all to see. Players can also compare their progress with each other in specific games. This instantly encourages replayability in games and extends their longevity, as gamers try to eek out every possible point and improve their achievements score.

TIME

Time is often manipulated in a variety of ways during the course of the game. The passage of time is not always in real time. There may be no distinction between day and night or the seasons, or they could pass by in sped-up cycles. Time is often used as a source of conflict and challenge to the player. Time can even be manipulated by the player.

Passage of Time

The passage of time in games is rarely based on real-world passage of time, as it would be extremely tedious in most cases (*Animal Crossing* being a notable exception). A distinction is made here between games in which time does not pass at all, save for the progression of the story (if you were to stand in one place for hours, the time of day in the game world would not change) and those that use a day/night cycle. Some games (such as *Half-Life 2*) show a perceived shift in the time of day by changing the lighting conditions between levels to make the player believe time is progressing.

A day/night cycle is generally highly accelerated (as players are unlikely to play a game for 24 hours straight). In *Grand Theft Auto* one real minute is equal to one game hour. This is a pretty good yardstick, meaning it takes 24 minutes to complete a day/night cycle.

Time of day can affect events that occur in the game. In *Animal Crossing* events occur based on the time of the day (and even the time of the year) that the player is playing the game, so certain characters perform particular actions at set times, and certain events occur at very specific dates on the calendar.

While day/night cycles are common, it is much rarer for this to be taken further to a yearly cycle of seasons. However, seasons could affect several things:

The weather: The world is more prone to snow in winter and sunshine in the summer (unless in the southern hemisphere of course). These weather conditions may have a direct impact on gameplay, such as opening up routes via frozen water and making the ground more slippery in winter.

Game events: Festive events could occur with the passing of the seasons such as the appearance of Santa around Christmas or the Easter Bunny during spring.

Time-Based Challenges

Many parts of a game may feature time-based challenges, where the player must perform some action or accomplish a certain goal within an allotted time. There are potentially limitless challenges that could be set, but most follow one or more of the following formulas:

Rescue: Save someone from death before the time runs out.
Escape: Escape from an area before time runs out.
Race: Beat a set time around a course.

Survival: Stay alive for a set time while being chased or attacked until an event occurs that removes the threat.

Manipulating Time

The ability for a player to manipulate time can lead to some very interesting design possibilities, but it also tends to open up a massive can of worms. Some time manipulation methods are easier to implement than others. Time manipulation can take several forms:

Slow time (aka bullet time): Time is slowed to allow the player more time to react. This has been used heavily in games since Max Payne used it as a major game mechanic.

Bend time: Slow the world around the player but keep the player's speed as normal.

Rewind time: Reverse time to correct a mistake.

Fast forward: Accelerate time to skip sections or increase the power of an attack.

Note: It is probably a very bad idea to include time manipulation in multiplayer games. It would become very annoying for all concerned if time kept being altered during play—except for the player actually performing the skill.

Slowing Time (Bullet Time)

Time being slowed down is either automatically performed during a particular action or is assigned to a button press or skill to allow the user to choose the right moment to initiate the attack. Automatic bullet time tends to be used only to emphasize a move or attack. Manual activation allows players to strategize, utilizing the slow down to improve their reaction times.

Bend Time

Bending time alters all conception of the rules by allowing a character to move at normal speed while all around are slowed down. This must be a skill that is limited by consuming a resource such as magic points, as it offers a huge advantage for the character.

Bending time does have extremely problematic aspects that are very tricky to solve. The problems arise if the player is able to perform the skill at any point. If they are able to do this, then they can potentially interfere with sequences that are timed correctly for normal play but can be interrupted when time is manipulated (e.g., the player could run in and kill one of the participants of a scene). The solution is to prevent the player from being able to bend time at certain points (which would seem inconsistent) or to ensure that the player cannot interfere with any critical event (put it behind some form of barrier or do it within a cutscene).

Rewind Time

Reversing time really needs to be user controlled, as it would become extremely confusing if used automatically. *Prince of Persia: Sands Of Time* introduced the extremely useful method of reversing a small section of time to allow a user to correct a mistake. However, the number of uses of rewind allowed needs to be limited; otherwise, all challenge would be removed. This is best done by forcing the player to collect a certain maximum of rewinds or rewind time. Each time a rewind is used, it costs some of these resources to perform.

To perform rewinds, all player, AI input, and physics interactions need to be recorded. This can be fairly expensive in terms of memory footprint for large sections of time. Hence, usually only small fractions of play time are buffered (10 seconds or so).

Fast Forward Time

Fast forward is a fairly unusual manipulation of time. There are obvious examples such as being able to skip cutscenes, but in gameplay terms it can be more tricky. One possibility is to use it to increase the power of an attack, so when an attack is made, the player can speed up to slam into an opponent.

LIVES AND SAVES

Most games make the player character vulnerable to death. Without some kind of punishment, there would be no threat and thus no challenge. However, death is not always the end. While it can often spell Game Over, it doesn't necessarily mean that the player has to start again from the beginning. There are several ways a player's death can be handled.

Lives and Continues

The old-school idea of having lives or continues is used less and less these days. The player has a set number of lives or continues, and each death will reduce this number by one. When the player dies, he is placed back at the last reached checkpoint or the beginning of the level. When the player reaches zero, then it's Game Over.

Giving the player infinite lives or continues tends to be a more popular method these days, as previously strict limits of three or so lives tended to alienate the casual gamer. It does make for a fairly retro arcade experience to reintroduce a set limit of lives/continues, however.

Arcade-style continues often have a 10-second countdown—time where more money needs to be inserted on a coin-op machine—but this often is translated to an arcade console game to give it that authentic feel.

Level Unlocking

Many arcade games separate the game into distinct levels or missions. These can be used effectively as restart positions. If you die, you are sent back to the beginning of the level or mission. However, if levels or missions are particularly laborious and long, this can be extremely frustrating.

Checkpoints

In order that the player doesn't have to start right from the beginning of a level, checkpoints can be utilized. The checkpoint can manifest itself in several ways. Usually the checkpoint is a physical object in the world, but it can often be an unseen trigger.

Exactly what is stored at a checkpoint can vary. All information could be stored in memory, such as what has been triggered, how much health the player has, how much ammunition, and so on. This information could be stored to the player's save game, making it an auto-save feature.

Keeping a snapshot of the entire situation can require a vast amount of information, taking up far too much memory. An effective way of making the checkpoint simpler is to place players back at a checkpoint with their health replenished and possibly added ammunition or other goodies to a capped level (to enable them to continue if they wasted all their ammunition, spells, etc.).

Restart Points

A similar idea to the checkpoint is the restart point. This is a location where the player will always restart after death. A great example of this is the Hospital in *Grand Theft Auto*. Whenever you die, you wake up outside the Hospital with your weapons removed and $1000 taken from your funds. This kind of punishment is really a requirement of this kind of system; otherwise, death is no longer a danger.

The Hospital is a particularly good metaphor to use in this situation, as it instantly places information in the player's mind. Immediately they assume that their character was picked up at the scene by ambulance, patched up by doctors, and is now healthy and ready to get back out into the world. Using metaphors like this can enrich the game with very little effort. The players fill in the blanks themselves.

Quicksaves

PC gamers are used to the quicksave. The hard drive allows them to save as much data as they want, a luxury that usually eludes most console owners. Essentially the player is able to save a snapshot wherever they want. The sheer size of a snapshot can mean that only a handful will fit into a save game file on a console without a hard drive, so having the luxury of saving anytime is not possible without overwriting old saves.

The problem with quicksaves is that they can lead to load and save conditions where the player fails a section and thus loads up the last quicksave. This in turn can lead to lazy design, as the designers rely on the quicksave feature to get players through a section. A quicksave also has the danger of being saved at a dangerous moment, which can potentially break the save, as the player dies as soon as the game loads. This can be avoided by making the player invulnerable for a short period on loading.

That said, quicksave also allows players to stop playing whenever they want and not have the frustration of having to reach the next savepoint before they can turn the console off.

Savepoints

Savepoints are similar to checkpoints, but they store a snapshot of the current situation and they are usually activated by the player specifically. These savepoints take the form of some kind of object in the game world that can be interacted with. When accessed, they allow the player to save a game to a slot on the memory card. Most games will allow more than one slot for saving.

When the player dies in game, he is prompted to load one of his saved game slots. This tends to be a very successful method of dealing with death, as savepoints can be specifically placed right before difficult game sections. They allow the player some choice as to when to save. However, it is important that the player cannot save the game in a potential broken-game situation—a position where the player instantly enters the Game Over state when the game is loaded (e.g., during combat on low health). Therefore, savepoints are usually placed in slow-paced areas where there is little or no action occurring.

A slightly more complex version of the standard savepoint is the tokenized savepoint. This requires the collection of specific items (tokens) before it can be activated. These items are used up when the save is made, thus effectively limiting the number of saves a player can make during a play session.

This can be an interesting, but often frustrating, mechanic. It is important to properly balance the number of items collected throughout the game. The earlier titles in the *Resident Evil* series use a Typewriter with Ink Ribbon in this manner. Each Ink Ribbon offers a limited number of saves.

Ultra-Realism

Some games aiming for ultra-realism have death as a definite end point. *Steel Battalion* takes this to the extreme. If you don't press the eject button before your mech explodes, it will cause your death, promptly wiping your saved game in the process. This is the same game that had a unique dual-stick, 40-button controller sold alongside (which originally was going to include a glass panel over the emergency eject, but that had to be scrapped because of health and safety reasons).

This is an extreme version of death in games and can frustrate many people. However, it does add a high level of threat for the players and a great motivation to keep themselves alive. This should only be used if you are really pushing for a realistic angle and are expecting a very small but loyal audience.

Party Death

Party-based RPG games may often "knock out" player characters rather than kill them, meaning they are revived once combat is complete. If they are considered dead, then there is always the opportunity to resurrect them in some way (unless their death was an intended part of the story).

A Game Over state is only reached if all members of the party are knocked out during combat. Then the game may use any of the above systems (though RPGs usually have savepoints) to place the player back into the game.

SUMMARY

Economics can be found in many more areas of games than just monetary reward. The use of various economies needs balancing to ensure that there are no golden paths or degenerate strategies. The topic of component balance is discussed in detail in the later game balancing chapter. We covered a number of topics in this section:

Character economies: Economies can be found within the construction of the characters:

- **Attributes:** The proficiency of the character in key areas. An attribute will either be static or dynamic.
- **Character creation:** There are several elements of character creation—name, type, appearance, attributes, skills, and inventory.

Progression: Several aspects of progression can be utilized in a game world:

- **Item progression:** Items can be improved through point spending or augmentations.
- **Character progression:** Improvement of the character can be performed by unlocking of content, basic point progression, experience points and levels, event-based progression, complex locking, or even character augmentation.

Wealth: There are three main sources of wealth—treasure and trade items, inventory items, and raw materials. These can be obtained through:

- **Collection:** Finding raw materials or treasures and trade items.
- **Manufacture:** Turning raw materials into valuable items.
- **Trade:** Buying and selling goods to receive currency.
- **Gambling:** Testing luck to gain wealth.

Inventory: A character's inventory can act as a defining characteristic, allowing the character to perform actions and abilities. Alternatively, it can be used as a reward for others.

- **Player inventory:** Items can be acquired through purchase or collection. The scope of an inventory might be as little as a single item or be unlimited, slot based, size based, weight restricted, or class based. There may even be storage boxes around the world to store extra items. Multiplayer games may feature several differencing methods—collection, player classes, equipment selection, or opposites.
- **Enemy inventory:** An enemy will generally either have carried items or have some form of bounty that is dropped on death, or possibly even both.
- **Ally inventory:** An ally may act as support for the main character, offering health replenishment or more ammunition.
- **NPC inventory:** An NPC may offer particular quest or mission items or may act as a merchant to enable trading.
- **Environment inventory:** The environment itself may have simple placement of items, smashables, lockers, and recharge points.

Rating: The grading and assessment of a player's skill can also be considered an economy, where there are several resources that players seek to accumulate to improve their score.

- **Single player:** A single player may be scored on particular events.
- **Multiplayer scoring:** Different scoring methods are applied to each of the different game types.
- **Online ranking and achievements:** Scores can now be shared online and, particularly with Xbox 360 Live, can turn into a competitive event across many games.

Time: The use of time in games can also be considered an economy.

- **Passage of time:** The passage of time may take the form of a day and night cycle or even seasons. Game events can be tied into different times of day or different seasons of the year.
- **Time-based challenges:** There are several types of time-based challenge—rescue, escape, race, and survival.
- **Manipulating time:** Time can be slowed, bent, rewound, or fast forwarded.

Lives and saves: The application of lives and saves can have a profound effect on the experience for the player. Several methods might be used:

- **Lives and continues:** An old-fashioned system of lives and continues might be employed.
- **Level unlocking:** A game may only progress one level at a time, requiring the previous level to be completed before progress is saved.
- **Checkpoint:** A very common system is to have points within the level where the player will restart on death.

- **Restart points:** A similar system to checkpoints might be used in more free-form worlds, where there is a particular location where the player will restart at on death.
- **Quicksaves:** The ability to save at any point.
- **Savepoints:** The ability to save progress at a particular point in the level.
- **Ultra-realism:** A very difficult system that models realism, with only one life.
- **Party death:** RPGs tend to not enter a game-over state until all members of a party have died.

Economies in games exist in many places beside those detailed above. Every game will likely have a unique economy of its own. Strategy games place a particular focus on the use of economies and manipulating them to get the best results. This is an element you might like to explore in detail in your own games. Certainly, the designer should know how to balance and implement economies to give the most enjoyment to their audience.

WORLD BUILDING

Games create worlds—virtual spaces for the player to explore. Designers are the originators of these worlds, as they create level designs and characters to fill these worlds. From these initial ideas, the rest of the development team makes realities. A concept artist will take a designer's imaginings and turn them into sketches—something tangible for the rest of the team to work with. The environment art team builds the levels imagined by the designers and visualized by the concept artists. The character art team turns character designs into textured and rigged models ready for the animation team to animate or apply motion capture data to. All of these elements are then tied together by the design team to create the final product—a game world.

In this part of the book we will examine several aspects of world building. The first two chapters in this part look at level design, from the basic principles of form, function, and flow to the implementation of content in the game.

The next two chapters examine the use of artificial intelligence (AI) in games. First we explore the basic elements needed to create AI agents—characters that are able to navigate and perform actions. Then we look at how to turn these agents into believable characters that will make our world appear much more realistic.

The fifth chapter in this part of the book looks at physics. We examine how physics simulation can increase the believability of a game world and how physics can be incorporated into the game.

Finally we take a look at audio in games and how we can use music, speech, and sound effects to enhance our game world.

12

LEVEL-DESIGN PRINCIPLES

In This Chapter

- Function
- Form
- Flow

The core mechanics are essential to creating the basis of a great game, but it is the scenarios in which they are placed and the spaces in which they are played out that ultimately determine the final game. It is crucial to get level design right. There is plenty of theory and opinion on level design—and plenty of budding young designers with fresh ideas. It is perhaps what most people envisage game design to be about.

To create good levels, a level designer needs to grasp three principles of level design:

- Function
- Form
- Flow

FUNCTION

Every space has some purpose—some reason for existing. Within the game world a space has three reasons for existing:

Physical function: Function of the space within the context of the world
Ludic function: Function of the space in relation to the game
Narrative function: Function of the space in relation to the narrative of the game

Physical Function

The physical function of a space is the purpose that space serves in the game world. Many level designers have problems with defining physical functions, as they create very contrived spaces that fit the ludic function but pay little heed to the space within its world context.

For natural, organic environments, the laws that determine how things would naturally grow and change should be applied—unless of course we are deliberately breaking those laws to create an alien-looking environment. Man-made (or indeed alien-made) environments should ask themselves one very important question: why would I have been built? A room full of boxes could be recognized as a warehouse, but does the space support this? For example, are there doors big enough to get goods in and out? How are the goods moved around? How come there are so many warehouses in games?

Make sure each part of the environment has a function and a reason to exist. Creating a backstory for each area and working out how the spaces are or might once have been used will allow you to build believable spaces instead of contrived rooms that serve no other purpose than to act as a backdrop. That also applies to every object within the space.

Ludic Function

Ludic function is very different from physical function. Each space will have particular elements of gameplay that occur within them. This is their ludic function. When creating spaces, much attention should be concentrated on making ludic function work. However, this can often result in a very contrived feeling for the physical function of a space—as though the space was constructed merely for the purpose of gameplay. Striking a balance between the two is an important design skill.

A mistake many amateur (and even professional) designers make is to model a level on a real-world space and then expect to shoehorn the gameplay into it. This is essentially taking the pursuit of physical function to the extreme. Doing this is unlikely to satisfy the ludic function needs and is likely to severely hamper the ludic flow as well (see later section on flow).

Gameplay Type

The design of a space hinges primarily on the type of gameplay contained within:

- **Melee combat:** These areas are generally flat with no major obstacles in the center of the space. This allows more space for the combat moves and prevents awkward AI navigation problems.
- **Ranged combat:** In contrast to melee combat, ranged combat requires plenty of cover points and vertical movement. Long spaces also allow room for AIs to retreat and regroup.
- **Stealth:** Stealth requires lots of places to hide, as well as areas of darkness. It also needs lots of points of clear vision so that the players have a good idea of what is going on around them.
- **Exploration:** Much of exploration gameplay involves traversing a space for the simple pleasure of seeing it. Hence, exploration spaces should have interesting elements and feature a variety of routes and methods of traversal.
- **Spatial puzzles:** Where environment traversal is the heart of the gameplay, the environment is constructed around the control patterns. Look at *Prince of Persia's* elaborate environments as a particularly good example of this. The environments are like giant makeshift obstacle courses for the player to navigate. However, such seemingly makeshift environments need meticulous planning.
- **General puzzles:** Other types of puzzle often need very specific objects in the environment. Often these puzzles act as physical barriers to the player's progression, such as a locked door that must be opened.
- **Chase sequences:** Areas where the player is to be chased are generally long thin spaces that funnel the player. This space may wind around within a larger volume, but essentially it is the same concept.
- **Races:** Races are often set in very specific courses that are tailored to have bends and obstacles to test the competitors. However, makeshift courses might be constructed out of the existing environment, such as the many car races around the city streets that are a feature of *Grand Theft Auto*.

Ludic function's importance is likely to dominate much of the designer's thinking. Often ideas are created for individual set pieces, and the spaces are constructed around these. However, there are other methods. Spaces such as cities are usually created by physical function foremost, and then specific parts are tailored to meet the needs of ludic function.

Systemic design (which is discussed in the next chapter) is also likely to involve a lesser degree of ludic function design, as generic building blocks are used to create a space. However, linear games such as *Half-Life 2* are often a series of set pieces placed one after the other. Each of these spaces is highly driven by ludic function.

Signposting

One very important aspect of ludic function design is to give information to the player about any potential threat that may occur within an area—particularly if that threat is likely to be very damaging. To inflict damage on an unsuspecting player without any kind of warning is pretty unfair and is likely to frustrate. The method of providing information is often called signposting, as some kind of visual or aural clue is used.

For example, a mountain path that is prone to rockslides may have rocks strewn around it and sections that look very flimsy. An axe that falls down from a gap in the ceiling may have left grooves in the floor below. All of these provide clues that something nasty is about to happen. They put the player on tenterhooks.

Narrative Function

The third function of a space is its use as a narrative tool. The narrative function of a space is a stage for actors to perform on. There are usually points in the story that require very specific environmental features. The space often defines the mood of the actors at that time and plays a part in their situation. A deserted mining station on Mars presents very different narrative opportunities than a magic castle in the clouds. The stage should suit the play. Mass murder in the magic castle might be an interesting juxtaposition but is unlikely to be a believable experience for the player (though it might be a very comical one).

FORM

The aesthetics of a space play a very large role in the player's interpretation of a space. How a space looks will be the true yardstick by which a player will judge whether a space is believable or not. Essentially, creating believable space is about creating illusion.

Visual Style

The most immediate aesthetic quality of a game is its visual style—the method of rendering and the art choices that have been made. Many games aspire to a photo-realistic method of display—replicating the real world as closely as technology will allow. While this can be impressive, it also suffers from what is known as the "uncanny valley effect," in that the more real a simulation appears to be, the more we notice things that are not quite right, which shatters the illusion altogether.

The other problem is that it is not necessarily artistically creative or even desirable to simply model reality. Game worlds are supposed to take us on journeys into virtual worlds. Why do we have to recreate reality when we can use imagination to create truly awe-inspiring places to visit?

There are infinite art styles that could be applied to game worlds. We have so far seen very little in the myriad of possibilities. All too often we are bogged down in over-familiar styles such as bold, brash American sci-fi or Tolkienesque fantasy worlds. It's definitely time for some originality.

A few rendering techniques can be used to create unique visual styles such as toon-shading, which was introduced to the game community with *Jet Grind Radio*. This renders a black line around the character, and flat colors are used for texturing to create a very bold style. There are plenty of other rendering techniques that might drive art style in the future. Perhaps we might see some kind of Monet Impressionist rendering sometime soon.

World Scale

World scale is the size of the players in relation to the world they inhabit. For most games, real-world scale is desired—or at least an approximation of it. A typical way of recreating real-world scale is to assign one unit of game measurement as a real-world unit—generally 1 meter. A typical human will be around 1.5–2 m in this scale. Using a real-world unit enables the world builders to construct the level to the correct proportions. You can often see scale mistakes in existing games, where furniture is huge or doorways too small.

Rules are meant to be broken, but bending the rules of scale and proportion can create visual tricks. Scale tricks are used in the real world. Disney World's Main Street second and third storeys are built at smaller scale to create a forced perspective. Snow White's castle also uses smaller bricks toward the top for a similar effect.

Another trick that is widely used in games is the "Tardis effect" (named for the space vehicle in the cult sci-fi series *Doctor Who*; the inside of the Tardis is considerably bigger than it looks like it could be from the outside). This effect is used when entering an interior location that is separated from the exterior. So when a door is entered the new space is loaded. This new interior does not need to match the scale of the outside, as it is separate. You can see this trick used a lot in RPGs such as *Final Fantasy*.

Scale may be played with in a completely different manner. Like Gulliver in his famous travels, a player character may be very large—a giant who can stomp around his environment. Alternatively, he may be diminished in size—perhaps no bigger than the average rodent. Now the same world is viewed from very different eyes. The scale of objects is completely changed and with it the player's perception of the world.

We may even work on a different scale altogether. Imagine that we are working on a microscopic level. Now our world units would take on a very different real-world measurement. However, working in very small units in our world builder makes little sense. We would scale up the real-world measurements to something that we can easily interpret rather than the other way around.

Cohesion

It is important that a space be cohesive with those around it and that it fit within the structure of the game. If a Chinese pagoda were to pop up in the middle of a South American gangster game, it might seem somewhat out of place.

Details matter. While most of us might not know the exact details of architecture, we can often tell when something is out of place. This is where extensive research comes into play. Study what architecture a space might use, particularly if it is based on the real world. Get the details right and the space will be believable.

Consistency is also key. While progression is an important element in narrative function, too much deviation can seem glaringly wrong. If it is supposed to be one continuous space, then its appearance should seem consistent—or build slowly into its new form. Moving from a ruined palace, crumbling on the outside, straight into a well-maintained, opulent interior is likely to be too jarring and will destroy the believability of the space.

Expansion

Game spaces are often fairly small in size, as we don't necessarily want hours of aimless wandering. The trouble with this is that it suggests very confined spaces. The trick is to create an illusion of more space than there actually is. There are many ways to do this:

Unreachable areas: Windows that show outside spaces offer restricted views so that only a small section of this space has to be built.

Billboards: Create large images in the background that create the illusion of a expansive environment (see Figure 12.1).

FIGURE 12.1 Expanse: using a billboard to give the illusion that there is more to the world than there really is.

Façades: Create building fronts that suggest that there is more behind them
when there actually isn't (just like a film set).

Architecture

The way a space is constructed has a very large impact on the feelings it evokes. It
can drive human emotions and direct our thoughts. The choice of materials and
color impacts on our perception of these structures. All in all, the architecture of a
space is extremely important in level design. The power of a structure's form is often
underutilized. Flat walls and simple geometric lines are often presented to the
player. So much more can be done with spaces that will impact on the way players
react and even how they behave.

Man-made spaces have been thought about, studied, and constructed for thousands of years. As such, there is a wealth of inspiration just waiting to be explored by
budding game designers. All designers should try to learn some basic information
about architecture and start to think more and more about how these real-world examples can influence their designs. Game designers already have a major advantage:
the practical problems of construction do not apply, and costs are minimal in comparison to real-world construction. Also, the laws of physics do not necessarily have
to be obeyed. So why is it that so many games feature such bland, pointless spaces?

Many influences drive the design of a real-world building:

* Practical function
* Expression
* Symbolism
* Surroundings

Practical Function

The function of a building is often the driving force behind much of its design. Its purpose must be fulfilled for it to be a useful building [ConwayRoenisch94]. Different
types of buildings are needed for train stations, stores, residential properties, offices,
banks, and so on. Form often reflects the function of a building, so a bank looks imposing and secure and a train station is large and open to allow the trains to reach the
platforms.

Spaces are arranged in a particular order for practical purposes—the kitchen
being near the dining space for example. However, in the days of open fires the
kitchen was often separate to prevent the possibility of fire spreading. The practical-
ity of space changes over time. The needs of a modern space are vastly different from
historical spaces, so new additions are often made to a building. Extensions are
added, new areas built, and old ones taken away. The result is a building that can be
very different from its original form.

There are also several elements to a building: interior, exterior, and transitional
spaces such as porches. There are the functional spaces within the interior where activities occur, and for moving from space to space, additional spaces such as corridors, halls, lobbies, elevators, and staircases exist. These prevent people from having

to go through functional spaces unnecessarily. Often these spaces are very enclosed, which can promote feelings of claustrophobia. Windows and large open spaces remove these feelings and change the perception of a space.

The exterior form of a building often reflects practical needs due to climate. For example, a sloped roof prevents the buildup of snow and drains rain away—hence their prevalence in the temperate climes of Northern Europe.

Modern buildings have requirements for infrastructure: electricity, water, air conditioning, and so on. These need to be housed somewhere. They may be hidden away from the main areas of a building and kept behind the scenes. Alternatively, like the Lloyds Building in London, they may be on display for all to see.

Expression

While buildings serve a practical purpose, they also reflect the human desire for self-expression. Much of showpiece architecture is considered to be true art, but even the humble dwelling is an expression of some style or period.

There have been many movements and styles in architecture, from the classicism of Ancient Greece and Rome, to stark modernity. These styles promote the use of particular elements such as columns, buttress, simple geometric shapes, and so on. Proportion is also an important element of form. Proportion is the relationship of scale between certain elements, such as the size of windows and the height of ceilings. Particular styles may have very specific proportions, even to the point of having strict mathematical relationships between elements. Some styles promote symmetry and harmony, while others use asymmetry to challenge the viewer.

The various approaches to building design through style have a massive impact on the forms of buildings. Classical architecture starts with a basic geometric form as a shell for the building, and then space is divided inside accordingly. Modern styles tend to first create the functional spaces and then create the links between them.

A building can even change throughout the course of day. Shadows cast by sun can dramatically affect the appearance of the building, highlighting or subduing particular elements. Modern buildings can be completely transformed at night because of lighting. What can be mirrored glass during the day is transformed into lit up pictures at night; we now see into the building rather than seeing the reflection. In game worlds where dynamic time of day is used, the visual differences should be highlighted, allowing a whole different world to come alive when darkness falls. In static lighting conditions, buildings and light sources should be placed where the most pleasing appearance is created.

Every building tends to have a façade—the front of the building being a dramatic showpiece. The other sides of a building can be somewhat plain in comparison. These façades often present much of the expression of the building, particularly when surrounded by other buildings. Free-standing buildings have much more space for expression on all sides.

Symbolism

Symbolism is often expressed in public or commercial buildings where power, wealth, superiority, or seriousness is to be reflected. Religious buildings in particular are structured around symbolism. For institutions and corporations, the portrayal of their importance is uppermost in the architecture of their buildings. Scale is often used to create an imposing or even overwhelming feeling of grandeur. Cathedrals often feature huge spaces inside that fill their patrons with awe; height pulls their eyes skyward in worship of God. Corporations use scale as a sign of their power and dominance.

Symbolism also occurs in many other ways, for example, in the features of New York's Chrysler Building that resemble the cars that they built. The forms of the Sydney Opera House resemble ship's sails—a reflection of the city's naval history.

Castles, banks, and other secure buildings are built to look secure. Thick walls large heavy doors, and security devices give a message that unwanted entry will not be easy. This gives the people that use them a feeling of safety.

Religious buildings are even constructed to form basic symbols. Most spaces are rectangular, but religious spaces are built to forms that are meaningful to that religion—the cross of the Christian Church for example. There are few practical uses for nonrectangular shapes, the oval stadium for an athletic track being one.

Surroundings

A building's surroundings have a huge impact on its form. The geography of a location has a major impact on construction technique and the type of materials that can be used. For instance, the dwellings in Vietnam are often built on stilts because of the marshy land on which they sit.

The surrounding buildings also have a large impact on form. Usually the building will be made to fit in with its surroundings, to conform to a particular style. However, there are many occasions where buildings will look completely different than their surroundings. This is due to progress, as old buildings are torn down and new ones built in their place, or as a result of drastic upheavals such as war.

Landscape

As well as creating structures, level designers may want to create organic, natural-looking environments or even alien landscapes. Creating organic environments is a little tougher than building more geometric structures and is often much more difficult to get right. Technical limitations have traditionally made it difficult to recreate landscape, as they require very intricate detail, particularly foliage, such as trees with their hundreds of branches and leaves that blow in the wind.

These days it is much easier to create believable landscape. However, the imaginations of designers still tend to be a little stilted. There is a gaming cliché where every game has a lava and an ice level, and, more often than not, it is true. With such a massive potential for possible settings, it seems lazy that the same scenarios are used again and again. There are reasons why these two are used, of course: lava is a deadly surface to fall into and ice has reduced friction, but there are plenty of other potential gameplay possibilities in other settings.

There are potential problems with landscape. Landscape generally has very few flat surfaces which are desirable for melee combat and smooth movement. Undulating surfaces also make for a complex collision mesh. Landscape can, of course, be leveled somewhat and still look fairly natural.

Landscape tends to be fairly wide and open. This can be difficult for many renderers to handle but is fairly easily solved. Placing the action in valleys or canyons and using high ground to occlude sections allows the designer to split the map into suitably sized sections. LOD is extremely useful for landscapes, especially for trees and other complex forms.

A look at more extreme landscapes that exist on earth is bound to spark ideas in a good level designer's mind. Games should take us to breathtaking worlds that we might never visit in real life.

Procedural landscape generation enables landscape elements to be generated on the fly. It is unlikely that this would be used to generate the level geometry, but rather landscape elements within this, such as trees and other plants. Foliage generation allows easy placement of complex forms and also allows it to be scalable according to the constraints of technology.

Destruction

Destruction of the environment in a game can be fairly difficult. The problem is one of technology restrictions. Deformations and destruction can result in vastly increased polygon counts, changes in lighting, and other thorny issues. *Red Faction* on the PS2 and PC used a technology called GeoMod to deform the terrain. While this worked to some degree, it created a very generic-looking destruction, and once large chunks had been blown out of the level, the framerate often slowed to a crawl.

Another problem with unlimited destruction is boundaries. If the player can destroy walls, what is to stop him from advancing? One of the failings of *Red Faction's* gameplay was that it didn't often utilize the main new mechanic of the game in its level design. It was almost redundant.

The solution to problems of boundaries is to only allow certain objects to be destructible. Instantly this breaks one of the most important game design rules: consistency. Why can you blow a hole in one wall but not destroy a tree with the same weapon? A way of overcoming this is to have a game language that defines particular elements to be destructible, perhaps by using particular recognizable materials, such as a crumbling wall or rotting wood.

The actual destruction of an object can be handled in a number of ways:

Despawn: The object is simply removed. This removal is covered by a cloud of particles. Obviously, this can look a little contrived, particularly with the power of today's technology.

Multiple meshes: A number of different meshes are created for various stages of destruction. These are then swapped as the object is damaged. This is also covered by a particle cloud.

Chunks: The object is constructed from a number of chunks that can be detached and controlled with the physics simulation. The only problem with this method is that larger chunks may end up blocking the player and getting in the way. This can be potentially game breaking but can be avoided if the chunks are small enough to be pushed out of the way.

Physics: The object can be deformed and fractured using physics simulation. These can be potentially costly and may suffer from the same problems as chunks but give a good-looking and different result each time.

Flow

The final of the three basic principles is flow—the movement through a space. Much like function, there are three forms of flow:

Physical flow: The physical connections and boundaries of space
Ludic flow: The arrangement of gameplay through a space
Narrative flow: The progression of narrative through a space

Physical Flow

Space is connected and bounded in a myriad of ways. These connections and boundaries define the physical flow of a level.

World Boundaries

Every virtual space must have some sort of physical boundaries [Adams03]. Some styles of game would suit the automatic generation of terrain and would thus not necessarily need defined boundaries, but most action–adventure games require predefined content. Because predefined content must be created by humans, it is finite.

We must place boundaries to prevent the player from leaving the confines of the predetermined space and effectively reaching the edges of the world. Beyond the edge is simply a void, and it can be fairly illusion destroying for a player to witness these areas.

Interior Spaces

Interior spaces have an immediate advantage: they are already confined spaces with predefined boundaries. The way to suggest that there is more than what the player can move through is to create false doors or glimpses into areas that cannot be reached, although false doors can be somewhat annoying when they are in a reachable position, because they break the believability of the world as there is no interaction. The more consistent interaction there is, the more believable the world becomes. If a false door looks sturdily locked so that the player obviously can't use it, the player is more likely not to question its placement.

Exterior Spaces

Exterior spaces are a little more tricky to place boundaries around, but you need to contain the player somehow. There are two basic methods to do this:

- An impassable obstacle surrounding the level
- An infinite plane surrounding the level

The most widely used boundary is some form of impassable obstacle, for example:

- Ocean
- Steep mountains
- Swamplands
- Buildings and walls

It is important that these don't seem too contrived. A great big box wall around the level is just wrong. A very popular confinement method for large environments is to set them on islands in the middle of the ocean. If the player cannot swim, the water becomes an impassable barrier. Smaller environments such as an urban street can use the geography of buildings and roads, but they may require the occasional oddity such as a road block or line of cars to prevent further travel. Alternatively, there might simply be invisible collision, but this tends to look and feel really wrong.

The idea of an infinite plane is to allow the players to wander off but make them so utterly bored in doing so that there is no reward (though sometimes there might be the occasional secret). An infinite plane can be:

- Ocean
- Desert plain
- Auto-generated terrain

If the player can swim or use a vehicle on water, then an ocean is no longer an impassable boundary. There might also be negative effects for going too far out, such as drowning when swimming the ocean or suffering from heat exhaustion when walking across the open desert. These effectively become impassable obstacles.

Space Connection

Most levels are a collection of spaces connected together to create a whole. The organization of these connections determines how the player will move though the world.

Several parameters affect the choices made when organizing the structure of a level:

Occlusion: The setup of a level that optimizes rendering performance. Being able to see the whole level at once will more than likely make the render engine struggle.

Navigation: The organization of a space to maximize the ease of navigation.

Progression: The organization of a level to lay out visible goals for a player to achieve.

Occlusion

The most technical influence on space connection is that imposed by the render engine. The need for occlusion is heavily dependent on the capabilities and restrictions of the rendering engine. There is likely to be a higher demand for occlusion where high detail is required in each space.

The basic principle of creating a level for occlusion is to separate space into distinct sectors and ensure that there are not spaces on the map where too many sectors can be seen at once. This is done by placing obstructions between sectors, so that there is no direct line of sight through to another sector. Methods such as kinks in corridors or entrances placed at different angles or positions so sectors are not aligned are effective methods of occlusion.

This need for occlusion is a generally negative force in creating flow, meaning that plans for an open level may have to be curtailed because of technical requirements. If these limitations are considered during the design phase, there will be far fewer problems later in development.

Navigation

Navigation is a very important aspect of level flow. Three main techniques can be used to aid navigation:

Landmarks: Almost every building or landscape has some kind of difference or feature that marks it out. Some of these features are more prominent than others. They instantly tell us where we are and allow us to orient ourselves. In game worlds we also need these landmarks to help us understand where we are. Landmarks can be used in very localized areas as an indication to the players that they have been there before. A whole series of localized landmarks would act like a breadcrumb trail, telling the players that they are doubling back on themselves. However, they do not allow players to orientate themselves within the level as a whole. Larger landmarks really need to stand out. Tall buildings or features that stand above everything around them offer a point of reference. If the players can see where they are in relation to such a landmark, they will have a good idea as to exactly where they are. These landmarks are often used as goals—places to aim for that lead the player through the level. *Half-Life 2* uses this technique excellently, with the large citadel tower at the centre of City 17, which can be seen from all around. This is also the final destination of the game [Valve04].

Themes: Themes are powerful ways of marking out areas of a level so that the players know what section they are in. In multiplayer maps these themes become especially relevant, as they enable the players to know where they are and where they should be going. Themes may be very simple, such as having specific colors or motifs within a particular area. The lighting might be used so that one area is themed with red lighting and another with blue. Themes may also be more complex. Whole areas might be dedicated to a particular physical function. For example a ship-based map might have an engine-room-themed area and upper decks, which are visibly different. This separates each section of the map from the others. There should still be cohesion in its form, though, as a mishmash of styles is likely to look ridiculous.

Architectural Form: The architectural form of a space can be used to guide the player. Different angles within a space cause natural responses to move in specific directions. As Tito Pagán describes in his article on gamasutra.com, "Where's the Design in Level Design?" [Pagan01], walls with long horizontal space make us want to move around them, whereas walls with long vertical space make us want to ascend them. Angled walls also affect the motion of space around them. A popular method for navigation is to create corridors that funnel the player in a particular direction. Grand doorways grab the player's attention and indicate that this is the direction in which to move. Clear paths show the players that there is a route that they should follow.

Progression

Progression is used on narrative-based maps that might otherwise be completely linear. Progression in respect to flow is about setting visual goals for the player. This can be done by placing the targets a player must reach in sight at various points in the level. Having a number of crossover points is a good method of introducing progression. When players see a feature in the landscape that appears to have some physical access, they will begin to question how they will be able to reach it. Later, when they do reach the feature, they can look back to see where they were earlier. This gives them a satisfying feeling of making progress.

A game that used spatial progression to superb effect was the original *Tomb Raider*. Much of the gameplay was based around trying to reach goals that were seemingly impossible to reach. Also, there were lots of crossover sections, where there would often be a long gap of time before they were revisited. All of these factors lead to a very real sense of progression through the space.

The flow of a level may lock areas that the player has passed through or leave them open to allow the player to retrace his steps. Locking areas behind the players ensures that they continually progress and prevents them from moving the wrong way but can sometimes feel like a contrived mechanic. It also makes it difficult to enable cooperative play (this is usually solved by teleporting the player lagging behind near to the further advancing player). Typical methods of locking include slamming or locking doors, rockslides, explosions, collapsing bridges, and hordes of enemies. Quick time event sequences can also be used to lock backward progress if they transition the player between two points that are not linked by the course of normal actions. Retaining the ability to retrace steps allows the designer to use backtracking or allows the players to return to collect items they might have left or missed along the way. However, enabling backtracking requires that information about previous sectors be retained.

Spatial Organization

Real-life buildings, towns, and cities are built around a group of organizational patterns [ChenBrown01]. These patterns can be used to structure the form of a level (see Figure 12.2):

Centralized: The main function of a space is in the center, and all of the spaces radiate out from this (e.g., a football stadium).

Linear: Organized along on axis such as a street or tower.

Radial: Built out from a center point, but functional space occurs in the outer areas rather than the center.

Clustered: Grouped together in a lump. For example, this might be a neighborhood that has gradually changed over time rather than having been built on purpose.

Grid Organized in a neat pattern of any tessellating shape. Modern planned cities are often built on a grid system (e.g., New York).

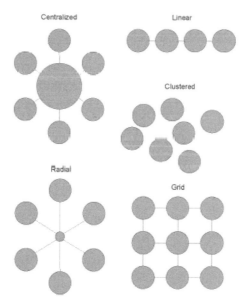

FIGURE 12.2   Methods of organizing space.

Ludic Flow

While physical flow is concerned with the connection of space and the ease of movement within it, ludic flow is concerned with how gameplay is connected through the spaces of the level. Ludic flow separates levels into two distinct types:

Narrative: A single-player or cooperative experience where the player(s) face a set of challenges laid down by the designer.

Competitive: Spaces where individuals or teams of players fight for victory. The challenge is in beating rivals, not completing a narrative.

Narrative-Based Levels

Narrative sets goals for the player to accomplish. These goals can be broken into three levels of abstraction:

Ultimate goal: The main goal of a game such as rescue the princess or save the world from evil (who says games are clichéd?)

Short-term goals: Missions and side quests that are a means to reaching the ultimate goal, such as gaining entry to a military base or rescuing a comrade

Immediate goals: Very short-term goals such as getting past a door or taking out an enemy

Each level or mission is composed of one or more short-term goals and often hundreds of immediate goals. A series of levels or missions moves toward eventually attaining the ultimate goal.

The goal of the designer is to create interesting combinations of immediate goals to build up an interesting scenario. This becomes a short-term goal. Thus, if we wanted to set a goal such as "enter the military base," a series of immediate goals might be:

1. Snipe the guard in the watchtower.
2. Sneak past the searchlight.
3. Break into the truck.
4. Drive the truck through the gates.
5. Take out the guards that respond to the alarm.
6. Steal the pass card from the lieutenant.
7. Gain access to the door.

Interesting diversions in flow appear when multiple options are given for a situation. A very linear game will demand that all of the above steps are followed. More free-form games would allow the above as one of a number of possible solutions.

Putting the mechanisms in place for these scenarios is based on the design methodology applied to level construction. This is discussed later.

Several elements can be used in narrative flow:

- Pace
- Backtracking
- Enemy placement

Pace

The pace of gameplay is another important aspect of narrative-based level flow. The players need action to keep them stimulated, but over-stimulation can lead to desensitization. The pace needs to keep the action moving in ebbs and flows—moments of intense action followed by moments of calm—to give the players time to relax or lull them into a false sense of security.

Several elements can create changes in pace:

Passages: Passages are long narrow spaces that encourage the player to move swiftly through them onto the next area.

Arenas: Arenas are sections where the player is locked in. Here the flow of enemies can be tightly controlled. One interesting technique is to make the arena empty at first until some event causes the action to begin. This allows the players to get their bearings before the action starts.

Mazes: Areas of tight corridors and rooms often create a slowed pace, as the player must meticulously search each nook and cranny.

Expanses: Vast open areas often slow the pace down, as they require lots of exploration or time to traverse. Filling large spaces may quicken the pace, but it is much harder to completely fill a large space than a much more contained one.

Actions: Actions will naturally have their own pace. Combat is often high speed. Stealth is much slower and methodical. Acrobatics tend to be set at a pace that the player is comfortable with.

Puzzles: A puzzle will usually slow the pace of the game down, especially if it is a cerebral puzzle.

Forced pace: A forced pace challenge, puzzle, or enemy wave brings the pace up sharply, as the player is under pressure to complete the section before the clock, health, or some other commodity runs out.

Backtracking

One method of getting multiple uses out of a single space is to force the players to backtrack through areas they have already encountered. This is a very efficient use of what can be very costly spaces to create but can irritate the players if done too often or if there is no new gameplay in these areas to reward them.

Enemy Placement

For melee-based combat the placement of enemies is not as important as the number and formations that they use. Placement of enemies is a key component of good ludic flow for games that feature ranged combat or stealth. A number of placement strategies might be employed:

Shock Ambush: A very well worn tactic is to surprise the player with a hidden enemy or group of enemies. Used in the right place, this can be an excellent tactic, building up a feeling of tension in the player. However it is also very easy to overuse this tactic to the point where the player becomes desensitized—something *Doom 3* was criticized for.

One major issue with the shock ambush is to try to keep the event in the player's view. Enemies that appear and attack unexpectedly from behind are usually frustrating and annoying.

Waves: Waves are patterns of enemies that approach or spawn at timed intervals. The shape, movement speed, timing, as well as the numbers and types of enemies in these waves, determine their complexity and difficulty. Waves are deeply rooted in gaming history. Early games such as *Space Invaders* and *Galaxians* are built around these patterns.

Waves can be used in modern games to bring enemies into play. They generally don't follow specific movement patterns like *Galaxians*, but move under AI control. Wave placement is often used as enemies' initial spawning positions or to govern the number and types of enemies that are in play at any one time.

Strategic Positions: A common tactic in many games is to place enemies in strategic positions such as at bottlenecks or in a sniping position. The key to strategic positioning is to offer a challenge to the player but not put enemies in such a strategic position as to make it almost impossible to defeat them. The player should believe that the positioning was well thought out and that enemies were not just placed arbitrarily. Placing groups of enemies in bunkers or guards in watchtowers lends a sense of believability to the world.

Patrols: Patrols are groups or individual enemies wandering the environment in set patterns. These patrols are looking out for the player who is trying to infiltrate their territory. Generally these are found in most ranged combat games, as well as being a large part of stealth games.

The important part of a patrol is its sensory AI and the route laid out for it. The player learns a patrol route and then can seek to avoid being detected as the patrols pass by. Careful placement of these patrol routes will create some interesting game scenarios such as overlapping routes that require the player to concentrate on multiple enemies. Care must be taken to ensure that there is an opportunity to move undetected.

Turkey Shoot: A turkey shoot is an enemy or group of enemies placed purely as cannon or sword fodder. These are enemies that are unaware or seriously disadvantaged and offer the player the opportunity to take them out with ease. These should never make up the entirety of a game, as there is no real challenge involved, but they are a great reward to give the player from time to time.

Sequences: The final placement of enemies is to have them performing some scene as the player approaches. The player is then either seen by these enemies and they drop what they are doing, or the player takes them by surprise. For example, a player might stumble into a room full of enemies tucking into a huge feast. On sight of the player, they might leap up and throw their food to the floor and grab their weapons, kicking out tables and chairs as they stumble into action.

Sequences add a very rich feel to the world and dramatically increase the believability for the player. They are, however, expensive in terms of resources and require a lot of animation or motion capture data to get right. They are a serious undertaking, but they can really pay off.

Competitive-Based Levels

Competitive-based levels are very different from narrative levels and generally require a different set of skills to be employed in their creation. These levels are merely stages in which individuals or groups play. The flow of a competitive level is based on the number of players, the strategies of the players, and the type of game that is to be played in the level. A level that works well for one game type does not necessarily lend itself well to all others.

The space itself becomes a playground of sorts, and it must offer tactical opportunities for the players in its spread of cover, distance, and the arrangement of space. Multiplayer games have a strong repetitive structure, so players will become very aware of the layout of space and the various tactical opportunities that are presented to them. On single-player, narrative-based levels events are triggered as the player moves though the space. In multiplayer, competitive levels it is only space that can be manipulated. The actual gameplay will vary according to the players and the tactics they use. That said, there are methods of biasing a level toward particular types of gameplay.

Game Type

Ludic flow for these levels should be broken down according to game type:

- Free-for-all
- Territory
- Mission based

The number of players can heavily influence the flow of a game. Some maps may be far too big for certain numbers. Often maps are built with specific numbers of players in mind. Alternatively, parts of a level can be shut off to allow the size of the map to expand and contract according to the number of players.

Free-for-All: Every man for himself is most commonly seen as Death match, but there are all sorts of variations on the theme. The important fact for ludic flow is that players can be anywhere on the map at any time and no one has allies (unless they forge some alliance by themselves). This requires several things to ensure good flow around a level:

Multiple exits and entrances: Dead ends are death traps for players. Once a map is learned, these areas will become dead areas—unless there is some reward.

Good routes: Players tend to learn their own patrol routes, which they circle looking for action. Make these routes prominent and action will build around them.

Gathering points: Areas where a number of routes overlap or combine result in action hotspots where players congregate.

There tend to be a few models that work particularly well:

Arena: One large area with multiple routes around it that all lead into the main area. The arena often makes use of vertical space as well as horizontal

Circular: A main circular route with branches leading off. This creates a well-worn patrol with side detours if need be

Meshed routes: Routes that all overlap each other at key points

Linked arenas: A series of three or four mini arenas with very short connections between them

Open space: Wide open area with scattered cover and buildings to hide in

Overly complex areas or areas that are too large mean players hardly ever see each other and result in a very dull game.

Territory: Territory games involve two or more teams fighting for possession of areas of a level. Territory maps generally start with each team having bases at opposite ends of the map. Often these bases cannot be taken by the enemy. Alternatively, one team can start with a major advantage by having nearly all of the bases in their possession but without a permanent base, so they are vulnerable to being completely wiped out.

The key to a good territory map is allowing for a variety of capture strategies and having a good spread of capture points without too great a space between them. Bases close together promote close-quarter fighting but also encourage spawn camping, where players are shot as soon as they are spawned. It can be extremely frustrating to be on the receiving end of this. Too wide a distance between points means far too much aimless wandering, unless there are vehicles or teleporters to get from point to point.

The number of bases is also important. Too few means the action is very intense but can mean little in the way of available strategies. It often becomes all-out chaos. Too many bases mean players see too little action, as there is less chance of being in the same vicinity as an enemy. Three to four bases in addition to the two team start bases tends to make for a good balance of action and strategy (depending, of course, on the number of players).

Each base can have strategic advantages and disadvantages or methods of defending or attacking them:

Easy to defend: A heavily fortified base allows the defenders to dig in and have a good view of all attackers.

Hard to defend: Bases that are easy to attack are high-action spots and tend to change hands regularly.

Directional defense: A base that is easy to defend in one direction but is prone to attack from another makes the defenders more nervous.

Resource base: A base that is rich in resources is a very attractive base to capture. These should be quite hard to defend, as it makes them too powerful otherwise.

The position of the capture zone is also important, as it makes the base easy or hard to defend and attack. A zone that is out in the open is generally easier to defend, as the attacker is vulnerable and easy to spot. Zones that spread over buildings or through walls are much harder to defend because attackers can hide in buildings to capture the zone.

The balance of resources on territorial maps, if there are any, is also key. Teams should begin with a similar amount of resources, though not necessarily of the same type. For example, a team with an air advantage might start with only one base some way from the main cluster of bases. For every attack strategy, there should be a balancing strategy available, so certain bases might be equipped with anti-tank or anti-aircraft weaponry. Having one resource-rich base encourages a rush to take it, but it should not be so resource rich as to leave the other team without a chance. This is heavily dependent on the balancing of the resources themselves, but a lot of care and playtesting should be used when attributing resources to each base.

Mission Based: Games like *Counter-Strike* have very specific levels where there are very clear mission objectives. The type of mission has some bearing on the layout and flow of a map, but all good mission-based maps are based on a core set of concepts:

Routes: Two or three main routes through the various areas of the map. Too many routes will result in not enough chance of action occurring. Routes need to be balanced so there isn't always a golden path for one team. There should be no unfair advantages.

Collision points: Areas where the two teams meet. Good maps time the collision point to be at specific points in a level. Collision points will only occur if the defenders are drawn away from their starting positions. Otherwise, they have the advantage of having plenty of time to prepare ambushes. Having more than one objective placed in a level away from the defender's starting position forces teams to move toward collision points to prevent the attackers from reaching them. However, any more than two objective points may make it hard to defend. Games such as Capture the Flag naturally have two objectives: each team must take their opponent's flag while defending their own. Collision points will naturally occur between these two objectives.

Strategic areas: Places on the map where ambushes can be set up or good teamwork will pay off. There might be sniping points to cover another team member aiming to complete a mission objective. Defense of an objective needs to tread a fine line between being easy to defend and possible to attack. Too many confined entrances and ambush spots make defense easy but attack very difficult. Having only one entrance will make attack nigh on impossible. The objective should be quite difficult to take if there are many defenders but offer enough options for strategies to be employed.

Strong themes: Players connect more with a level if there is a strong and believable theme.

The key to creating successful mission-based levels is strenuous playtesting. Only by playing this kind of level extensively will all the possible strategies or exploitations be found. This is true of all levels, but mission-based maps in particular benefit from repeated scrutiny.

Player Strategies

No matter what the game type, every player has a preferred way of playing and a number of strategies that they use. These strategies should be catered to in every map to keep players happy, but some strategies may be encouraged more than others to give a level a distinct feel:

Camping: Although hated by many, camping is a perfectly valid tactic. Camping is aided by providing areas of darkness or plenty of objects to hide behind. Don't go overboard with catering for this strategy; otherwise, no one will be able to find each other, as they will be trying to camp and it will be too hard to know where you are being attacked from. Keep camping spots fairly minimal, as this allows players to learn the prime camping spots and approach them with caution.

Sniping: Sniping sections require long, narrow view areas for optimum sniping potential. Wide areas are harder to scope. Sniping alleys should offer some kind of cover for potential victims. Snipers should be vulnerable to attack from behind to prevent them from becoming too much of a nuisance.

Rushing: The charge-in all-guns-blazing approach generally demands small areas of cover in a fairly open area. Thus, the rusher can circle strafe around an opponent and dive out of harm's way if need be.

Cautious: The cautious approach is enabled by offering lots of cover points so that players can advance from cover point to cover point, always ensuring that they are not left vulnerable. Of course, it is nice to make such players nervous by forcing them out in the open at certain points.

Spaces

Long, tight corridors are particularly bad for competitive shooter levels, as they offer no place to shelter from attack. Areas that require tricky movement to negotiate are also bad, as players are easy targets while traversing them, or they may prove to be the downfall of a circle-strafing player. Geometry should not feature protruding elements that might snag players as they move about. This becomes very frustrating.

In areas with many entrances it can be very difficult to watch your back, making unexpected ambush while you are already engaged in combat a real problem. A simple method of solving this is to use audio clues, such as placing doors that make sounds at entrances to alert players of other people's movements.

Item Placement

Item placement can be used to control a player's movement through a competitive level. By placing ammunition away from the weapon it is used with, the player is forced to keep moving to stock up on ammunition. Keeping ammunition in the same place as a weapon is often a bad idea, as it creates a holding ground where players can circle around, collecting the items as they spawn.

Narrative Flow

A space can define narrative beyond the performers acting out the script and beyond simply being a stage for them to perform on. An environment can act as a commentary for the game world and the story that is being told. It can be used as a measure of progression to indicate to the players how the world is changing around them, and how deep into the game experience they have gone.

This kind of narrative has been used in many games. It was used in both *Half-Life* and its sequel. As the players progress, the creatures they encounter become ever more alien and the world around them begins to change as well. At the end of *Half-Life* you enter the alien world itself. In *Half-Life 2* you see the human city being consumed by the alien machine. These are great examples of changes to the world that can hold useful narrative details (though the alien world Xen in *Half-Life 1* was somewhat disappointing after the wonderful Black Mesa complex).

This can also be flipped on its head so that the world changes for the better as a result of the player's actions. Imagine a once-dank swamp suddenly blooming and singing with life once you clear out the evil lurking in its midst.

SUMMARY

In this chapter we have focused on the basic principles of level design. These principles should guide designers through the basic steps of level design and allow them to start thinking about the elements that go into producing the very best level designs.

Function: The purpose of a space. Function aspects of level design are broken down into the following elements:

- **Physical function:** The purpose of a space within the context of the world.
- **Ludic function:** The purpose of the space in relation to the gameplay. This will depend on the types of gameplay that occur within the space.
- **Narrative function:** The purpose of the space in regard to the narrative.

Form: The aesthetics of a space. This is broken down into a number of elements:

- **Visual style:** The art style used in the game.
- **World scale:** The physical relationship of character to game space.
- **Cohesion:** How a space works in relation to its backdrop and within the narrative.
- **Expansion:** The creation of more than there really is.
- **Architecture:** The study of how real-world spaces will allow designers and artists to construct awe-inspiring virtual spaces.
- **Landscape:** The study of real-world landscape to create natural, organic spaces.
- **Destruction:** The deformability of the world by the players and their actions within it.

Flow: The movement through a space. There are several aspects of flow in games.

- **Physical flow:** The world boundaries, connections between spaces, and organization of spaces in relation to each other.
- **Ludic flow:** There are two types of ludic flow—narrative and competitive. Narrative flow relates to single-player or cooperative story-based levels, whereas competitive levels are designed for multiplayer gaming matches.
- **Narrative flow:** The use of the level as a narrative tool, such as changing the feel of levels to suit the mood of the story.

Level design brings together all the elements of a game and lays out gameplay into something tangible. It is an aspect of game design that requires skill and a range of abilities in a designer but many consider it to be a lesser area of design. All the best mechanics in the world won't count for anything if they are not utilized in interesting and meaningful ways.

LEVEL IMPLEMENTATION

In This Chapter

- Design Methodologies
- The Level Design Pipeline
- Logical Structures
- Construction Methods
- Tools

The implementation phase of level design is where the most differences between projects occur. Potentially there are almost limitless approaches and combinations of technology that can be employed to make levels a reality. In practice there are good and bad ways of approaching the problem. This chapter will allow you to realize the best approach for your game.

When tackling implementation, several things must be considered:

- Design methodologies
- The level design pipeline
- Logical structures
- Construction methods
- Tools

DESIGN METHODOLOGIES

Design methodologies are approaches to level design that heavily influence a level's construction. Essentially they are theories of level breakdown that define the manner in which play elements are constructed and how they relate to each other. There are two main approaches to level design, and a third approach that is a mixture of the other two:

- Systemic
- Specialized
- Hybrid

Systemic

Systemic design is the creation of a set of base elements that can be placed together to form more complex scenarios—almost like a giant *Lego*® set. Each entity within the world is defined as a rigid set of interactions. For example, there may be a set number of door types: one light door that can be broken down, unlocked with a key, or lock picked; a heavy door that can only be unlocked with a key or lock picked; and a secure door that can only be unlocked with the key. When a player encounters a door, he knows immediately what he can do and thus creates strategies quickly.

Complexity starts to build when all the elements are brought together, but this is where interesting situations begin to arise. For example, if we encounter a light door and we can hear the sound of guards on the other side, we are presented with the following options: break down the door and face down the alert guards, pick the lock and hope we are quick enough so they don't hear, or get hold of the key to quickly gain entry and surprise the guards.

Harvey Smith, one of the designers of *Deus Ex*, is a big advocate of the systemic method. He talks extensively about the power of systemic design in his web lecture "Systemic Level Design for Emergent Gameplay" [Smith02]. He explains the advantages and disadvantages that this methodology offers. The advantages are:

Efficiency: Having building blocks in place makes it very quick and easy to set up gameplay scenarios. Changes made to an object will be made across the entire game so refinements can be distributed to the team quickly.

Consistency: The players knows exactly what to expect with each object they encounter, which in turn allows them to quickly formulate plans. A consistent world is generally a believable one, so the players are likely to feel a sense of solidity within the game rules.

Emergence: Having a set of base rules enables more complex and unexpected strategies than the designer may have conceived. This can be both good and bad, as some strategies may mean breaking free of the map and losing the sense of solidity of the game world.

Some of the disadvantages are:

Shoe-horning: Not all game elements may fit in a generic mold, so they may have to be forced to work in a certain manner.

Uncertainty: This could also be read as "bad emergence," like being able to break out of the confines of a level.

Conformity: While having a base set of rules to create scenarios is consistent, it leaves little room for individualism or truly one-off game elements. Some of the more individual elements in games can be the most memorable.

Perception: From a designer's point of view, this methodology might seem very restrictive on the imagination, but this is not necessarily the case.

Specialized

Specialized design is very much the opposite approach to systemic design, in that every design problem is approached individually. This means every case is considered to be unique and will have its own behaviors and interactions. This approach has very different results than the systemic approach. It has some powerful advantages, but also a number of problems. The advantages include:

Uniqueness: Every situation is unique and can therefore be made as elaborate and spectacular as the designer wants or has time to do.

Certainty: Because every situation is tailor made, every possible interaction can be accounted for and dealt with. While there is no emergence, there is also less risk of something bad unexpectedly occurring.

Style: Levels become a very personal thing, where the designer is heavily involved in the feel of the level. Individual styles can be seen, though this is not always an advantage where consistency is desired.

The disadvantages include:

Inefficiency: Every scenario needs specific implementation, which is very time consuming and needs good technical know-how on the part of the designer.

Inconsistency: While it is possible for level design to be consistent in this methodology, it requires much more collaboration and communication on the parts of all involved in the implementation process.

Lack of freedom: The constrained nature of the design means that the players are limited to what the designer wants them to do.

Hybrid

The ideal solution may seem to be combining the two methodologies to get the advantages of each with none of the disadvantages. That is a good ideal to aim for but is not as easy as it may first seem.

The biggest problem is that when placed side by side, the contrast between two elements created by different methodologies can be very noticeable. The key to solving this problem is to apply the methodologies to suitable elements. This forms two types of level elements within a game:

- Generic entities
- Level-specific entities

Generic Entities

Generic entities are those created from the systemic vision. These are entities that will be used across levels in multiple situations. They might include doors, weapons, furniture, scenery such as trees and bushes, and other bits and bobs. Each entity might belong to a specific group, such as doors, where a basic set of interactions and attributes can be applied. Each specific type may have specific settings for these interactions and attributes.

Generic objects give the feeling of consistency that allows players to formulate plans and enables emergent gameplay.

Level-Specific Entities

Much more elaborate scenarios can be approached from a specialized methodology and be custom built. Keeping this methodology for the elaborate set pieces means that there are far fewer of them, so more attention can be paid to them. Having limited numbers ensures they can be polished to a high standard and have a number of interactions catered to. This makes them fit well with the generic objects.

Level-specific objects might also use generic objects within them to keep a high level of consistency. The identification with a known object helps communicate possible interactions to the player.

THE LEVEL DESIGN PIPELINE

The workflow for level design can be approached in many different ways. Some designers like to jump straight in and start building geometry. Others like to sketch out some rough ideas first. Level design in the past has been an ad hoc journey for all involved.

The increasing pressures of commercial game development mean that such a laid-back approach to level design is no longer a viable way to work. Game design is no longer a solitary pursuit. Teams sometimes break the 100 people mark these days. Proper work pipelines need to be developed so that every member of a team knows what needs to be done.

Pipelines are likely to differ from company to company and even project to project, as different construction methods require different working practices. On some projects level geometry is created using bespoke world builders. Other projects have geometry created by environment artists in 3D packages such as Maya. There are, however, a number of key phases that should be implemented to ensure the production of quality levels, no matter what the construction methods.

- Concept
- Gray box
- Playtesting
- Balancing
- Refinements
- Sign-off

These phases are not run through in order but are often intermingled so that information is fed back to another phase. This process of revision builds up a solid pipeline and should produce well-designed levels (see Figure 13.1).

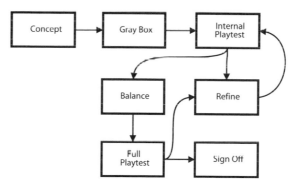

FIGURE 13.1   Level design pipeline.

The pipeline is the ideal method for designing a level. However, the realities of game development often throw a spanner in the works.

A publisher is spending a large sum of money on a project and is likely to want to see polished work as early as possible. Our advice is to build small areas of the level up to high standards first, so that the publisher can see the intended direction of the project as a whole.

Another demand is the demo for marketing purposes, and this can be a whole different beast. Projects can be severely affected by the constant need to produce demos for a number of different people, tradeshows, and so on. Be very wary of doing too many of these. They can mean months out of the schedule and mean lots of hackery introduced to make the demos work, which causes huge problems later on.

Concept

Each level is taken in turn and planned out on paper to determine the gameplay and to start building up sketches, diagrams, and documents for the team to work from. The basis of the level should be taken from a story overview if there is one for the game, so that the designers know how the level fits into the bigger picture. The first level should never be designed first. There are several reasons for this. First, it is possibly the simplest level and might not feature enough risky game elements that need tackling as soon as possible. The second problem is that early design work is usually improved later on. The first level needs to grab the player's attention and as such needs a "wow" factor. Third, it is likely to be a tutorial level, and some elements might not make it into the game, meaning it might get rewritten anyway. Finally, being the first level, it will be fairly easy, meaning that the difficulty level will not be a good indication of the average. It is best to start with a level somewhere in the middle of the game.

There are several stages to the conception of a level:

- Research and brainstorm
- Document ideas
- Level specifications
- Blueprints and concept art

Research and Brainstorm

A very important stage of level design that often gets skipped is the research phase. This is when information and reference that is applicable to the level should be gathered. This is gathered from a number of different sources:

- Real-life spaces and themes
- Historical evidence
- Media such as films and books
- Other games

Let's say we are creating a level set in ancient Rome. The first port of call would be to find as much literature and history as we could on the subject. Go to the library, search the Internet, and gather as much information as possible. It is also useful to gather as much visual reference as you can. This can be acquired from photographs, drawings, artwork, films, and so on. Finally, looking at other games with similar themes or mechanics can garner some very useful reference.

If a real-world space is to be emulated, then there is no better research than going there in person and experiencing it firsthand. Even ancient civilizations still have remains that can be seen, which give an idea of what life might have been like. A contemporary theme makes it even easier to get a feel for how a space feels. You can see and experience them directly. Of course, some places might be too dangerous to visit.

Researching more fantasy-based worlds is slightly more difficult. However, there is such a wealth of film, art, and literature that can spark the imagination that there really is no excuse for not being able to conceive some truly spectacular worlds. It is advisable to try to avoid the usual clichés such as high fantasy Tolkienesque worlds, as these have really been done to death. There are plenty of other references for many other styles.

Once you have gathered a mass of information and reference for a level, a group of designers and artists should gather for a brainstorming session. Try to keep numbers fairly small for these, as they tend to be much more vibrant with fewer egos to shout over each other. All ideas should be considered and listened to. They may spark other ideas in someone else. It is also important that someone takes notes, or you could even record the session.

Document Ideas

An often-missed step is to document all the ideas that come out of a brainstorming session and, of course, from the minds of team members outside these sessions. There may often be several brainstorming sessions and meetings as these ideas are discussed and formalized.

This documentation should describe the rough concept and suggest methods of implementation so that all know the viability of ideas and what is required to make them work.

All the various ideas are then evaluated and compiled to a final level flow, either by one designer or through a meeting. The file Design-LevelDesign.doc on the companion CD-ROM, shows an example of a level-design document that might comprise this final level-flow document.

ON THE CD

Level Specification

Once the ideas for a level have been chosen and laid down, a detailed specification of a level should be drawn up. The level specification breaks down in detail every scene and object that is needed for the level. The form of this breakdown can vary. Usually it takes the form of a standard document. This is then stored somewhere on the server so everyone can access it. This may be an adequate solution, or more likely it will simply get forgotten and never read by anyone except the author. A more dynamic solution is to create web pages so that the team can easily access them. Using a Wiki-style web page system is great for sharing information quickly and easily. Our preferred method is to create a database for level specifications, where all of the relevant information is broken down. A GUI interface allows easy data entry. Once in a database, the data is easily manipulated and can be used as needed. A database makes searching and cross-referencing possible and allows all manner of reports to be generated.

A level specification should contain the following:

- A breakdown of all the areas in a level
- All the events that occur in each area
- All the puzzles and traps the player encounters
- All the enemy waves

- All the actors in a level
- All the sequences and cutscenes in a level
- Any audio that is needed
- All the props and scenery needed
- Any special effects required

Blueprints and Concept Art

Once a full level specification has been written, a layout should be formalized. In many regards this resembles an architect's blueprints. The form that the blueprint takes varies. It may take the form of a 2D image, possibly done using CAD tools, though usually drawn in Visio®, Adobe® Photoshop®, or some similar visualization tool. There are also some more sophisticated ways of visualizing, such as a very handy package called SketchUp™, which allows 3D models to be generated and annotated quickly. This allows a designer to create a 3D walkthrough that gives everyone on the team a much clearer idea of what happens in the level and how things fit together spatially.

At this stage a concept artist should also be brought on board to create some concept work on how the level will look—the visual style and some details of particular elements. Concepts should be broad ranging and should offer a variety of different avenues to be explored. The best of these can then be pursued further until the lead artist, lead designer, or creative lead is satisfied with their direction. Often the publisher will also have a say in the concept art and the direction for the visual style of a project. Sometimes opinions can clash. You should always try and be resolved amicably through compromise. All too often communication can break down even at such an early stage. Everyone wants to have their creative input to the project, after all.

Gray Box

Once the concept phase is complete, then it is time to build the level in gray box form. This basically involves building the whole level using placeholder artwork. The level should be built to such a standard that the art can be dropped in later without having to rework large parts of the level. It is at this stage that any necessary changes should be made to the design and to the layout of a level to make it work. It is much more costly to do this later when artwork is nearer to completion.

A gray box should be completed in stages:

- Art mockup
- First implementation
- Complete implementation

Art Mockup

The art mockup is an interpretation of the blueprint as a 3D model that can be used in the game. Many FPSs use world editing tools to build the geometry. If this is the case then it is likely that the level designer will build this mockup. If level designers are building geometry, it is imperative that they have an artistic eye. Most games have dedicated environment artists who build the level. These are the guys who would therefore create the 3D mockup.

With the mockup completed, the designers can run through the level and get a feel for the scale of areas and the physical flow of the level. Changes can then be made quickly to make the basis of the level feel right.

First Implementation

The first implementation is a phase to get all of the basics of the level laid out. This results in a framework, which can be used to assess the ludic flow. This first implementation tends to be very rough, and often sequences will just be a note that appears on screen to say what is happening. Any scripts will be basic just to show the general gist. At this point the designer gets an overall view of how the level fits together and can quickly adjust geometry to fit the necessary ludic flow. To actually play through the level requires quite a lot of imagination.

It is during the first implementation phase that many ideas might come to the designer about changes and improvements to the level, or the designer will discover bits that need attention or simply don't work. These changes are fairly easy to work into the design at this point. The designer should remember to document and share these changes across the team, as necessary components to instigate the changes may get left off the schedule until it is too late.

Complete Design Implementation

A longer phase then begins in which the whole level is fully implemented from a design perspective. Art and animation departments will need to provide the design team with placeholder work that can be used to construct all the sequences and events that occur. It is during this time that a lot of unforeseen code issues will arise. Good communication from the level designer is essential for this phase of the project. Designers will often be calling on several people at once and keeping track of numerous tasks.

A complete design implementation will have all the basic gameplay in the level and all the sequences in placeholder form. By this point there may also start to be finalized sections of art going into the level, but this is not essential for design progression. With a complete gray box, the design team is ready to move into the next phase.

Playtesting

There are two main types of playtesting that teams tend to use, which are used at different stages of level development:

- Internal playtesting
- Formal playtesting

Internal Playtesting

Internal playtesting is an ongoing phase that begins as soon as the gray box level is approaching completion. Most playtesting is done by the level designers as they build the level, constantly playing through and checking their work.

The quality assurance department is also good to get on board at this early stage, providing they don't inundate the designers with bugs. They should be assessing the bigger picture rather than picking out flaws in what is essentially placeholder work.

A good system to use is an inter-design team playtest or peer review every so often by taking each other's levels and playing through them to give constructive criticism to each other and improve the overall design. This playtesting will produce a lot of refinements that are then made to the level. In extreme cases this may even mean trashing whole sections or going back to the drawing board.

Formal Playtesting

Formal playtesting is not used by every team or company. Some publishers such as Microsoft® have in-house groups that specialize in usability testing, where large groups of the general public are invited to play the game. The results are recorded and data is produced that is given to the development team.

These formal playtests need to be conducted toward the end of the development cycle, when the game is looking polished with the correct assets in place. The general public is likely to be negatively influenced by placeholder work still in place. The idea of the tests is to gather useful information about how the players respond and how they play the game. This should not be used to completely redesign the game but to balance the difficulty and adjust areas where players struggle or have no idea what to do.

One important thing to remember is to take the findings with a pinch of salt. Just because one player struggles with a section doesn't mean it should be completely revamped. Consider the majority in your decision making.

Often the playtesters will offer design ideas and improvements. Maybe 1 in 1000 of these will be worth listening to, but don't try to pander to the public consensus too much or you will end up diluting the vision of the game. A lot of the time the public doesn't know what they want or just wants to incorporate familiar elements into the games they play.

Good playtesting data will give you all sorts of invaluable balancing data, such as the most- or least-used combo. This can be used for spotting ways of improving a system or preventing golden paths. Read the data wisely and make adjustments sensibly and balancing will make the game just right.

Balancing

Balancing is the very tricky art of tweaking numbers, formulas, and placement of entities to get the level of difficulty and the intensity of the gameplay just right. It is such an important stage that a whole section of this book is dedicated to it. Balancing tends to be the final stage of the level construction before it is signed off, although it will have been an ongoing process throughout implementation.

From a level perspective, there are several things to balance:

- Enemy placement
- Item placement
- Difficulty ramping
- Pace

Refinements

Refinements are a stage in the process that is likely to be visited many times as the game takes shape. It is the process of playtesting, balancing, and refinement that will produce a quality title at the end of the process.

Sign-Off

The sign-off phase is a fairly mythical beast. Ideally, once a level is done, it would be nice to put it aside and say it is complete, but in reality this unlikely to occur until the very end of the project. Most projects tend to do a content freeze at some point toward the end. This is where no new content goes in, and only balancing and bug fixing is allowed. This should probably be followed by another deadline where balancing is also frozen to allow a period where only bug fixing takes place.

LOGICAL STRUCTURES

A level is essentially a collection of entities with associated data and links between them. To create a working level, there needs to be structures put in place to determine the course of action that will be taken.

Entities

Entities are the basic building blocks of level construction. They are the bricks, whereas the events, schedules, and responses are the mortar that binds them together.

Entity Types

Various types of entity can be instanced in the level. Each has a number of attributes that can be assigned. The attributes depend on the type of entity. The types of entity used in a level fall into several classes:

Physical entities: Entities that have physical presence and have a position in world space

Manager entities: Entities that control and manage other entities

Abstract entities: Entities that are used for aiding construction, such as timers or script entities

Logic entities: Entities that are used to perform logical operations on data being passed in messages

Physical Entities

Physical entities are those that have a position in 3D space. We can use a metaphor of a movie or play to describe different types of entity.

Actors: Actors are any player- or AI-controlled entities in a level. This can mean human characters, animals, aliens, or whatever oddities might be included in a game world. An actor may have several parameters that describe it:

- **Model:** The model the character uses.
- **Skin:** Models may have a number of different skins (different costumes or textures) so that variations can be assigned to the same model.
- **Animation container:** The list of animations an actor might have.
- **AI type:** Determines if the actor is a player (no AI), an ally, an enemy, an NPC, or a boss.
- **AI controller:** The controller behavior the actor uses.
- **VO pool:** The pool of voice over speech the actor uses.
- **Voice type:** The specific voice the actor uses.

Props: A prop is any object that is interactive within the game world. This could be a moving platform, door, switch, key, or any number of other objects. There are a number of distinct types of prop, each with several parameters:

Pickup: An item that is collected such as health or an armor boost. Might be used immediately or go into the player's inventory.

- **Model:** The model the prop uses. Often a model is much bigger than it would be in real life or has effects attached so that it draws attention and stands out from its surroundings.
- **Function:** What function the pickup serves for the player.

Diegetic: An object that can display text or an image on collection or inspection.

- **Model:** The model the prop uses.
- **Diegetic element:** The text, image, or sound that is activated.

Thrown: An object that can be picked up and thrown to cause damage, to provide a distraction, or provoke a reaction.

- **Model:** The model the prop uses.
- **Physics properties:** The mass, center of gravity, friction, or so on
- **Damage states:** The various states of damage an object might be in.
- **Health:** How much damage the object can take.

Pushable: An object that can be pushed or shoved around the world. Might be used for block-pushing puzzles (though rather clichéd) or for a form of attack.

- **Model:** The model the prop uses.

- **Physics properties:** The mass, center of gravity, friction, or so on.
- **Damage states:** The various states of damage an object might be in.
- **Health:** How much damage the object can take.

Weapon: An object that can be picked up to cause damage in melee or ranged combat systems (weapon parameters are covered in the combat section). This is often a form of pickup.

Turret: A fixed weapon that cannot be moved but only used in its current position.

- **Model:** The model the prop uses.
- **Projectiles:** The type of projectile it fires.
- **Ammo:** The amount of ammunition the turret has, although this is often unlimited.
- **Health:** How much damage the object can take, although turrets are often invulnerable.

Vehicle: An object that can carry one or more actors around the world at speed.

- **Model:** The model the prop uses.
- **Physics properties:** The mass, center of gravity, friction, how the vehicle moves, and so on.
- **Damage states:** The various states of damage an object might be in.
- **Health:** How much damage the object can take.
- **Speed:** How fast vehicle can move.
- **Weapons:** What weaponry the vehicle has.

Collapsable: An object that breaks up into smaller components (this can often be a property of other props).

- **Model:** The model the prop uses.
- **Physics properties:** The mass, center of gravity, friction, and so on.
- **Damage states:** The various states of damage an object might be in.
- **Health:** How much damage the object can take.

Switch: An object with two or more states that cause events to be triggered when activated.

- **Model:** The model the prop uses.

Key: An object that opens locked doors. Often these are disguised as other objects such as an emblem, but they are a key in essence.

- **Model:** The model the prop uses.
- **Lock:** The lock to which the key belongs.

Door: A physical barrier between one space and another that can be made to move. May need a key to operate. Doors might be animated or may be moved procedurally (extra variables are needed if moved procedurally).

- **Model:** The model the prop uses.

- **Health:** A door might have health if it can be broken through.
- **Speed:** The speed at which the door moves (procedural).
- **Acceleration:** The rate it moves to full speed (procedural).
- **Deceleration:** The rate at which the door slows (procedural).
- **Animation container:** A list of the animations for a door (animated).

Traverser: A traverser transports other entities from one location to another by moving itself, for example, a lift or crane. A traverser may be moved through animation or procedurally. If moved procedurally there will be extra variables that determine its movement.

- **Model:** The model the prop uses.
- **Speed:** The speed at which the traverser moves (procedural).
- **Acceleration:** The rate it moves to full speed (procedural).
- **Deceleration:** The rate at which the traverser slows (procedural).
- **Animation container:** A list of the animations for a traverser (animated).

Space link: Facilitates movement between areas without moving itself (e.g., a ladder or rope).

- **Model:** The model the prop uses.

Scenery: Scenery is the basic background art that is used to create the surrounding world. Each level is often broken down into chunks of scenery for sectorization purposes. Also, smaller elements of scenery such as bushes and rocks can be easily reused. There are relatively few parameters associated with scenery:

Static: Nonanimated scenery such as statues or pillars.

- **Model:** The model the prop uses.
- **Effects:** Any effects the scenery might use.

Animated: A basic model that uses animations. Could be used for wind blowing through trees, turning windmills, and so on.

- **Model:** The model the prop uses.
- **Animation container:** A list of animations used by the scenery entity.
- **Effects:** Any effects the scenery might use.

Physics based: A non-prop object that has physics properties such as a rock. There are many types of physics object that might be used such as a rigid body, soft body, and so on.

- **Model:** The model the prop uses.
- **Physics properties:** The mass, center of mass, and so on.
- **Effects:** Any effects the scenery might use.

Cameras: Cameras as entities only really exist for third-person games not using the basic chase camera. Otherwise, games only need to have one camera, unless cutscenes use multiple game cameras.

For games that do require lots of cameras to be placed, they will be a very important influence on the game architecture. The parameters for cameras are discussed at length in the camera chapter, as they depend very much on the type of camera being used.

Lights: Lights are essential for providing illumination to the scene. Depending on the available rendering technology, they can also be dynamically adjustable. Static lights are usually baked into the environment art, but dynamic lights will be able to change in real time and must thus be calculated on the fly. Lights fall into one of the following types:

> **Omni:** A point light with a hotspot and a fall-off radius. The hotspot is the bright part of the light, and the fall-off fades the light to nothing at its outer extremity.
>
> **Spot:** The light faces in a direction with a conical volume of effect. It will have two conical volumes—one for hotspot and the other for fall-off.
>
> **Directional:** The whole area is lit by a light from one direction, for example, sunlight.
>
> **Ambient:** The light is applied to the whole of its volume in all directions.

A light is assigned an RGB value and might also be given a function curve to alter color or intensity over time. The individual parameters of a light such as hotspot or fall-off might also be altered dynamically.

Effects: Effects are any particle systems, animations, or trails used to emphasize action, add atmosphere, or create special FX. Effects can be broken down into several types:

> **Action trails:** Those used for enhancing movement
>
> **Atmospherics:** Effects used to enhance the environment
>
> **Announcement:** Effects used to emphasize important moments or events for gameplay
>
> **Object effects:** Any special effects associated with an object such as smoke, explosions, and so on
>
> **Hit effects:** Any effects used when objects collide

Mechanism Entities

Physical entities are linked by underlying mechanisms that enable the whole system to work.

> **Volumes:** Volumes are used for many purposes: triggering events, activating cameras, describing the AI navigation graph, loading sectors, and more. A volume has few parameters:
>
> - **Position:** The x, y, and z coordinates of its position in the world
> - **Orientation:** The x, y, and z rotation
> - **Dimension:** The size of the volume in length, breadth, and height
> - **Active:** A flag that determines whether the volume is currently active

Locators: These are perhaps the most simple entity in a game, as they generally consist of only a position in x, y, z. Locators might also have orientation and even a radius dependent on their usage (an AI might use radius for AI node graphs).

Paths: A path is a collection of locators with a spline between their various points. The way in which this line is drawn is dependant on the spline algorithms used in the game. They might use Catmull-Rom or nurbs, for instance.

Paths are used by various entities in different ways. A camera might use them as a guide or movement rail. An actor would use them to describe a path to follow. A traverser might use them to describe its path that will be procedurally followed.

Checkpoint/Autosave: These are entities that save the current state of the game and write game data to the memory card or hard drive or offer a restart point should the player die.

Navigation Graph Set: The navigation graph is used to create the AI interpretation of the world and might consist of volumes, nodes, or a grid. Different systems have different parameters but each is a collection of either volumes or locators.

Navigation Graph Links: These join together navigation graph sets to allow entities to navigate between them. This allows them to be dynamically adjusted to be turned on and off as needed, so if a bridge blew up, the navigation could be severed for this section. Types of links are:

- **Direction Link:** One way A→B, one way B→A, two way. Determines if the link is navigable in only one direction and if so, in which direction.
- **Active:** Determines if the entity is active or not.

Hints: Hints are indicators used by the AI to ascertain information beyond basic navigation of world space. There are all sorts of hints that might be useful to AI and could be point or volume based:

Window: Defines a space as being a window that overlooks another area.
Action: Determines that a particular action can be performed at the location.
Sight/sound/smell: Determines a specific point of interest. This can be assigned a particular value to elicit a suitable response in the AI. For example, a nasty smell would result in disgust for the AI.
Cover: The location offers cover that might be full or partial.
Wait point: A character leading the player will wait here for him to catch up.
Retreat: A point to retreat to if combat is not going well.
Rally point: A point to meet up if the AI gets separated.
Climb: An area where the AI must climb to move to the limited area.
Sniper point: A place good for sniping.
Sniper target: A good place for snipers to aim at.

Camera Transition: Transitions link two cameras together and determine the transition between the two:

Transition type: The type of camera transition.
Transition time: How long the transition takes.

Manager Entities

Managers are entities that are used to control and monitor groups of entities and relay information to and from their subordinates. A lot of these entities are used in systems where scripting is kept to a minimum.

Spawner: A spawner is used to spawn individuals or groups of actors (or even other types of physical entities) in a timed or event-driven schedule. There are several parameters for a spawner:

- **Actor list:** The individual or list of actors to be spawned in any one group.
- **Spawn groups:** The list of spawn groups.
- **Trigger event:** Each group has a specific trigger, which may be anything from an external influence to a self-timed event.
- **Spawn points:** List of locators for where a group will spawn. Actors could be assigned to specific locators or could be spawned randomly at any free locator.

Actor Manager: The actor manager monitors the status of a group of actors. This can be used by other elements to query the state of the group. Thus, if a group of enemies is getting small, reinforcements can be called in. Parameters include:

- **Action queue:** A list of actions for the actors to perform.
- **Number of members:** The amount of members left in the group.
- **Member type:** The type of entities that are held in the group.
- **Other information:** All kinds of information about the state of its members could be stored, such as individuals' health.

Player Manager: The player manager monitors the status of the player, providing these entities with statistics to keep track of. Thus, if the player was low on ammunition, this could be tested for and more ammunition spawned for him. Parameters include:

- **Player health:** The player's level of health.
- **Player score:** The player's score.
- **Player ammunition:** The amount of each ammunition a player has.
- **Other information:** Any other pertinent information. For example, an RPG might want to track attribute values.

Game Manager: The game manager holds all important game information, which is mostly relevant to multiplayer games. This information includes:

- **Round time:** The length of a round.
- **Score table:** The list of player and team scores.

Scripted Sequence: A scripted sequence overrides AIs and tells them to perform a sequence of actions. This entity needs to have:

- **Actor list:** A list of the actors in the sequence.
- **Action list:** The list of actions to be performed in the sequence.

HUD Manager: The HUD manager is used to interface with the heads up display, allowing the posting of text messages, for example.

Quest and Mission Manager: This manager looks after all the possible quests and missions, indicating whether they are active or not. The status of any completion prerequisites, such as number of items left to collect or objectives left to complete can also be shown.

Abstract Entities

Abstract entities are those that do not have a physical presence within the game world but provide functional uses for the construction of levels. In a world editor abstract entities are used to contain script or data-based objects or to activate events in a particular schedule.

Script: A script is used to link from a world editing tool to a script. As such, the entity parameters simply point to the desired script. Having an entity within the world tool allows the script to be operated like any other entity—depending on the system.

Time Line: The time line is a schedule of events that occur during a set time frame. Nodes along the time line activate the desired events. Therefore, a time line would have the following parameters:

- **Node events:** A list of all the events and their positions on the time line.
- **Duration:** The total duration of the time line.
- **Branches:** The time line may be an interactive tree rather than a simple list, having conditions for particular nodes.

Data Controller: There are usually fairly generic scripts that have a lot of associated parameters. Rather than having to create individual scripts for each of them, we might instead want to turn these kinds of situations into data so that we can create better interfaces for the design team to utilize. We might want to move control of enemy waves, spawning, or formations away from script into data. We might also want to control sequences via data rather than through a complex script. These are called controllers. Instead of having to write a script to perform these functions we can create tools to write data or expose the parameters to our world design tool.

Let's look at a wave controller. We could expose the following parameters to our world editing tool:

- **Troop pool:** A list of all the actors in a wave
- **Formation:** The formation by which the wave is organized
- **Attacks:** The types of attacks that are available to the wave
- **Next wave event:** The event that will move to the next wave, such as on two troop deaths

Generic objects or sequences should be moved to this data-driven system to provide maximum efficiency. The only drawback with doing it in this way is a loss of flexibility. It is often best to prototype a system in script form before turning it into a data-controller entity.

Function Curve: A function curve describes the value of a variable over a length of time. This allows designers to draw curves for use with various other entities. Let's say we wanted to dim a light or adjust game speed. If we apply a function curve to the brightness or game speed, the value is adjusted over the specified time frame according to the curve.

Procedural Movement: This is an entity used to apply translation and rotation (possibly even scale) to another entity.

Level Entity: A level entity is an entity that describes the parameters of a level such as its name and any functions or flags it might have.

Distance: A distance entity draws a line between two entities and calculates the distance between them. This then outputs a distance value that can be used by other entities.

Logic Entities

Logic entities are required for complex levels where scripting is not used. They offer script-like functions that can be placed in the standard entity-linking flow.

Counter: A counter is used to store integers or floats. This could have several message handlers such as Add, Subtract, Multiply, Divide, Set Max, Set Min, and so on. A counter's parameters are:

- **Maximum value:** The maximum value the counter can reach
- **Minimum value:** The minimum value the counter is allowed to drop to
- **Start value:** The initial value of the integer or float
- **Thresholds:** Values assigned to kick off events when the values are reached

Filter: A filter is used to sort incoming data and process it before it is passed on. This could be used to restrict data to certain values or omit particular undesirable elements.

Branch: A branch is a logic entity that can accept a number of inputs. A condition is created for these inputs. An `OnTrue` event is fired if this condition is met or an `OnFalse` event is fired if the condition is not met.

Case: A case entity contains a list of preset conditions and fires an event if the input matches any of these. An Otherwise condition might be used to catch any value that does not match any of the cases.

Compare: A compare entity takes two inputs and compares them against each other. An `OnEquals`, `OnLessThan`, or `OnGreaterThan` event is fired according to the result.

Entity Persistence

Entities are either spawned and despawned as they are needed or they are permanently contained within a level but switched off until they are required.

Spawning entities as needed causes problems with serialization that will need to be solved by the engine programmers but has the advantage of being a flexible system for the designers and means they don't have to worry about finding space to fit all of the entities. Spawning may also cause issues if too many entities are spawned at one time. Older or extinct entities may have to be despawned to accommodate these newer ones, or new ones may not be able to be spawned until older ones become extinct.

Persistent entities need to be turned on and off as needed. This is done by splitting the level into sectors (these may be distinct spatial sectors or just conceptual ones). Each entity is assigned to one or more sectors. When that sector is active, those entities are activated and will be updated. Be aware that if the player crosses into a sector that entities are not set up for, they will be deactivated and the player may witness this. Entities should be confined to particular areas and only deactivated when the player is not in view.

Entity States

State machines are not only used for controlling AIs. They come in handy for all entities. If a messaging system is to be used, the state machine system is particularly apt, as it can be considered calls to switch between states.

Looking at an example of a door, we could say it has two states: Open and Closed. In truth it actually has four: Open, Opening, Closed, and Closing. The Open state handles a `Door_Close` message and the Closed state handles a `Door_Open` message (messaging is discussed later in this chapter) that move the door into the transitional states before reaching the goal state (see Figure 13.2). Opening and closing can be done either procedurally (by the game code) or by playing an animation. Procedural movement it easier to interrupt and manipulate, but animation can be much more elaborate and impressive.

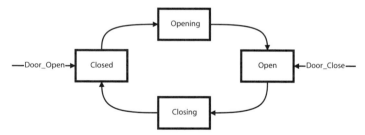

FIGURE 13.2   An FSM for a simple door.

Objects tend to be somewhat more complex than this, but the basic principles remain the same. A notable point is that using objects in third-person viewpoint games generally requires animation for the object and the player character, unless you cheat and zoom into the object and omit the player character, as they do with certain object interactions in *Resident Evil 4*.

Sequences

Sequences are series of actions that are strung together. They are set piece scenes that the player either watches or interacts with. There are several types of sequence that might be used in a level:

Scripted sequence: An in-game, interactive sequence

Background sequence: A noninteractive sequence that occurs in the distance or in an unreachable location.

Cutscene: A sequence where control is taken away from the player

Interactive cutscene (quick time event [QTE]): A sequence where normal control is relinquished but button presses are required to progress

Full motion video (FMV): A cutscene not made in game, but rather prerendered and played back by video

Full motion animation (FMA): A cutscene made using the game engine but recorded and played back by video

Events

Levels are primarily event driven, responding to actions that the player performs and the player's physical location in the level. Thus, there are two primary types of event:

- Action-based events
- Space-based events

Action-Based Events

Numerous potential actions can occur in a game, all of which could be classed as events. For the purposes of level design, we probably want to filter these somewhat. For example, the following events are often used:

OnConstruct: Called when an entity is created

OnDeconstruct: Called when an entity is despawned or destroyed

OnDeath: Called when a character is killed (essentially the same as OnDeconstruct, but specifically for characters that are not removed from the world on death)

OnHit: Called when an entity is hit by another object with an attack

OnTouch: Called when an object physically collides with another (without the need for attack data)

OnAction: Called when a particular action is performed on an entity (an OnGrab, for example)

OnHealthValue: Called when the health reaches a certain threshold

OnSighted: Called when the player is first spotted by an object or AI agent

OnLevelStart: Called when the level is loaded

Potentially limitless action events could be applied. The usefulness of an event is determined by the requirements of the game mechanics. A game that features a lot of stealth would likely make good use of an OnSighted event. This could be used to sound alarms when the player is spotted by a security camera or an AI character. In a high-action game OnSighted is likely to be of less use.

Each type of entity might also have its own specific actions, such as an OnComplete event for a script entity. There are potentially limitless events that could be assigned on a per-entity basis. The problem with having lots of specific events for each entity is the limitations of the designers' memory. Names need to be self-explanatory, and some kind of reference is essential for projects where there are hundreds of possible events. Valve's Hammer tool for the Source engine can be somewhat overwhelming at first sight, as it has hundreds of events unique to each entity.

Space-Based Events

Knowing where the player is in world space, or at least a rough approximation of the player's position, is essential. A game would not be able to synchronize game events unless the game knows where the player is in relation to the event.

Therefore, space-based events form the core of every level. There are generally two methods of determining position, which are in fact the same system at heart: trigger volumes and sectors. Both are volume-based systems, the difference being that sectors break the level down into areas and trigger volumes can be placed pretty much anywhere. Trigger volumes might be appropriated in any desired shape, but only a few are really needed: cubes, spheres, and cylinders.

A volume can have one of four possible events:

OnEnter: Called when the activator enters the volume

OnExit: Called when the activator leaves the volume

OnAction: Called when the activator performs a certain action within the volume

OnLook: Used in first person games to activate when a particular volume is being looked at (highlighted by the targeting cursor for a period of time)

The activator is the entity that causes the event to occur in that volume. There could be one potential activator for the volume or a different activator for each event. The activator is usually the player but could be any other entity, such as an enemy. There could be a list of any type of entity or even a very specific entity by name. However, as already mentioned, more often than not, it is the player.

Schedules

Schedules are lists of actions that occur in a specific timed sequence. Schedules are very useful for certain things, such as playing animation sequences, but do not offer the possibility of replacing an event system since they are not as interactive. Schedules are initiated by a particular event occurring. They act as timers to count down the time till an event or series of events is initialized. In effect they are a schedule of events.

Response Mechanisms

Once detected, an event must be dealt with. This response is handled by one of two potential mechanisms: functions or messages.

Function-Based Response

A function-based response is generally made with heavily script-based world construction. With each event a specific function is called. This is a simple and very flexible system, but it makes creating tools difficult, as there are not simple links from one entity to another. The result is that it is best suited to a system where scripting is going to be the basis for level creation as building an entity-linking tool around this system is unworkable.

Another issue is the sheer number of functions that will need to be kept track of. With a lot of designers on a project, this could turn into a nightmare.

Message-Based Response

A much clearer way of setting up the level is with message-based response. Instead of calling a function each time, a message is sent to a target entity. The target has a handler to deal with the received message and can then act accordingly. This object-oriented approach makes visualizing the links between entities much simpler and makes it far easier to build entity-linking tools for much better designer productivity.

Any type of message can be sent from one entity to another, but there are several generic messages that have wide-ranging uses:

Trigger: Tells an entity to perform its main action.
Activate: Tells an entity it is active and can receive messages.
Deactivate: Tells an entity to switch off and to ignore any received messages.
Kill: Kills the entity, possibly removing it from the world.

As mentioned, we do not have to stick to generic messages. We could be far more specific in the messages that we send to an entity. We could send a door a Door_Open or Door_Close message to tell it to directly perform those specific actions. If the world editing tool exposes the possible messages that can be sent to the target entity, then it makes it even easier to quickly link the two together. Valve's Hammer tool for the Source engine does exactly that with its Input/Output linking system.

Let's look at the messaging system at work. Let's say we have a door that we want to open with a switch, which automatically closes behind us as we walk through it (see Figure 13.3).

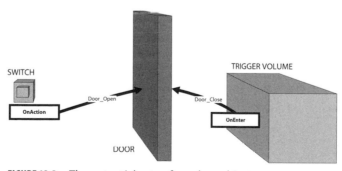

FIGURE 13.3   The potential setup for a door object.

To achieve this we set a Door_Open message to be sent on the OnAction event for the switch, which targets the door. A trigger volume on the other side of the door has a Door_Close message on its OnEnter event, which also targets the door.

With a message we might also want to pass data to the target entity. For example, if we had a light that changed color when the player entered the room, we could send a Change_Color message to the light with the RGB value that we want the light to change to.

There are a number of other parameters that we might want to apply to a message. First, we want a maximum amount of times that we want to send this message from the triggering of an event. Second, we might not want to send a message until an event has occurred a certain number of times. Finally, we might not want to send the message immediately, but rather some time afterward.

All of this means that a message has the following parameters:

Target: The entity the message is to be sent to. This could even be a list of entities.

Message type: The type of message to send to the target entity.

Data: Any associated data that might be required (this is not a required parameter).

Max sends: The maximum number of times the message will be sent. This is usually once or an infinite number (–1 is often used to represent infinite) but could be any number.

Trigger threshold: The number of times the event must occur before the message will be sent. This is useful to count up to a certain value, for example, if you wanted to count the number of deaths of characters before triggering an event.

Message delay: A time delay in seconds before the message is sent.

CONSTRUCTION METHODS

There are many potential methods of creating levels:

- Hard coding
- Scripting
- Data driven

Hard Coding

The old-fashioned method of implementing a level was to build each individual element within the code itself. When games were very simple, this was a viable option. On today's complex projects this approach is simply madness. Amazingly there are still projects where level design is implemented in this way. It will be difficult to continue this approach as the scale of content continues to increase.

Scripting

Scripting is a very popular and powerful method of implementing level design. Scripting is essentially programming outside of the main game code. A virtual machine runs scripting languages such as Python, Lua, or some bespoke language.

The level to which scripting can be used is extensive. Effectively the whole game could be written in script to interface with a render engine. Knowing where to draw the line is a difficult task. Scripting runs slower than traditional compiled code, so it makes sense for only the high-level gameplay code to be written using scripts and keep low-level game mechanics in faster game code. Script code can reference functions in the main game code (known as bind functions) to keep things moving as fast as possible.

Scripting facilitates all areas of level design, allowing a designer to produce scripts that control level flow, operate all the various sequences in the level, control all the states of objects in the level, and much more. It also supports any kind of level implementation structure.

Scripting is extremely powerful, as full control is given to the designer. The immediate drawback of doing everything in script is that designers need to have programming experience in order to be able to use the system. This means many good designers simply will not have the necessary skills to be able to create levels. Many technical designers who have good scripting skills do not also have good creative skills. This makes it problematic to assemble a solid level-design team that can think of great creative ideas and implement them. It often means fracturing the design team into two camps: those who script and those who come up with concepts.

Pure scripting is becoming less popular and is now often used alongside data-driven structures and world editing tools. This keeps the flexible structure that scripting affords but increases productivity and ease of use for the design team.

Data Driven

Data-driven level design moves away from coding a level by hand toward the simple allocation of data to the properties of entities and allows them to be linked together. This kind of system needs an event-message structure in order to be able to work, as this is the only system that provides direct physical links between entities.

The data itself can be exposed from code to these data sets but must be stored in some kind of structured data format so that it can be read by the game. This data format could be anything—often binary or ASCII. Binary is a particularly bad option, as it offers no ability to be hand tweaked or manipulated outside of any tool that creates the data. ASCII files are more appropriate, as they can be read in their pure form. The ideal format for data these days is Extensible Markup Language (XML), which allows bespoke markup formats to be created. This allows readable data and facilitates easy code manipulation of the data itself. The actual format of an XML file is dictated by the project, and a standard will have to be set—usually by the programmers.

Data is generally edited via the use of some kind of design tool. The beauty of this is that no programming experience is required for the designer, which generally allows more creative types the ability to get their hands dirty with implementation. Also, it greatly improves potential productivity, since it is much easier to edit data than it is to produce a script for every item.

TOOLS

These days tools are essential for commercial game development, or at least they should be. It is amazing how little regard many studios pay to getting design tools right.

Tool Requirements

There are several areas where a variety of design tools are extremely useful:

Scripting: There are already plenty of good text editors out there that have functionality to improve workflow for the scripters—from simple things like the color of keywords, to more feature-packed editing environments. However, if scripting is used in conjunction with entity-placement tools, it is very desirable to integrate the scripts into that tool itself, or at the very least have the tool link to the editor and automatically fetch the right script.

World building: The creation of geometry in a bespoke design tool is something of a peculiarity to the FPS. Technical restrictions drove the need to construct levels in very particular ways, but these are needs that are falling away. Most geometry these days is built in 3D packages such as 3DS Max, XSI, or Maya.

Entity creation: Creating entities within a tool makes it much simpler and more efficient, providing it is intuitive to use and flexible enough. Various elements of entity creation can benefit from the use of a well-designed tool:

- Entity parameters
- Animation setup
- Combat data
- State machine creation
- Physics properties

Entity placement: Without the use of a tool it can be very difficult to place entities at all without guesswork or by copying position and orientation values from a 3D package. The role of the level editor is to allow easy placement of entities in the world and the ability to export this information in a game-readable format. A world editor therefore needs to be able to render 3D scenes and needs to have various editing modes to allow placement of a variety of entities.

Entity linking: Many editors stop at entity placement and let scripting do the rest. However, the tool can be expanded to allow linking of entities to create communication channels between them. This idea can be taken to the extreme so that scripting is abolished altogether, as in Croteam's Serious Editor and Valve's Hammer editor.

Debugging: Because everyone is fallible and bugs of either logic or usage will occur, debugging is a necessity. On the highly complex projects that console games inevitably become, this can turn into a serious issue. Having a good set of debugging tools can make the process of game development, much, much easier.

These features might even be incorporated into a single design tool. It certainly makes it easier to keep everything together in one place.

World editing features are often built into complex 3D packages such as Maya. This can be rewarding and work well to begin with. More often than not, it becomes incredibly unwieldy and slow as the level grows and can grind the package to a halt in a complex scene. A bespoke editor can be tailored for speed and only needs to contain level functionality rather than the whole host of features that the 3D packages contain.

Tool Features

Features that make a tool easy to use will improve the efficiency of the design team. This has a knock-on effect with creativity. A good tool encourages experimentation, which can lead to some of the best gameplay experiences.

Work Flow

Commercial game development on console titles can mean fairly large teams of designers working together on the same levels. To make level creation viable across a team of designers, the level data needs to be set up in a particular manner—by using layers or by creating a database that the tool interfaces with.

Layers

Layers are separate files that store particular game elements or break a level down by areas or both. By separating data in this way, different users can work on different layers at the same time without conflicts. Breaking down by area can be completely arbitrary or might be based on sectors. Breaking a level down by element is generally more constrained. For example, a level might be broken into the following layers:

Geometry: All the major geometry for the level
Scenery: Any secondary geometry used for detail
Props: All the prop entities needed for an area
Triggers: All the triggers for an area
Cameras: All the camera rigs and triggers
Actors: All the NPCs, enemies, and allies
Effects: All the effect emitters and so on
Volumes: All the volumes used to describe the spatial aspects of a level

Designers should have the ability to move objects between layers, turn the visibility on and off, and control the export of these layers.

Database

Most game developers probably get very nervous when the word *database* is mentioned—either that or their eyes glaze over. However, a game is effectively a database with a fancy interface, so it makes perfect sense to use one in its creation. This is the ideal solution, as a database is designed for multiple users to access, insert, and manipulate data.

Setting up a design tool to interface with a database is not a trivial task but is well worth the effort. Being able to run Structured Query Language (SQL; a language designed to work with databases) searches or create complex data reports is a real boon. The file Design-Database.mdb on the companion CD-ROM, shows an example of a simple database that can easily be extended to fit the needs of a large project that has a lot of potential data.

ON THE CD

Profiles

A complex design tool is likely to have a pretty complex interface. It might be used by a number of different people with a range of job specs: the designers, scripters, artists, audio engineers, and so on. Therefore, it is highly useful to have a number of profiles—setups for individual job roles. Furthermore, it is important to allow the users to customize the layout to their liking and be able to save their own custom user profiles.

Live Editing

An extremely powerful feature is that of live editing—being able to adjust entity data and run scripts on the fly. To enable live editing, the game either needs to run on a PC or there needs to be some kind of network communication with the console development kit. Running the game on a PC makes connection to the game simple, but means a whole extra version of the game has to kept up to date. Using a console connection can require some complex networking code but means that the tool on the PC can directly influence the game on the console. This connection system is also useful for multiplatform development. Ideally editing an entity in the tool on the PC would automatically update the entity on all connected consoles at once.

WYSIWYG

WYSIWYG, or what you see is what you get, is pretty much a standard for all windows tools these days. It really goes without saying that this should apply to level design tools.

SUMMARY

Level implementation is a myriad of possibility, but the design team will need to make sure that their strengths are being used. Otherwise, a game's technology may dictate the types of designers that are able to work on a project.

We looked at several aspects of level implementation in this chapter:

Design methodologies: A few different approaches can be taken when implementing levels:

- **Systemic:** Creating universal elements that can be used across the game. The advantages of this methodology are efficiency, consistency, and the possibilities for emergence. The disadvantages are shoe-horning elements to be generic, the uncertainty that comes from emergence, and the rigid conformity to set types.
- **Specialized:** Creating unique characteristics for each element in the game. This has the advantages of uniqueness, certainty that the elements will behave as expected, and the possibilities for different styles. The disadvantages are inefficiency, inconsistency, and the lack of freedom for the player.
- **Hybrid:** A hybrid system takes the best of both systems by having generic entities and level-specific entities.

Level design pipeline: An important consideration of the implementation process is the work flow that the designers use to create their levels. This process should follow a number of stages:

- **Concept:** The creation of the initial level concept.
- **Gray box:** The creation of a basic working level.
- **Playtesting:** The continual testing of a level to refine and improve it.
- **Balancing:** The act of taking playtesting data and adjusting the difficulty balance, number of enemies, and so on to get the balance just right.
- **Refinements:** The continual revisions of playtesting and balancing to produce the finished game.
- **Sign-off:** The approval of the finished article.

Logical structures: The elements that make up game systems and enable the production of methods. We need to consider a number of different elements:

- **Entities:** There are a number of different types of entity—physical entities, managers, abstract entities, and logic entities.
- **Sequences:** There are a number of different types of sequence—scripted, background sequences, cutscenes, interactive cutscenes, full motion videos, and full motion animations.
- **Events:** There are two basic types of event—action-based events and space-based events.
- **Schedules:** Essentially a list of events that should happen over a period of time.
- **Response mechanisms:** A response is either performed via functions or via messages.

Construction methods: A number of approaches can be taken when it comes to building the levels:

- **Hard coding:** The levels are built directly into the code base. This is not a recommended method of building levels.
- **Scripting:** The levels are built using a scripting language. This means designers will need to have scripting experience.

- **Data driven:** The levels are built through data constructs. This is generally the most intuitive way of building levels. Often a data-driven approach will be used in conjunction with a scripted approach.

Tools: The use of tools on a project can really boost productivity, as long as the tool is suitable for the job.

- **Tool requirements:** A tool will need to suit the method of construction, so it might have scripting elements, world building functionality, entity placement, and linking as well as debugging features.
- **Tool features:** A tool should have a good work flow, might use profiles, possibly even have live editing, and really should be WYSIWYG.

Level implementation is an area that will really benefit from some investment in the creation of tools and process. Even the very best tools are ripe for improvement. The increase in productivity and the knock-on effects for a design team's motivation will return tenfold any time and money invested in creating a great tool.

14

ARTIFICIAL INTELLIGENCE FUNDAMENTALS

In This Chapter

- AI Components
- AI Communication
- Methods of Choice
- AI Construction Methods
- The Mechanics of Actions
- Group Management

A I is an essential component of game design. Without it, the computer-controlled actors would not be able to perform any actions, and the game world would seem lifeless. There are many approaches to AI, and many ideas from the burgeoning field of computer intelligence offer exciting prospects. However, game AI is generally more smoke and mirrors than true AI.

In this chapter we will explore the following aspects of AI:

- AI components
- AI communication
- Methods of choice
- AI construction methods
- Mechanics of actions
- Group management

AI COMPONENTS

To understand the structure of an AI system it is useful to break it down into its constituent parts.

Behaviors

The highest level of AI component is a behavior. A behavior is composed of any number of states, actions, or reactions that describe the functionality of an agent (an AI-controlled actor). An agent generally has one behavior but may possibly switch behaviors according to their use within a particular situation. Behaviors might be shared across many different actors or may be peculiar to just one.

A behavior contains a set of rules for choosing which actions are performed during which states. These rules may be specified in different ways for each part of the AI system.

States

A state separates actions and reactions according to their use in a situation. These states are transitioned between when events occur in the game, according to rules prescribed within the structure of the behavior. Complex AI systems may need several states in order to accurately respond to a situation. However, not every AI system needs states. Some simple systems do not need to distinguish different rule sets and actions for different situations.

States dictate what actions and reactions are available. The rule set for each state will vary from state to state. One particularly useful definition is between exploration and combat states, as the needs and goals of an AI agent between these states differs drastically.

Many more states may be found where more fidelity in describing a situation is required. For example, if the game were to allow the player to hide from the enemy

AI, it would require aware states, in which the AI knows the player is in the vicinity but not currently within their cone of vision.

Actions and Reactions

Actions are the physical performance of a decision made by the AI. There are many actions and reactions that can be incorporated into a system and possibly separated into a variety of states:

Idle: Stand around playing an idle animation or some incidental animation. Idle could translate to several states, so that normal idle is standing around as normal, aware idle is looking around for an actor, and combat idle is idling with weapons ready.

Patrol: Follow a prescribed path looking for intruders. This would only be used in an unaware state. As soon as the actor is spotted, aware or combat state would initiate.

Wander: Like patrol, except that the AI agent does not follow a prescribed path but instead moves randomly.

Use object: Interact with a particular object. The type of object dictates what kind of action will be performed.

Seek: Search for a hidden actor.

Close in: Move within a specified range of a target.

Back off: Move away from a target to a specified range.

Melee attack: Perform a close-range attack on a target.

Ranged attack: Perform a long-range attack on a target.

Flee: Keep a fixed distance away from a target to avoid being attacked.

Cover: Use a sensible place in the environment for cover.

Ambush: Lie in wait until the target is within range, remaining as hidden as possible.

Block: React to an incoming attack.

Recoil: Play recoil animation on being hit.

Counter: Perform a counterattack on an attacking enemy.

These are a tiny fraction of the vast number of actions and reactions that could possibly be created. The more that are created, the richer the AI system can become.

Animation of Actions and Reactions

Actions and reactions are intrinsically linked to animations. Every action and reaction will have one or more associated animations. An action cannot exist without some form of animation.

Actions and reactions often have more than one associated animation. This may be needed to do a series of complex maneuvers to perform an action. Also, an action may have several different animations depending on the context in which it is to be used. An action may also have a number of variations of an animation so that a more organic feeling is brought to the system and the actors aren't just doing the same animation over and over again.

Animation is vital in conveying the intelligence of an actor to the player. All the most sophisticated AI in the world won't help if the actor has a bad walk and run animation.

Incidental Actions

If we are to make more believable worlds, we need to increase the amount of incidental actions and animations performed by actors in our game. At present many games simply have the actor performing a basic walk cycle along a patrol path. In reality we greatly vary our actions. We don't loop the same actions over and over. We look around, move our arms in different ways, scratch our noses, stop to tie our laces, and much more. Incorporating some of these actions into games will help increase the believability of game worlds.

AI COMMUNICATION

In order to be able to make decisions, an AI agent must have information about what is happening within the world. This requires lines of communication from objects and other agents in the game world. There are two basic methods of communication: polling and event messaging.

Polling

Polling asks objects in the world for information about their current status and gathers this information to make a decision. This means a lot of exchange of information as many objects request information from many other objects. The result is likely to be a system that is bogged down by far too much information. Polling has certain advantages in that it does not rely on other objects for information and can therefore gather the relevant facts as and when they are needed. More often than not, however, much of the resources are being wasted by needless communication. With lots of objects in a game world, this can become an unmanageable loss of resources.

Event Messaging

Event messaging is a much more efficient system. Messages are only passed around to other objects when a particular event occurs. A message can be broadcasted to all agents or can be targeted to one or more agents specifically.

Every event can be of a specific type and can contain data that can be passed with the message to another object. Objects in the world have message handlers that accept messages and interpret them so that the objects can perform actions based on those messages. If an object receives a message of a type it does not have a handler for, the message will be ignored.

The depth of the messaging system determines how much information an agent receives. The more information is given to the agent, the more-informed will be the decisions that are made. For instance, consider an attack message that is sent when an attack is made on an agent in range. On receiving this attack message, the agent could then decide to block, counter, or get hit.

The only problem with an event system is that agents may end up waiting for messages that never arrive. The solution is to carefully design situations so that agents are not reliant on any one particular message that might not ever occur or ensure that they have a suitable message handler in every possible state.

METHODS OF CHOICE

With a collection of AI components assembled, we need a way of tying them together. We need to create a set of rules for how those components fit together—a system of choosing which actions to perform.

Different parts of an AI system might use different methods of performing these choices. An AI system might be composed of several subsystems that control choice for certain aspects. For example, the choice of macro action (high-level actions such as Patrol, Seek, etc.) might be governed by one system (such as a finite state machine), whereas low-level micro choices, such as which particular attack to perform, might be made by another (e.g., a weighted random system).

There are several well-used methods of choice ranging in their level of complexity:

- Sequenced
- Decision trees
- Weighted random
- Scoring
- Finite state machines
- Learning systems

Sequenced

The simplest method of choice doesn't involve any real choice at all. Instead, the AI follows a specified set of rules. It meticulously follows this set of instructions, only being interrupted to perform any reactions that might occur, such as recoiling from a hit. Sequenced AI is extremely basic and is only used where AI can be dumb (usually in large, relentless numbers), in games such as *Serious Sam*, for example.

Decision Trees

Decision trees are more advanced sequences that allow branches of choice. Tests are made at particular points to decide on the next course of action. Therefore, they need to be meticulously planned out and are rigidly set once created. An example is shown in Figure 14.1.

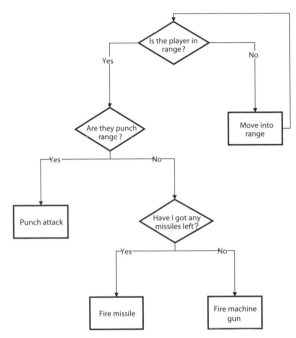

FIGURE 14.1 A decision tree.

Decision trees are often used for boss fights, where attacks can be highly scripted. Decision trees require a fair amount of time to build and are generally constructed via scripting. This makes them fairly inefficient to produce.

Weighted Random

A weighted random system assigns a bias (a weight) to each action and then randomly selects an action based upon these biases. The higher the weight applied to an action, the more probability there is of it being selected. This can be visualized by imagining a pool into which actions are put. By assigning a weight of three to attack and one to flee, there will be three attack actions in the pool and only one flee action. It is easy to see that there is much more chance of selecting the attack action.

Each action may be assigned one of several values (see Table 14.1).

TABLE 14.1   Action Values

PARAMETER	DESCRIPTION
Weight	The relative selection weight for the state compared to others in the group
Fall through	The chance, even if the state is selectable, that it will not be selected

$\rightarrow$

PARAMETER	DESCRIPTION
Time out	The amount of time before the state times out (i.e., cancels) and another state is selected
Cooldown	The time before the state can be activated again once completed
Min/max offset	A min/max distance the agent must be from a target (usually the player) to perform the action

A weighted random system is often used to select combat actions. It can also be used for higher-level actions such as Patrol, Seek, and so on but has the disadvantage of being unpredictable and hence could perform actions that don't make sense in the situation.

A weighted system might be combined with a state system so that random choices are made within a more rigid structure. Actions are split into several states that are switched between. During these states the choice of action within that state is determined by the weighted random system (see later examples of how this would be implemented).

Scoring System

A scoring system uses a set of rules to calculate a score value and identify the best course of action in a given situation. The key to creating a working scoring AI system is to create sensible rules that can accurately describe a situation. These rules determine a score value for each possible action based on the situation, which is broken into a number of variables [Tapper03].

As an example, let's look at two situations and their possible outcomes.

Example 1

The AI is low on health and the player has it targeted. The possible actions here are Attack, Block, and Back Off. For each of these actions a score is attributed to a factor that concerns that action:

- Attack
  - Player health: +10
  - Player proximity: +5
  - AI aggression: +5
  - AI difficulty: +5
  - AI health level: −10
  - AI is targeted: +5
  - Total: 20
- Block
  - Player health: +5
  - Player proximity: +5

- AI aggression: 0
- AI difficulty: +5
- AI health level: +5
- AI is targeted: +5
- Total: 25
- Back Off
  - Player health: +5
  - Player proximity: +5
  - AI aggression: 0
  - AI difficulty: 0
  - AI health level: +10
  - AI is targeted: +5
  - Total: 25

The result is that this AI will either Block or Back Off.

Example 2

The AI has a high health level and is very aggressive. The player is on very low health. Again the same three actions apply:

- Attack
  - Player health: +20
  - Player proximity: +5
  - AI aggression: +10
  - AI difficulty: +5
  - AI health level: +5
  - AI is targeted: +5
  - Total: 50
- Block
  - Player health: +10
  - Player proximity: +5
  - AI aggression: 0
  - AI difficulty: +5
  - AI health level: 0
  - AI is targeted: +5
  - Total: 25
- Back Off
  - Player health: +10
  - Player proximity: +5
  - AI aggression: –10
  - AI difficulty: 0
  - AI health level: –5
  - AI is targeted: +5
  - Total: 5

In this situation it is clear that the AI will try to attack.

You may have noticed a flaw of the system already: it is too perfect, as it will always choose the correct action for a situation. This means that AI will become far too predictable, and it might be too hard to defeat if it performs the right action each time. To counter this we need to add an element of chaos to the mix. There are lots of ways this could be done, but two are particularly sensible:

Range for each factor: Every score is random within a range, so instead of receiving 5 points, the score might lie between 3 and 7 points. Over all the factors this will create a random element without producing wildcard results that a random weighted system might produce.

Random from top choices: In the above examples we have three actions, but there could be many more. We could take the top two or three actions and choose randomly between them. We could even use their scores as a weighting for random selection.

Finite State Machines (FSMs)

FSMs are extremely useful for creating fairly complex and believable AI. They are also fairly simple to comprehend. Essentially, a state machine can be thought of like a flowchart. Different states are transitioned between by conditions or events that occur [Brownlee].

FSMs are perhaps the most widely used AI technique in games, as they offer a great deal of power with relatively little complexity. They are also simple to visualize and offer the opportunity for intuitive construction via graphical editing if enough time is spent creating the right tools.

Basic FSMs

At the most basic level an FSM simply moves from one state to the next via a defined set of rules. It has no memory of any previous states. For example, let's look at a popular behavior where an actor transitions from patrol to suspicious to combat state when he has spotted the player (see Figure 14.2).

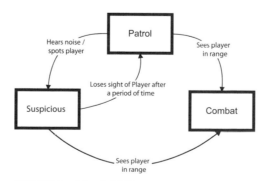

FIGURE 14.2   A basic FSM.

Each of these states is built up from a number of actions:

- Patrol
  - Normal Idle
  - Patrol
  - Use Object
- Suspicious
  - Aware Idle
  - Seek
- Combat
  - Combat Idle
  - Combat Close In
  - Block
  - Melee Attack
  - Ranged Attack
  - Combat Back Off
  - Combat Flee

An FSM consists of a start state, a number of accepting states, inputs, and transitions. The start state is the actor's initial state—its default actions. Accepting states are the possible states the actor can enter. Inputs are stimuli from the world that cause a transition from one state to the next to occur.

Often states will have certain actions occur when initialized. These are controlled via an `OnEnter` function. This could, for example, play a specific animation to mark the transition into a new state. Also, a state may have an `OnExit` function, which is generally used to clean up existing actions before transitioning to the new state.

Stackable FSMs

The basic FSM has no memory of previous states, meaning it relies solely on a good state flow to make it appear intelligent. A stackable FSM, on the other hand, allows states to be remembered and returned to on finishing the current state. The stack allows a history of states to be stored. New states can be pushed onto the stack and popped off when needed. States can also be replaced on the stack, effectively removing the last remembered state.

This is very useful, as actors can now return to a previous action that was being performed before they transitioned to the new state. For example, an actor is involved in a complex patrol that requires doors to be locked and unlocked. When he enters the suspicious state, the previous state is pushed onto the stack. If the actor then finds nothing during his Seek action, he can return to the point where he was during his patrol state by popping it off the stack.

Hierarchical FSMs

This is a very powerful way of expressing a system, by allowing FSMs within FSMs. Each state can be represented by a contained FSM of its own. Looking at our previous example, the Patrol state might be constructed of further FSMs (see Figure 14.3).

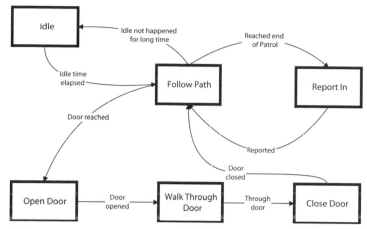

FIGURE 14.3   A hierarchical FSM.

Learning Systems

Learning systems react to stimuli in the world and base future decisions upon the outcome of their interactions with these stimuli. Learning systems are a field of true AI, where much progress has been made, but much of this does not have a direct influence on game AI. Game AI is generally about creating an illusion, not trying to actually produce intelligence. Much of the reason for not using true AI systems is that we want to control the experience for the player. We are trying to entertain them, not beat them.

Learning systems are one area where this mantra must surely ring true. If we are too efficient, we will create an increasingly complex and challenging AI that in all likelihood would eventually crush the opposition. Learning AI in games should learn from its mistakes and react to a player's actions, but must never become infallible.

Reinforcement Learning

Reinforcement learning involves gaining experience from your mistakes. By learning what is a good outcome and what is a bad outcome, the AI can choose a good tactic over a bad one. Punishment for a bad outcome reinforces that the good outcome is preferable. Imagine a rat in a cage pressing one of two buttons. One drops a piece of food into the cage, and the other administers an electric shock. It won't be long before the rat learns not to press the shock button [Hopson01].

An AI will do well to learn the risk reward mechanism. This can often mean suffering a bad outcome to achieve a better outcome at the end. Going back to our rat, we add his favorite food as an incentive for pressing the shock button. He gets a shock, but he also gets a much better reward for his troubles. Does he take the easy option and get the normal food or take a little suffering in exchange for his favorite food?

How do we represent this in AI? Outcomes need to be defined in numerical terms, such as the level of damage received or amount of damage inflicted on an enemy. With these definitions and values in place, the AI can determine actions that have a positive effect from those that have negative implications.

Learning from the Player

When an AI learns from the player's actions it is effectively dynamically adjusting its difficulty. This also means there are no easy solutions for the player, that is, strategies that will always defeat the AI. However, the AI should never become too difficult. There must always be some way for the player to beat them—built-in stupidity. An AI might learn from the player but shouldn't necessarily always employ what it has learned.

AI CONSTRUCTION METHODS

With all of these elements of a system mapped out, we still need a way to create them. There are several basic ways that AI is implemented in a game:

- Hard coding
- Scripting
- Visual editing

Hard Coding

Hard-coded AI is programmed in the same language that the main game is written in (generally C++) and is usually done directly by the AI programmer. With hard coding many of the underlying variables of the AI might be exposed (often called soft data), so that they can be adjusted and balanced with ease in an editor.

However, this offers a very limited amount of flexibility for the designers. Hard-coded AI is likely to need the AI programmer to be involved in any changes that are made to any behavior, except any changes that can be performed through the limited amount of exposed variables. This can be fine for very simple AI systems such as sequenced AI, but for more complex behaviors it does not offer enough flexibility and efficiency for the design team.

Scripting

Scripting is a big step up from hard-coded AI, as it allows the systems to be created in a specific scripting language that the designers are more likely to have access to. This offers designers wide scope in what they can achieve with the system, as they can create any behavior they want and have full control over every aspect of the AI.

This in itself poses a problem, as many designers tend not to be efficient programmers. Often what can result is a pile of cut and pasted code, which would make most programmers weep. This also makes debugging a nightmare, as designers must try to visualize their code and often don't have the necessary debugging tools within the scripting language editor. Often it can be confusing as to whether the problem lies with the script or within deeper engine code.

This method offers designers a lot of power but it requires a team of technically proficient designers or a good support team of coders. Not all creative designers are particularly technical and vice versa.

Visual Editing

This is the ideal solution if you have tools and programmers available to implement such tools. Using visual editing has many advantages that make it worthwhile to invest the time to make the necessary tools:

- Easy to understand
- Easy to visualize and debug
- Much faster and more productive

The actual representation of the AI system is dependent on the systems being used. For a weighted random or scoring system, a slot-based system is ideal. The designer can drag actions onto a page with a number of slots. These actions hold a number of variables that can then be tweaked.

FSMs are particularly well suited to visual representation, because they can easily be visualized as a flow diagram. The designers can drag states onto a workspace and link these states together with transition arrows and conditions for transitioning. Using such a system, even a nontechnical designer should easily be able to create behaviors. This removes the need for the whole design team to be technically orientated but still offers a lot of flexibility.

Building Further on AI Systems

AI systems can be further built upon to optimize and encourage particular aspects that may be beneficial to gameplay.

Emergent Behavior

A word you might hear a lot of in AI is *emergence*. Essentially, emergence is unexpected but useful behaviors that come from using a set of carefully designed rules. This has advantages and disadvantages—particularly for action–adventure games. The advantage of basing behavior on base rules and letting the AI agents get on with it is that you have a system that will play differently each time. Any good emergent behaviors then add to this system, making it fun to interact with. The disadvantage comes from its main strength, in that you are never completely sure what will happen, and bad emergent behaviors then make the AIs appear completely dumb.

Emergence is very useful but perhaps better suited to other styles of game than those we are concerned with in this book. Games with strong narrative rely on the designer being able to carefully craft all the behaviors of the AIs in the world.

LODed AI

LOD (level of detail) is used extensively for graphics but can also be applied to other game systems. One of those that can benefit from LODing is AI. Initially it may seem that there is little that can be changed to create different levels of detail. However, AI can be very processor intensive, so there are lots of systems that can be shut down to save on resources. When the player is some distance away from an AI, you only need to track its position and what its basic behavior is. All systems beyond that can be shut down such as:

Sensory AI: The actor will not need to sense until the player is in sensing range.

Internal states: There is no point expressing emotions if the player is too far away to appreciate them.

THE MECHANICS OF ACTIONS

Actions are built up from one or more basic AI mechanics. These are the mechanisms that give an AI the ability to perceive the world and form the basis of the higher-level choices made by other parts of the system:

Navigation: The AI's ability to negotiate the game world

Sensory AI: The ability to spot stimuli in the environment

Combat: Performing attacks and defending against enemy attacks

Navigation

An essential task of AI in any game to navigate the game world. There are several parts to navigation that may or may not be needed by the game system:

- AI representation of the world
- Movement and Animation Control
- Pathfinding
- Autonomous Steering
- Seeking
- Dynamic obstacle avoidance

AI Representations of the World

AI agents need to know information about the world in order to be able to navigate around it. The way in which this information is imparted to an agent may differ from game to game. The AI representation of the world is something that designers definitely need to know about, as it is likely to be their task to implement that representation. There are a variety of ways in which the world might be represented:

- Grid
- Corner graph
- Waypoint nodes
- Space-filling volumes
- Navigation mesh

Grid

A grid is a network of triangles, squares, or possibly hexagons that are laid out to form the structure of the level (see Figure 14.4).

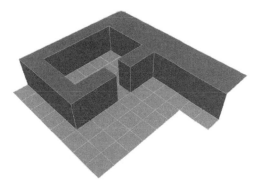

FIGURE 14.4   A grid-based AI representation.

The edges of each shape can be set to a specific type:

Two way: An AI can move from either direction through the shape.

One way: An AI can only move from one shape to the other in one direction (e.g., the shape is on a cliff edge and the actor can drop down but cannot climb back up).

Boundary: The edge is at the limit of the world and forms an impassible boundary such as a wall. This may not be a physical boundary but a place where the AI should not go (into a lava pit, for instance).

Region connections: These include ladders, elevators, transporters, and so on.

Restricted actions: In some areas only specific actions can be performed such as wall runs.

Creating these AI maps is traditionally done by designers via an editing tool. This tool allows them to lay down the grid over the level geometry to match the environment. The size of the grid shapes is determined by the amount of fidelity required. The smaller the shape, the more fidelity is offered. Often the grid is created in unison with the collision data, as they are likely to match up pretty closely. It might be the role of a collision artist to build these AI grids rather than the designer's task.

One possibility for grid-based AI representation is auto generation. This greatly reduces the amount of work involved in creating the grid but is still likely to need a human eye to refine and perfect the grid.

The biggest problem with a grid system is that it is a 2D representation mapped onto a 3D world. It offers no navigation for any AI that does not move along a surface with a grid mapped to it. Thus, flying enemies would not have the needed data to operate.

Another problem is also associated with the 2D nature of the grid. Different levels that pass over each other must be identified so that the AI knows which space to move to next. Each part of the grid thus needs to be separated into various sections. These sections then link into each other and allow the system to know exactly where the AI can move to next.

Corner Graphs

Corner graphs are a rarely used representation that work in a different manner from all other systems. All corners are marked out to form a detailed plan of the environment (see Figure 14.5). The AI agent can move within these areas marked out by the corner boundaries.

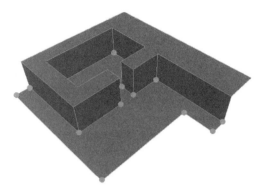

FIGURE 14.5   A corner graph AI representation.

The truly great feature of corner graphs is that it is easy to auto-generate the data required to make them. However, automatic generation of corner graphs may provide results that aren't entirely as expected. Sometimes better results can be acquired by hand, even if it is a much more time-consuming process.

The problem with corner graphs is that they don't really offer any way of setting up one-way links or provide much information other than where the AI is allowed to move. An AI may require further information to actually navigate the world, such as the little ability to add hints or topological data to specific areas, and as we shall see later, hints are extremely useful.

Waypoint Nodes

One of the most popular methods of representing the world in recent times has been via waypoint nodes. These are nodes that are dropped into the world and then linked together to form a network that describes the layout of a level. Each node can also be given a radius that describes the area covered by that node. Anything within that area is considered a navigable zone (see Figure 14.6).

Node links can be either one or two way and can have restricted actions to cross between nodes.

One issue with waypoint nodes is that it is extremely difficult to generate this data automatically. This means it has to be placed by hand. However, this is not necessarily a bad thing, as it allows the designer to tailor the representation exactly. As long as the placement and linking of nodes is made as intuitive as possible, this should be a fairly simple process—albeit a very important one.

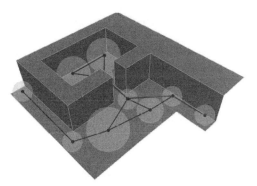

FIGURE 14.6   A waypoint node AI representation.

The biggest problem with waypoint nodes is only being able to describe angular worlds with spheres. This is not a huge problem, however, as the fidelity usually does not have to be absolutely perfect. A rough approximation is usually enough.

In all waypoint nodes are a reliable and fairly simple system to use.

Space-Filling Volumes

A great method of representation is to use space-filling volumes. The idea is to fill the whole of the space that an AI can navigate with "safe" volumes (see Figure 14.7). These volumes tend to butt up against each other or overlap. Alternatively, the volumes could map the unsafe zones—walls and other features that the AI should avoid.

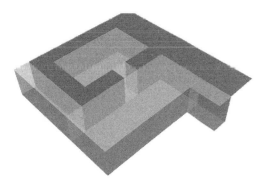

FIGURE 14.7   Space-filling volume AI representation.

Links can also be drawn from one volume to another and one- and two-way links established between them.

It can be possible to auto-generate volumes, particularly in interior locales. In exterior locations it may be tricky to define the limit of volumes. However, it is not too difficult to manually create volumes that describe the environment, and this offers much more opportunity for refinement.

The problems with space-filling volumes concern overlapping areas at different levels but are easily overcome in much the same way as for the grid system. Volumes are broken into smaller parts around an obstacle so that the two volumes are not linked to each other.

It can be tricky to lay volumes down manually when there is a mass of them on screen. This mishmash of volumes can become confusing to look at, but there are easy ways around this such as allowing the ability to hide volumes from view.

Navigation Meshes

The perfect representation would be to use the world mesh itself, or at least a stripped down version of it, as the representation. However, the biggest problem has been the sheer amount of resources that would be consumed by doing that. As power increases, though, this technique is likely to see more use in the future.

Hints and Topological Data

So far, our representation has only allowed us to find basic paths through the world—how to get from A to B. However, we can do much more with our representation by using hints or topological data. This data provides extra information about various points around the map. For example, different sections could be flagged as cover points. Now when the enemy needs to find cover, they can plot a path to the nearest sensible cover point and use it.

Plenty of other snippets of information can be included in the representation. The amount of data will depend entirely on the depth of the AI system, but some popular hints are:

Jump: Points to where the AI can jump up
Climb: Points to where the AI can climb to reach a higher level.
Ambush: Ideal spots to start an ambush.
Snipe: A perfect spot for sniping.
Cover: Use a cover point to hide from enemy attacks and return fire.
Interesting: The AI is curious about the location.
Danger: The AI responds as if something is a threat.
Disgusting: The AI responds with a vocal "eurgh!" and moves away.
Amazing: The AI stops to stare with mouth agape.
Frightening: The AI responds by running away or reacting nervously.

Movement and Animation Control

The physical movement of an actor is done via the animation system, but this system needs to be instructed as to which animations to play and when. This is an AI interface called a movement controller. Once an action has been decided upon, the tasks required to perform that action are instigated by the movement controller.

Tasks and Schedules: An action can be broken down into a schedule of tasks that need to be done to complete that action. This schedule is stepped through in order, and each of the necessary animations is played.

As an example, let's look at a Follow Path action. This would be made up of the following tasks:

1. Find Patrol Path.
2. Plot path to get to nearest point on Patrol Path.
3. Follow plotted path to Patrol Path.
4. Decelerate to move onto Patrol Path.
5. Accelerate to full walk speed and follow Patrol Path.

When performing an action there are a set of conditions that the actor will need to check during each think cycle. These conditions may cause a change in the schedule, new tasks to be implemented, or the conclusion of an action. In the case of the Patrol Action, the end of the Patrol Path will require the actor to turn around and walk the other way. New tasks are added to the schedule on the end of path condition being met.

1. Decelerate to meet end of path.
2. Idle at the end of path for fixed period.
3. Turn 180°.
4. Accelerate to full walk speed and follow Patrol Path in opposite direction.

In addition to conditions that are checked on each think cycle, there are interruptions that will occur. These will flush out the current schedule and instigate a whole new set of tasks to be added. In our Patrol example an interrupt could be the player being spotted.

Playing Animations: Tasks in a schedule will often cause animations to be requested. Once an animation has been selected, there may be several other alterations made on top of this:

Animation speed: The animation might be played at a different speed.
Partial animations: The animation may blend over the currently playing animation or may be layered so that it only affects a particular part of the body (for instance, the actor could be made to wave while idling or walking).
Joint control: Particular joints could be rotated or adjusted to make a head turn to look at the player or point a gun in a particular direction.
Inverse kinematics (IK): The animation can be altered to, for example, adjust the IK to make an actor's feet fit steps.

Movement Parameters: Physical movement of the actor in world space (translation) can be done in two ways or by a combination of the two. Animations can control all physical translation of the actor so that every footstep corresponds to real-world movement. This seems desirable but can be very tricky to implement. Certainly, much of the animation can be done in this way, but more complex motions are dealt with more simply. Often turning uses the parameter methods rather than direct animation to world space correlation.

Movement parameters describe certain values of movement that are directly applied to the actor. The animation simply plays as the movements are performed procedurally. The biggest problem with this method is that sliding feet can occur if the animation and movement speeds are not properly synched. A variety of parameters can be applied:

Speed: The speed of movement.

Acceleration: The rate at which the actor can accelerate.

Deceleration: The rate at which the actor can decelerate.

Stationary turn rate: How quickly the actor can turn when stationary. Smaller actors can turn very quickly when stationary.

Walk turn rate: How quickly the actor can turn when walking, which is likely to be less than when stationary.

Run turn rate: How quickly the actor can turn when running, which is likely to be much less than stationary or walk speed.

Pathfinding

Pathfinding is one of the essential elements of actor AI. Without this ability, the actor would not be able to move from point A to point B without running into walls. Pathfinding allows them to turn and follow a route through the world.

Basic path following allows an actor to follow a predefined path laid down by the designers. All movement can be made along these paths. For some games, such as on-rail shooters like *Time Crisis*™, this would be acceptable. However, any form of interaction beyond pointing and shooting would show obvious flaws. The paths that actors follow would be too rigid. Also, they would not be able to react dynamically to the player's actions unless an interwoven mess of paths were laid down by the designer. This is impractical and is an utter waste of time.

The solution is to get the AI to plot its own route from one point to another. Doing this it requires knowledge of the game world and algorithms to calculate the best path through it.

The A Algorithm*

The algorithms are the domain of the AI coder, and there is little need for designers to know exactly how they work, but we describe them briefly here.

The A* algorithm is the most recognized and most widely used algorithm for determining the best route through a world. However, simply plotting a route from point A to point B isn't always enough. There are more complex considerations to make than the shortest route between two points.

Fastest Route: The shortest route might not necessarily be the quickest. The short route might mean swimming, climbing, or wading through mud, which will take a longer time than running. The fastest route might be a longer distance, but it doesn't require time-consuming actions to traverse.

Safest Route: When moving in a vulnerable situation, such as in the heat of a gun battle, the shortest route might leave that actor vulnerable. Choosing the safest route would bear in mind cover points and defensive positions, should they be needed, and would avoid the actors placing themselves in open positions.

Natural Motion: The shortest distance between two points is a straight line. When plotting a course through the world, the A* algorithm produces a series of straight lines and sharp angled turns. However, real people don't walk in straight lines and make sudden angular turns. They move smoothly around corners and constantly adjust their paths as they walk [Pinter01]. This can be achieved by smoothing the route through the world as much as possible. Even slight noise can be added to a path to make it less regimented (see Figure 14.8).

Plotted Path
Smoothed Path

FIGURE 14.8 Adjusting a path to create more-natural movement.

Autonomous Steering

A method that is used for many tracking, seeking and obstacle-avoidance behaviors is known as autonomous steering [Reynolds99]. This uses a basic set of controllers and allows them to be combined to produce more complex behaviors:

Seek: Steers the AI toward a target.

Flee: The opposite of steer, causing the AI to run away from a target.

Pursuit/Evade: Seek or flee applied to a moving target so that the agent can predict the future position of the enemy.

Arrival: Slows the speed of the AI as it comes to a stop at a target.

Obstacle Avoidance: Alters the direction of heading so that an obstacle is no longer in the line of sight.

Wander: Move in a random path without having twitchy movement; maintains a smooth movement by remembering previous movement.

Collision Avoidance: Avoids other AIs as they all move around.

Separation: Method of avoiding collision for AIs moving in the same direction (cheaper than collision avoidance).

Tracking

One AI mechanic that is highly used is tracking, or following, where an individual or group must track a target in some way. In order to close in on a target to attack, the AI needs to be able to follow that target. To do this, a seek or pursuit action is used, though this may be combined with A* pathfinding over longer distances. Steering is used on a more local level. There are different methods of tracking with individuals and with groups of AI.

Leader Following

Leader following at its most basic form allows the actor to steer toward a target. Its goal is to get within a certain range of this target, so if a target keeps moving away from the actor at the same speed, it will keep moving indefinitely.

Leader following can be used in several situations. The most-used method is to close in on an enemy or to give chase, but it can also be used to have a group of actors follow a leader ally. This could be an individual or a group. When a group is following a leader, several autonomous steering behaviors would be used: pursuit to follow the moving leader, arrival to slow down when the leader comes to a stop, and separation to avoid bumping into squad mates. The shape of the following crowd might be a random mob of enemies, a straight line, or a rigid formation of enemies.

Flocking

Flocking is a method of controlling an organic group of actors and making them "flock" in a realistic manner. This is particularly useful when modeling crowds of animals, such as birds, that move in a large huddle with little discernable structure. Three variables control the motion and arrangement of a flock:

Separation: The amount of distance to maintain between each member of the flock

Alignment: The steering toward the average heading of the group

Cohesion: The steering toward the average position of the group

Seeking

Seeking AI is essentially tracking AI without any fixed target to move toward. Instead, it must calculate a point to move to and search that area for the target. There are plenty of ways the AI could go about this, depending on the desired sophistication of the system.

Diminishing Point

One method of seeking out a player is to cheat. The AI can easily find out where the player is and then use this information to plot a course in his direction. Obviously, this isn't entirely fair to the player. The solution is to pick a point in the vicinity of a target and head to this point. This point could get ever closer to the player unless he moves. This means the player will have to constantly move about to avoid being spotted.

The flaw with this system is that it can seem very unfair and unrealistic. Exactly how does the actor know where the player is? This should only be used in high-action games, where stealth is not the main element of the gameplay.

Spot Search

A spot search uses information the agent has acquired to search. It begins by investigating the source of suspicion—the place where the player was last seen or where a sound was heard. On reaching this point, it will thoroughly investigate the spot by looking in all directions. It may be satisfied that nothing is there or decide to pick a number of surrounding spots and investigate those.

Thorough Search

A thorough search involves much more elaborate movement through an area in order to seek out the player. Again the search will start from the point of suspicion. From this point, a network of paths will be plotted that cover the local area. These paths could be laid down by the designers or could be automatically generated by the AI system. These paths should not be so thorough that escape is impossible, however. If more than one actor is involved in a search, then each actor can take a path that covers a particular area rather than all covering the same ground.

The advantage of the spot and thorough searches is that they appear much more natural than the other searches. They take a little more work but are worth the effort, and if stealth is an important game mechanic, then they are fairly essential.

Dynamic Obstacle Avoidance

Using pathfinding to negotiate the game world is all very well, but often the path will be obstructed by a dynamic object that wasn't there when the path was calculated. Also, the AI will need to avoid other AI agents in the world so they don't look stupid running into each other every five minutes.

One way of doing this is to use autonomous steering to guide the AI out of the way of an incoming object. It can then alter its course to circumnavigate the object. Another method is to use repulsion to push either an object or an actor away. This works well against small objects that the actor pushes or large objects that push the actor, but can look odd for those in between. A good dynamic obstacle avoidance system can be created by using a combination of these two systems.

Sensory AI

Without senses we are nothing—and the same rings true for agents. An agent must be able to read the situation in the game world in order to be able to respond to it. At the most basic level, enemies respond to the player's proximity. They are spawned into the world and follow a very prescribed behavior. The only thing they would need to know is the player's position. You can immediately see that there is a limited intelligence being simulated here. In a game world with more intelligent actors, we need to see what happens before they perform their reaction.

We can base sensory behavior on what tangible experience we have of our own senses. We can emulate any of these senses, but usually it is vision and hearing that are modeled [Leonard03]. Smell and touch have feasible use within a game world, but taste might be a rather difficult sense to use and has seemingly little relevance—but you never know how creative designers can get.

Vision

Most games use vision as part of their actors' AI sensing. There are many levels at which this can be set up. The rules that determine whether the player can be seen dictate the complexity of the system. Most games keep it fairly simple. If the actor has a line of sight to the player within a certain range, then the player is spotted. However, systems could conceivably be much more complex than this. Movement, light, camouflage, and situation are some of the factors that might be considered.

Vision Cones

We all have a cone of vision, that is, a restricted view of the world at any one time because of the setting of our eyes in the front of heads and our direction of facing. We can simulate this with a cone in the actor's direction of facing. This restricts the actor's ability to spot a player to this limited space. Often this might be a 2D shape, in which case actors can see the player anywhere in the third dimension. However, it is perfectly possible for this cone to be 3D.

When the player enters this shape or volume, a ray is cast from the actor to the player. A more complex system might cast multiple rays to different parts of the player to determine if a part of the body is not hidden, even if most of the body is. If these ray tests show a clear line of sight, then the actor can see the player (depending on other factors in more complex systems).

Games that rely on stealth for most of the gameplay might have more than one view cone to model different aspects of vision, such as movement. This emulates peripheral vision, where our ability to detect movement is much stronger than our forward vision. However, it is less capable at determining shape.

If a detection is made with peripheral vision, then a confirmed spot would not be made. This would simply make the agent suspicious. An agent would not confirm a detection until the player was caught in the forward vision cone in a vulnerable position (they might be hidden in shadows and thus not be visible).

Movement

Movement is only detected when the player is moving above a certain speed threshold—effectively, how far the player has pushed the analog stick. Spotting movement might provoke different reactions in different AI agents. For example, a guard would become suspicious, but a motion sensor would immediately sound an alarm if a detection is made.

Light Levels

Using shadow to hide is a very common feature of stealth games such as *Thief* and *Splinter Cell*. Essentially, player characters' visibility is measured by the amount of light currently cast on them. The more light there is, the more visible they are. This analog measurement means there could be different reactions from an agent at different visibility levels. This could be tied to proximity. For example, if a player character is at 0.5 visibility and is 20 meters from the guard, the guard might be suspicious and move in for a closer look. At 2 m with the same visibility, it would be an instant detection. Different actors might have different thresholds for visibility so that normal guards have high thresholds before they can spot a player, but a guard with night vision would be far lower and would spot a player much more easily.

Camouflage

Camouflage is tricky to model, as it is difficult to assess when a player is camouflaged. How could you model camouflage? One fairly simple way might be to mark out areas of the map as particular types of scenery. Each camouflage uniform would be rated for each of these different scenery types, so a jungle camo would score a 10 in the jungle, but a 0 in an urban scenario.

A more complex and processor intensive method would be to assess the image seen by the actor and measure the color difference between the player character and the background. This is likely to consume a fair amount of processing, however.

Situation

In many circumstances it might be perfectly feasible for players to walk around freely without concern of being detected, as long as they are not performing certain actions. For example, in *Grand Theft Auto* some civilians react to you pulling out a gun by panicking and running away. The reactions could also be much more dramatic. Modeling such reactions is discussed in the later implementing AI chapter, but the basic premise is that different actions will spark different reactions from an actor in the world.

Hearing

Hearing can be modeled in many ways, from fairly basic to very complex.

Basic Hearing

Sounds made by the player can be heard within a sphere volume around them. Any actor within this volume will hear and react to a sound of a certain level. Ascertaining the level of a sound requires applying either the volume of the sound or a score to each action in a situation.

Actions and Materials

By using the level of a sound, the effect of actions and materials should be natural, the sound of a player moving across gravel being physically louder than walking across grass. However, if we are using a scoring method, a matrix of values will need to be built up of every action in relation to a material (if such a relationship exists; for example, shouting would have no relation to grass) (see Table 14.2).

TABLE 14.2   Cross-Reference of Action Against Material

	CREEP	WALK	RUN
Grass	1	2	5
Gravel	2	3	8
Concrete	1.5	2.5	6.5

Other actions, such as firing a gun, will have a much larger score value than these actions and thus be far more likely to be heard.

Cover Noise

Cover noise will prevent an actor from hearing a noise as much, as the sound may be lost in the noise from the environment. In our score-based system the cover noise is represented as a value. If the noise the player is making is within a certain threshold of this score, then he may be heard (see Table 14.3).

TABLE 14.3   Cover Noise Values

COVER NOISE	VALUE
Heavy machinery	20
Computer equipment	5
High traffic areas	10
Listeners are talking	10

When we are using pure sound values to calculate the detection of noise, we can work out whether the ambient noise in the area is louder at that point than the noise made by the players. If it is, they will not be heard.

Distance Scaling

With either system it is generally a good idea to scale the level of the sound across the range of the sound sphere of the actor. Using the actual volume of the sound at a particular point should naturally include this drop in sound level. With a score system some kind of multiplier should be applied over distance from the player, for example, half volume every 10 meters.

Complex Hearing

This basic system works fine for many games, but where stealth is the major game mechanic, a little more effort is needed to make the system believable.

Sound Bounce: Sound reflects off walls and bounces around an environment. This can be both beneficial and detrimental to the player. It is beneficial, as it means that a sound from behind a physical barrier is not likely to be heard on the other side unless it can bounce around it. It is detrimental to the player, as sound may bounce to a point around a corner.

Physical boundaries come into effect during a test to see if the agent can hear. A ray is cast to the agent to see if there are any obstructions. If there are, then the ray can bounce a number of times to test if it ever bounces into the area where the actor is. The number of bounces is likely to depend on the level of the sound and the area where the sound is being played. Some systems may have sound bounce as a natural part of the system and thus can calculate the sound level at the agent's position.

Sound Absorption: Some materials absorb sound much more readily than others. When a sound bounce is made, its level can be reduced by a multiplier based on the material it has come into contact with.

Sound Leakage: Materials may not fully reflect the sound when it is bounced. Some sound might continue through the material as well as the reflection being made. The amount of leakage depends on the material and its thickness. A thick wall of concrete will have far less (if any) leakage in comparison to a thin pane of glass.

Directional Sound: Not all sound is cast in every direction. Some sounds may be cast in a specific direction. A cone volume is more appropriate when calculating volume for these types of sound, though it should be noted that this sound could still bounce behind a player who is standing facing a wall. Loud sounds, even when directional, are going to cast sound all around to some degree, so they are best modeled with the forward-facing cone volume and a weaker sphere volume to represent this radiating sound.

Touch

Touch is a pretty simple sense to implement and doesn't need to be made complex. If an actor is touching the player character, then he should sense that the player is there, so as soon as the player touches an actor he should be alerted. However, it might be fun to allow the player to creep up behind the actor to tap him on the shoulder or something similar. In this situation the actor would react much more sluggishly, perhaps muttering "Huh?" as he dumbly turns around.

Smell

Smell is a much more peculiar concept to model in a game world, as it is not really tangible (at least until we have odor-creating consoles). Frontier's *Dog's Life*™ put the player in the paws of a dog. It created the sense of smell by representing it as something visual—in this case colored clouds of scent.

Smell is not used in games much at all, but there is plenty of potential to be had with the idea of smell. Imagine that wind and time affected the strength of these smells. Imagine that you were playing a hunter. To sneak up on your prey, you would have to make sure your scent trail wasn't blown in its direction.

Normally smell is a sense that is ignored, but we might see a few more games that try to tackle the more subtle of the five senses (perhaps even taste—who knows).

Extrasensory Perception

Not one of the five senses, but often known as the sixth, extrasensory perception (ESP; the ability to see the future) might be modeled by using a learning system. Essentially, ESP would predict the next action of the player and perform countermeasures before the event occurs. It bases these predictions on the player's previous patterns of actions, working out the preferred tactic for a given situation. The more a player uses a tactic, the higher the weight attributed to the selection of a particular countermeasure.

The result is a system that requires the players to constantly vary their tactics to ensure that they can defeat their opponent.

Combat AI

Any AI agent that will perform combat must be able to attack or defend. There are two possible types of combat that require very different approaches from the AI system: melee and ranged.

Melee Combat AI

Creating a melee combat AI system requires knowledge of which move is suitable to be used in a particular situation and the ability to choose suitable actions to perform at the right time. The two modes to melee combat are defensive and offensive.

Defensive

To know which move to perform for defense, you need to know what the opponent is doing. Thus, attacks can be described in their various parts: buildup, strike, recovery, and lead out. Moves can be accorded to each of these parts:

   Block: The attack is blocked before and during the strike window of the assailant's attack. A maximum number of blocks within a specified time might be applied to prevent the AI from blocking indefinitely.
   First strike: A long buildup window offers the defendent a chance to get his strike in first.
   Riposte: The strike is blocked and then an attack can be made when the attacker is in his recovery period.
   Counter: The strike window is anticipated and a counterattack is performed at this moment.

Injury attack: The defendant can attack even if hit.

Evade: The evade move is made just before the assailant's strike window occurs. The type of evade is dependant on the attack:

- Sidestep for vertical attacks
- Backstep for horizontal swipes
- Jump for low attacks
- Duck for high attacks

A random weighted or scoring system might be used to model the choice of defense. For example, all defensive moves are given a weight. A value between 0 and 1 is given for the probability of a defensive move being performed. An easy enemy that mostly blocks is shown in Table 14.4.

TABLE 14.4   An Easy Enemy with a High Chance of Blocking

Defense chance	0.2
Block	2
Evade	0.5
Counter	0.1
First Strike	0.1
Riposte	0.1

A harder enemy would have a higher chance of defending and would use more offensive defense, as shown in Table 14.5.

TABLE 14.5   An Enemy with a Higher Chance of Defending

Defense Chance	0.5
Block	1
Evade	0.5
Counter	0.4
First Strike	0.4
Riposte	0.4

These values could be dynamically adjusted to different values for different situations or as the enemy learns the player's tactics.

Offensive

The choice of which attack to perform is often modeled using a random weighted or scoring system but could be a simple sequence. By using probability to determine outcomes, a more natural, organic feeling is produced, which is great for humans or animals, but a static sequence might work very well for a robotic enemy.

AIs are generally given a difficulty and aggressiveness rating that determines how often they will attack and with which attacks. A higher level of difficulty will mean an increased likelihood of selecting more powerful attacks and getting farther with complex combo chains. Each move in a combo string would have a diminishing probability, which will differ according to the actor's difficulty level. For a group attack combo, any offensive property will be controlled by the commanding AI, so that actors are not making these decisions themselves, but simply following orders.

A higher level of aggressiveness will indicate an actor that attacks with a much higher frequency. With high difficulty levels this produces a very difficult opponent. With low difficulty levels it may seem more like enemy frustration.

Ranged AI

Like melee combat, there are likely to be both defensive and offensive modes for a ranged AI.

Defensive

For slow-moving projectiles, evasion, or possibly block, could be used, but defense moves against ranged attacks are generally based on finding cover. An AI might remain behind cover while in the player's cone of view, but once outside of this, it will likely move to a position from which it can fire, unless its current position offers this opportunity.

Offensive

Offensive moves are based on finding a firing spot. This could mean standing up from behind low cover, turning out from tall cover, or simply standing out in the open. Generally an AI should try and seek a good firing point dependent on their type; a sniper will want a firing point farther away than a pistol wielder would, for instance. A good firing point must obviously have a view of the player and be in range but should also have good cover nearby and possibly have a good fallback route if the player gets too close.

Choosing when to fire can be based on a scoring or weighted random system. This can be based on a desired action or what the player is doing. For example, it is less desirable to fire when the player is hiding behind cover.

When controlled as part of a group, it would be the commanding AI's responsibility to provide the instructions of when to shoot and where to move.

GROUP MANAGEMENT

So far we have talked about AI on an individual level. We haven't really looked at how AIs interact with each other and work as a team. With the exception of fast-paced, numbers-based shooters, it is extremely important that AI can work as a unit because if all AIs performed their behavior unregulated, the player would likely be swamped in seconds.

What is needed is a method of managing groups of agents and communicating between them. There are numerous approaches to this problem, but a few are particularly suited to different game requirements.

Basic Group Management

The simplest method of controlling a group of attackers is to have a maximum number of attackers at any one moment. The other actors then mill around waiting for their opportunity to attack. If these waiting AIs were simply to stand watching, it would feel like a very flat and lifeless system. Instead, these spectators should perform some suitable idles, be able to circle the target, and, further still, barge in and replace the current attackers from time to time. This barge-in action moves them onto the attacking list and sends the AIs they are replacing into the spectator mode.

Formations

Formations are organized groups of actors that form shapes around or toward targets in the world. A formation might track the target or remain stationary once formed up until an order is given. Formations are particularly useful for simulating groups of human (or human-like) opponents. They might also be used to align friendly allies to the player so they follow in a more organized manner. This makes combat much more organized and makes the AIs look like they are behaving more intelligently.

There are limitless shapes that formations could potentially form, but there are two basic shapes that really make sense:

Line: The group members form a line in a fixed direction from the target.
Circle: The group members form a circle or part circle around the target.

While these seem basic, we can add parameters to improve them. The concept of ranks allows us to specify how deep a shape becomes. We can form shapes like a wedge with the basic line shape by putting fewer members in the front ranks. Thus, a formation might have the following parameters:

Formation type: Line or circle
Number of ranks: How many ranks deep
Rank members: How many and the type of members in a rank
Width: The width of a line rank
Circle arc: The angle of an arc of a circle
Spacing: The spacing between members
Distance/radius: The distance of each rank from the target (each rank has its own distance)
Direction: The direction vector from the target

Offset: A world offset from the target

Facing: The direction the members are facing, not necessarily toward the tracking target (e.g., the formation is guarding a door but facing the player)

Commander AI

Having a commander AI is a significant step up from the previous management system, as it allows much more synchronized patterns and attacks to be employed. This commander AI may be an actor in the world or might simply be an ethereal concept used to direct the troops. The advantage of having it as an actual actor in the world is that the group can then fall into disarray when the commander is killed.

Commander AI is basically a way of organizing a group. The commander issues orders to each of the individuals and they carry out the action. In this respect it is much like an individual AI, in that the methods of choice for selecting an action can be a state machine, score system, randomly weighted, or sequenced. The only difference is that individuals may still have the ability to act by themselves, even if this is limited. For example, they can block or counter incoming attacks without the commander AI having to issue an order.

The beauty of this system is that complex tactics can be put into play by controlling the agents' attacks in a synchronized manner. Enemies can be told to attack from specific directions with specific attacks. They can be told to guard a particular part of the environment or to attack a specific location. This makes for a believable and strategic style of gameplay that will convey a true feeling of intelligence.

SUMMARY

The secret of good game AI is not the underlying system that powers the AI, but rather the appearance that is given to the player. A character can be very simple in its technical implementation yet exhibit apparently intelligent behavior. The game designer tries to create a challenge for the player that is fun and believable. They do not try to create an infallible opponent. As such, much of AI is about designing illusions, not clever programming of heuristics or neural networks.

AI components: There are several components that make up an AI system:

- **Behaviors:** The sets of actions and states an AI will perform.
- **States:** Separates actions and reactions according to their use in a situation.
- **Actions and reactions:** The base units of physical performances that an AI will use.

AI communication: AIs will need to communicate information about the state of the world with each other. There are two methods of doing this:

- **Polling:** Constantly requesting information from the world.
- **Event messaging:** Receiving information from the world when particular events occur.

Methods of choice: An AI will need some method of making decisions. A number of methods are used to choose what actions to perform:

- **Sequenced:** AIs follow a very rigid sequence of instructions.
- **Decision trees:** AIs follow a branching structure of decisions.
- **Weighted random:** Choices are made randomly, with particular weightings toward certain choices.
- **Scoring:** Choices are scored according to the situation.
- **Finite state machines:** AIs follow a set pattern of states that react to events that occur in the world.
- **Learning systems:** AIs learn to decide what are the best choices in particular situations by learning from mistakes or learning from the player's actions.

AI construction methods: A number of methods might be used to construct AI systems:

- **Hard coding:** The act of writing a behavior entirely in game code. This makes it efficient but inflexible.
- **Scripting:** Designers are able to script various elements of the AI.
- **Visual editing:** The most intuitive method is to allow the player to build elements of the AI visually.
- **Building further on AI systems:** We looked at how emergent behavior can be utilized, as well as how we can make AI more efficient.

The mechanics of actions: The methods of how AIs function was looked at in depth in this section of the chapter. Designers need to consider several elements of AI functionality:

- **Navigation:** How the AI moves around the world.
- **Sensory AI:** How the AIs can sense their environment and entities within it.
- **Combat:** How AIs make decisions and react to combat situations.

Group management: We investigated the following management systems to control groups of AIs:

- **Basic group management:** Using maximum attackers on a target to prevent a player from being swamped.
- **Formations:** Using more advanced structures to order and control the movement of attackers.
- **Commander AI:** Using a singular entity that issues orders to the group.

The bulk of the time spent in AI development should be spent looking at ways of communicating the actions of the AI character to the player. Anything that occurs "under the hood," no matter how clever, will never be seen by the player unless some method of communicating those actions is created. Feedback is essential. The next chapter concentrates on making AIs much more believable, so that the illusion of intelligence is given to the player.

IMPLEMENTING AI ACTORS

In This Chapter

- Player Expectation and Feedback
- Enemies
- Nonplayer Characters
- Allies
- Bot AI

All the techniques discussed in the previous chapter can be utilized, along with animation, to create the AI actors themselves. AI breathes life into these actors, and the strength of this AI will have a huge impact on the player's experience. Poor AI will destroy the illusion and quite possibly the gameplay entirely. It is important that AI is just right to make the game work.

When it comes to implementing AI, there are lots of situations and types of actors to consider. The types of actors will have an enormous impact on the techniques used to create the AI and the demands that will be placed upon it. This chapter focuses on the following aspects of AI development:

- Player expectation and feedback
- Enemies
- Nonplayer characters
- Allies
- Bot AI

PLAYER EXPECTATION AND FEEDBACK

With each type of game the player has a set of expectations from the AI. The higher the quality and complexity of AI, the higher these expectations become. If AI is kept at the most basic close-in and attack formula, the only real expectations a player will have is that the AI can move without bumping into objects. However, once you start adding more complex behaviors, expectations rise. Now the AI must take into account additional issues. If two guards are standing together chatting and you take one of them out with a headshot, the player expects the other guard to react. With more complexity, the number of different situations increases exponentially. The consistency of a game world is paramount; if something happens to break this consistency, the illusion of intelligence can be shattered.

Besides the maintenance of consistency, players have several other expectations of the AI:

To provide challenge: The player must feel enough challenge to not get bored, but not so much that it is frustrating.

To provide interactivity: The AI reacts to the player's actions and acknowledges his presence.

To provide various scenarios: The player wants new challenges and expects to witness new sights as often as possible.

One key aspect of communicating intelligence to the player is providing feedback of the AI's actions and behavior. The golden rule here is that without some form of feedback to the player, an action shouldn't be included at all. Make every detail of an AI's state be transparent to the player in some way, whether this be through animations or even icons above the actors' heads. Use speech to communicate actions to the player, such as "Cover Me!" or "Attack!" Make each enemy announce an attack before lunging forward to give the player time to react.

By combining a strong set of AI rules and good feedback to the player, a solid feeling of intelligence will emerge. Players will also start to read more into a situation than there really is—start to interpret intelligence that hasn't been modeled. Solid AI rules also allow for emergent behavior and allow the player the reward of trying new strategies and having them pay off. Good AI will solidify the game experience, so spend some time getting it right.

ENEMIES

By far the most common type of AI that will be implemented is enemy AI. This is what provides the bulk of the challenge in most action games, particularly games that involve combat.

Types of Enemy

The variety of enemies in any game will vary greatly, but many of them can be classified into a particular type depending on their usage within a game situation:

Fodder: The lowliest of the low, fodder tends to be dumb and is thrown at the player in abundance. These are usually simple to dispatch and only really serve as a nuisance. Their only strength is in numbers.

Soldiers: The basic enemy type. They are not throwaway like fodder but present a brief challenge. Soldiers might be found in small groups or in fairly large numbers. They lack any real fighting skill unless coordinated by a commander AI.

Commander: A much tougher version of the soldier, who dishes out tactical plans to a group. He is also likely to be proficient at combat himself.

Heavy units: Slow, powerful enemies that might be found mingling with a group of soldiers or in a small group of their own. They offer crushing attacks but little in the way of speed or dexterity.

Light units/scouts: Very fast, but cause little damage. They might be found in groups of soldiers or in small groups or as individuals in an advance scouting party.

Ranged fighters: A group that remains at a distance and uses ranged attacks to whittle down the enemy. They may appear as part of a larger group of soldiers or form a group of their own.

Snipers: Units that fire from long ranges and remain static and fairly hidden from view. They will appear alone or in very small numbers.

Assassins: Enemies that hide from view and strike quickly before running back into hiding. They tend to move as individuals or very small groups.

Elites: The very best of the soldiers, fighters, or gunslingers. They are difficult to overcome and use plenty of tactics. They tend to appear as individuals or small groups but might also lead a larger group of lesser enemies.

Subbosses: A specialized enemy who is very proficient at combat. They are usually one-off individuals or a tiny group of individuals. They are different from true bosses in that they do not have highly scripted patterns or use specific environments, but use standard combat systems.

Bosses: Something of a gaming cliché but well-loved features of many games. They usually use a very particular pattern and use a specifically designed environment.

Enemy Attack Strategies

An enemy can employ any strategy they want. Many of these strategies will be fairly useless, but many can be seen in a variety of games. The level of AI strategy is dependent on the style of game that is being made. High-action games with a multitude of enemies have fairly basic and forthright strategies. Tactical games, on the other hand, employ much more advanced strategies against the player. Strategy is also heavily dependent on the types of enemy that are involved.

Individual Strategies

Strategy is used on an individual level in games where there is a relentless number of attackers (such as *Serious Sam*) or where there are very few attackers at any one time. Individual strategies place no emphasis on the communication with other AIs, but instead simply act out their behavior.

Melee Strategies

For an individual melee actor a number of strategies might be employed that are concerned with the manner of the actor's movement around the player:

Close in and attack: The most basic strategy is to simply get within attack range and perform attacks. This could even be a suicide attack (such as the headless, screaming bombers in *Serious Sam* that run directly toward the player and explode when they reach a certain distance from the player).

Darting attacks: The actor runs in to perform one or more attacks and then backs off for a period before returning to attack again.

Charging attacks: The actor gets within attack range and then performs a charge attack in a straight line, which forces the player to sidestep or evade.

Directional attacks: The actor keeps moving around the player to vary attacks. This might include slowly circling or performing much faster leaps over the player's head.

Ranged Strategies

Melee attacks require the actor to get up-close and personal. Ranged attacks present a threat that can be much trickier to deal with. It can be hard to know where attacks are coming from, so ranged attacks might need slow-moving, obvious projectiles or may need to only fire when in view. There are a number of strategies that a long ranged attacker might employ:

Close in and fire: This is generally a slow-moving, well-armored enemy, as they leave themselves totally vulnerable.

Circle and fire: Remain at a distance, circling the player's position and firing.

Cover and fire: The agent remains behind cover and emerges to shoot frequently. Relatively little movement is involved.

Seek cover and fire: Move between cover points to fire. This feels more dynamic than staying put.

Close in, cover, and fire: Get closer to the enemy, but use the cover to get there.

Camp/ambush: Remain hidden and wait for the enemy to get close.

Snipe: Remain hidden at a long distance and fire on the enemy.

Group Strategies

While individual strategies can be interesting, you get much more mileage from developing group strategies, where the enemies can work together and different skill sets of different agents might also be put into play.

Melee Strategies

With groups of melee attackers, much more can be done to coordinate attacks and hem the players in to a degree. Melee combat tends to involve having a number of active attacking AI units and a number of spectators that wait for their turns. This may be a disheveled group or an organized formation.

Formations: We have already covered the basics of creating a formation, but there are a variety of ways in which these formations can be employed. From a simple circle or line formation we could select attackers to move in on the player and fight. However, we can make the formations much more interesting

Line formations are good for protecting objects or people, as they form a wider barrier and tend to be much more defensive. Circle formations that encircle the player are more aggressive. One nice setup is to have two circles of enemies around the player—one offensive and one defensive. The inner circle is offensive, and potential attackers are chosen from this group. The outer circle is defensive and acts as a wall to keep the player in. Enemies can swap between these two circles as combat progresses.

Synchronized Attack Patterns: Each AI in a group could attack the player one or two at a time, but while this can be interesting, we can do much more with a group situation. We can synchronize attacks so that one attack can lead into another, and specific types of attack can lead into the next. For example, one enemy could knock the player up into the air for another to juggle. This creates a group combo attack, where the player must defend against a coordinated series of moves as though it was from one individual. The difference is that attacks can come from all directions.

To create a system for choosing attacks we can specify:

Attack type: The move that we want an enemy to perform
Direction: Where in the formation we want the attack to come from (compass points)
Time: Delay to next strike

To set up an attack we might have:

1. Power Attack, North
2. 1 second delay
3. Fast Attack, West
4. 0.5 second delay
5. Power Attack, South
6. 0.5 second delay
7. Fast Attack, East & West

Ranged Strategies

With ranged groups there are lots of strategies that could be used. Real-life soldier tactics are extremely good references for looking at how AI should behave (often this is precisely what we are trying to model). A modern soldier employs lots of subtle tactics (often this means splitting agents into squads or units that work together):

Cover and move: One team provides covering fire while the other team moves into position.
Flanking: One squad attempts to move around to the side or rear of the enemy so that the enemy is pressured from more than one angle.
Fire channel: The AIs create an ambush in a bottlenecked area or pinch point. Any enemy that walks into this area is caught and attacked on two or three sides.
Flush out: The squad uses grenades or charging attacks to flush the enemy out.
Directional fire: The unit moves together facing separate directions so that they cover all directions.
Hold ground: The team digs into position and communicates any threat they see to each other. They try to hold their position and prevent the enemy from reaching the area.

Mixed Strategies

Many groups employ both ranged and melee attackers, but they can be difficult to get working together. The problem is that the melee guys can get in the way when ranged attackers want to perform an attack. One solution is to alternate attacks, so that melee attackers move in for a period, then disperse to allow ranged attacks to be made. Ranged attacks can also be made while melee attackers flank the player and then move in to attack from the side or the rear.

Support Strategies

While there may be many direct attackers in a group, there might also be a number of support actors (particularly in fantasy RPGs). What does a support actor do? Well, they can heal their allies or boost their attributes to make them better fighters. They might also afflict the player with negative statuses to give the attackers in the group an advantage. Support actors can become a real nuisance to the player, and their deaths can be key to the player's survival.

Bosses

Bosses traditionally involve one-on-one fights against a particularly difficult and often spectacular enemy. Boss patterns and behaviors are generally tailored specifically to match their character. There are several well-used themes that might be employed.

Use of Environment

Either the player or the boss may utilize elements in the environment in the following ways:

Boss movement: The boss uses the environment to its advantage, being able to move quickly around it.
Player movement: The player must use the environment to move and attack in a specific way.
Environment attacks: The boss uses the environment to attack the player. For example, it could destroy a section of the floor space with a certain attack.
Environmental weakness: The player must use the environment to destroy the boss, for example, destroy four shield generators before he can attack the boss.

Attack Patterns

Bosses often use particular patterns that the player can memorize:

Set patterns: The boss performs set patterns of attack that can be learned.
Multiple stages: The boss has several (often three) stages of attack that get steadily more ferocious.

Weak Spots

Often a boss may have a weak spot that the player can use to his advantage:

Single weak spots: The player must hit a specific spot to cause damage. The weak spot is generally made fairly obvious; otherwise, the player will be confused as to how to defeat the boss. Plenty of player feedback is given when the boss is hit (such as flashing red).
Attrition: The player must destroy parts in order to weaken the boss and eventually defeat it, for example, chipping various parts of armor away to reveal the vulnerable underbelly.

Attack Types

The boss may use a number of different types of attack against the player:

Melee: Close quarter attacks with high damage.

Charge: Charges at the player, forcing him to evade.

Direct shots: Fire a volley of projectiles or a beam straight at the player's current position.

Scatter shots: Fire a series of shots around the player's current position, forcing him to move away.

Radial attacks: Use beams, slams, or spinning attacks that rotate around the arena or cause circular waves to expand outward, forcing the player to jump.

Mines: Drop a series of mines that makes the battleground far more dangerous.

Minions: A number of lesser creatures are brought in to keep the player occupied.

Negative statuses: The boss inflicts negative statuses on the player, making him more vulnerable.

Defense

A boss character may have a number of defensive tricks up his sleeve:

Shields: The boss has shields that have gaps that must be fired through or that must be deactivated somehow.

Heal: The boss is able to heal himself and replenish energy. There might be a destructible device that facilitates this, and the player is required to destroy this first.

Positive statuses: These make the boss or his minions stronger, faster, and more deadly.

By using a variety of these strategies with flair and good environments to interact with, you can create memorable, challenging, and enjoyable boss battles.

Bosses with Multiple Player Characters

With party-based games (usually RPGs) it is possible to pit multiple actors against the boss. In a turn-based game this can work very well, but in a real-time game it can be a little different. There are several problems in a real-time scenario:

Focus: It is difficult to determine who the boss should attack during its patterns: the player or the AI? If it attacks the player, then the AI is free to attack and never gets threatened. If it attacks the AI, then the player never feels threatened. Finding the balance is difficult.

Control: If the AI is attacking the boss without direct player influence, there is a distinct lack of control on the player's behalf. The players may feel cheated that the AI did all of the work and feel deflated from a lack of challenge.

Babysitting: With AI actors who are not too powerful, the opposite problem arises, where they require constant looking after.

This does not mean that multiple party boss fights should not be used in real-time games; they just need careful consideration of the problems, and suitable solutions need to be devised. One technique that works well is to have a number of minions in the boss battle. The AI party members can concentrate on the minions while the player-controlled actor concentrates on the boss. A different solution to the problem is to give the player greater control of the AI actors. If players are able to issue commands to their teammates in the heat of battle, they will have a greater feeling of victory and not feel cheated that the outcome was not of their making.

Building Fair Enemy AIs

While we are aiming to create the illusion of intelligence, we must remember that we are trying also to create an enjoyable experience for the player. This means we have to make sure AIs don't behave so well that the single-player experience is no longer fun because the challenge is too great.

We have to build in certain rules that warn the players and give them a slight advantage. Lars Lidén, of Valve fame, talks in his presentation "The Use of Artificial Intelligence in the Computer Game Industry" [Liden] of several techniques that can be used:

Proper use of senses: Rather than cheating to find the player's position, the AIs actually engage in sensing the world.

Miss first time: The first shot made by a ranged actor does not hit the player but instead acts as a warning, giving the player time to react.

Bad aim: The shots made by a ranged actor scatter around the player but rarely hit. The smarter an AI gets, the less this is likely to happen.

Don't immediately attack: The first action is to get the agent into place rather than instantly attacking. This gives the players time to react or prepare themselves for an onslaught.

Warn the player of attack: Use animation or voice acting to announce an attack. This again gives the player time to react.

Give tactical clues: Let the player hear speech to indicate the group's next move, such as shouting, "Cover me!" when about to provide covering fire.

Be vulnerable: Allow an AI to be caught out in the open, fumble an attack, or even beg for mercy.

Pull back: When a player is nearly dead, ease off and allow him some breathing space.

Using Distraction Against Enemies

The focus of many games may be combat, but there are other behaviors that can be given to the AIs so that the player can employ different methods of tackling an enemy. Stealth games often use distraction to draw an opponent away from the player, but it can also be used in nonstealth-based games too.

A stealth-based distraction is intended to make a noise that will attract the attention of the enemy, who will then move to investigate that area. The players must still be careful when moving, as they will attract attention if they are making too much noise. Other distractions can be used to move attackers away from the player. For example, a hologram might fool enemies into attacking, or a juicy bone could be thrown to dogs to keep them busy. A large explosion might be set off to make the AI investigate and clear the route ahead.

Another form of distraction might be tear gas or a flash grenade that temporarily renders the victims incapacitated and offers the player the chance to attack or move past the threat.

Building Character

So far we have talked about very functional elements of AI, but there are many more techniques that can be added to increase the depth of an enemy's character. We can increase the number of states that an enemy can be in by using incidental animations and voice acting and by modeling emotions.

Initial Behaviors

One technique that is often used, as it allows for a very high level of control, is moving AIs from a scripted initial behavior to their standard behavior. The scripted behavior allows for very complex actions to be used and even tailored to a specific area. This is also the easiest way of doing one-off animation rather than having to build whole states for one use. As soon as the player is sighted or a message is sent to the entity, the scripted behavior changes to a standard AI behavior.

Extending Enemy Behaviors

The flow of an actor's behavior is generally modeled with an FSM. These allow us to easily build up complex AI systems. Choosing the flow of the states carefully and logically will enable us to breathe life into the AI actors.

Patrolling Guard

A very popular behavior to model is that of a patrolling guard that will attack when he spots the player. We have already looked at this behavior when we examined FSMs, but this can be taken much further (even to the point of making the guard go for a toilet break). This extended FSM is shown in Figure 15.1.

Police Officer

Imagine a game where you play a criminal on the run. We want to create a police officer AI that will seek out the player and then give warning before opening fire (see Figure 15.2).

Venomous Beast of Doom

Just to show that more complex behaviors can be applied to any kind of enemy, let us consider a horrible slathering beast. This beast has no vision and must sense

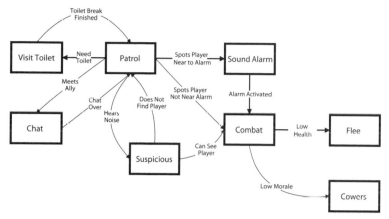

FIGURE 15.1   Extending a basic FSM to add character.

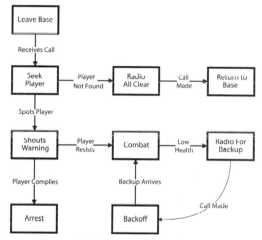

FIGURE 15.2   An FSM for a police officer.

things by sound. When the player first encounters it, it lies slumbering in relative peace. If the player can quietly sneak by, it will not hear him. The beast is on a large chain that irritates it. This FSM is shown in Figure 15.3.

Incidental Animations

Adding personality to an actor is a great method of increasing believability, and one of the best ways to do this is with incidental animations. These are not necessary for the gameplay but add color and life to the scenario. The possibilities are limitless here, but there are many common themes that might be employed:

Everyday activities: Sharpening swords, staring at the daisies, or going about their general business before the player is spotted

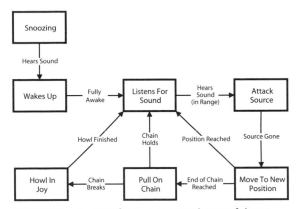

FIGURE 15.3   An FSM for a venomous beast of doom.

Spectating: Watching the fight and performing several types of action, depending on the current situation

Cheering: If the player is doing badly or has been knocked to the floor

Jeering: If the player is doing well or has floored or killed a colleague

Cowering: If the enemy is doing particularly well or performs a stunning move

Fumbles: Bungling an attack

Voice Acting

A lot of personality can be added with good-quality voice acting (however, bad acting can be extremely detrimental). By adding several layers of chatter, communication, and banter to a group of AIs, a deep level of atmosphere can be added to the game.

While speech can be used for story exposition, the dialog used for enhancing characters tends to belong to an actor type, which may include several voice types. As much variation as possible should be used to avoid constant repetition (it is extremely annoying to hear the same line over and over, and it breaks the believability of the world). There are many types of voice over (VO) that can be used in different situations.

Characters who are unaware of the player may voice:

Idle banter: AIs discussing something mundane like the weather or their daily lives

Incidental information: AIs discussing story-based events, giving little snippets of information that enrich the world

Warnings: AIs being ordered to move out or search the area by a commanding AI, giving the player an indication of what is happening

Characters who are searching for the player may voice:

Warning: Announcing that they are suspicious (e.g., "What was that?")

Commentary: Describing their actions so the player knows how to react (e.g., "I see something over there!")

Threats: Describing what they will do when they find the player (e.g., "I'll skin you alive when I find you!")

Communication: Talking and instructing other AIs during a search (e.g., "You take the right corridor.")

Characters engaged in combat might voice:

Threats: Telling the player that they want to cause damage to them

Taunts: Mocking the player when they perform badly

Awe: Becoming frightened when the player performs well

Cheers: When a fellow AI is doing well against the player

Jeers: When a fellow AI is doing badly against the player

Communication: AIs talking to each other and offering tactics

Orders: A commander issuing orders to his subordinates and motivating or chastising them

Voice acting is discussed in further depth in the audio section.

Modeling Emotion

By modeling emotions, we can add another layer of depth to actors, as we show that they can be affected by the player's actions and can react in different ways by making variables different for each actor. Many emotions could be modeled, some that we will look at when we deal with NPCs and allies. There are only a few that are worth modeling with enemies.

Morale

Morale is not so much a visible emotion as a measurement of an actor's confidence. We can use this measurement to elicit different responses from an actor. The response can vary from actor to actor or even from instance to instance.

There are two ends to the morale scale—high morale and low morale—which can be used to instigate positive or negative emotions. While this may be seen as black and white, we can add shades of grey in between (see Table 15.1).

TABLE 15.1   Positive and Negative Emotions

	POSITIVE EMOTIONS	NEGATIVE EMOTIONS
Confidence	Brave	Timid
	Heroic	Cowardly
Mood	Enthused	Deflated
	Elated	Distraught
	Triumphant	Devastated

These have been broken down into confidence and mood. Confidence emotions concern the actor's self-perception and manifest in their behavior. Mood is more of an outward appearance.

Morale is gained or lost depending on the actions of the player and those of an actor's fellow AIs. Thresholds are set for stages of morale and then an emotion or choice of emotions applied to each of these. These thresholds can differ for each actor to create different personalities. For each action performed within sight or hearing range of an AI actor, a morale modifier will be applied (see Table 15.2).

TABLE 15.2   Actions and Morale Modifiers

Player kills fellow AI	−10
Player injures fellow AI	−1
Player surprises AI	−5
AI injures player	1
AI floors player	5
Player performs special	−5

A commander being present in an attack group can have a positive effect on morale, so that any negative emotions are reduced by a modifier and positive emotions are boosted. This models the commander keeping his troops motivated by issuing commands and shouting encouragement.

There could be a virtually limitless number of actions and resulting modifiers, but the important element is the reaction of an AI when it leaves the normal threshold and enters the outer morale states. For example, a weaker AI might be set up as shown in Table 15.3.

TABLE 15.3   The Effect of Morale Shown as a Reaction by the AI

MORALE	REACTION
Very low	Cowardly/devastated
Low	Timid/distraught
High	Cocky/enthused
Very high	Brave/elated

A more dangerous AI would be set up with less debilitating negative emotions and stronger positive emotions (see Table 15.4).

TABLE 15.4 A More Dangerous AI's Reactions to Morale

MORALE	REACTION
Very low	Timid/distraught
Low	Cautious/deflated
High	Brave/elated
Very high	Heroic/triumphant

Alternatively, AIs might be set up with an entire emotional spectrum as shown in Table 15.5.

TABLE 15.5 An AI with the Full Emotional Spectrum

MORALE	REACTION
Very low	Cowardly/devastated
Low	Timid/distraught
Quite low	Cautious/deflated
Quite high	Cocky/enthused
High	Brave/elated
Very high	Heroic/triumphant

Emotional Responses

An AI will become more confident and will be in a better mood when its morale is high. There are lots of positive emotions that might be applied, but not all fit the idea of being an enemy. We want to model emotions that are relevant to situations the AI will face.

Confidence: Confidence adjusts the behavior of an AI according to its morale. We must be wary of a self-feeding cycle where the game gets harder for the lesser player and easier for a better player. The solution to this might be to have dynamic, shifting morale thresholds based on a player's skill, so that a poor player will encounter more demoralized AIs and a better player will be pit against actors that are highly motivated. It's a difficult decision to employ any technique that can cause this problem and must be considered carefully.

Cowardly: The actors are highly likely to flee the combat area or cower in a corner. They are unlikely to launch any attack unless provoked.

Timid: The actors back away easily and do not like to engage the player head on. They will try to attack when the player's focus is away from them. They are more prone to fleeing.

Cautious: The actor plays more defensively and uses less impressive attacks.

Cocky: The actors are feeling particularly confident but may lack the experience to perform. They would become more aggressive, but lowly AIs might overstretch themselves, leaving them vulnerable. Experienced AIs will simply perform better than normal.

Brave: The actors are fighting much better than normal and will perform more impressive attacks, have better aim, and become more difficult opponents.

Heroic: The actors are fighting on top form, much better than they normally might. They perform moves that dazzle the opponent.

Mood: A much safer method of employing morale is to simply add a visual appearance of morale and the occasional action, although this can also be used in combination with confidence.

Devastated: Actors are in awe of the player and cannot cheer at all. The commander is screaming at his troops that they should all be shot, hung, murdered, flogged, and so on.

Distraught: Actors begin to mutter among themselves, showing they are scared to approach the player. They jeer less regularly than when deflated but with more passion. A commander will be hurling insults at his troops.

Deflated: The actors are fairly quiet and cheer rarely. A commander would begin to order his troops to work harder. Jeers are made when the player does well.

Enthused: The actors cheer fairly regularly and throw a few taunts at the player.

Elated: When not in combat the actors cheer, perhaps while stomping their feet or slamming their swords against their shields. They throw plenty of insults at the player.

Triumphant: The actors sense victory and are cheering almost nonstop, making plenty of noise and moving about in anticipation of the kill. Insults are hurled forth.

Frustration

When we try to do something repeatedly, but repeatedly fail, we tend to get very frustrated. We can also model frustration for our AI actors. We could have several levels of frustration, which produce different behaviors:

Frustrated: The actors lash out wildly for a few moments with heavy attacks that leave them vulnerable for a while after the strike. Ranged attackers might stand in the open to fire a volley of bullets, but then leave themselves vulnerable.

Angry: The actors do a series of long buildup and long recovery attacks for a slightly longer time and completely forget to block or cover. This leaves them very vulnerable.

Enraged: The actor performs a long series of heavy attacks or rapid shots that are poorly aimed and are likely to miss altogether. An actor firing a gun might even carry on firing when it's empty (causing the gun to click on the empty chamber) while screaming at the top of his lungs and being completely ineffective.

Frustration works on a scale also, but only with one target. Points are added to frustration each time a frustrating move occurs. This will reset after a period of time or after a number of successful attempts to attack are made. Different actions will have different levels of effect (as shown in Table 15.6).

TABLE 15.6   Effects of Actions

ACTION	EFFECT SCORE
Attack is blocked	1
Attack is countered	5
Attack is evaded	2

A cooldown period will be needed once a frustration event has occurred; otherwise, the actor could be constantly performing the action!

Fear

Some games might allow the player to instill fear in his opponent. This could be used as the main gameplay mechanic, so that instead of fighting opponents, you must try to shock them. As with the other emotions, we may want to have a number of grades of fear that determine the enemy's response:

Nervous: The actors are twitching and are suspicious of the slightest sound. They may even chase after shadows.

Fearful: The actors are visibly shaking and are calling out to every shadow. They will attack anything they see move.

Terrified: The actors run away screaming and are unable to defend themselves.

Fear should be based on a time-adjusting scale, so that fear slowly diminishes when no fearful stimuli are applied to an actor. Thus, actors must be constantly "topped up" to make them more and more scared.

Again we can score actions to create an effect of the fear scale. Some actions will have a positive effect on fear, and others will take fear points away when the mystery is solved (see Table 15.7).

TABLE 15.7   Fear Scale Based on Player Actions

ACTION	FEAR SCORE
Noise heard	1
Attacked without seeing aggressor	10
Player is sighted	−2
Player is sighted in costume when fear is high	10

We could have all sorts of actions here if we were really investing in the fear-inducing mechanic. Imagine the player was pretending to be a poltergeist and had to terrify the AI subjects. The player could have all sorts of abilities, such as switching on appliances, pushing objects, smashing objects, and so on. Perhaps the player would have to do all this while remaining out of view.

NONPLAYER CHARACTERS

NPCs are actors the player meets while traveling through the game world. Players never get to play as these actors, nor do these actors fight alongside players (those that do are termed ally AIs).

NPCs need few complex AI behaviors, but they can be modeled with fairly complex behaviors if a high level of depth is sought in the game world.

NPC Types

NPCs may have several uses, and their use will determine the sort of AI structures they will need to be equipped with.

Incidental Actors

Incidental actors are like extras on a movie set. They need the ability to patrol, wander, and perform actions. They might be able to interact in a minor way such as speaking a line. They might also respond to actions or events triggered by the player. They might be able to turn into enemies and engage in combat if provoked or might simply run away or die quickly when attacked.

Minor Actors

Minor actors are not quite key actors but have more of an involvement in the story than the incidental actors. They are often involved in scripted sequences, but not in any scene that might suffer if they were to die. If they are killed before their big scene, then the scene simply does not occur (or possibly another actor is chosen to perform the scene instead).

Key Actors

Key actors (that are not allies) are essential to story exposition. They are involved in complex cutscenes or scripted sequences. The death of a key actor is a thorny issue, as it is a potentially game-breaking situation. Often games end if the key actor is killed. The other option is to make the actor invincible, but this can break immersion (as well as a source of fun) for the player. A compromise might be to give them infinite health but let them be attacked and have a reaction. Often this reaction might be to scold the player for his actions.

Merchants

Merchants buy from and sell items or commodities to the player. Generally they need a specific user interface (UI), but their AI is likely to be limited to patrolling, incidental animations, and conversing with the player. Merchants might not be attackable, as they are often essential to player progression.

VIPs

VIPs are actors that are used as part of a mission or quest that need to either be protected or assassinated but are not able to fight by their own means. The target generally follows a set patrol path, which the player must help VIPs along or intercept. If the AI is to be assassinated, then it will often be flanked by a group of enemies who fight back (the enemies are in a formation that has the VIP as the formation target).

Another type of VIP follows the player around. It will always try to keep within a minimum radius of the player character and try not to stand in the player's view cone. A VIP such as this might be given simple commands such as follow or wait, and possibly hide actions are allowed where appropriate. To keep the game from being frustrating, the follow command should be usable at any distance so that the VIP pathfinds to the player's position rather than the player having to navigate back to the VIP's position. When crossing loading zones, the VIP should follow the player. The loading zone cannot be crossed until either the VIP is in range (a suitable message can be displayed on screen such as "must wait for the VIP") or a cut to the next area occurs. Then the AI can simply be popped near the player's location during the cut.

Patrols and Wandering

An NPC may simply be static in the world, waiting for the player to arrive, but usually they follow a patrol route through the world, going about their daily business. Designers can lay out a patrol path through the environment and can fix actions to specific points along the path. The problem with fixed patrol paths is that unless they are extremely long, they are very regular and repeat fairly often.

A different solution is to wander in sensible regions (i.e., keep to a footpath). Actions could then be performed by objects requesting to be used. A suitable NPC AI might then wander over and interact with it. This gives a much greater feeling of randomness but requires more AI processes to be running. Also, if things are left to AI alone, rather than being directed precisely, there is always a chance of it going wrong if the system is not robust enough.

Conversations

One of the most common interactions between a player and an NPC is a conversation.

Simple Conversation

At its most basic, conversation with a character is an entirely linear experience. On triggering the conversation, the avatar and subject will engage in a predefined conversation. This is such a simple system that it is easy to determine all the necessary voice over lines and is straightforward to implement. However, it is not an interactive system and requires no skill or thought on the part of the player other than to listen.

Reaction-Based Conversation

Reaction-based conversations use different conversation strings according to the subject's opinion of the player character. An opinion is classed as the degree of liking the subject takes to the avatar and possibly a level of suspicion as well. This opinion may be based on a number of factors:

- The subject's mood
- The avatar's reputation
- The subject's friend network

Subject's Mood

Characters can be assigned a number of different moods and temperaments that determine what mood they are likely to be in. Some characters may be naturally happy and carefree, whereas others are grumpy and suspicious of strangers. There may be factors that affect the mood of a character such as:

Story events: Character's mood can change over the course of the story time line.
The weather: Rain and gloom are likely to make some characters miserable, or maybe some like the wet weather.
Time of day: Some characters might be morning people; others may be in a better mood later in the day.

Characters' moods have an impact on how they speak and react to the player and will show in their facial animations, their body language, and their voice acting. There might need to be several inflections of each line of speech for each mood of the character.

There are plenty of possible moods for a character, but there are a few standard moods that tend to be used:

- Neutral
- Happy
- Sad
- Angry
- Upset
- Puzzled
- Laughing
- Disgusted
- Serious

The Avatar's Reputation

A reaction is often guided by the avatar's reputation. If the avatar has a reputation for being dishonest and mean, characters are more likely to be suspicious and take a dislike to the avatar (though they may be frightened enough to do as they are told). If the avatar has a reputation for being a nice guy, then they are more likely to respond well to him (but might take him for a fool and try to con him). Other characters might be criminally inclined and respect the player for being dishonest, reacting to him as a friend. It all depends on the subject's motivations and outlook on life.

The Subject's Relationship Network

Characters in a game world often appear isolated from each other, as they don't seem to interact with each other beyond the player's own interactions. This can be solved by building a relationship network, which will determine a reaction based on the opinions of a character's relationship to other characters. If the player does harm to a character the subject likes, then that subject is likely to dislike the player. If the player harms someone the subject dislikes, then the subject will more likely welcome the player's actions. Conversely, helping another character will have the opposite reactions for each relationship.

There are generally five types of relationship, which may be concealed so that a different reaction is shown when interacting with that character than is actually felt by the actor in question:

- Loves
- Likes
- Neutral
- Dislikes
- Hates

The relationships between characters can be expressed as a network of reciprocal relationships as shown in Figure 15.4.

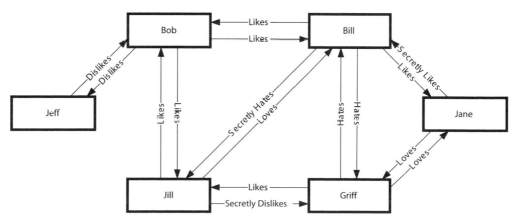

FIGURE 15.4   A character's relationship network.

One important element to consider is the time it will take for the player's actions to filter down through the network. If a player performs an action on one character and then talks to another soon afterward, the second character shouldn't immediately base its reaction on the previous action, unless the new subject witnessed the action directly. There should be some length of time before the action is registered, to simulate word spreading through the network (simulating gossip).

Conversation Trees

Conversation trees are a popular method of approaching conversations, as they offer a level on interaction for the player. The basis of a conversation tree is that there are choices as to which question or statement can be said to the subject, which will illicit different responses—different branches on the tree. Certain choices of phrase will open or close further branches of the tree, so that the conversation develops (if this is not done, then it is just a way of choosing which information to gather, not a skillful exercise in selecting the right phrase). As such, phrase choices can be broken down into a number of types:

General questions: Asking a general question to obtain information about the plot, objects, environment, or another character.

Probing questions: Asking a particular question to illicit information on a specific topic.

Personal questions: Asking a personal question about the character could potentially offend or please the subject and may close or open branches, respectively.

Request: Asking the subject to perform a favor or particular task.

Reassuring statement: Giving a positive response that is designed to please the subject (although it might make him feel patronized). This generally opens branches.

Insulting or threatening statement: Giving a negative response that is designed to anger or frighten the subject. This will often close branches, though it may also open them if the subject is frightened.

Neutral statement: Giving no particular response to the subject will generally keep the conversation on an even keel.

Correct answer: Giving the correct answer to a subject's question will generally open branches or provide a reward.

Incorrect answer: Giving an incorrect answer to a subject's question will generally close branches or result in insults.

Accept statement: Accepting an offer made by the subject.

Decline statement: Declining an offer made by the subject.

Subjects can have a number of phrases in return:

Salutation: A greeting to the player based on the subject's opinion of the avatar.

Positive response: A positive response to a player's phrase.

Negative response: A negative response to a player's phrase.

Neutral response: A general response to a player's phrase.

Information statement: Giving information known about the subject of the player's question. This may be given willingly or reluctantly.

Refusal statement: Refusal to give information known about the subject of the player's question or request.

Accept statement: Accepting a player's request to perform a favor or task.

Decline statement: Declining a player's request to perform a favor or task.

Denial statement: Denying or lying about knowing anything about the subject of the player's question.

Question: Asking the player a question in order to solicit a response. The subject may give a reward if the question is answered correctly.

Offer: Making some form of offer to the player such as a quest or mission or some form of trade.

Parting: A goodbye to the avatar, dependent on the subject's opinion of him. The subject may use this in response to a player's choice if not happy with it.

One important factor in choosing a phrase and its response is whether it can be repeated. All important information responses should be repeatable to allow the player to gather information if they miss it the first time (though there may be variations on the reply phrase to keep it from becoming stale). Other phrases are only selected once, and then they are closed, generally when some positive, neutral, or negative statement is made and the subject responds.

Skills could be associated with conversation such as persuasion or intimidation, so that tests are made against these skills when a particular phrase is selected. If a test is successful, then a success branch of the conversation is initiated; otherwise, a failure branch ensues.

A reaction system can be used in combination with a conversation tree system so that reputation, the subject's mood, and the subject's relationship network can be taken into account.

With a conversation tree it is also possible to base the reaction on the outcome of previous conversations with the player, so that characters remember the previous conversation history and limit their response. They might also refuse to talk to the player until the player does some action to redeem himself.

Conversation trees require a lot of dialog for each of the various branches and variations for those branches. This can mean it is not entirely viable to use voice over acting. Many games in the past that were dialog heavy (RPGs mainly) simply displayed text. These days, however, speech is the more desirable option (though subtitles are a must for the benefit of deaf gamers). Organizing this volume of speech can be a fairly daunting task. Often the avatar's line will not be spoken, as it has already been read by the player and this saves on both time and resources.

Phrase Parsing Systems

A very different approach to conversations is the idea of parsing phrases of words or symbols to initiate conversation. This reads text or a set of symbols and interprets them, thus providing a much more interactive method of conducting speech, but it also raises a number of issues. First, the player has to deal with fairly abstract or very simplistic phrases to construct a sentence with a console input; otherwise, the process is far too lengthy. Second, the player may find it difficult to know what questions to ask and may miss out on important information. Third, it is a more complex system to grasp than simple choice selection.

There is plenty of potential in the system, but we remain unconvinced that it offers much more scope than the conversation tree method (certainly as it currently stands). Maybe in the future this will be a viable option, but at the moment it has fairly little reward in relation to the amount of time that needs to be invested in making it work well.

Persistence

A problem that many PS2/Xbox/GameCube® era games had is that they created fairly believable worlds, but there was a lack of actors making up a scene. In a city there would be only a handful of actors milling about at any one time. This is something that is changing with later-generation machines.

Games like *Grand Theft Auto* managed to have what seemed like a well-populated city by cheating somewhat. Crowds were created on the fly locally; not every AI in the city was kept track of at any one time. As soon as the player was a certain range away, the actor was despawned. This gave the impression that everyone was performing their daily lives around you, but if you were to turn around and try to follow someone who had just moved out of range, then you would find that they had disappeared.

Persistence is the tracking of entities in a game so that they perform actions according to game world time. If an actor is persistent, then we should be able to find him somewhere in the game world performing his routine. Say an armored car were to collect cash every Friday and take it to the bank. This is an event that we can observe and track. It is persistent.

The basic NPCs of the *Grand Theft Auto* world are perceived to be persistent, but they are not. However, important NPCs are persistent. This allows the player to make plans and interact with NPCs on a whole new level. By having only selected NPCs be persistent, a huge amount of data tracking and processing time is saved. You only really need to have persistence for any NPC that can be interacted with in a meaningful way.

Emotions and Reactions

We could model limitless reactions for an NPC, but there are several context-based reactions that serve the basis of much of the interaction. An NPC's reaction is dependent on several things: the action being performed, who is performing the action, who the target of that action is, the reputation of the actor, and the target's state of mind.

Action

Several types of action can be performed on an NPC:

Converse: The player tries to strike up a conversation. Most games have some level of conversation between the player and the NPCs, but in some cases this might be restricted. Some actors might refuse to speak to a player with a certain reputation or one who has committed an unkind act upon a friend of that NPC.

Attack: The player attacks the target. Some games allow the players to freely attack whoever they want, although this may have an effect upon their reputations. Different NPCs have different responses. Some might attack, and others might flee.

Touch: The player touches the target. Bumping into an actor might elicit a response, often a verbal ticking off. However, this reaction might differ depending on the player's reputation. The player might receive a "Watch out mate" or something much more stern.

Approach: The player comes within a certain range of the target. Comments might be made by an NPC as a player approaches. There are all sorts of comments that might be used:

Player's appearance: Different costumes, hair cuts, or change in physical appearance may result in a variety of different comments.

Player's reputation: Speaking highly of the player or speaking in hushed tones about him.

Player's progress: Congratulating the player for killing a monster, or some other feat.

Player's wealth: Commenting on the state of the player's cash flow.

Threaten: The player threatens the target. This elicits a response from the NPC, which may be based on the player's reputation. If the player has a tough image, the response might be an apology or running away screaming. If not, it might be an insult right back, or the NPC might even start attacking.

Give item: The actor gives an item to the target. Giving an item will often result in some kind of reward—maybe just a nicer reputation or perhaps even love and respect.

Actor

The person performing the action is most likely to be the player, but there is no reason to not have AIs interact with each other in a similar manner. Often these will be scripted sequences, as there needs to be pretty tight control over exactly what is going on, but a whole world of actions could be going on around the player. NPCs could be chatting to each other, insulting each other, robbing and fighting, or any number of other actions.

Target

A target is generally the immediate receiver of the action, but there are also indirect effects. An action is therefore either direct or witnessed. Direct actions have a much more potent effect than witnessed ones. However, more depth can be added by linking AIs as groups (friend networks). These are considered to be like groups of friends—other NPCs they "know." When an NPC witnesses an action performed on a member of its group, the potency of that action is magnified. NPCs could belong to more than one group.

Reputation

Reputation is a means of measuring attitudes toward the player or even other AI actors. There are several ways in which reputation can be implemented. First, reputation can be on a very simple numerical scale of 0 and up. Second, reputation can be applied to good or evil—a positive and negative score. Third, reputation can be split among several groups. Finally, reputation can be based on specific actions.

Simple Reputation Scale

The most basic method of measuring reputation is with a 0 and up scale. As the player performs actions and deeds in the world they are attributed a number of reputation points. This scale can be split into various sections, which could be given specific names. For example, in a game where you must play an aspiring criminal the reputation ranks might be as follows:

1. Pickpocket
2. Mugger
3. Burglar
4. Thief
5. Heister
6. Grifter
7. Gangster
8. Crimelord

Each of these ranks has a threshold—a number of reputation points that must be earned before that rank is achieved. NPC reactions are based on this scale so that much more respect is paid to a player with a higher reputation, whereas a player with a low reputation might be treated like dirt.

Good and Evil Scale

The eternal struggle between good and evil might be something you would like to map as reputation. *Fable*® on the Xbox used this as the central premise of the game, and *Knights of the Old Republic*™ also featured this game mechanic. Essentially, it is a positive and negative scale as opposed to a purely positive one, so an action will either add or subtract from the reputation score. Negative points symbolize a leaning to the side of evil, while positive points move you to the good side.

Many of the actions performed by the player are attributed a score based on their effect on the target and witnesses. For example, killing an NPC will be a huge negative score, whereas rescuing a damsel in distress would be a high positive score.

Different actors will react differently to this reputation, based on their own leanings. Thus, an evil actor will have much more respect for a player who has a negative score, whereas others may run away screaming. Good actors will cheer on a heroic player with a positive score but will boo or be scared of an evil player.

Group Reputation

Group reputation distributes the scale among several groups or factions within the game world, so that while you may have a high score with one group of people, a different group may have an entirely different opinion. This score with each group is based on actions performed and previous encounters with that group. For example, if you have done lots of missions for that group in the past, then they are likely to be very receptive. If, on the other hand, you killed one of their group members, you will have a very poor score, and they may be likely to attack you on the spot.

Reputation by Action

Another way of integrating reputation is to define scores for each type of action such as:

- Aggressiveness
- Defensiveness
- Friendliness
- Generosity

Each of these action groups can be assigned a value, which could be positive or negative. They could even be applied to groups or factions of NPCs within a game world. Reputation groups could also be accorded based on these scores:

Stoic: The actor is very defensive and unfriendly.
Thug: The actor is very aggressive and unfriendly.
Hero: The actor is very aggressive but friendly and generous.
Mean: The actor is unfriendly and miserly.

There are plenty more groups that could be created, and more action groups could be thrown in the mix to create a complex reputation system. Again different NPCs will react differently according to the reputation group to which the player belongs.

NPC Emotions

Many emotions can be modeled for NPCs—pretty much the whole emotional spectrum. Some emotions naturally group together and work with specific game mechanics. Note that not every game needs complex emotion modeling for NPCs.

Fear and Courage

Fear and courage are essentially opposite emotions. We could model them in the same manner that we did for morale—a single sliding scale with fear at one end and courage at the other. However, there are plenty of other ways it could be done. One of those ways is to have two separate scales that can adjust independently based on the action, so we have a fear scale and a courage scale. When one reaches a reaction threshold, the other is reset. Actions will have independent effects on each scale, as shown in Table 15.8.

TABLE 15.8   Fear and Courage Change According to Player Actions

ACTION	FEAR	COURAGE
Player pulls out gun		
Actor is targeted	8	−8
Actor is facing player	5	−5
Actor has gun drawn	5	3
Actor is behind player	2	4
Actor is behind player with gun drawn	1	10
Player shoots fellow AI		
Actor is next to AI	10	−5
Actor is behind player	5	2

Fear will tick down over time if no stimuli are applied to the actor. Courage might increase over time if no stimuli are applied.

The emotional reaction of a target can be broken down via thresholds within each scale (see Table 15.9).

TABLE 15.9   Emotional Reactions to Fear and Courage

FEAR	COURAGE
Nervous	Cocky
Terrified	Brave
Hysterical	Heroic

Notice that these are similar to emotions we have discussed previously concerning enemy AI. However, the reactions for NPCs when in these emotional states are likely to be very different. They can also differ drastically from NPC to NPC. For example, if we had a pregnant lady, her reactions might be:

Hysterical: Scream at the top of her lungs about saving her baby.
Terrified: Sob uncontrollably.
Nervous: Visibly shake.
Cocky: Get frustrated and ask what's going on.
Brave: Insult the player.
Heroic: Scream for help.

Alternatively, if we have a cocksure young male, his reactions might be completely different:

Hysterical: Wets his pants and faints.
Terrified: Begs not to be killed.
Nervous: Stutters when talking.
Cocky: Brags that he could take on the player.
Brave: Openly insults the player and challenges them.
Heroic: Makes an attempt to attack the player.

Different actors also have different thresholds for fear and courage. A security guard would most likely have a lower courage threshold and higher fear threshold than the average citizen. It might be comedic to have certain unexpectedly high courage, such as an old lady, who would then proceed to beat the player with her handbag should she enter a heroic state.

If we were using crowd control as part of a game mechanic (in a bank robbing game, for example), this system would fit really well. The player would try to keep actors away from either extremity so that they would follow orders. An hysterical actor would be as much of a liability as a heroic one.

Like and Dislike

Like and dislike is a single opposing scale that has many shades in between. Like and dislike for the player character in respect to an NPC is based on the player's reputation. This system could also be used between NPCs or may simply exist as hard-wired connections (a friends network).

The level of feeling toward an actor might be described by one of the following:

Despise: Cannot stand him whatsoever.
Hate: Wishes him harm.
Dislike: Does not take kindly to him or may be suspicious of his motives.
Indifferent: Has no real leaning one way or the other.
Like: Has respect for him.
Love: Has very high regard for him.
Adore: Thinks he is the best thing ever created.

The reaction of one actor to another is based on this scale and will differ from actor to actor. It may also differ according to gender and sexual preference. For example, the NPC is a hot-blooded female and the player character is an Adonis-like figure:

Despise: Will openly attack or insult the actor.
Hate: Will mutter things about the player character to other actors.
Dislike: Will simply ignore the player character or make her dislike known.
Like: Will openly flirt with the player character.
Love: Will very actively flirt and compliment the player character.
Adore: Will swoon over the player character and worship the ground he walks on.

If the NPC is a gruff, surly male:

Despise: Will start a fight on sight.
Hate: Will slander the player character.
Dislike: Will mutter under his breath.
Like: Will laugh and joke with the player character.
Love: Will slap the player character on the back and laugh heartily (as all good friends do).
Adore: Will consider the player character his bosom buddy and lay his life on the line for him.

Of course, playing with sexual preference and gender could create some interesting narrative moments, sources of humor, or potentially uncomfortable moments for some people—something that games have not yet properly tackled (at least not with any level of maturity).

Joy and Sorrow

Joy and sorrow are generally not modeled in depth but can be interesting emotions to play with. Joy and sorrow tend not to come directly from player actions but are more likely to be based on narrative events—the birth of a child or death of a loved one, for example. The implications are usually purely visual but could also be accorded to gameplay:

- When in a joyful state, an NPC will be more likely to converse and share information, offer good prices, and so on.
- When sorrowful, NPCs are much less likely to do any of the above and might not respond at all. Sorrow might express itself as anger if provoked.

Direct Action and Reaction Correlation

Instead of modeling emotions as we have been doing in the previous sections, we might instead want a simpler system, where each action has a corresponding reaction. These reactions can be different for each actor. An example of an actor's reactions is shown in Table 15.10.

TABLE 15.10   An Actor's Reaction to a Specific Action

ACTION	REACTION
Attack	Cower
Compliment	Blush
Flirt	Become coy
Proposition	Slap
Insult	Cry

Motivations

Motivations are an NPC's internal needs. These motivations will provoke actions to occur when the need rises to a certain point. Most action games are unlikely to need anywhere near this kind of depth, but RPGs might use such a system if it fits in with gameplay. Choosing which motivations to use is important, as too many can become overcomplex and monotonous.

All sorts of motivations could be included: hunger, thirst, comfort, toilet, sleep, entertainment, passion, and so on. Each of these needs will have a resulting action once their threshold is reached. They might also have another action when the need cannot be satisfied and has reached maximum (see Table 15.11).

TABLE 15.11   Needs and Corresponding Threshold and Maximum Actions

NEED	THRESHOLD ACTION	MAX ACTION
Hunger	Seek food	Die of hunger
Thirst	Seek drink	Die of thirst
Comfort	Seek comfort	Break down crying
Toilet	Seek toilet	Wet themselves
Sleep	Seek bed	Collapse
Entertainment	Seek entertainment	Be bored
Passion	Seek passion	Cry from loneliness

Motivation can be adjusted in particular ways:

Over time: The most basic method is that the need slowly accumulates. Points are added at a set frequency.

By received actions: Actions inflicted upon the actor will increase or decrease a need. For example, an insult will increase an actor's need for comfort, whereas a hug will decrease it.

By their own actions: Performing energetic actions might increase an actor's need for food and drink and sleep more quickly than standard behavior. Other actions an actor performs will have a positive or negative effect on them.

ALLIES

Allies are friendly AIs that help the player in some manner (generally in combat). In order to do this, an ally AI could be equipped with many of the following:

- Formation AI
- Combat AI
- Command response
- Communication

- Roles
- Emotions

Ally Formation AI

Any squad or AI that closely follows the player is likely to use formation structures to allow the character to follow sensibly. These are generally very different from enemy formations, as they are based on more defensive tactics.

Ally AI will generally choose the player as the formation follow target and try to remain in a particular position around him. This position will never be in front of the player so as to obscure him. It should probably move to rotate so there is never a position where the player's field of view is obstructed by an ally AI.

Some very accurate real-world squad formations might be modeled, such as the four-man special forces unit where one faces forward, two cover the sides, and the final man covers the rear. More offensive formations might occur when a player commands allies to attack a specific target or to hold ground. This might also occur at scripted moments if there is no player control over allies.

Combat AI

A very fine balance needs to be observed when creating combat AI for an ally: providing enough help to be useful but not taking the feeling of control and achievement away from the player. There may be an exception to this rule if these AIs are player built, such as party members in an RPG.

Combat Behaviors

Limitless potential behaviors can be employed for combat. In practice, some behaviors are more useful than others. The types of behavior available to allies will reflect their abilities as characters:

Standard Attack: Standard move to attack.
Defend: Move into a defensive position.
Hold: Stay in a particular place and hold ground.
Covering Fire: Provide covering fire for the player.
Seek Cover: Move to find cover from enemy fire.
Retreat: Avoid combat at all costs and move back from enemies.
Berserk: Attack enemies relentlessly.
Guard: Remain close to the player and attack incoming enemies, but break away from combat if the player moves away.
Aid Attack: Help attack the player's current target.
Targeted Attack: Specify a target to attack.

Behavior Selection

The actual combat behavior of an ally can be set in different ways:

AI controlled: The choice of AI behavior is selected by the AI system.

User command: The choice of behavior is determined by commands given by the player.

User modes: The choice of behavior is set by the player selecting a specific mode.

User scripts: The choice of behavior is set by the user via a series of predefined instructions.

AI-Controlled Selection

When the AIs are not commanded in any way by the player, they will have to select behaviors to perform themselves. These are drawn from a set of available behaviors for a particular character. For example, a swordsman might have a pool of behaviors such as: Attack, Defend, Berserk, Retreat, and Aid Attack. To select between these attacks, the AI might use a weighted random system, a scoring system, or an FSM. A scoring system works well in this situation, as points can be attributed to the player's current situation (as shown in Table 15.12).

TABLE 15.12   A Scoring System for Behavior Selection

PLAYER ON LOW HEALTH	SCORE
Attack	2
Defend	0
Berserk	3
Retreat	0
Aid Attack	10

Thus, the actor would most likely rush to aid the player.

An FSM also works well in this situation, as shown in Figure 15.5.

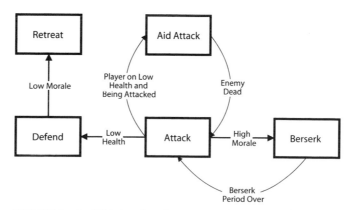

FIGURE 15.5   An FSM showing the states and transitions for an ally.

User Command

A user command is an instruction given to an ally AI. The ally AI responds to this command with a certain behavior. Commands might also have context, dependent on where the player has his cursor or crosshair on screen. The item under the cursor or crosshair is a target. If no commands are issued, then the actor will follow its normal behavior and make its own decisions. For example, we might have the following commands:

Hold Ground: Holds the ground where they are currently.
Follow: Keep in formation with the player and attack enemies when they are sighted.
Cover Me: Provide cover in the direction of a target.
Attack Target: Attack the highlighted target.

The command structure might be much more complex than this, but each command is effectively selecting behaviors for the ally to perform.

User Modes

A very different approach to selection is to allow the player to select from a list of available behaviors for a character. This is really straightforward. It just requires a suitable user interface.

User Scripts

These are the most complex but can be extremely powerful. Essentially, detailed plans of attack can be created, or a list of actions to be performed might be assigned to a slot for easy selection. These are two different mechanisms. The first is a planning stage that might be part of the gameplay. This is a one-shot deal, where detailed plans are created. The second is a shortcut, which allows a player to quickly and easily perform a complex set of actions. They both amount to the creation of a list of actions for an AI to perform. The UI for doing this is the more complex element that needs to be well considered. It might require a map of the area, waypoints, hints, and so on.

Command Response

We briefly touched on commands in the previous combat AI section, but there is much more possible depth to a command system. Several questions need to be answered when issuing a command:

- What is the command?
- Who is it issued to?
- How do they respond?
- When do they stop performing the command?

Structure of a Command

To understand what a command is, it needs to be broken down into its constituent parts:

Locomotion: How the actor moves to fulfill the command
Target: The desired point in the world or entity to be targeted
Action: The action or series of actions to be performed (often a state change)

Each of these parts is attributed a value to make up a command. For example, the command Hold Ground would be made up of:

Locomotion: Stationary
Target: The current position of the player
Action: Enter sentry state

The command Attack Target would be:

Locomotion: Move to target
Target: Highlighted entity
Action: Attack highlighted entity

The command Guard would be:

Locomotion: Enter guard formation
Target: The player
Action: Enter guard state

Command Scope

Who the command is issued to is fairly straightforward. It can be issued to one or more ally AIs within range. This range might be within shouting distance or could be limitless if we were to use radios or telepathy as the suggested means of communication to the AIs. The biggest problem with issuing commands to groups of people is the UI to select which people to command. The player will need some method of selecting all, a group, or a number of individuals to whom to issue a command.

Response

An AI responds with either success or failure. If a command is successfully issued, then the desired action is performed. Acknowledgement of this success should be fed back to the player, perhaps by using a voice over of "OK Sir!" before heading off to perform the action. If a command is failed, feedback should be given that the action cannot be performed—even better if a reason can be given.

There are several reasons why an AI might not be able to perform an action:

Locomotion: The target cannot be reached or the AI is unable to move.
Target: The target is invalid or the target gets destroyed before the action can be performed.
Action: The action is invalid for the target, or a state cannot be entered for some reason (e.g., attack cannot happen because the ally AI is too scared).

Command Termination

The AI stops performing a command when either another command is issued or the action becomes invalid. Many commands may have actions that never become invalid, such as holding ground or guarding. Others, however, will be invalid after an event has occurred, such as the death of a target when an attack command has been issued.

Ally Communication

Communication between AIs and the player can be incorporated to truly enrich the game experience. There are two styles of communication that might be implemented:

- AI to player
- AI to AI

AI to Player

AI communication to the player is based mainly on the player's performance and events relating to mission objectives. An ally should be a useful method of providing information to the player as well as inflating his ego.

Mission Objectives

Using voice over for mission objectives allows the designers to weave important game information into the game world, meaning they don't have to rely on screen furniture to get the message across. For example, an ally might call out to the player, detailing that they need to get a door open to progress.

Complimenting the Player

Ally AI should make the player feel as though he is the hero. This can be achieved by having a pool of speech for certain actions. There are plenty of actions to which these compliments might be attributed:

- Hitting a small target
- Hitting a moving target first time
- Killing an enemy
- Saving an ally or NPC from an assailant
- Performing an acrobatic feat
- Pulling off a special move

AI to AI

AI to AI communication makes the world feel much more alive. It feels like the player is part of the world and that it doesn't just revolve around him. Lots of different types of speech might be implemented:

Story based: Plot extrapolation; would be heavily scripted

Chit chat: Idle banter between AIs; could be scripted or used on a more ad hoc basis

Battle communication: Shouting out orders or information to each other based on the events currently occurring

Roles

One method of dictating an ally's actions is to base his behavior on his assigned role. The role of an actor within a team determines his behavior in a given situation. This situation could be anything, but in most games this tends to be combat.

An ally will have a standard behavior for the normal, nonconflict situation, which is likely to be a simple follow the player in formation action. Once a combat situation arises, the allies then perform their behavior according to their defined roles. Thus, a vulnerable helper would do his best to remain behind the player character or to hide away from harm. A bodyguard would do the opposite and get between the player and the enemy.

Individual personalities also come into play. A gung-ho character would charge into action with all guns blazing, whereas a well trained soldier would remain cool, calm, and collected.

Emotions

Allies, just like NPCs and enemies, can be modeled with emotions. For allies the whole spectrum explored with both NPCs and enemies could be applied. The only thing that we must be wary of is making sure that we don't take the feeling of achievement away from the player should an ally be boosted by high morale and go on a rampage.

BOT AI

Bot AIs differ from single-player AIs in that they are not merely providing a performance to fool a player. A Bot is trying to replicate human behavior to provide challenge in a multiplayer game [Booth04].

This is where some of the rules previously applied get thrown out. We are less concerned with the player being the center of attention and more concerned about making the Bot appear to be a believable opponent. What we really want is for the Bot to pass the gaming equivalent of the Turing Test (an AI test that basically says an AI can be perceived to be intelligent if it can fool a human into thinking it is human).

A Bot may take on the role of an enemy or an ally, depending on the type of game being played. Death match games are every man for themselves, but team-based games such as *Counterstrike* or *Battlefield* pit one team against another. As such, a Bot may contain aspects of both of these AI types.

Bots are usually assigned a difficulty level that adjusts several things:

- How quick they are to respond to attack
- How good their aim is
- Where they aim (for the head if they are set to difficult or perhaps the torso if not)
- What strategies they use

Each Bot may also be given its own personality that dictates several things:

- Which strategies they use (camping, rushing, sniping, etc.)
- What weapons they prefer to use
- Their level of team cooperation

SUMMARY

In this chapter we entered into an in-depth discussion of how to create character in AI actors. This subject is such an immense topic that we have only really scratched the surface. There are many techniques for making characters more believable. The trick is in choosing elements that will have the most impact for the least amount of effort.

We covered the following topics over the course of the chapter:

Player expectation and feedback: Players expect certain characteristics and actions from the AI actors. Providing these will create the illusion of intelligence.

- **Consistency:** The player expects the AI to be consistent and not perform ridiculous actions.
- **Other expectations:** AI is also expected to provide challenge, offer interactivity, and provide various scenarios for the player to explore.

Enemies: The standard form of game AI is generally the enemy.

- **Type of enemy:** There are a number of different types of enemy that will provide different levels of challenge to the player.
- **Enemy attack strategies:** Enemies will attack individually or as part of a group. Bosses have unique strategies of their own.
- **Building fair enemy AI:** One thing that must always be considered is the creation of fair AI. After all, the player is playing the game for enjoyment, not work.
- **Using distraction against enemies:** The gameplay may allow for the ability to bypass enemies rather than engage them in combat. This will extend the use of the enemy's sensory AI.
- **Building character:** We have explored a number of ways to build character in this section, such as initial behaviors, extending basic behaviors, incidental animation, voice acting, and the modeling of emotions.

NPCs: The use of NPCs as supporting characters can add real color to the game world and make for a much more convincing universe.

- **NPC types:** We looked at the use of incidental actors, minor actors, key actors, merchants, and VIPs.
- **Patrols and wandering:** NPCs can seem more believable if they have places to go and actions to perform beyond interaction with the player.
- **Conversations:** Vibrant interactions can be made with an NPC through the use of conversation. This may be performed in a number of ways— simple conversations, reaction-based conversation, conversation trees, and phrase parsing systems.
- **Emotions and reactions:** The modeling of emotions and reactions in NPCs makes for a much more diverse and interactive world for the player to engage with.

Allies: Allies can fight alongside or provide support for the player during game-play.

- **Ally formation AI:** Allies need to move intelligently as the player moves around the world and avoid getting in the player's way.
- **Combat AI:** An ally may be able to join in combat with the player, but they don't want to take all the action away from the player.
- **Ally communication:** More life can be expressed by having the allies intelligently converse with the player and each other.
- **Roles:** More interesting characters can be made by giving allies roles to play within a team.
- **Emotions:** Emotions can also be modeled for the allies.

Bot AI: The creation of AI characters that try to mimic human behavior to produce suitable opponents for multiplayer games.

Time is very well spent trying to make more believable characters. It is a field of AI that is likely to get more and more attention over the coming years, as technology allows ever more emotion to be expressed through facial animation. However, while big-budget games will push the envelope of what was thought possible, there are plenty of ways of imbuing character that don't cost the earth.

PHYSICS

In This Chapter

- Physics Simulation
- Physics in Gameplay

Physics used to be restricted to very simple modeling of forces such as gravity, simple collision detection, and very little else because it can be very processor intensive to perform lots of physics calculations. Modern console architecture is at a point where a physics simulation can now truly be performed with many objects. In addition, middleware physics solutions such as Havok make integrating a physics engine much more feasible.

Even so, very few games have delved deep into the gameplay possibilities that a physics engine can supply, mainly because there are so many possible problems. Unlike traditional methods of interaction in a game, such as a set animation, physics can be very unpredictable. A large building collapsing may look great in physics and may not pose any problem 99% of the time, but there is always a possibility that a chunk of rubble will land in such a way that it will block the path, preventing the player from proceeding.

Half-Life 2 is a great example of how physics can be integrated into gameplay. Instead of just being a superfluous feature to enhance the world aesthetically, physics was integrated into puzzles and into the combat itself. Objects can be picked up and used to weigh down a see-saw or used to build a makeshift ladder. The Gravity Gun allows the player to pick up objects and hurl them around the world with abandon, meaning that almost any object in the world can become a makeshift weapon.

The possibilities of physics are bounded only by imagination, but the designer must first understand a little of how physics simulation works to know how their imagination can become a reality. The following aspects of physics will be covered in this chapter:

- Physics simulation
- Physics in gameplay

PHYSICS SIMULATION

Several fields of physics simulation are currently useful and feasible in game worlds.

Dynamics

Dynamics is the real meat of a physics simulation. It is the calculation of movement of objects when forces are applied. Several fields are covered in dynamics, encompassing a wide range from Newtonian mechanics to conservation of momentum. The depth of a physics simulation is based on the depth of dynamics calculations. The actual calculations for much of these can be very complex, so they are not within the scope of this book. A designer does not really need to know the absolute workings of the physics simulation but is required to know what is possible within a system.

Forces

Games have utilized basic forces for a long time in some manner, gravity being the most obvious example. Besides gravity, friction is also a popular force to be utilized. Other forces come from powering mechanisms, such as the thrust of a rocket.

Gravity

Unless you are setting your game in the weightlessness of space, it is very likely that your game will feature gravity. Gravity is not usually modeled exactly on the earth's gravity. In fact, Earth's gravity (9.8 m/s^2) often doesn't feel right. Usually gravity in a game world is stronger than this, as it feels too "floaty" otherwise. This seems strange, but the perceived feeling of gravity is more important than factual accuracy.

The effects of gravity are not always all encompassing. A character is nearly always influenced directly by gravity, but there are many other areas where gravity may or may not have influence. For instance, it is fairly rare for gravity to be taken into account when calculating the path of a bullet. However, many other projectiles, such as grenades or mine launchers, do consider gravity, resulting in a trajectory. Even in these calculations, concessions may be made for feel against fact. They may even differ from gravitational forces applied to other objects.

Friction

Friction is a measure of resistance to movement between two surfaces. In gaming terms this may have several influences. With a correct physics simulation, friction will determine the conservation of momentum of each object in the world. Without friction, an object would never come to rest.

Friction does have applications beyond pure simulation. It can be used to affect player movement, for example. In an area with high friction the character will have good grip and will come to a stop almost the instant the player releases the movement control. Low friction will produce sliding, where the character will slide along the surface for a time before coming to rest. This might be used to simulate an icy surface. This is often used into gameplay to force the players to be more cautious in their actions.

Applied Force

Applied forces are those that are applied to an object by another object or character. An action of some sort applies this force, affecting the object in some way—usually moving it, unless the object can no longer be moved. It might deform the object if movement is not possible. Wind might also be considered to be an applied force.

Spring Force

Springs store energy and release it as a force. This spring force is dependent on the amount of potential energy put into the spring and the strength of the spring itself.

Momentum

Momentum is essentially mass in motion, so any object that has mass and is moving has momentum. The faster an object is moving, the more momentum it has. Also, the more mass an object an object has, the more momentum it has.

Two forms of momentum are applied in 3D space:

Linear momentum: The translational momentum of an object in 3D space
Angular momentum: The rotational momentum of an object in 3D space

Momentum in a system is conserved, so when two objects collide, the momentum is transferred between objects in a collision. Collision response deals with these issues.

Center of Mass

The center of mass is a point on an object from which mass-based physics calculations are performed. This is an important variable to manipulate, as it has a very large impact on the behavior of an object in the simulation (see Figure 16.1).

In Figure 16.1 the left-hand object has a very high center of mass. The result is that it will be very easy to tip over. The right-hand object has a relatively low center of mass. It will be much harder to tip over. With its curved bottom, it will wobble, so that it will roll upright again.

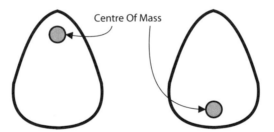

FIGURE 16.1   Different positions for center of mass will affect the behavior of the object.

Kinematics

Kinematics is the calculation of movement to achieve a desired position without the need to consider forces. Its use in a game environment is generally to dynamically modify a character's skeleton position. Inverse kinematics (IK) is used to move the extremities of a skeleton so that feet are positioned on stairs or a character turns to face a particular point.

A new branch of development in kinematics seeks to automate character animation. Instead of creating animations, the movements of a character are simulated. This may take several cycles of learning for character movement to start looking natural, but even then, current results are fairly limited. At present it is a fair way from being a suitable replacement for animation, but as it gets better, it will allow simulation to be taken further. For example, it can already be used to get a character back to a target pose from a ragdoll hit reaction.

Physical Structures

The physical structure of an object determines how the object will behave as it is flung around the environment. There are several aspects of the physical structure:

- Body type
- Connections and constraints
- Materials

Body Types

One of the most basic attributes of physical structure is the object's type of physical body.

Rigid Bodies

By far the most common type of physics body is the rigid body. This is an object that has no elasticity or change in its physical state when a collision is made. This makes it the most efficient in terms of processing power.

Simple rigid bodies are usually objects such as bottles, tables, or stools. They may become damaged, but this will be via the swapping of the physical mesh rather than by using physics simulations.

Rigid bodies can be loosely grouped together to form another damage system. When the health of the item reaches zero, the group is unbound and the various objects are free to move by themselves. For example, a table might be made of four legs and several wooden planks. These separate when the table collapses. More complex rigid body structures can be constructed by linking them together with bones, such as a human skeleton. These ragdolls can then be thrown around, and the joints will constrain the motion in the correct manner. There are limits to the total amount of bones that can be used within an object.

Soft Bodies

Soft bodies are much more processor intensive. A soft body will deform when sufficient forces act upon it. Soft bodies may be constructed in different ways. A very common simulation is to use springs. Groups of springs (arrays) can form structures such as rope, cloth, or even gelatinous solids.

Connections and Constraints

To properly simulate objects that are joined together or can move and flex within their own mesh, a physical structure of bones and joints is required. Constraints ensure that these joints behave in a proper manner and do not exceed their possible range of movement.

Several types of joints are feasible in game worlds (at least at present):

Hinge joint: A hinge allows rotation in one axis. This may be limited to certain angles. An elbow is an example of a hinge joint.

Ball and socket: A ball and socket joint is a very flexible joint that allows movement in two or even three axes. Movement is constrained to the physical limits of the socket. A shoulder is an example of a ball and socket joint.

Rail: A rail allows sliding along a predefined line. The limits of the rail create self-imposed constraints.

Materials

Every object in the game world must be made of some kind of material. Materials have a very big impact on the object's behavior in a physics simulation. For example, wood behaves in a different way than metal. This extends to several things:

Collision response: The collision between two different materials may have very different responses. For example, metal may break wood but not other metals. Elasticity is also dependent on the type of material applied.

Buoyancy: In conjunction with shape, material determines an object's buoyancy value.

Sound: A physics-based sound system depends on knowing the materials that are colliding to produce the sound effects.

Collision and Response

Collision is an essential game system that is often considered to be a stand-alone issue, but it is becoming more commonplace that the collision system is considered to be part of the physics engine. Collision is essentially the physical boundaries of objects within the world. Without it, the objects would not be able to rest or move within the world, as they would pass through surfaces (they wouldn't even make contact with the floor).

Collision Volumes

Generally the actual model and the collision representation of a model are not the same. There are several reasons for this:

Performance: Most collision is performance intensive. While for static objects complex mesh collision may be feasible, for moving objects it is impractical.

Boundaries: There may not be a physical boundary. The world must be restricted to prevent the player breaching the boundaries of the level.

Different collision: One object may have several types of collision to prevent a player from passing through but allowing the passage of projectiles, for instance.

Models usually have simplified geometry to represent collision. Dynamic objects tend to have very basic collision primitives such as spheres, cubes, and cylinders. A few of these can be combined to make complex shapes; for example, a barrel might be represented by a cuboid and a sphere (see Figure 16.2).

Having simple primitives vastly speeds up collision calculations.

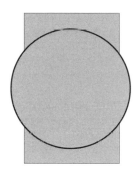

Physical Object   Collision Primitives

FIGURE 16.2   A barrel collision mapped as a sphere and a cuboid.

Collision Response

At the simplest level, a collision results in preventing an actor or object from moving through a surface. A projectile is often destroyed when a collision occurs. A more physics-based collision response is to reflect the object, or to conserve momentum in a collision between two movable objects. This reflection is often very simple, where the motion is reflected exactly. Deeper simulation will use the elasticity of an object to determine the reflected velocity. An inelastic object will drop to the floor almost immediately. A perfectly elastic object will rebound with the same velocity. Most objects fall somewhere in between.

When two movable objects collide, the momentum is transferred between them. The objects move away with almost the same momentum as before the collision.

Fluid Dynamics

Fluids are a particularly processor intensive part of physics simulation, so much of their behavior is heavily abstracted. The movement and interaction of a fluid is particularly difficult to simulate. The simulation rarely extends to the point of creating droplets, but instead studies water as one body. Splash effects are usually animations or particle effects rather than simulations.

There are two variables associated with water:

Viscosity: Another dissipative force like friction. The more viscous a liquid, the harder it is to move through (e.g., water is not very viscous, whereas molasses is).

Buoyancy: Determines the ability of an object to float in water. This is a number based on the material of the object and its shape. However, shape can allow a material such as metal to float, but it may sink if not aligned in the correct manner (an open can might sink if it fills with water). When damaged, the shape can become compromised. For example, a punctured plastic barrel would eventually fill with enough water to cause it to sink. This is a fairly difficult physics simulation, so it would probably be faked somewhat.

Physics in Gameplay

Early attempts at physics generally kept its use as an aesthetic improvement—something that made the world seem more real. However, much more interesting possibilities are presented by player interaction with these physics objects.

Physics Interactions

Physics allows much more meaningful interactions with objects in the world, as these interactions have a much greater scope of possibility. Pretty much any physics interaction will become an emergent experience, which is both a great boon to sandbox gameplay and an absolute nightmare for the testing department.

Initially it can be fairly daunting to think of uses for a physics simulation, but once you start to think of a few ideas, they tend to start flowing faster and faster. Physics is an area where there is plenty of innovation ripe for the plucking. Our early forays into physics-based interaction have been fairly limited. At present there are really three main uses for physics interactions in the world:

- Puzzles
- Makeshift weaponry
- Traps

However, there are probably many more potential uses for physics interactions that have yet to be tapped into.

Puzzles

Traditionally puzzles have been very rigid: perform x function to see y result. The use of physics turns this all on its head and allows much more analog interpretation of a scenario. There are plenty of physics interactions that could be turned into puzzles of some sort:

Gravity: Using different local gravities can make for a very confusing experience and also allows full use of 3D space. Enemies could come rushing toward the player across the ceiling, or the player might be able to switch gravity to different settings to progress through an environment.

Forces: Using forces to manipulate objects can range from the mundane pushing of a block to more impressive explosions or cannon blasts. The player might have to aim an object by detonating a carefully placed explosive pack or use some giant piston to fling an object at a decaying wall to break through.

Weight: The weight of an object might be used to affect another object in the world. This may be as simple as putting a heavy object onto a pressure pad to open a door, but could be much more elaborate. *Half-Life 2* has a puzzle where bricks must be piled at one end of a see-saw to lift the opposite end. *Tomb Raider: Legend* has an even more elaborate version of this, where the player jumps on one end of a see-saw to catapult a box on the other end up to a higher platform.

Mechanisms: Springs, cogs, ropes, pulleys, and so on might be used together to form some kind of mechanism that the player can interact with. The player might pull a rope, turn a cog to utilize the mechanism, or jam something in its works to prevent it from operating.

Construction: Objects can be manipulated to construct various structures. The player might need to build a makeshift staircase to reach a higher ledge or perhaps build a bridge across a gap. Construction could become even more elaborate. *Garry's Mod* for *Half-Life 2*, a physics sandbox modification, allows the player to stick objects together, create a number of physics connections, build wheels and thrusters, and more. The players could build almost anything if they so choose.

Destruction: One of the more popular uses of physics is destruction. This can easily be woven into the game as an obstacle the player must destroy to proceed.

Fluids: Fluid dynamics could be used for all kinds of puzzle elements, such as channeling fluid in the right direction, changing the volume of fluid in a particular area, and so on.

Buoyancy: Objects that float could be used to make rafts to cross treacherous stretches of water or prop up a sinking platform or could be used against a group of enemies who were coming toward the player by shooting the objects keeping them afloat.

These are just a few of the myriad of possible interactions that could be used to make interesting puzzles.

Makeshift Weaponry

Having a world full of physics objects is great, but being able to use them as a makeshift weapon during combat is even better. Larger objects in the environment might even be smashable and break down to provide a number of smaller weapons. To facilitate this, the player might have some kind of gravity gun, be able to use weapons to flick debris at an opponent, kick objects, or be able to physically pick objects up and throw them.

Object Pickup

Doing these kinds of interactions in a first-person game is simple. *Half-Life 2's* Gravity Gun is particularly elegant, as it solves interaction and the problem of physics objects getting in the way in a manner that improves gameplay. The gun sucks objects up and holds them just in front of the gun. Picking an object up can be done by simply hovering the object in front of the player.

Third-person object interaction is much more difficult. Here we need to see the character actually interacting with the object. A device similar to the Gravity Gun would pose few problems, but it becomes more difficult when we want the character to physically pick the object up. In this case we need to synchronize the animation of the character and the object. However, because the object can be in any position, we need some method of getting the object or the character into the right position.

The simplest method is to pop the object to the right orientation before performing the animation. This may not be noticed for certain objects, especially if you cover it with particle effects. However, it can be very noticeable for objects with one dimension significantly larger than the others and for objects with significantly different colors on different faces.

More complex methods might try to blend the orientation of the object across the course of a pickup animation, though this runs the high risk of the object moving through the character or the world as it does so.

Throw Object

When throwing an object in first person or from the Gravity Gun, there is little that needs to be done. The object is thrown from its floating position with a particular force. When throwing an object in third person, the character will perform a synchronized animation before relinquishing control to the physics simulation. Often this will inherit the velocity and angle described in the preceding animation.

Hit Behavior

On collision with a surface, an object might do one of several things:

Smash: The object simply smashes into pieces. This is often done by despawning the object and covering it with a particle effect. However, it may break into smaller physics pieces or even other types of interactable object.
Bounce: The object bounces off the surface. The amount of bounce is dependent on the elasticity of the materials of the objects and surfaces involved in the collision.
Embed: Sharp objects might even embed themselves in the surface with which they make contact.

This hit behavior is often determined by the material from which the object is made. For example, you might set all objects with the pottery material to instantly smash on impact, whereas metal objects will always remain intact. An object made from rubber would bounce with a lot of elasticity, whereas a concrete object would hardly bounce at all.

Collision-Based Interactions

An object might not need really close interaction, such as actually picking it up. Instead, the character might be able to kick the object or use a weapon to slam or flick the object in a particular direction.

There are two ways to do this:

Create a force: Once the action is performed (such as a kick animation or a specific attack), the object is fired in a particular direction with a set force.

Collision-based force: The speed of the collision between the two objects is used to calculate the resulting movement of the object. The trouble with this is that erratic results can arise if weapons are moving particularly quickly.

Traps

Traps are elements in the world that use physics to cause damage indirectly to an opponent. They might also be used against the players themselves. There are all sorts of physics-based traps that might be used:

Breakable support: The breakable support is perhaps the most common physics-based trap. By damaging some support mechanism a heavy object can be dropped onto an opponent. It might be the chain on a chandelier or a brace for a shelf holding a group of heavy objects.

Spring: A spring could be used to catapult a victim into danger or could be connected to a dangerous device to deliver a serious amount of damage.

Pendulum: Pendulums are a staple of traps, such as the traditional swinging axe that is something of a video-game cliché. However, there are plenty of other objects that could swing to create a trap. The pendulum might be a timing challenge for the player or might be activated by the player to swing into a group of enemies.

Rolling object: Another cliché is the rolling boulder. However, rolling physics objects are often used as potential traps to injure the player or can be used by the player to take out opponents.

Thumper: Closing-in walls or dropping blocks are often done in animation, but if done in physics, they offer a much greater level of interaction. For example, in *Tomb Raider: Legend*, there are several walls that slam together, crushing the player if he tries to move through. However, the player can use a push block to jam these walls and pass through safely.

A particularly sophisticated physics system might allow the players to construct traps of their own. They might be able to link together a series of ropes and pulleys or springs to create mechanisms to inflict damage on their opponents. They might be able to place a pile of objects above the entrance to a room and then shoot out the supporting beams to collapse them onto an enemy's head. With this kind of system all sorts of emergent behavior can result.

The Limitations of Physics

While physics simulation opens up a world of interactivity and believability for the player, it also poses a vast array of nightmares for the designer. The biggest problem arises from its unpredictability. This makes it possible for potentially game-breaking situations to arise. Consider, for example, a tower that is made to collapse using physics. It is possible that this might collapse in such a way that it blocks the path ahead and prevents the player from progressing.

Physics, when used directly for gameplay, can be particularly complex. Usually some limitations are placed upon the simulation so that any problems are encapsulated in a localized area. The following guidelines make implementing physics less of a design and testing nightmare:

Keep physics to noncritical objects: Allow the player to throw incidental objects around with abandon, but ensure that any critical objects cannot be broken by these events (e.g., knocked out of the world or stuck behind another object). Critical objects should really be left out of the simulation.

Keep physics localized: Allowing the player to pile hundreds of objects into one area is asking for trouble. Place boundaries between areas to prevent the player from gathering too many together. For example, these boundaries might be ladders that require the players to drop their currently held items to continue.

Keep large-scale physics-based destruction in the background: Using physics-based destruction is risky, as it is unpredictable how the pieces will land. Using animation for large-scale foreground destruction ensures that the pieces will fall as desired and not block the player's path. Alternatively, if large physics objects are used up close, there should be some way of moving them out of the way (such as the Gravity Gun in *Half-Life 2*) or some method of destroying them.

SUMMARY

Physics is a fascinating field that is really improving the feel of games and expanding the level of interaction a player can have with the game world.

We looked at several aspects of physics in this chapter:

Physics simulation: The act of simulating phenomena in the real world and possibly enhancing it for use in a virtual world. There are several elements in a typical physics simulation:

- **Dynamics:** The motion of objects in reaction to forces
- **Kinematics:** The movement of objects without needing to consider forces or mass
- **Physical structures:** The body type, materials, connections, and constraints placed on objects
- **Collision and response:** The detection and reaction of objects when they collide
- **Fluid dynamics:** The movement and behavior of fluids

Physics in gameplay: A physics simulation is easy to use to enhance the aesthetic quality of a game world, but it can be fairly difficult to weave it into gameplay. We explored several methods:

- **Physics interactions:** The types of interactions that might be handled with physics, such as puzzles, makeshift weaponry, and traps
- **The limitations of physics:** The problems that might occur and ways to solve those problems

While physics is advancing quickly, there is still plenty more that can be simulated with a physics engine. We are barely scratching the surface. Physics tends to be processor intensive, but this is becoming less of an issue as processors increase in power. We are even seeing the beginnings of what could be a revolution in physics: dedicated physics chips (a physics processing unit [PPU]). Their success is as yet unknown. This suggests that games in the future will become more and more reliant on physics simulation. This is both a good and bad phenomenon. Physics greatly increases the player's ability to interact with the environment, but it also adds much greater room for error. Physics also greatly increases the complexity of testing and debugging.

What might we see in the future? Certainly improvements can be made to the current simulations. Being able to deal with more physics interactions is one immediate answer. There are more complex simulations we can start to explore, such as much more convincing fluid dynamics. We could also start to model complex events such as explosions and the movement of gases in accurate ways. We could look at all manner of other more fantastic effects that require ever more intensive processing power. We could delve into all manner of subjects that physics can provide.

Physics does present a good prospect for future gameplay improvement, and we can only begin to imagine what scenarios will be possible with the physics engines of the future.

AUDIO

In This Chapter

- Designing with Sound
- Types of Sound

S ound is a very emotional sense—far more so than vision. It can immediately evoke feelings and put the listener in a specific time or place. As such, audio is an essential part of a game experience, but one that is often forgotten. Sound engineers are usually tucked away in a hidden part of the office to create the sounds in peace. However, this isolation can often mean that they are left out of the loop in many vital aspects of development communication.

While the sound engineer is the person who will actually create the sound, it is vital that every game designer understands sound's importance and how to use it to embellish and improve the player's immersion in the game world. It is also vital that the design team liaise closely with the audio department and ensure that their existence is not forgotten.

We will explore two main aspects of audio in this chapter:

- Designing with sound
- Types of sound

DESIGNING WITH SOUND

From the very start, the audio engineer should be involved in the design process, as there are many elements that can be fleshed out and ideas that can be sparked at even a very basic stage. Rather than giving audio engineers a list of desired sounds and music, they should be briefed on the design itself. The audio engineer is going to have a much better appreciation of what atmosphere will be required. In order to design a good soundscape, audio engineers should have the freedom to work with ideas and play with elements that don't affect gameplay without the need to go through a designer. This will enable them to experiment with different concepts. Having a good game design tool that integrates sound easily is key here.

The design of the game itself can be influenced by audio issues:

Setting: Choosing locations that have a potentially rich palette of sounds will make the audio engineer's life easier and more enjoyable. This will create a much better aural atmosphere.

Symbols: Certain sounds can be used to symbolize characters, events, and so on. These sounds can personalize elements to a surprising degree.

Silence: Knowing when not to use sound is as important as knowing when to use it. Too much noise at once becomes a barrage on the senses.

Visual and aural synergy: Tying sound to visual elements will emphasize particular shots or elements of a scene.

Gameplay: Using sound as a gameplay device can be very successful. This can vary greatly, from puzzles such as Simon Says, or items based around sound such as musical instruments. Sound can be used as a positional device to indicate the direction of a potential threat. Sound can also be featured as an element to alert the enemy in stealth-based gameplay.

Emotion: Sound can be used to convey or elicit emotion. It is very successful in building tension and heightening the climactic moment.

Sound in the environment: The effects of sound in the environment can be tremendous. Sound can reverberate, be muffled, or be amplified by volumes of space. Good use of environmental effects will increase the believability of the world. Volumes can be flagged with information about how sound will behave within it.

TYPES OF SOUND

Three main types of sound are used in games:

- Sound effects
- Music
- Speech

All sounds are one of two forms:

Diegetic: Sounds based within the world itself, such as a fist hitting home or an actor's line of speech.

Nondiegetic: Sounds beyond the fourth wall that do not exist within the world but provide information or seek to set the atmosphere. For example, music is generally nondiegetic, as is narrated speech.

Sound Effects

Sound effects are any sound element that is not a composed piece of music or a line spoken by an actor. This can therefore include all manner of sounds, from atmospheric wind to the sound of a sword hitting against metal.

Sound is also important in highlighting events in a game. The human brain reacts more quickly to aural stimuli than it does to visual stimuli—a legacy of our animal instincts.

Sourcing Sound Effects

The audio engineer can use a multitude of ways to create sound, but there are several well-used methods:

Recording sounds: The engineers record a sound source using microphone equipment and then edit the sound to how they require it.

Stock libraries: The sound is pulled from a library of sounds (which must be licensed or there will be severe repercussions later on down the line).

Foley: Footage of the target for a sound effect is played as foley artists create sounds on the fly using all manner of props. For instance, the sound of an insect moving in *Star Wars Episode II* is actually a fork being squished into a grapefruit.

With the basics of a sound in place, the audio engineer will generally build up a number of other elements up on top to beef-up the sound or to give it more depth and character, particularly if it is sourced from a recording or a library. Many real sounds actually seem lackluster in comparison to our experiences with movies and television, so this process of strengthening the sound is important.

Sound Effect Types

A number of different types of sound effect are used:

- Atmospherics
- Actions
- Physics events
- Game events

Atmospherics

Atmospherics are any form of background or ambient noises that set the scene. Good use of atmospherics will build up a detailed, personalized sound for each area that gives it a unique identity. Atmospherics can be used to psychologically deepen believability in the world. For example, the faint sounds of a city when wandering through dark alleyways will encourage the player to imagine a whole world beyond the physical limits of the current space.

Atmopherics can also enhance the physical feel of the spaces within the levels, such as the faint hum of computers in an office or the louder bangs and clanks of machinery in an industrial building.

Actions

Actions are perhaps the bulk of the sound effects work, as every action performed in a game is likely to need some kind of sound effect to match. There are potentially thousands of actions in games, so keeping track of each sound effect can become a mammoth task. Action sound effects are generally tied to specific animations and attached to events within that particular animation.

Action-based sound effects can cover a multitude of areas:

Character movement: Sounds made as the characters run, walk, jump, roll, creep, and so on across different surfaces. Establishing sounds for each surface means every type of material will need to be assigned information in the collision hull to specify what type of surface it is.

Attack: Each particular attack may have a number of effects associated with it (as well as potential speech such as grunts and groans).

Weapons and gadgets: The various states of using a weapon or gadget will have sound effects including firing, reloading, recharging, and so on.

Items: Using particular items will likely have associated sound effects such as picking up and using.

Objects: Various objects in the world will have sound effects when they are being interacted with and possibly while they are idling as well.

Physics Events

Physics sounds are those made by collisions between objects in physics simulations. Each collision tests the two colliding materials, their mass, and a type of collision that determines what specific sound will be played. There might be several types of collision:

Impact: The two objects slam together and are potentially damaged in the impact.
Bounce: The objects collide and one or both objects are bounced away.
Roll: One object rolls across the surface of another.
Slide: One object slides across the surface of another.
Puncture: One object punctures another.
Break: One object smashes on impact with another.

The mass of the object and the speed of the collision will affect the sound. Heavy objects produce louder or different sounds than lighter objects of the same material.

One issue with using a physics-based sound system is that it can become extremely chaotic, as it is out of the strict control of the audio engineer. Restrictions must be placed on the system so that it can only play a maximum number of sounds at any one time from the same source.

Game Events

Game events are often nondiegetic sounds that signal specific game events such as a mission being started or completed, game over, time running out, and so on. These sound effects highlight the event in question to bring it to the players' attention, so they can then take the appropriate action.

Variation

One very important factor in the use of sound effects is the ability to play a variation each time to avoid repetition. Too much repetition shatters the believability of the world and can start to become extremely irritating to the player. This is solved by having a large pool of sound effects for each potential sound, so that one can be randomly selected to be played. The drawback of this is that more memory is consumed to store all these effects. At this point they might be streamed from disk or cycled through memory so that there are not too many loaded at any one time.

Spatial Use of Sound Effects

Sound effects are used to position elements spatially. Classic stereo features two speakers that can take advantage of binaural perception (the ability of the brain to interpret the sound received by each of the two ears and use the differences to locate the position of a sound) by panning sounds to a particular speaker. However, this is localized to the direction of the speaker source.

With modern surround-sound technology, this can be used to pinpoint sound to a location. However, this requires a number of speakers placed around the player to the sides and at the rear. Not everyone has this technology at home, so it cannot be relied upon.

Music

The film industry has long understood the powerful role that music plays in our lives and has spent years perfecting the art of visual and audio synergy. Watch a film without music and it can often seem hollow and empty. Music has such a massive impact on the tension and feeling of the narrative. Music can be used to build tension, to signify triumph, to elicit sadness, and to wrap us in the joy that the characters we see on screen are feeling.

There are two main approaches to producing music for games:

Composition: Music is composed for use in the game. This may be done by an in-house composer but is often outsourced to a big-name composer. At the small end of the scale a composer will create all of the music single-handed. At the larger end of the scale, whole orchestras might be used to perform the composition.

Licensed tracks: A completely different approach is to compile a series of licensed tracks from known artists. This has the advantage of bringing instant kudos to the project but suffers from the static form the music takes. There is much less scope for tailoring the music to requirements. This approach seems best suited to extreme sports or racing games. Having licensed music also allows the option for the players to select their own tracks to be played.

Assuming that we take the composition approach, there are a number of considerations to bear in mind.

Style

The style of music used in a game will have a large impact on the overall feel of the game. A number of factors will influence the style of the music:

Setting: The basis of the setting can determine particular genres of music or particular artists used. For example, a game set in an Eastern-based world may be heavily influenced by Asian styles of music.

Plot themes: The types of plot the game features will have very different emotional moods for the pieces of music. For example horror titles have a very different feel than epic battle games.

Gameplay: The types of gameplay that will be experienced will require different styles of music. Some sections may require fast-paced, adrenaline-fuelled styles, whereas others may be more laid-back and atmospheric.

Instrumentation

Musical style is in a large part determined by the instruments used. In a setting that is based on real locations, indigenous instruments will reinforce the sense of place.

Conversely, using unexpected instruments may have the result of either being refreshing and interesting or feeling completely out of place.

The time period of the setting may also have a large influence on the types of instrument used. Many modern synth sounds will feel completely out of place in a period setting but may be perfect for contemporary or futuristic settings.

If composing with realistic instruments, there is no substitute for recording a professional musician performing on the real thing. Sometimes synth sounds just don't cut it.

Tempo

The overall pace of a game is often reflected in the average tempo (speed) of the music. A fast-paced action game will be enhanced by having a score that matches the pace of the action, getting the players into the rhythm of the action and enabling them to deepen their concentration. Slower-paced games use music to heighten tension, set moods, and build atmosphere and are thus more likely to have a slower average tempo.

Genre

The choice of music genre is a difficult one. People's interpretations of genres tend to be very selective. What some people might find pleasing to listen to can be grating and annoying for others. This is why more classical orchestration works so well, as it has less opinion cast upon it and is not subject to whimsical changes in fashion. Movies are very often scored in a traditional way, though there have been a number of successful contemporary scores over the years.

Above all, the choice of any particular genre should be made in relation to the game itself and not based solely on the personal preference of the development team or led by the current marketing fad.

Leitmotifs

Leitmotifs are repeating pieces of music used to signify a particular character, object, or event. These are composed to create connections with various elements and to strengthen the mood with which they are associated. For example the *Star Wars* films feature leitmotifs for a number of elements in the film such as "The Imperial March" for Darth Vader. Themes for the other characters also play throughout the movies. Indiana Jones has his own leitmotif every time he performs a particularly spectacular action, as does super-spy James Bond.

The use of leitmotifs will create stronger emotional ties with the characters and provide reward for the player. Every time we hear the Bond music playing we know some great action is about to unfold.

Implementation

The implementation of music in games to date has been fairly simplistic given the possibilities offered by the interactive nature of the medium. The reason for this is that creating a dynamic music system is rather hard.

Basic Music Implementation

The basic method of using music in games centers around the use of triggers to play a specific piece of music for the duration of the composition or to loop the piece until told to fade out. One advantage of a basic system like this is that it gives the audio engineer absolute control over how the music will sound but it does not react in any real way to the action on screen.

Chunking and Layering

A more dynamic method of playing sound is to divide it up into chunks or layers. Chunking divides a particular piece of music up into a number of clips that have different intensities. The chunk can then be played according to the action occurring at the current time (see Figure 17.1).

Intro	Building 01	Intense 01	Intense 02	Falling 01	Outro

FIGURE 17.1   Music chunking.

Layering is a similar method that divides a piece of music into clips, but more than one of these clips can be played at a time. This allows clips to be layered one on top of another to build up the intensity of the piece. Often these may be broken down by groups of instruments (see Figure 17.2).

			Strings Light	Strings Heavy	Strings Outro
	Horns Light	Horns Light	Horns Heavy	Horns Light	
Percussion Intro	Percussion Light	Percussion Heavy	Percussion Light	Percussion Light	

FIGURE 17.2   Layered music tracks.

One problem with this system is that transitioning between moods will be delayed from the actual action, as it has to be registered and, without breaking rhythm, it cannot immediately switch. A different way to do it might be to ensure that quiet sections have no rhythm-based section such as drums, so that the more intense clips can be faded quickly in without horrible clashes of sounds.

All sorts of conditions can be used to determine the intensity of the music:

Number of threats: The current number of threats to the player.
Player's action: How often the player is performing particular actions such as attacking.
Level of danger: The types of threat currently facing the player.
Closeness to death: How low on health the player is.
Closeness to victory: How far from winning the player is.

Music Usage

Music is used for a variety of purposes in games, such as:

Tension: Building up suspense of an impending event. Can be used to unnerve the players and make them jumpy.

Shock: Used to emphasize a shock. Will help surprise the player.

Announce: Introduces a new or known area or character and announces their arrival (see Leitmotif).

Dramatize: Emphasizes the drama of a current situation, which can build up the adrenaline in the player.

One mistake many games make is to arbitrarily use music where it is not necessarily needed, playing it constantly in the background, for example. This can detract from the game and potentially annoy the player.

Speech

Until the advent of mass storage devices such CDs, DVDs, and now Blu-Ray, the use of speech was fairly prohibitive because of the sheer size of memory required. These large disc sizes allow speech to be streamed from the disc rather than having it resident in memory.

Types of Speech

Two basic types of speech are used in games:

- Script based
- Voice pools

Script Based

Script-based speech is that used to tell the story and is based around the story script. This type of speech is used during cutscenes or sequences triggered during play. There are two forms of script-based speech:

Narration: Nondiegetic speech, where a character relates parts of the story directly to the audience.

Dialog: Speech within the game world, where characters converse with each other. This might be some manic speech by the villain, an overheard conversation between a group of enemies, advice from a mentor, and so on.

Voice Pools

Voice pools are a more dynamic form of speech used for characters performing actions such as patrolling or fighting. They can draw on a pool of speech to react to the current situation. This can really increase the believability of a scene if the characters match the appropriate line of speech to the current situation.

Matching speech requires the determination of context so that the appropriate line can be selected. Voice lines are separated into groups according to their context, for example:

- Combat:
  - Player hit/knocked out/killed
  - Ally hit/knocked out/killed
  - Enemy hit/knocked out/killed
  - Low health (self)
  - Low health (player)
  - Allies all dead
  - Low morale
  - High morale
  - Player performs impressive attack
- Patrolling:
  - General patrolling
  - Alerted
  - Suspicious
  - Investigating
  - Player sighted
  - Player lost
  - Returning to patrol

This system could be applied to all manner of different systems such as racing or squad speech. Careful consideration and grouping of sounds and their trigger conditions will ensure that they are used in the right context.

Voice Acting

The quality of voice acting in the average game is, frankly, awful. It seems that little thought is given to the need to select the right actors and direct them in such a way as to get the best performance out of them.

The image of games among the acting community is fairly lackluster. A lot of actors view game work as little better than advertising voice overs. The truth is that the games industry really needs to wake up and get organized in order to get the results they desperately need.

There are several stages in the process of recording voice talent:

Casting: Choosing the right people for the job is crucial. Some games are even voiced by members of the development team. This might be fine for placeholder work, but games really should be voiced by professionals in the final product (unless the development team happens to be particularly talented). The casting role needs to be taken seriously and is likely to need a dedicated team member to manage casting sessions, book actors, and so on.

Directing: Another stage that is often poorly handled is the process of directing the actors. All too often the responsibility is shouldered by a team member entirely unsuited to the job. A director needs to be skilled at the job. Even a really good actor requires good direction, especially in games, where many actors know little about the final product or the processes involved in development.

Recording: Using a professional recording studio is essential, as the quality of voice recording must be maintained.

As games get higher budgets and incorporate more cinematic techniques, we are likely to see the quality of acting in games improve. Motion capture is now becoming a recognized field of acting, with great actors such as Andy Serkis making names for themselves playing digital characters such as Golem and King Kong. Motion capture combined with voice acting can get top-notch performances out of actors, as they can really get into the characters. In the not-too-distant future we might start to see digital actors being as well recognized as mainstream movie actors and deservedly winning awards for their work.

Implementation

Even the best acting in the world can be ruined by poor implementation. Many game scripts fall victim to very poor implementation of often fairly good voice acting. The main problem is poor timing, with large pauses between lines, and acting not flowing correctly. The source of this problem is usually the voice implementation being out of the hands of the creative departments. The solution is the ability to be able to craft scenes with good tools to match up audio and animation.

Lip-synch is often a large concern for the implementation process. There are two ways to approach the problem:

Phoneme matching: Phonemes are the base units of speech. These basic units have matching face shapes when spoken. The speech is broken down into the basic units so that a face shape can be applied to match. Often further tweaks are made on top of the face shapes so that mood can be expressed along with the sound shape. Some form of tool will be needed to create the sentence-based animations.

Facial motion capture: An increasingly popular method of lip synching is facial motion capture. Here the actor's facial movement is captured along with the audio so that the two can synch up. We are moving steadily toward the capture of virtual performances being used extensively in games. Such techniques are likely to dramatically increase the quality and perception of storytelling in games.

SUMMARY

Audio is a vital element in creating a believable world. We have only taken a brief look at the possibilities of audio, mainly because the job of implementation is done by specific audio engineers. However, it is vital that a designer understands the importance of audio and does not overlook it when creating designs for the game. We investigated several aspects of audio:

Designing with sound: When designing the game, we should consider audio in the setting we choose, the use of audio as symbols, the use of silence, visual and aural synergy, audio in gameplay, the use of audio to elicit emotion, and the use of sound in the environment.

Types of sound: Sound takes one of two forms—diegetic (in the world) or nondiegetic (outside the world). We looked at several types of sound:

- **Sound effects:** The use of sound effects in atmospherics, for actions, for physics events, and for game events
- **Music:** The use of music to provide tension, elicit emotion, and provide themes for particular elements in the narrative
- **Speech:** The use of speech to enhance narrative and increase the atmosphere

Audio will continue to play a very important role in creating emotion and enhancing gameplay. Sound engineers have always been the types of people to embrace the new, so the future is likely to utilize new technologies and explore more complex interactivity that the medium of games offers.

USER INTERFACE

A good UI is essential. It controls the way a player interacts with a game. Get it wrong, and a player will be confused, frustrated, and possibly annoyed. Get it right, and the players will barely notice. That's when you know your UI is working as it should.

There are several prerequisites that a good user interface will have:

Simplicity: Every interface should be as simple as possible. Adding complexity where it is not needed will only confuse the player and steepen the learning curve.

Consistency: An interface should have common navigation and functionality. Having to press different buttons for the same actions each time will lead to confusion and frustration for the player.

Familiarity: Interfaces that people are used to and comfortable with are generally more successful, unless the new system is far more intuitive.

Intuitiveness: The time it takes for different types of players to learn the interface and how its elements are interconnected.

These principles should be applied to every element of UI design.

The first chapter in this part of the book takes a look at the front end—the system of menus used to set up various options and to allow the player to start the game. The second chapter examines in-game interfaces used to relay information to the player and allow them to interact with various game systems.

THE FRONT END

In This Chapter

- Front End Elements
- Flow Schemas
- Visual Style
- Technical Requirements
- The Back End

The front end is a player's first experience of a game but is very often one of the last aspects of the game to be designed. First impressions count, and as all good chefs say, "The first taste is with the eye." A poorly presented front-end system will immediately make the game seem cheaper, and, worse still, a very badly designed front end could even put players off playing the game.

Thus, it is essential that the front end is right. It is important to bear in mind the main purpose of the front end: to get the players into the action with everything they need as quickly as possible, but it must also offer enough choice and options to give players the ability to tune the game to their liking. A front end needs to have good flow.

Typically a front end is composed of a series of menu screens. The presentation may differ dramatically, but the basic premise remains the same. Action–adventure games tend to be somewhat simpler than many other types of game, but there are several key elements that must be accessible. The action depth of a menu system (how many menu actions must be performed to achieve a goal) should be as minimal as possible, preferably requiring one or two button presses at the most to perform the main functions.

We will examine several aspects of the front end in this chapter:

- Front end elements
- Flow schemas
- Visual style
- Technical requirements
- Back end

FRONT-END ELEMENTS

Many elements can make up the front end. Their use is dictated by the structure of the game and information that needs to be ascertained before play can begin, such as equipment selection or even character creation.

Logo Screens

All commercial products have logo screens as the first part of the game loading cycle. These display all publisher and developer logos and often any middleware that has been licensed for the game. Publishers are often extremely specific as to how these function, as are console manufacturers, so there is not really any room for changes in this area.

Language Selection

After the logo screens there is often the option to select the desired language for front-end menus and possibly for in-game speech as well. This is more desirable in the European territory, where there is a wide mix of languages. In this territory support for the six main languages is encouraged.

Each language is usually displayed by that country's flag along with the language name written in that language for maximum clarity. Language selection is often less of a necessity in the North American and Japanese territories (though North America is well served by providing Spanish, because of the huge Hispanic population, and French for the Canadian market).

Main Menu

The real meat of the front end begins with the main menu. This allows the player to navigate to all the various functions that the game presents. Different schemas will have different options presented on the main menu.

Start Screen

Many older games had a start screen—a picture screen where the start button must be pressed before moving onto the main menu. These are still often used today, but they are often completely unnecessary. It is a wasted button press for the player.

Attract Mode

When the main menu is left on screen for a period of time, the game often enters attract mode. This mode plays a demo, some FMV, or something similar to attract the player's attention. These should disappear as soon as the player presses a button or direction and return to the main menu instantly.

Difficulty Selection

On choosing a new single player game, the player is perhaps presented with a difficulty selection screen. Typically this will be a menu listing the difficulty settings and, ideally, a brief description of what the player can expect from each difficulty setting, for example:

Easy: Enemies are easier to kill and not as smart as usual.
Normal: Enemies are generally smart and present a challenge.
Hard: Enemies are much harder to kill and use complex strategies against you.

Often these settings will be named to suit the portrayal of how the player would be perceived, for example, Wimp, Average, Tough, God. Alternatively, they might be themed to the style of the game itself, so in a gangster game it might offer Runner, Thug, Made-Man, and Crime Lord.

There may be much more esoteric difficulty selection screens, such as asking the player a series of questions to determine his personality and adjusting the challenge to suit. Generally these can be a little too abstract. Often it is much easier to offer the player a simple choice and explain the options.

Select Save Game Menu

The vast majority of modern games allow players to save their game progress (it hasn't always been this way; classic arcade games required the player to start from the beginning every time). Usually it allows them to make more than one save so that they can replay different sections if need be, but some games simply have one save game that records what has so far been unlocked during play (a level or mission select schema).

On loading the game, the player is usually able to pick which save game to load, although some games might automatically load the save with the latest time stamp. While this is often the save a player wants to load, it cannot be guaranteed. More than one person might be playing the game at one time and each have their own save games. Loading automatically keeps action depth to a minimum but can prove frustrating if several people are playing through the game separately.

Profile Creation

Many games ask the player to create a profile, which will be used to store progress and possibly statistics as well. The player is asked to input a name for this profile. On a PC this could be easy, but on a console with a typical joypad it is not so simple. The solution is to display a keypad that the player can navigate by moving the cursor to the right letter with the analog stick or digital pad. The norm for this process is to have a grid displaying the letters. Letters are arranged alphabetically or in a QWERTY keyboard.

There are other methods that can be used, such as pressing left or right to cycle through the alphabet and pressing the action button to select a letter. One particularly different and elegant solution was created by Ubisoft's *Beyond Good and Evil* team, where letters were arranged on a large corkscrew. Players rotated the analog stick left and right to rotate the corkscrew. A cursor on the corkscrew indicated the letter to be selected.

Level or Mission Select Menu

A slightly different approach to the save game is to have distinct levels or missions that are unlocked as the game progresses. Thus, no actual level data needs to be saved—only the unlocked position and perhaps rating values such as score.

With such a system the front end requires the player to select which level or mission to start the play session from. This is a popular choice where there are short levels. For example *Halo* and *James Bond: Everything or Nothing* both use this kind of level select system.

The really big bonus with this system is that it makes replayability extremely easy to initiate. The players can jump right in wherever they want. However, it makes it somewhat frustrating to have to complete a level before being able to save the game, especially if it is particularly long. People like to be able to turn off their console and go to bed at some point.

Options Menu

The options menu allows the player to set various aspects of the game, the in-game interface, and controls. There are generally three types of options:

- Game options
- Interface options
- Audio and visual settings

Game Options

Game options adjust settings that pertain to the game mechanics themselves. Typical game options might include:

Difficulty setting: The player is usually asked to set difficulty before starting the game, but might also set the difficulty from the options menu.

Round time: Beat 'em ups usually allow the player to set round time as a game option, but other multiplayer games will often set this up in the multiplayer game setup screen.

Number of wins: The number of rounds needed to win a match. Again this is a setting usually applied to beat 'em ups, as other multiplayer games tend to offer these options on the multiplayer game setup screen.

Interface Options

Interface options allow the player to adjust various aspects of the UI, usually the in-game UI and controls. Some typical options are:

Controller layouts: Allows the player to select between a number of predefined controller layouts

Button assignments: Allows players total customization of controller layout by assigning the various actions to buttons of their choice

Invert look: Switch the vertical movement of an analog stick when looking to either inverted or not

Controller sensitivity: Allows the player to adjust the sensitivity of the analog sticks

Controller calibration: Allows the player to calibrate analog sticks or more exotic controller devices such as light guns

Hints: Allows players to turn help hints on or off in game, so that they can choose to receive helpful information when learning the game and remove it when they have learned it all (or when they simply don't care)

Language: Allows the player to select which language to play the game in

Audio and Visual Settings

Audio and visual settings allow players to tune the game to their entertainment systems. Typical audio and visual settings might include:

Screen ratio: Choose from some standard screen ratios such as 4:3 and 16:9. This is likely to disappear in the future, as most games console manufacturers are pushing for games to only support 16:9 ratio.

Display mode: PAL games often allow the player to choose between 50 and 60 Hz display modes. 60 Hz can only be shown by multisynch TV sets in PAL territories. HDTVs have different settings based on screen resolutions: 720i, 720p, 1080i, and 1080p.

Screen position: Adjust the placement of the image in screen space.

Sound system: Select the type of sound technology such as Stereo, Dolby 5.1, DTS, and so on.

Subtitles: Turn subtitles for voice acting on and off. This should be an essential part of every narrative-based game, but as yet isn't. The consideration of disabled gamers needs to be looked at in much more depth. Game events that rely on sound should also notify the player via subtitles or closed captions.

Split screen: Determines whether a two-player split screen game splits the display vertically or horizontally. With the move toward 16:9 ratio, the horizontal split is becoming a fairly redundant option.

Intro Movie

Many games feature a prerendered movie to introduce the game and story. This is most likely to be played before the level loads. However, if the intro is using the game engine, the resources will need to be loaded before it can be played.

Loading Screens

Loading screens are generally a necessity. Even in a streamed world such as *Grand Theft Auto* there needs to be an initial point where data is loaded into memory—perhaps when the game is started. Loading is more of a problem with disc-based consoles. In the days of cartridges it was much less of a problem, but with the demands of modern gaming, with streaming music and copious amounts of data, cartridges are just too expensive and impractical these days.

There are ways of making loading screens more interesting:

Hint screens: Static screens that display text and images that explain elements of the game. Some people hate these because they break the fourth wall, but they are a useful way of communicating information such as controls or strategies to the player

Ambience screens: Suitable images or movies that set the ambience of the proceeding level. These are often considered useless, but they are preferable to hint screens, as they get the player into the mood of the game if done well.

Linking: The best method of utilizing load times is to create some kind of link piece: a cutscene that justifies the loading time. The perfect example of this is the planet-hopping sections in Insomniac's *Ratchet & Clank* series.

Story exposition: It is technically possible to play movies while loading (though not always), so an FMV for story exposition could be used to hide the load time (this would not be skippable, however).

Character Selection and Creation

Some games feature different selectable players or the option to create your own character. Often these can act as the difficulty selection. For example, in the first *Resident Evil* selecting Chris Redfield made the game much harder than chosing Jill Valentine. Character creation is a very well used mechanic in RPGs originating in the West, which reflects a cultural difference in that Japanese audiences like to play predefined characters and Western audiences tend to like more control over their avatars and want to mold them to their own liking.

Character selection is much more likely in multiplayer games, particularly beat 'em ups, where each character represents a different set of skills. Multiplayer character attributes in FPS games tend to be more basic, usually just changing the model used to display the players to their opponents. *Timesplitters 2* was an exception to this rule, where selecting different characters gave players different attributes such as speed and stamina.

Mission Briefing

Mission-based games often have some kind of mission briefing before the level begins. This mission briefing outlines all the main objectives that the player needs to complete. A mission briefing might also offer equipment selection, giving the players the opportunity to kit themselves up ready to meet the mission objectives that they face.

Multiplayer Match Menu

Selecting a multiplayer match can be pretty quick and simple. For example, starting a versus game in *Tekken* is simple a case of selecting a character and a handicap. Then the players are thrown straight into the action.

Multiplayer modes can be a lot more complex than this, however, particularly when going online.

Creating a Match

Starting a match to play locally on one machine is generally not too complex. Usually there are match settings, player settings, and map selection to be performed before a game is initiated. Player settings are based on the choice of profile that contains name, model, and control preferences, or preset characters and control setups are chosen before the commencement of each match.

Depending on the genre of game, there could be all manner of match settings such as:

Match type: The type of match to be played: death match, capture the flag, and so on

Round time: The length of time a round lasts

Score target: The number of rounds or points to be reached for the match to be completed

Weapon sets: The available weapons if such a system is being used

The selection of which level or map to play the match on is an essential part of the match setup process. The level itself should show a picture and give a clear overview of the level, specifying the optimum number of players.

Online

Playing online console games requires an extra layer of depth in the front end to allow the player to connect with other players.

Match List

The simplest approach is to display a list of all the available matches. Players simply peruse this list and select a match, playing a map they like that has enough free spaces. When the player creates a match, it is added to this list so people can connect and join the action. Some multiplayer matches require all players to be present at the start of the game; people cannot join once the game has started. Such games have a staging area called a lobby. The lobby is a meeting place where the players wait for all the necessary players to join before the action commences. Players can chat and brag about the forthcoming match while they wait. Lobbies tend to be used for race and strategy-based games where late-arriving players would be at a severe disadvantage.

Interfaces for online play can get a lot more complex than this, but much of the online interface can be brought in as middleware, such as GameSpy's Arcade. This makes the complexities of server setup and interface creation less of a concern for developers and is likely to be a major growth area in the future.

Online Models

Online games require a host machine to act as the game server. There are two basic models for rolling out online features: official servers and peer-to-peer.

Official Servers: The expensive option is to host online space for serving games to the audience. This promotes a strong online community and enables developers to roll out extra content with ease. It also leads to games with less lag than the peer-to-peer structure, allows much larger game spaces, and enables much tighter control of the active players. The costs of this are so high, however, that charging some kind of subscription fee is generally a must. Official servers are usually reserved for massively multiplayer games that do charge monthly subscription fees but require a constant stream of content to be created to keep players interested. For most this approach is simply a waste of money.

Peer-to-Peer: By far the most popular model is a peer-to-peer system, where a multiplayer game is hosted on the machine of one of the players. Other players can connect to this machine and do battle. The main problem with this system is speed. Peer-to-peer systems are a lot slower than dedicated servers. Broadband has done much to ease this problem, however, and speed is likely to be far less of an issue in the future.

Online Content

The most desirable online content is the ability to play with other players; however, there are lots of other possibilities for interesting online content:

Score boards: High-score tables and league tables for players to upload their best performances.

Replay videos: Watch other people's replays for some spectacular action.

Machinima: Watch, make, and share films made with game engines. Some series such as Red vs Blue made using *Halo* are extremely popular.

Content: Download new levels, characters, equipment, and so on. Extra content is a very big driving force in the longevity of a game. This could either be developer-created content, which moves gaming toward an episodic structure, or user-created content if editors are provided to enable players to make content.

Extras Menu

Often a game will include unlockable extras or secrets. These can often be accessed via a menu option on the main screen. A whole host of extras might be included here:

Gallery: Browse concept art

Making of: DVD-style making-of documentaries, bloopers, and so on

Cheats: Any cheat modes that have been discovered or could be entered

Trophy room: A display of all the trophies the player has accumulated

Stats: A number of statistics for the player's profile, such as time played, miles traveled, and so on

FLOW SCHEMAS

The following flow schemas represent possible game flow in very broad brushstrokes. However, they do indicate the basic structure of many game front ends and show how you might structure your own.

Classic Single-Player Game

The classic single-player game has a very simple and elegant flow. Not too much information is needed, and relatively few features need to be added. This schema assumes a very linear style of game (see Figure 18.1).

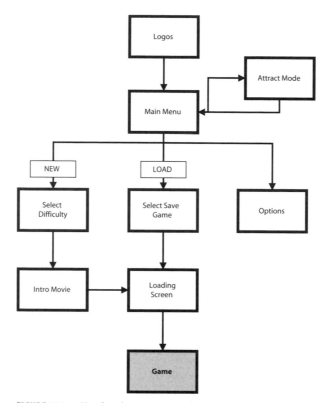

FIGURE 18.1   Single-player game schema.

The main menu usually contains just three options:

- New Game
- Load Game
- Options

When the game is first loaded, the New Game option is selected by default, but when a saved game is detected on the memory storage device, the option defaults to Load Game so the player does not need to navigate to the most likely option.

This schema is very easy to extend. For example, it is quite possible that a character creation screen could be placed after selecting a new game.

The Minimalist Front End

Grand Theft Auto did away with the front end as much as possible. Instead the game automatically chooses between creating a new game or loading an existing saved game. On booting, the data storage device is checked for saved games. If none can be found, then a new game is created. Otherwise, the saved game with the latest time stamp is loaded. The player can choose to create a new game or load a different game from within the in-game menus.

Select Level or Mission Game

For less linearly structured games the front end is tailored around the ability to select a starting point (see Figure 18.2).

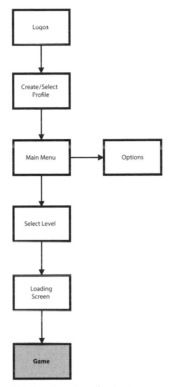

FIGURE 18.2   Level select structure.

Level or mission select schemas are designed for games with very distinct levels or missions. The schema is designed to get the player into the action as soon as possible. The main menu is a level or mission select screen, although there is often a higher-level menu if a variety of game modes are available.

Multiplayer Games

Many action-centric games feature multiplayer options. To reflect this, the main menu contains options to select between single-player or multiplayer modes (see Figure 18.3).

The multiplayer schema is likely to have more action depth simply because there are a greater variety of options to choose from. Multiplayer options will depend on the scope of the mode. If it only offers multiplayer options on one machine, then only a Create Game option will be offered. If the game allows players to go online, the player will be able to see a list of available games to join.

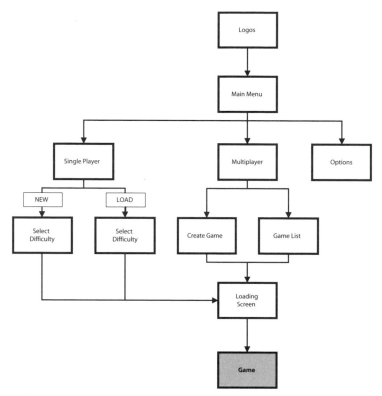

FIGURE 18.3   Game UI with multiplayer options.

VISUAL STYLE

The visual style of a front end can vary tremendously, from very minimal 2D interfaces to complex 3D rendered scenes. Getting a clear visual style is extremely important, and simplicity is essential, but this does not have to mean boring.

There is a vast array of potential styles for a UI, but there are a number of common design concepts:

- Simple menus
- Metaphors
- 3D environments

Simple Menus

The biggest bonus of simple menus is familiarity, since games began with very simple menu systems. A simple menu is based on a highlighted region that is moved with the D-pad or analog stick. An option is selected by pressing the action button. Pressing an option will initiate another menu screen or the game will load. On a lower-level menu screen a button can be pressed to move back up one or possibly all tiers of the menu tree.

While conceptually simple, these menus can be wrapped in designer clothing and appear ultra-sleek. Take a look at *WipEout® Pure's* übercool menus. Then examine the mechanics behind them to discover that they are very simple indeed.

Simple menus can promote lazy and even shoddy design because of their simplicity. Take the typical picture with a menu by the side. Sometimes it can look very cheap, as though someone could not be bothered. A little bit of good design thought goes a long way. *Half-Life 2's* very simple menus still have a great impact. The backdrop is created using the game engine, so a beautiful animated scene with ambient sound is presented to the player. Laid over this is a very simple point-and-click menu, which translates very easily to the console highlight bar method. One word of warning here: running the game engine may mean a significant load time just to show the menu.

Simple menus can appear extremely complex in terms of movement and style yet still have a basic mechanic underlying them. Take, for example, the menus used in *The Chronicles of Riddick: Escape from Butcher Bay*. A 3D cube contains the text, and when a menu option is selected, the cube is rotated and the text assembles itself from a selection of much smaller cubes. The effect looks extremely complex and gives the feeling of some impressive device, but it is all just fancy animation. The core of the menu is still a simple highlight selection mechanic.

Simple menus may use other devices, a popular one being the idea of a wheel. Menu options are organized around the radius of this wheel. The player rotates the wheel by moving left and right, bringing the desired choice to the front. This could be extended to rotating spheres or cubes, adding the use of up and down movement.

Metaphors

Using a metaphor for a UI is very common in commercial applications, as it helps the user identify with a real-world system. The Microsoft Windows® desktop is a classic example, presenting the idea to the user that there is a desktop space where they can place objects, a bin where they can throw their rubbish, and so on.

The use of metaphor for a game's front end is still a fairly rare occurrence, though in-game menus do tend to use the idea of metaphor more often, such as a menu being a PDA or something similar. One good example of a metaphor in a front end is *Gran Turismo*. The main interface presents a map of a city where there are various race venues, car showrooms, and garages for the player to travel to.

Metaphors create an immediate atmosphere for the game. Consider a sci-fi game where the UI takes the form of an advanced-looking login terminal. With such a metaphor we create an almost seamless link from the front end to the game world itself, never destroying the illusion of the player inhabiting a game world. Even the loading screen could be made to be part of the experience, perhaps having the idea of connecting to a mainframe computer to initialize the virtual reality simulation. We see loading metaphors fairly often, such as the act of moving through a door in *Resident Evil*, where a door is shown animating on screen while the next section is loaded in the background.

This kind of design keeps the player's mind on being in character, focusing on the immersion in the game world.

3D Environments

Using 3D environments for the actual menu rather than just as a backdrop can create a very impressive-looking menu system, which can also be very immersive. 3D environments allow the player to inhabit some space and interact with objects that represent menu functionality. For example, we could be in a lounge where various elements in the room represent different menu selections. The computer could represent an options menu. The door could represent the act of starting the game. Trophies on the wall could represent the player's scores and achievements.

The environment could be navigated in simple menu style, using movement of the stick or D-pad to focus the camera on different objects in the room. When a selection is made, a 2D menu will often overlay the 3D environment so that simple menu selection can then be performed. Otherwise, the devices themselves could be interacted with in a way that suits their function, for example, moving a mouse pointer on the computer screen to click on a file to save the game. Sometimes this can make the menu functionality ambiguous and overly fussy, so care must be taken to overcome this problem.

This could be taken to a further extreme, using actual game movement of the avatar to allow the player to move around and interact with the objects. Now we might as well integrate the front end into the game itself, as indeed *Grand Theft Auto* does to great effect.

Remember, there may be significant work involved in creating a 3D environment menu, both in coding and art resource terms. Plus, there can be loading time issues that may make this approach more trouble than it is worth.

TECHNICAL REQUIREMENTS

The UI is one of the most heavily scrutinized areas when the technical requirements checks are made during the submission process (see later console requirements section for the lowdown on the submission process). Therefore, it is a good idea to design the UI with knowledge of what requirements will need to be met. A number of requirements have a large impact on the front end:

Default buttons: Each console manufacturer tends to have guidelines for which buttons should be used to select options and cancel actions. These may even be different in different territories.

Memory interfacing: Loading and saving game data from the hard drive or memory card usually has strict rules on providing messages to the user.

Loading screens: Whenever the game is loading, the screen should indicate that loading is occurring so the player doesn't assume it has crashed.

There are plenty more requirements for a front end, but each manufacturer tends to have different rules that change over the course of time. Make sure you have all the latest details for all the platforms for which you are developing.

THE BACK END

The back end is composed of UI elements that are used once the main gameplay has completed, for instance when a level has been completed or when the player dies.

Level Complete

On completing a level, there may well be level complete screens. These may serve several purposes:

Success acknowledgement: Rewards the players by acknowledging their success in completing the level.

Replay: Sports games or quick level-based games (such as *Super Monkey Ball*) often have replay functions to allow a player to watch and review the action. It may even allow them to save that replay.

Rating: Often in arcade-style games players are given a rating for their performance for a level. It has become something of a tradition for this to be graded like an exam paper (A+, A, B, C, etc.), but there are plenty of other potential rating schemes. Ratings are generally based on various stats such as accuracy, amount of kills, secrets found, or a score value. Each rating has a certain threshold score set for each level by the designers.

Stats: A display of the player's achievements during the level (which are often used to create ratings). As well as accuracy and the usual suspects, there might be more exotic stats such as number of miles traveled.

Save game: Often at the end of a level the player is presented with the opportunity to save the game.

Game Over

A screen that might be employed is the Game Over screen. This occurs when the player has no more lives. This screen will likely offer the player the choice to continue or quit. Sometimes there may be a countdown (usually 10 seconds) before automatically quitting.

The Continue screen is a hangover from the arcade days, where the screen appeared to pressure the player into pumping more money in to continue the game. To be honest, Game Over screens are fairly redundant on home consoles, unless the game is trying to emulate an arcade experience at home. They are a level of action depth that is redundant, and forcing the player to restart from the beginning can be a very frustrating mechanic. On death, the player should restart from the last checkpoint or be given the option to load a saved game.

SUMMARY

The front end is the player's introduction to the game and as such should be an inviting experience. The concepts covered in this chapter should spark some ideas for developing an interesting front end for your game.

Front-end elements: We looked at a number of front end elements that might be featured in a game. Not every element would be needed, as a front end should only include elements that it really needs to keep it as simple as possible. There is no point in complexity just for complexity's sake.

Flow schemas: After examining the possible elements, we looked at several possible schemas that might be used to guide the front-end design:

- **Classic single-player game:** A standard schema that is used where there is only a basic narrative game mode.
- **The minimalist front end:** A schema that seeks to remove as much of the front end as possible and drops the player straight into the action.
- **Select level or mission games:** A schema used where the player is able to quickly jump between levels.
- **Multiplayer games:** A schema used for multiplayer games.

Visual style: The visual style of a front end can completely change the player's initial perception of the game. There are several potential styles:

- **Simple menus:** The use of basic menus to take the player through the settings into the game.
- **Metaphors:** The use of metaphors to put the front end into context with the game.
- **3D environments:** The use of the 3D engine to place the player within the world itself.

Technical requirements: When developing a front end, it is important to know the technical requirements of the console manufacturer, so that time isn't wasted revising the system later on.

Back-end: The screens that greet the player on completion or failure of levels:

- **Level complete:** A summary of the player's achievements in the level or a congratulatory message.
- **Game over:** A message informing the players of their failure and the option to continue or quit.

The power of the current generation of consoles means we are likely to start to see more elaborate front-end systems being created. As with any new technology, there are likely to be some horrible mistakes before some truly brilliant material is created. The process of evolution will always weed out the weak systems and leave the strongest as the survivors.

IN-GAME INTERFACE

In This Chapter

- HUD (Head up Display)
- Pause Menu
- Inventory Screen
- Treasure or Experience Screen
- Map Screen
- Objectives Screen or Quest Log
- Information Screens
- Game Hints
- Character Advancement Screen
- Save Games
- Store or Merchant Screens

The in-game interface refers to all the visual information that is provided to the player, as well as any menu-based control presented during a game session. An in-game interface is an important method of communicating with the player. It is not essential to display every piece of information—indeed, some games are seeking ways of removing much of the in-game interface altogether.

The in-game interface may consist of several parts:

- HUD (Head up Display)
- Pause Menu
- Inventory Screen
- Treasure or Experience Screen
- Map Screen
- Objectives Screen or Quest Log
- Information Screens
- Game Hints
- Character Advancement Screen
- Save Games
- Store or Merchant Screens

HUD (Head up Display)

HUD is a term taken from military aircraft, where information is projected onto a screen in front of the pilot's eyes rather than requiring the pilot to look down at the cockpit panels. In a game this information is placed at various points around the screen. The space occupied by HUD elements is often referred to as screen furniture. A lot of screen furniture can be counterproductive, as it blocks the view of the action or becomes confusing. The goal of a good HUD system is to present the most relevant information as it is needed in a clear and concise manner.

One important consideration with HDTV-era gaming is the use of static elements on screen. High-definition sets can suffer from screen burn if a static image is left on screen for a long period of time. This has to be taken into account when designing the HUD. Making it translucent will alleviate the problem fairly easily.

HUD Components

A HUD is composed of several components that provide different information to the player. Many types of components may be used, but there are a number of popular components that many players will recognize instantly:

Bars: A scaling bar that indicates the current value of a particular variable
Counters: A numeric representation of a variable
Text: Messages and subtitles
Icons: Warnings and notifications of game events
Targeting reticule: A visual indicator of where a weapon is being aimed
Cursor: A pointing device under the player's control

Highlighters: Effects that highlight particular elements in the environment
Equipment selection: The ability to quickly select equipment
HUD map or compass: A mini map or compass displayed on the HUD for navigation purposes

Bars

Bars are a visual method of displaying a value without having to display a number. These are an extremely popular component, particularly as a method of displaying a player's health. Bars are also very useful for representing armor, shields, rage, magic points, specials, and so on. The bar typically has a finite maximum length. The size of the bar moves between this maximum and zero according to the described value. The maximum length of this bar may be permanently or temporarily increased by collecting special objects.

Bars might also double up, so that the bar changes to a different color once it has filled up to a sufficient size and then begins to fill again. This could be done multiple times. The secondary bar could even represent another value. For example, if armor is collected, it may replace the health bar until it has run out.

Bars may be analog, so that they represent a granular value, or may be divided into chunks. These chunks represent whole values that are removed in one piece. It is also worth noting that these bars may not be the suggested rectangle but could be any shape, such as a circular pie chart.

Bars are often used to represent enemy health. These bars might appear in a screen corner to represent the enemy that is targeted or perhaps only appear for a boss enemy type. Otherwise, bars might be positioned above the heads of enemies, a feature that might best be served by a toggle button to remove them for better viewing.

Counters

Counters are numeric values displayed as numbers on the HUD. They can be used for any numerical value but should remain limited to only essential information. There are plenty of practical uses for counters:

Score: Monitors the player's current score.
Combo counter: Displays the current number of consecutive hits. This would only be displayed when necessary.
Health armor, magic points: A player's health, armor, or magic points might be represented as a number or percentage as well as, or instead of, a bar.
Ammunition: A very important piece of information is the remaining amount of ammunition in a weapon and the total in the inventory.
Countdown timer: Displays the remaining time left in a time-based challenge.
Damage amount: Displays the amount of damage inflicted on an enemy. This would usually float above the victim's head.

Text Messages and Subtitles

At particular points in the game, text messages might need to be displayed, such as information about the next mission objective. These appear on screen for a short duration before fading after a suitable length of time.

Subtitles are used to display dialog. As such, they must remain on screen long enough to be read but need to match the pace of the dialog.

Displaying text is not usually a big problem, but there is one major issue to bear in mind: localization. Don't embed the text into script or code, as it cannot be easily localized. Each line printed to the screen should reference a coded string that can be replaced with text according to the selected language.

Icons

HUD icons are generally used to highlight certain events, such as the need to reload, whether the player is in a hazardous environment, and the like. If a common language of icons is established, they can be used without the need to back them up with text, but they must be clear, concise, and easily understood.

Targeting Reticule

The targeting reticule is a device that displays where the player character is currently aiming his weapon. This is widely used in many games and is almost a certainty in an FPS. A reticule usually takes the form of a crosshair. In a first-person game the crosshair is usually static in the center of the screen. However, games such as *Timesplitters* allow the cursor to be moved by holding down a button to allow more accurate aiming.

A crosshair might also expand and contract to indicate the accuracy according to player actions. When the player is running, the crosshair would expand, indicating poor accuracy. If the player is stationary in a crouched position, the crosshair would contract, indicating a more accurate shot.

Different weapons often have different targeting reticules to differentiate between them and to display their differing firing properties. For example, a shotgun might have a wide circle, whereas a sniper rifle might have a tight crosshair.

Reticules might have other features such as lock-on. A lock-on is a highlight over a target to indicate that the target has been acquired. This is often used to show the currently targeted object.

Cursor

The cursor is a mainstay of PC gaming but is far less practical in a console environment because of the lack of mouse control as standard. The cursor is a pointing device that is used to indicate the current focus. It is rarely used in console-based action or adventure games but might be used to select objects or elements on the HUD or might indicate a position in the game world for the player character to move to. The squad-based strategy game *Full Spectrum Warrior* uses a cursor-based system for movement of the squads, though in this case it is a context-sensitive cursor, which allows it to perform more advanced orders with ease.

Highlighters

Highlighters are effects placed over objects in the environment to indicate their use to the player. A good example of a highlighter is the twinkle effect in *Resident Evil* that denotes that an object can be picked up. Effects may be far less subtle than this, such as pickups that float and rotate while being surrounded by copious effects. This could be said to be immersion breaking, but it does ensure that the player understands the object's purpose. This has become such a well-known game element that most players accept it without questioning the reality of it.

Equipment Selection

Many games use an inventory screen to select equipment, removing the need for any HUD components. However, this can be a fairly slow system—too slow for many action-based games. When the player is selecting objects, the game either continues in real time, continues in slow motion, or is paused while inventory decisions are made. Such games require the selection to be made via the HUD.

List

A list of weapons is cycled through by moving to the next or previous item. If there is equipment as well, this would be probably be held in a separate list. In *Metal Gear Solid 2* the two shoulder buttons open either the weapon or equipment inventory, respectively, allowing the player to cycle through the available items. Once an item is highlighted, the button is released and that item is chosen. Alternatively, one button might open the list and a second button confirms a selection.

Slots

Weapons and equipment are organized into categories so that they can be traversed a little more quickly than a standard list. Essentially this is a collection of smaller lists laid out like a grid (see Figure 19.1).

The player moves left or right to select a category and then moves up or down to select an item in that category. A button press performs the selection.

Wheel

A list or slot system can have considerable action depth. The fastest method by far is to open a list of items and arrange them around the eight points of a wheel. A push in a direction selects an item (see Figure 19.2).

The immediate flaw is that only eight objects can be listed. There are a few ways around this, however. The first is customizing the menu via the main inventory screen, as is done in *Ratchet & Clank*. Alternatively, it can be extended as was done in *Serious Sam: Next Encounter* by doubling up the selection points, so that the first press

FIGURE 19.1   Slot-based weaponry system.

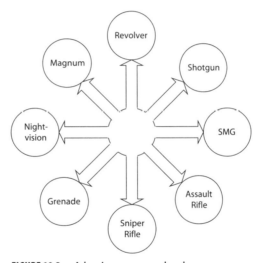

FIGURE 19.2   A basic weapon wheel.

of a direction selects the inner object, but a second push in a direction selects the outer object (see Figure 19.3).

This could be expanded further, but at this point action depth may become too deep and it loses its benefits.

HUD Map or Compass

HUDs often have a mini-map or compass to give the players an indication of the direction they need to head in or a basic overview of their surroundings. A compass is used to indicate the direction of the next objective. This is done with a wheel that rotates left and right or possibly by a rotating arrow.

A mini-map (often called a radar) shows a limited view of the surroundings in an abstract form. The mini-map might display the location of nearby enemies or NPCs, as well as showing the direction of objectives. Objectives out of radar range

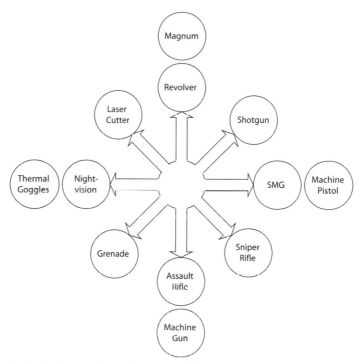

FIGURE 19.3   An advanced weapon wheel.

are often displayed on the very edge of the radar to indicate where they are. The icons used for displaying characters and objectives might also display a vertical relationship to the player. An up arrow could indicate that they are on higher ground than the player's current position, while a down arrow could indicate being lower. A standard icon, meanwhile, would demonstrate that they are at the same vertical level.

Component Positioning

One important aspect of a HUD component is its positioning. There are 10 basic positions that a HUD component might occupy: top left, top, top right, right, bottom right, bottom, bottom left, left, central, and entity relative. Most components occupy one of the four corner positions. Side positions are usually used to display taller UI elements that extend from the corners. Top and bottom positions are often used to display text messages.

The central position is not used for many components, as this is where the focus on the player character is in a third-person game or will be directly where a player is looking in a first-person viewpoint. Most components placed here would obscure the action. The main use of the central space is for targeting crosshairs, but it might also be used for button placement during a QTE sequence.

Entity-relative positions attach a component to a particular entity such as above a character's head or at the center of a volume.

The positioning of HUD components may be heavily influenced by the target audience. The preference for position is likely to be based on the way a person of a particular culture scans a page when reading. In the West we read from the top left of a page to the bottom right. In other cultures, such as in Japan, the page is often read from the bottom right to the top left. Thus, the placement of important HUD components is often biased to where the eye looks first. In the West components in the top left appear stronger, as we tend to look there first. In Japan most important HUD elements appear in the bottom right. Having the option to rearrange HUD elements may be of great benefit to games wanting to bridge the cultural divide.

The Death of the HUD?

HUDs have been around in games since the very start. Even *Pong* has a HUD to display the scores. However, many game designers feel that it detracts from the sense of immersion, so some games have tried to remove the HUD altogether. HUDs may also need to be removed to appeal to a wider market, as the complexity of many game HUDs is intimidating to the uninitiated.

Games such as *Ico* did this very successfully by removing the need for any visualization at all. Health does not exist; the only failure is to lose the girl to the shadows. Other games such as *Resident Evil* have not done away with health but instead reflect the status of the player character via animation and joypad vibration. As the avatar approaches death, it begins to walk with a limp while clutching its chest. The joypad begins to pulse like a heartbeat. This feedback is essential; otherwise, player death will be unexpected and seem arbitrary. Even with this feedback, it is important that access to an exact measure of health is still represented. In the case of *Resident Evil* this was tucked away as a pulse meter in the inventory, indicating with color just how close to death the avatar was. This is an added action depth that can frustrate many players.

A compromise is to have HUD components hidden for the majority of play and then slide into view when needed, only to disappear again once their use has been fulfilled. For example, a health bar might scroll onto screen when the player character is hit and then disappear once a few seconds without damage have elapsed.

PAUSE MENU

The pause menu's main purpose is to pause the game to allow players to eat, make a drink, or change the kid's nappies without losing their progress. A game that omits such a function is really not treating the player with respect. The pause menu can also provide a number of options to the player besides its main function:

> **Resume game:** Having been paused, the game should be resumed somehow. This might also be done with the same button that paused the game (usually the Start button).

Save game: Games that allow the player to save at any point require the player to enter the pause menu to initiate a save.

Load game: Giving the player the ability to load another saved game from within the pause game menu is very user-friendly, meaning users don't need to quit the current game and return to the main menu.

Restart level or mission: Often the player is given the ability to restart a level or the current mission in case things have gone horribly wrong.

Restart from last checkpoint or save: As well as restarting a whole level or mission, the player might also be given the option to restart from the last checkpoint or save.

Options: Having the ability to access the options screen once the level has loaded is truly lifesaving. Being able to adjust controls during gameplay should be essential, but all too often a player is forced to quit the level and return to the front end to make tweaks. This is simply crazy.

Quit to main menu: The final option of most pause game menus is to quit the current level and return to the main menu. This option should always prompt the users to make sure they did not select this option by accident.

INVENTORY SCREEN

Inventory management is often featured in action–adventure games. Often this is handled in a separate inventory screen that pauses the action while selections are made. Inventory screens are generally used in games where the inventory is more complex than a simple selection of the current item and where inventory management is required. This occurs when inventory space is limited or the player is able to equip his character or party of characters with more than one item at a time or party of characters. Possibly both systems may be in use.

Limited Space Inventory

Inventories with limited space are generally based around grids where the player must place objects of certain grid square size in an organized manner. There are two approaches to placement. There is the stack, where objects must be placed in the inventory in a certain order. Objects at the bottom cannot be swapped with objects above them. This can be very frustrating when trying to get an item out of the bottom. It's a bit too much like real life. The heap is a much freer system, where the player can rotate and drop objects in patterns and can easily select them as they are needed. This is a much more user-friendly system. *Resident Evil* uses this approach with great success.

The player has to discard objects when there is not enough space in the inventory to fit them.

Slot-Based Inventory

Slot-based inventories provide locations where objects of specific types can be placed—gloves on hands, for example. This system can either use a drag-and-drop system (which tends to be a little unwieldy with a joypad) or a replacement system. With a replacement system any object the player equips replaces any object that is currently equipped in that location.

Infinite Inventory

An infinite inventory system will only display a list of the available items. This list may get long, so some sorting and filtering functions may be extremely useful.

TREASURE OR EXPERIENCE SCREEN

Treasure or experience screens are used when a battle or objective has been completed. These are only used in turn-based RPGs, where they mark the end of the battle and show the players the treasure and experience they have accumulated from the fight.

MAP SCREEN

The map screen is a separate screen that pauses the game and shows the players their position in the world. Maps can be presented in many ways and in a variety of possible resolutions. The amount of information a map provides might vary drastically from game to game.

Auto-Mapping

In games where the environment requires easy navigation and where the game structure is very free flowing, such as *Grand Theft Auto*, the map screen will be fully open to the players from the outset, allowing them to see where they need to go. However, in many other games where you are going is generally not known. Where you have been might be important if there are branching routes that require backtracking (it is unlikely that purely linear games will require a map at all). In these instances an auto-mapping feature will most likely be required. This uncovers parts of the map according to where the players have ventured so far, so they know where they have been, but not where they are going. Consequently they know where they have not been.

Map Legend

The legend tells the player points of interest on a map. This is more likely to be useful in a free-roaming map, where it can be difficult at times to know where everything is. For example, in *Grand Theft Auto* it is often necessary to know where the nearest Spray Shop is to get away from the cops.

Looking at the main map is the easiest way of seeing exactly where something is located. *Grand Theft Auto: San Andreas* also offered the ability to lay a target icon down on the map that would then show up on the radar, allowing the players to pick their own objectives (a very useful feature in such a vast game world).

OBJECTIVES SCREEN OR QUEST LOG

The objectives screen or quest log is a record of any open objectives or quests and their requirements for completion. In games where objectives or quests are set, it is very important to be able to review these in case they were missed when originally set.

INFORMATION SCREENS

Information screens are used to record any useful information during the course of the game so the players can read or replay it if they missed it the first time. This may take the form of notes, sound clips, or videos. These may be tied in with a relevant metaphor, such as a notebook, dictaphone, or PDA, so that they make sense in the game world.

GAME HINTS

Game hints are clues or snippets of advice that are used to guide the players or help them when they get stuck. Hints can take many forms in the game world but are of two basic types: automatic and requested.

Automatic hints are triggered when certain events occur such as the player not completing a section after *x* number of attempts or on encountering a new game mechanic. Automatic hints can be frustrating to the player, particularly more-experienced players who are likely to not need hints as much.

Requested hints are those that the player must interact with for advice or hints to be given. *Super Mario 64* had a number of signposts placed around the environment that could be used to provide snippets of information. The problem with this is that by not using the relevant hint, players might miss information that could help them.

The presentation of these hints can have a large bearing on their perception by players. Text-based hints with button-press information are the simplest to implement but are generally the most intrusive and break the believability of the world. Another method is to have an advisor character who appears and hands out relevant information, such as the CODEC in *Metal Gear Solid*. Care must be taken to not make irritating advisors, such as the infamous *Microsoft® Office®* help assistant: the Paperclip.

Finally, advice might be given by characters or objects within the world itself, which runs the risk of being missed but maintains the fourth wall and doesn't break away from the believability of the world. It also tends to be the most expensive option in terms of time and necessary resources, needing VO, special animation, special objects, scripting, and so on.

CHARACTER ADVANCEMENT SCREEN

Character advancement is a mechanic that is almost essential to every RPG but often crosses into more mainstream games. Advancement screens are generally held in a similar place to inventory screens, in that the game needs to be paused to access them. The advancement screen allows the player to spend points to buy skills and so on. When a character receives enough experience to level up, the player should be notified so that he can enter the advancement screen. This is usually shown by an icon on screen or by having level-up text float up from the player character's head.

Some advancement systems are much more strict about where advancement can be performed, in that items or currency must be taken to specific characters to receive skills and attributes, or skill and attributes can only be altered on completion of the current level.

SAVE GAMES

Saving progress is an important aspect of game UI and can be performed in a variety of ways (although with a games console there are often memory restrictions that can have a large impact on just what can be saved):

Unlocking: Saves are only made on completion of a level. This level is then considered to be unlocked. Only one saved game is required for this, and the memory footprint is pretty small. This system should only be used where levels are quite small.

Profiles: Several save games may be used to allow several players to save their progress independently; otherwise, this system is similar to unlocking.

Autosaves: At various points in the level game data is automatically saved. This is done in safe locations, where there will be no danger of a broken save being created (as there would be when saving just as the player is about to die, causing a load/die cycle). The advantage of an autosave is that the player does not have to worry about saving during the course of play. However, when the player wants to stop play, it can be frustrating to not know when the last save was or where the next one will be.

Save points: A very popular console choice is to have save locations—often specific objects in the world that can be interacted with to create the save data. Each save is its own file, so as many can be saved as there is storage for them. These objects are scattered around safe areas in the level, where the player cannot be harmed while saving. Often AI will not follow or attack in these areas, to prevent broken save games.

Free-roaming saves: These allow the player to save anywhere; as many can be saved as the player wants. Free-roaming saves are often considered to be the most desirable. On a PC they are easy to implement, as the hard drive allows for large save game sizes. On a console they can be more problematic, as they generally require a save of the full game state; otherwise, everything will reset on loading. The other problem is that broken saves are very easy to create by saving at the wrong moment. This kind of problem can be overcome by making the player invulnerable for a short period after loading.

Save Game Data

The size of a game save is important, as data storage on the console tends to be limited. There are two approaches to save game data: player state and game state. Player state only needs to save information relative to the players' progress: how far they are in a level, how much health they have, ammo, score, and so on. Game state saves as much information about the game as possible, such as all player information, AI states, the state and position of objects, and so on. The player state saves take up far less room than full game state saves, but everything in the world is reset when loaded.

Tokenized Save Games

Tokenized saves are a dwindling technique for rationing the amount of saves the player can make, which we already discussed in the economics part of the book. The player must collect objects (tokens) in the world to be able to save the game. This means the player has to think carefully about when to save, adding the extra challenge of knowing when is the best time to save. This system is dwindling in popularity mainly because it is such an artificial method of introducing challenge and is not a particularly interesting challenge to beat. A better method is simply counting the number of saves made and perhaps offering rewards for completing the game with as few saves as possible. This offers choice to the players but does not constrict their play session.

Save Game Metaphors

Metaphor is often used in save point interfaces. A good example is the previously mentioned *Resident Evil* series, where players interact with a typewriter to record their progress. *Full Spectrum Warrior* also wraps the save game interface up in the game world, so that the soldiers call into base to give a reference for their location, rather than simply saving the game.

STORE OR MERCHANT SCREENS

Games that feature some form of currency will most likely have a store or merchant from which they can purchase items and possibly to which they sell items back. Two main functions are possible: buy and sell (though many systems will only have a buy option).

Buying Items

The interface for buying items is generally one of the following:

- **List of available items:** The player simply scrolls up and down the list to select items. Prices are displayed next to the item. The list may be separated into categories for easier browsing.
- **Store representation:** The shelves of the store are perhaps modeled and the player can cycle between the items. This method allows the player to see the item before purchasing it.

Selling Items

Where items can be sold, the player will be able to select items from inventory to sell to the store or merchant. This is generally done in one of two ways:

- **List of suitable inventory items:** Any items the player can sell are displayed in a list from which they can select items. The sale price is generally displayed next to the item.
- **Adapted inventory UI:** The normal inventory UI is brought up, but selecting items will sell them to the store or merchant. Prices are displayed when items are selected for sale.

Before selling an item, there is likely to be a message warning to ensure that the player is not selling an item by mistake (though for lesser items such as treasures this may not be necessary).

SUMMARY

An in-game interface such as a HUD may or may not be a requirement of your game, but it is certainly worth considering the ways you might want to impart game information to the player. Certain in-game interfaces, such as a pause menu, are a technical requirement for many console manufacturers. We covered a number of elements in this chapter:

- **HUD (head up display):** Information about the current game state displayed on screen during gameplay
- **Pause menu:** A menu that pauses the game and allows the player to select a number of options

Inventory screen: A screen that allows the players to adjust and inspect items in their inventories

Treasure or experience screen: A screen that displays treasure or experience the players have collected during their travels

Map screen: A screen that shows a map of the world that the player has explored

Objectives screen: A screen that recaps any objectives the player currently has outstanding

Advancement screen: A screen that shows a character's progress and allows the player to develop his character(s)

Game hints: Generally pop-up dialogs that give hints to the player as to how to progress

Store or merchant screens: Allow the player to trade with vendors in the game world

In-game interfaces are a reminder that we are playing a game, which is perhaps why some developers are seeking to remove them as much as possible. It is debatable whether it is a system we should embrace as part of our heritage or whether it is something we should phase out to appeal to wider audiences. In the end it comes down to the needs of the individual game.

PART

5

BALANCING

Balancing is the dark art of tweaking numbers and adjusting gameplay to make a game experience enjoyable. It is a vital stage in the creation of good gameplay. However, it is something that is often overlooked or not given the attention it deserves. Balancing plans should be started early in the game development process to allow them to mature and grow. A well thought out balancing plan will save a lot of headaches later on in the process.

The most important consideration in the process of balancing is ultimately creating a good game experience for the player. At the heart of all balancing lies the fact that the game designers must balance the game for their target audience, not for themselves. Ultimately the designers will have to imagine themselves in the player's shoes.

The first chapter in this part of the book explores the basic principles of game balance, from difficulty and player motivation to component balance. The second chapter looks at techniques that can be used to perform the act of balancing and produce a quality experience for the player.

CHAPTER

20

GAME BALANCE PRINCIPLES AND PRACTICE

In This Chapter

- Difficulty
- Motivation
- Component Balance

There is much more to game balancing than first meets the eye. The principles behind game balancing are still being explored, but several concepts have been examined in detail. These principles will continue to evolve as our understanding of games deepens.

There are three major balancing areas that will need addressing in any game:

- Difficulty
- Motivation
- Component balance

DIFFICULTY

One of the hardest aspects of game balancing to get right is difficulty, because difficulty is a very subjective area. The solution is to design for your target audience, so the first task of difficulty balancing is to establish what the limits of that audience are. With a difficulty model established, there are still many considerations to be made, such as how difficulty will ramp up during the course of play. A number of techniques can be used to make the game adjust to player abilities. A lot of variables and elements affect how difficult a game becomes for its players. The bulk of the difficulty in a game stems from its AI and the complexity of its puzzles.

Flow

Key to the creation of a well-balanced difficulty level for a game is the notion of flow. If you have read *Rules of Play* [SalenZimmerman04] or *21st Century Game Design* [BatemanBoon05], you may already be familiar with Csikzemtmihalyi's concept of flow. This studies the feelings people experience when performing a task, depending upon the level of challenge and the subject's level of skill in that task (see Figure 20.1).

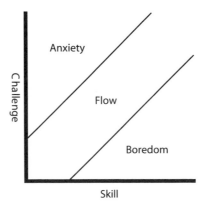

FIGURE 20.1   Csikzemtmihalyi's concept of flow.

The hypothesis states that a channel of flow exists that provides an optimal experience for the subject. The subject feels a high level of enjoyment and fulfillment when focused on the task at hand. Should the challenge become too hard, then flow is lost and anxiety begins to affect the subject. When the challenge becomes extreme, this anxiety may turn to frustration and even anger. Flow is also lost when the challenge is not great enough, as the subject becomes bored. Too slight a challenge results in apathy and, in the case of a game, probably a swift return to the game store.

Difficulty Settings and Dynamic Difficulty

To reach a wider audience, there are methods of offering players choice or adjusting the experience to suit the player's skills. The most popular method is to offer the player the choice of several difficulty settings. These usually take the form of easy, medium, and hard or similarly worded phrases that indicate the potential difficulty to the player. This poses a dilemma: how do the players know which difficulty setting suits them? If they choose the wrong difficulty setting, frustration or boredom could easily ensue.

Offering the option to change difficulty during play may satisfy their needs but it may not be immediately obvious to the player that the setting can be changed. *God of War* offers the player the choice of reducing difficulty after a certain number of deaths, but many players feel a sense of failure when they cannot rise to the challenge. Another major problem with difficulty levels is that the amount of testing required is significantly increased, as each setting will have to be thoroughly tested.

A more dynamic option is to tune the game difficulty to the player's skill level by adjusting difficulty parameters according to player performance. If the player is consistently performing well, difficulty can be increased to keep the challenge high enough to pique the player's interest. If the player is performing badly, difficulty can be lessened to eradicate frustration. The problem is trying to match the optimum level to fit the channel of flow for different players.

A good rule of thumb is the number of player deaths, as near-death experiences tend to heighten tension without introducing a high level of frustration and thus can be desirable. Casual players will probably not want to die in any particular area more than once or twice—any more than five and they might give up. For hardcore players this figure may be slightly higher. They may enjoy the higher level of challenge. It can perhaps be assumed that the higher the skill set, the more the challenge can be ramped up in a short space of time.

Another theoretical advantage of dynamic difficulty is that only one difficulty stream needs to be tested but will need to be approached via different play styles. It may turn out that dynamic difficulty actually requires more testing than static difficult settings.

Difficulty Parameters

There are a huge number of parameters involved in the difficulty level of a game, but many adjustments that increase difficulty might also increase the frustration for the player. Some aspects of game difficulty are much easier to tweak than others.

Combat

Combat is perhaps the easiest area to adjust difficulty, as there are a host of variables that can be adjusted with ease. However, some aspects can have serious implications on the feel of the game, so particular care needs to be taken when adjustments are made.

Damage and Health

The easiest and most immediately effective parameters to change are the damage values of attacks and the health values of characters. The ratio of damage to victim's health determines the duration of combat. The spread of damage values determines which attacks are most effective.

Care must be taken to not make enemies too weak or too strong. Enemies that are too weak will be too easily killed. Enemies that are too strong can be extremely laborious to kill. Differing attack values will reward the player for performing certain moves but may result in a dominant strategy (see later section on component balance). Enemies that perform strong attacks will encourage the player to be more cautious and thus will affect not only difficulty but also the way the player approaches the game.

The health level of the player is also a key element in defining difficulty. Little health may mean frequent death if there is not a steady supply of health replenishment. Conversely, too much health will remove challenge.

AI

Another popular area of game difficulty balancing is in the AI. Several parameters can be fine-tuned:

Aggression: An aggressive character will attack more frequently but not necessarily more efficiently.

Defensiveness: The more defensive capability an AI has, the better it is at dealing with incoming attacks. The way AIs handle an attack is also important. A character that counters more often than one that blocks will be more difficult to fight.

Attack choice: The types of attack that an AI makes will determine its efficiency at causing damage. Powerful, well-timed attacks will increase difficulty, as will more complex combo chains as opposed to single strikes.

Accuracy: Ranged-weapon-based enemies can be made more or less difficult very quickly by adjusting their accuracy.

Awareness: The ability of the AI to spot a player who is sneaking around can be adjusted. More alert characters or wider view cones will increase the player's need to remain hidden.

Tactics: The types of tactics that AI uses against the player will have a large impact on the difficulty. The effectiveness of these tactics can also be tweaked. For example, on hard difficulty levels a squad might try to remain hidden from the player and attempt to flank him.

These factors in combination allow the designer a wide range of possibility for game balance.

Movement Timing

It is perfectly feasible to increase difficulty by adjusting attack and hit reaction times to be longer or shorter. A longer player hit reaction would make it much harder, for example. This, however, is a very, very bad idea. Once a combat system has been balanced so that it plays well and all attacks and reactions are synchronized, it is not good to play with these, as it will ruin the entire feel of combat. If time is changed in any way, it should all be adjusted together relatively so it all speeds up together rather than going out of synch.

Item Placement

The placement of items may have a surprisingly large effect on difficulty, in particular, the placement of replenishment supplies such as ammunition, health, and armor. Judicious placement of items will keep the level of challenge just right. Not enough items will result in too great a challenge; too many will result in far too little challenge. The two approaches to item placement are predefined placement and dynamic "just-in-time" placement.

Predefined Placement

Predefined placement is the simpler of the two systems, but it requires much more conscious effort on the part of the designers. The designers must judge where to place items in the level according to where they think the items will be needed. This can be a very difficult art to master and requires extensive playtesting. One of the biggest problems with this system is that it has only one level of challenge represented. This can be solved to a limited degree by having different item placements for each difficulty setting, but this increases a designer's workload.

Dynamic Just-in-Time Placement

A different approach is to provide items as the player needs them. This has several benefits: the challenge can be adjusted to skill, the players will nearly always have what they need, and the pace of the game can be controlled by keeping the players on the edge of their seats with low health or ammo.

Determining when a player needs an item requires scrutiny of the player's inventory and current state. When the player is low on a particular ammunition, this can be spawned; when low on health, this can be provided. However, in certain sections the designer might want to purposely override what the player is given to force the player to use particular strategies. This can be achieved by giving weights to items. Triggers in the world can adjust these weights to the desired values in particular areas where gameplay demands it. For example, shotgun ammo weighting might be raised when in a very-close-quarters-fighting section.

Puzzles and Traps

Puzzles and traps are much harder to adjust for difficulty than other elements. Cerebral puzzles, in particular, are very difficult to adapt to different levels of challenge. However, elements of puzzles and traps can be adjusted to cater to different levels of challenge.

Time

Any puzzle or trap that involves a time limit is immediately open to adjustment. Allowing more time instantly reduces challenge, while reducing time increases challenge. There is an absolute point at which it becomes impossible to complete the challenge if there is not enough time, though this should never be the designer's target. There should always be some leeway to allow the player a chance of completion.

Consequence

The consequence of failure in many puzzles is a stop to progression, which is a game-terminating condition. The player must beat the puzzle to progress. With traps the consequence is usually damage or the loss of some commodity. This consequence can be balanced. Damage can easily be increased to boost challenge, even to the point of instant death for failure. Loss of a commodity is also a very simple element to balance.

Number of Elements or Complexity

The number of elements or the complexity of a puzzle or trap can be balanced but possibly with some difficulty. At the simple end of the scale, a puzzle for a code might require more numbers to complete. At the other end of the scale, it might be heavily tied into world geometry, for example, having four spinning discs to interact with instead of two. Changing elements such as these can have large impacts on the schedule and the environment team. However, that said, it is often easier to cut items out to reduce challenge than it is to add new elements to increase it.

Clues

Another method of balancing difficulty of puzzles and traps is to increase or decrease the number of clues given to the player. With a puzzle this might mean dumbing it down by making the answer almost obvious. A puzzle should never be obscure, but it can be made less difficult if enough information is given (without necessarily giving the answer away).

A trap can be made more obvious by giving more visual clues to its presence—short of sticking a great big signpost by it.

Difficulty Ramping

As a single-player game progresses, it is generally accepted that difficulty will ramp up. The obvious reason for this is that the player's skill in playing the game will increase, so the level of challenge will have to increase to meet that change.

Feedback Loops

Feedback loops are often used in games to balance the difficulty. Getting just the right amount of the right type of feedback ensures that the player is constantly kept at the right level of challenge [Adams02]. There are two forms of feedback loop: positive and negative.

Positive Feedback

Positive feedback is the increase of odds in favor of the player. As the player gets better or collects better equipment it becomes easier to defeat the enemy. This makes it easier to progress and get more commodities to become even more powerful. You can see that the more powerful a player becomes, the easier the challenge becomes. Positive feedback is an essential part of an eventual victory condition.

However, the speed of this positive feedback influences how quickly the challenge is overcome. If this feedback is too great, the challenge will eventually head into the realms of boredom. If this feedback is too little, the challenge will become too much.

Negative Feedback

Negative feedback is, as it suggests, the opposite of positive feedback—the move away from odds in the player's favor. This is used to temper the results of positive feedback. For example, in a single-player game the difficulty of the enemies will increase as the player's abilities increase. This keeps the level of challenge within the channel of flow. However, too much negative feedback will make the challenge too hard, and frustration will result.

Difficulty Phases

The amount of increase in difficulty is a tricky aspect to judge, as different people's skills naturally evolve at different rates. Many designers refer to a difficulty curve—a measure of the amount of challenge over the course of the game. This curve could be any shape but tends to follow a fairly steady increase. A good model is based on six phases of difficulty, as shown in Figure 20.2:

> **Learning phase:** The learning phase needs to hook the player and familiarize the player with controls. All too often this is done via an incredibly tedious tutorial. Learning should be fun, and if you don't hook players immediately, you could lose them. Get them into some limited form of action as soon as

possible and use this to teach them the basics. Puzzles and action will be simple in this phase, as core mechanics are gradually introduced.

Building phase: Once the basic core mechanics have been learned, these can now be layered to provide some more interesting challenges that require a mix of skills to overcome. The challenge starts to increase a little in areas the player has previously experienced.

Challenge phase: Now that the core mechanics and a variety of situations have been presented to the player, the challenge can really start to ramp up. This is the phase with perhaps the most dramatic change. For the first time the player is likely to feel a real sense of danger.

Mastered phase: The player has now mastered the nuances of the controls and feels comfortable with the game and starts to find strategies and solutions coming subconsciously. The difficulty starts to level out slightly as we enter the reward phase.

Reward phase: The player has now been playing for some time. Most, if not all, of the items in the game will be at the player's disposal. The player should now be made to feel powerful and very capable by leveling out the difficulty in preparation for the final challenge.

Final challenge phase: This often takes place as a boss fight but could be any more spectacular conflict than normal—perhaps a huge battle, for example. The final stage should be pretty challenging, as this is the finale of the game, but shouldn't be so ridiculously hard as to make the game almost impossible to complete. The player should have to work hard for the prize but not feel that it is a Herculean task.

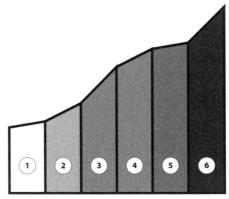

FIGURE 20.2   A six-phase difficulty curve.

Learning

One of the most important aspects of balance is easing the player into the game. The simpler a game is to learn, the faster the player will get to grips with playing it. However, if it is too simple, it will not hold the player's interest for long.

The Psychology of Learning

We can turn to psychology to study how people learn, and we can use this to work out better designs for games that let the beginner in but do not insult the expert.

Appetitive and Aversive Stimuli

The world around is a myriad of stimuli waiting to be experienced. The three senses of sight, hearing, and touch (through the control pad) are being constantly barraged with information—stimuli—during play. There are two different types of stimuli that a player can experience:

Appetitive stimuli: Positive stimuli that the player enjoys. In a game this will be the reward of completing a task, beating an enemy, completing a level, finding a secret—anything that is fun or rewarding for the player.

Aversive stimuli: Harmful or unwanted stimuli that the player does not enjoy. This can be loss of health, bad play, death, traps—anything that stops the player's progress or is frustrating. Even good things can become aversive; for example, someone who has had too much to eat will become sick. As a gaming parallel, this might equate to using the same gameplay over and over. It can become boring once players have had their fill.

Both types of stimuli promote learning. If we are rewarded for our actions, we will feel more compelled to perform those actions again in the future. If we are punished for our actions, we will be less likely to want to repeat those actions.

The designer should seek to introduce plenty of appetitive stimuli but must remember that aversive stimuli must also remain to add to the sense of danger. Play in a world where there is no risk or conflict has no sense of drama. The players may be happy setting their own goals and challenges for a while, but the conflict is really needed to drive them forward—particularly in story-based games.

The secret to good gameplay is to minimize the impact of aversive stimuli so that they present the danger but have none of the frustration.

Vicarious Learning

Vicarious learning is observing the behavior of others in order to learn. This is a very important human trait, as we all observe those around us in order to pick up experience, whether it is our parents, teachers, or peers.

Like all learning processes, the results of positive and negative responses have different effects on the observer. A positive effect on the subject is likely to encourage the observer to copy his actions. A negative effect is likely to prevent the observer from doing the same. An observer will go through four processes when learning this way:

Attentional processes: Observing what is happening.

Retention processes: Retaining the information that has been observed. Too much information at once will be difficult to retain.

Production processes: Modeling the observed behavior and applying it to one's own situations. The observations need to be clear enough for the observer to form these observations, or else they may miss the clue or simply not get it.

Motivational processes: Determining the results of the modeling as positive or negative.

Learning from others in games is essentially the act of a tutorial or giving the player hints. This can be done in obvious ways, such as a set series of goals within a tutorial framework, or it can be done in more subtle ways, via other characters in the game and their actions.

The Learning Curve

The learning curve is a conceptual element that is used to describe the initial stages of interaction with all kinds of interfaces. Within the context of a game it describes how quickly the player is able to get a handle on the core mechanics and to develop a degree of aptitude in controlling the game and the avatar. A typical learning curve shows the amount of knowledge and ability that the player gains over time (see Figure 20.3).

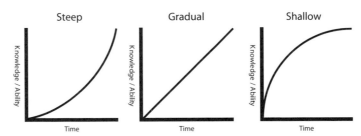

FIGURE 20.3   Potential learning curves.

Ideally the curve for a new player should be as shallow as possible. Experienced gamers find long learning phases to be particularly boring. Often it is a good idea to make the learning process optional or throw players straight into the action and offer advice as it is needed. Several elements affect the player's ability to learn:

Complexity of the interface: The most immediate hurdle the players must overcome is starting the game through the front end. The most important hurdle, however, is learning to control their avatars. The level of complexity of these interfaces will determine how quickly the player can begin to enjoy the game. For players new to gaming, a control pad can be very daunting, so they need to be eased into using it. A hardcore game player will be very experienced at using the pad and will be able to deal with a lot of complexity fairly quickly. Familiarity helps here. If the control scheme is similar to games that a player has experienced before, then the curve will be a lot shallower (of course, there is no way to know what games a person might have played).

Game language: Games have been around for a number of years, and during that time a number of conventions have developed for abstracting particular mechanics. Those who play a lot of games have come to understand these nuances and accept them as part of the language of gaming, but newcomers often find them very confusing. The system of lives and continues may frustrate and confuse new gamers, as it is an abstraction born out of the arcade era. Many of these old conventions that were created for technological or contextual reasons need to be buried if the games market is to attract new audiences.

Instruction: A good method of teaching the player the interface is to offer instruction or tutorials on how to perform particular actions. For the beginner these are essential to the learning process. To an expert gamer these can often be extremely irritating. The solution is to either make the tutorial optional or to be able to turn the instruction system off. Instruction could even be made dynamic so that it determines when the player might need guidance, perhaps when they are having difficulty performing a particular action.

MOTIVATION

What keeps players playing a game? Something must drive them to keep their hands on the joypad, keep their eyes on the screen, and keep the smiles on their faces. A good game elicits a feeling in the player that they must keep going—just a little bit further or just one more go.

This is achieved by "dangling a carrot," providing reward to the player. *In Rules of Play* Salen and Zimmerman [SalenZimmerman04] show us the work of Hallford and Hallford that defines several types of reward:

Rewards of glory: That feeling we get when we achieve something. Glory that is hard won can create real feelings of elation (known as fiero).

Rewards of sustenance: Giving a reward that replenishes lost health or ammunition. Sustenance enables the players to keep going on their quests.

Rewards of access: Exploration, the thrill of being somewhere new, and discovering what it has to offer. The treat of some visual splendor.

Rewards of facility: Receiving rewards that progress skills or abilities so that a character becomes stronger or receives a weapon that facilitates new attacks.

Scheduled Reward

A scheduled reward is that placed to keep player interest high, offering new gifts at particular intervals to keep them playing the game. How often these gifts are given is a delicate balancing issue that impacts on difficulty. Give too many gifts, and it can become too easy; don't give any, and player motivation can suffer.

The type of reward has a large impact on this. Two rewards can be given frequently with little impact on difficulty: Glory and Access.

Rewards of sustenance have a large impact on difficulty, but a good sense of urgency is achieved by only giving such rewards when they are needed. Rewards of facility should be the rarest. Gifts of this nature should be given on only a handful of occasions in the game. Rewards of facility usually require some form of risk to be taken in order to acquire them.

Risk and Reward

Life is full of risk and reward—playing the stock market, for example. Risk and reward is a concept that translates well to a gaming paradigm. Risk is a natural part of gameplay, as there needs to be conflict to keep the player interested. However, risk and reward structure tends to be used as a choice rather than as part of the main game progression. By placing a desirable item in a hard-to-reach location, the player is forced to make a decision, to choose whether taking the item is worth the risk. The balance is in knowing how much of a reward should be given for an appropriate risk.

Risk can have one of two outcomes: certain and uncertain. A certain outcome is one where all the relevant information is known and the player can make a calculated risk. An uncertain outcome arises when not all information is known or there is an element of chance involved. It is a gamble.

To achieve a calculated risk, both the risk and reward need to be immediately transparent to the player. Communicating the reward to the players means indicating exactly what they would receive for their efforts. If a standard language has been described, then this should be a simple task, as the player will instantly recognize the laid out items. Communicating the risk means being able to show the player the consequence of failure, whether this be damage, death, or loss of a commodity. Damage and death are fairly easy to convey, but it is more difficult to explain the loss of a commodity. Again a strongly established visual language will help; for example, a shimmering blue translucent wall represents a magic shield that will drain magic points.

Uncertainty arises when either risk or reward, or even both, are ambiguous. Let's say that rewards are placed in chests, so the player has no idea whether the reward is worth the potential risk. Disguising risk can be trickier, as it can present unfair damage and death. The player should have some information as to a potential danger, even if consequence is not immediately apparent.

Finally, the reward should match the potential risk, especially if uncertain, as the player may feel cheated if a large risk results in little payoff.

One balancing issue arises from reward—that of stockpiling items. If players stockpile a lot of items early in the game, it can make them much more powerful later in the game, and thus they will find it easier. One preventative method is to have a limited inventory system so players are only able to carry a limited number of objects. Alternatively, restrictions can be placed on the amount of each item that can be carried. This places much more control in the hands of the designer, but it is difficult to explain the reasons for these restrictions to the player.

COMPONENT BALANCE

Component balance is the task of juggling numbers to make each object and skill in the game work in relation to other objects and skills. This can be an incredibly complex challenge.

Dominant Strategies

The key to component balance is to ensure that there are no dominant strategies or golden paths—situations where one strategy completely invalidates all others or removes any sense of challenge.

A dominant strategy arises when a skill or item is too powerful. This issue is fairly easy to guard against with extensive playtesting. Another form of dominant strategy occurs when a logic error causes an exploitation to exist that players can take advantage of. This is often called a degenerate strategy. Degenerate strategy exploitations often occur against AI characters, where they have little defense against particular strategies, which can then be repeated ad infinitum. Unless the AI can learn from its error, it is doomed to fall victim to this strategy again and again. The key to solving such problems is extensive playtesting.

Component Relationships

Conflict-based components have relationships that determine the outcome of a conflict. This is often the case in melee combat systems, where different components clash to determine a result.

The simplest and most immediate relationship is winner and loser. Whenever a conflict between these two components arises, one will always win out over the other. This can easily be extended with the notion of a draw—neither component coming out on top. In a combat system this might represent an unguarded attack, a block, and a counter (lose, draw, and win for the victim of an attack or win, draw, and lose for the attacker). A simple model for this is the game rock, paper, scissors [RollingsAdams03]. A cyclic model of relationships exists where each component beats the other (see Figure 20.4).

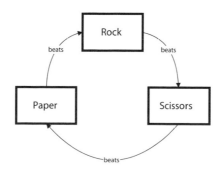

FIGURE 20.4   The cyclical nature of rock, paper, scissors.

Adding another component quickly increases the complexity of the dynamic, so that there are now situations where a draw is possible. Let's say we had a magical element system based around fictional elements: air, ice, fire, and earth (see Figure 20.5).

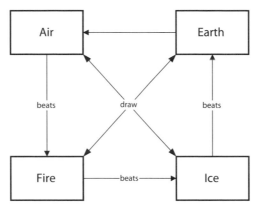

FIGURE 20.5   The relationship between four elements.

Moving much higher than a four-component relational system is likely to cause confusion for players, as there are not clearly defined, simple to understand relationships.

Redundancy

Redundancy occurs when items are replaced in their usefulness by a new item that renders the old items' functions obsolete. This frequently occurs in weapon- and equipment-based games as newer and better weaponry and equipment is found or bought. Redundancy may not be an issue, but if not considered can result in a form of dominant strategy, where the newest weapon or item is always the best to use.

Redundancy can be easily solved by ensuring that the function of each component is unique, so that every weapon or item will still have a use even when the new item has been collected. Another method is to provide limited opportunity for use of better weaponry or equipment by not supplying a large number of replenishment items such a component might require.

Player Relationships

In multiplayer games the relationships between players are extremely important. The balance between players is either symmetric or asymmetric.

In a symmetric relationship every player is on a level playing field. They all have the same abilities. This means it is pure skill that will decide the victor. If all players have the same skill level, this can result in a balanced game, but most players will have differing levels of skill, which can result in different game experiences for each player. Winners will probably enjoy the game unless it is too easy, whereas losers are likely to feel like the challenge is too great.

Asymmetric relationships mean that the player character abilities or parameters are not equal. This can be the result of different choices available to the players or handicaps applied according to skill. Where choice is concerned, each element of choice must have advantages and disadvantages that balance out so that there is no dominant strategy. Handicaps are applied to place players at similar relative skill levels, so that less-skilled players are able to compete. Bear in mind that asymmetric relationships often require much more playtesting than symmetric ones to ensure that there are no dominant or degenerate strategies with any particular choice.

Economic Balance

The various economies in the game (score, currency, health, etc.) will all need balancing in relation to one another. This economic balance can be a tricky task to perform, depending on how complicated a system you might want to create.

There are two forms of economic systems in games:

Closed: There is a set amount of resources and commodities and therefore limits on each economic element.

Open: There is not a set amount of resources and they can accumulate. Such a system represents a more realistic view of a real-world economy but is much harder to balance. RPGs often have open economy systems.

Worth

One of the most important aspects of balancing an economy is establishing the relative worth of all its components. Worth is a subjective element. Several aspects can be used to determine the worth of a component:

Game impact: The most immediate measure of worth is the impact the component will have on the game.

Lifetime: The duration of a component determines how far reaching the game impact will be.

Range: The spatial limits of how the component can be used will also affect the game impact.

Aesthetic quality: The desirability of looks, sounds, and so on of the component if it has physical form may also determine its worth but to a lesser degree.

Game Impact

The most important factor in establishing an object's worth is its impact on the game. Every component within the world will give some form of benefit or ability to its user or negative effects on its victims. To establish the impact of an item, its main purpose needs to be examined and compared with other components of similar use. Each component type therefore has different balancing elements associated with it.

Weapons and Attacks: The main purpose of a weapon or attack is to inflict damage on an opponent. Therefore, to measure the worth of a weapon or attack, its efficiency at causing damage should be measured—expressed as potential damage per second.

However, once this figure has been determined, it needs to be considered in relation to health in order to establish how quickly a target would perish.

Melee Attacks: Melee attacks are either single actions or strings of actions chained together and should be considered both in isolation and as a whole to establish the worth of each (and identify any potential dominant strategies).

The potential damage per second (D) of a melee attack can be expressed as

$$D = \frac{\sum_{n=1}^{N} s_n}{N} \times \frac{\sum_{n=1}^{N} d_n}{\sum_{n=1}^{N} t_n} \tag{20.1}$$

where:

d = damage value of each attack
t = time for each action
s = simplicity of the action (from 0 to 1)
N = total number of moves

The simplicity value is very subjective. Moves with complicated patterns will have a low value. Single button presses will equate to a value of 1. Few actions should have simplicity values below 0.5 unless they are extremely complicated to perform.

Melee Weapons: Melee weapons' worth might be based on the basic attacks with a few modifiers to describe aspects of the weapon. Thus, our calculation might look like

$$D = dWS \tag{20.2}$$

where:

d = damage value of a basic attack
W = weapon strength
S = speed factor of the weapon (a number from 0 to 1)

The speed factor describes how much (as an average) the character will be slowed by using this weapon as opposed to using a standard weapon.

Projectile Weapons: Calculating a weapon's damage per second is a good method for balancing weaponry. It allows us to compare and contrast the relative effectiveness of each weapon. First we need to find the fire time for a full magazine and then the full damage for a magazine. With these two figures, we can calculate the potential damage per second.

The complete calculation is shown below:

$$F = H(Md)$$

(20.3)

where:

d = damage of each projectile
M = magazine size
f = fire rate of the weapon (number of projectiles per second)
R = reload time
T = firing time
H = hit chance (as a value between 0 and 1)
F = full damage for a magazine

With a projectile weapon, we must always remember that its worth will also be affected by its maximum range.

Defense: When calculating the defense worth of a component, the potential threat the subject might face must first be established. This threat rating is based on number of attackers and the potential damage they can inflict. Thus, the potential damage received (R) from each attacker can be calculated by

$$R = a\left(\sum_{n=1}^{\infty} D_n\right)$$

(20.4)

where:

a = aggressiveness of the enemies (as a value between 0 and 1).
D = potential damage per second of the attacker

Armor (A) will protect against damage, so to find its worth it can be a good idea to find the difference between the potential damage per second without that armor and the potential damage with that armor, as follows:

$$A = R - R_A$$

(20.5)

where:

R = potential damage received per second
R_A = potential damage received per second with armor

These can then be compared against other armor ratings to determine how much worth the armor has.

Potentially armor can be restricted to work only with particular types of damage. If this is the case, then worth is determined by the number of threats the player will face during the course of the game that will utilize that form of damage. If there are very few threats that cause that kind of damage, the worth of the object will be far less, even if its impact in that situation is extreme (e.g., immunity to that damage).

The worth of armor is also influenced by negative effects such as any slowdown in a character as a result of the weight.

ON THE CD

The file Balance-Worth.xls on the companion CD-ROM is an example spreadsheet that shows how these calculations might be employed to determine the worth of components in the game world.

Attributes: Character progression is a great way to get players to input emotional investment, but it also poses a number of potential balancing issues. When attributes are increased, this will instantly have knock-on effects to all systems that utilize that attribute.

When considering balance for character attributes, it is first essential to establish all of the systems that will be affected by any changes. These affected systems can be more numerous than first expected. Take, for example, strength. Its primary use is likely to be in combat, but it might also factor in lifting, pushing, or other skills.

With each system established, the designer should then calculate the changes brought about by this increase. The impact of these changes determines the worth of the attribute increase.

Skills, Abilities and Equipment: Unlike many other components, skills, abilities, and equipment often offer functionality that wasn't available before their introduction. Therefore, they have an immediate worth. However, that worth is very much dependent on the skill it provides and the use of that skill within the game.

Let's say, for example, that our player character gains a set of night-vision goggles that allow him to see in the dark. In a game like *Splinter Cell*, where sneaking around avoiding enemies in the cover of darkness is the main game mechanic, their worth is extremely high. If the game has no darkness in it, they are useless and hence pretty much worthless (except for perhaps a little novelty value).

Support Items: These are not too difficult to determine worth for, as they are fixed elements. Each item will provide a particular benefit such as replenishing health, casting a status effect, and so on. Because each item has a predefined function, its worth is based purely on the effects of that function. Thus, a health potion that cures all health will naturally be worth more than one that only replenishes a few points.

Status Effects: Status effects are measured by the bonus or the detrimental impact they have on the subject. As such, the type of effect will have slightly different methods of measurement. Status effects are very heavily influenced by their duration, which will determine the real impact of that component.

> **Boost/Weaken:** Will either raise or lower the potential damage that attacks and weapons will perform. Therefore each weapon and attack needs to be looked at for its new potential damage per second.

> **Protect/Curse:** Will either raise or lower the potential damage that a subject can receive. Therefore, potential damage of attackers will need to be considered to see how quickly the subject could die.

Haste/Slow: Will either raise or lower the speed at which the subject moves. This alters the potential damage per second that they can inflict but also changes their ability to avoid enemy attack and thus also alters the potential amount of damage per second they can receive (though this is dependent on them not avoiding the attacks).

Regenerate/Poison: These opposing status effects both affect the potential damage per second that the subject can receive but need to be considered separately. Poison adds a guaranteed damage per second on top of any potential damage per second, so subjects will die much more quickly. Regenerate, on the other hand, adds health per second. The difference between this and potential damage of attackers per second then determines an overall damage received per second, which could easily equate to actually being an overall gain.

Scores: So far we have considered very physical components, but there are more abstract constructs within games that also have some kind of worth. One of these is score. Establishing the worth of a score is pretty simple. One point or set of points (they might be grouped in tens for example) should be worth the most basic action that will achieve a score. From this basic action the other more complicated actions can be assigned scores based on their increasing complexity.

Lifetime: One limiting factor of game impact is the lifetime of the component. The worth of an item is severely affected by the lifetime of its use.

Permanent: The most valuable lifetime is a permanent game impact, as from that point on the impact will remain.

Timed: If the component has a limited time of use or existence before it expires, its worth will depend on the length of time it is useful for.

Limited use: The component may only be used a limited number of times before it expires (often only once). The number of uses will help determine its worth.

Burst: The component may be used in bursts before it has to be replenished in some way, either by not using it or by requiring an external feed such as collecting more bullets for a gun.

Range: A component can have a very large game impact, but if it has a very limited range, that impact is minimized to a degree. The range of use for a component therefore has an effect on the worth of that component. Not every component is affected by range. For example, support items can generally be used anywhere.

The range of a component is relative to the space in which it will be used. For example, a shotgun that fires a wide spread of shot will be very effective in tight areas where there are very few encounters that are at long range. However, in a space with lots of wide open areas its use is much more limited and hence its worth would be much less.

Aesthetic Quality: In real-life we place worth on objects of all kinds. Many have practical utility, and others are just aesthetically pleasing to us, such as precious metals and gem stones. In a game there may be a number of items that are valued for their aesthetic quality as well as their function. Some items are even valued for their aesthetic quality alone.

Desirable Items: These serve only as an item to acquire, perhaps a hat that the avatar can wear. The worth of these items is purely arbitrary and based on opinion and tastes of the designers assigning values to them.

Trading Items: The worth of a trading item is extremely subjective and is generally some arbitrary figure plucked out of thin air. However, this worth has an important significance, as it will translate into a monetary value that can be used to purchase other items. Therefore, worth should be considered to fit within the cost of the items that have game impact and the frequency of occurrence of the trading item within the world, specifically focusing on how the item is acquired. The harder a player has to work or the greater the risk taken to get an item, the more worth it should have. Deciding which items are worth more should depend on the setting of the game. Let's say we have a fantasy game where you can collect animal hides. In this world there are plenty of rabbits and lots of dragons, but unicorns are extremely rare. Rabbit hides would be worth very little, as they are abundant and are easy to procure. There are lots of dragons, but they put up more of a fight than a lowly rabbit, so their hides are worth considerably more. However, because unicorns are so rare, their hides are by far the most highly prized and are therefore worth a small fortune.

Cost

Cost will immediately suggest currency, and while many games do use currency, cost can be applied to a number of other elements, most of which actually determine its worth. Therefore, there are really two basic types of cost for any component:

Intrinsic: The costs that have an impact on the functionality of the component and therefore affect its worth

Extrinsic: The commodity cost applied to an object to indicate its worth within the system as a whole

Intrinsic costs will be balanced based on the impact on the game rather than the impact on the items' monetary value. Thus, when we consider cost in this section we are really looking at the component's extrinsic cost—a monetary value.

When creating a monetary system, the first task is to determine what one unit of currency is worth. We must decide what one florin or one dollar will purchase in our world. Next we consider applying prices based on our model of either a closed or open economic system.

A closed economic system will generally have fixed prices, although different merchants or stores might offer different prices on different goods. Balancing a closed economy is pretty simple. Assign prices to each of the items as a whole or price them for each merchant or store. If you are to have different prices at various merchants or stores, then one area where you need to be careful is ensuring that there are no easy farming items available, meaning an item that is cheap to buy in one place and sells for a higher price in another. Otherwise, the player can easily earn cash by journeying between the two. Of course, if the two places are miles apart, or there is some cost associated with traveling, this is much less of a problem.

An open economic system obeys the laws of supply and demand and thus prices for goods will fluctuate over time. Implementing this kind of system can be time consuming and potentially unsettling for game balance but does offer great reward for the players, as they can use the laws of economics to their advantage, resulting in trading-based gameplay. The inherent problems in this system are ensuring that there is never too much or too little money available at any one point, so that the player advances too fast or too slow and breaks the channel of flow for the rest of the game.

Economic Feedback Loops

We have already discussed feedback loops in relation to difficulty, but they can also be used for economic balance, particularly in respect to multiplayer scoring.

Positive feedback loops: In multiplayer games positive feedback can often be undesirable. If characters become more powerful as they win, it will make it easier for them to win in the future. This creates runaway leaders in a match.

Negative feedback loops: Negative feedback in a multiplayer game is a fairly desirable way of evening out the field, so that winning players are perhaps handicapped in some way to allow the other players to catch up. This will result in much closer matches, but too much negative feedback can result in stalemates and wild swings in the lead.

SUMMARY

We have examined the basic principles of game balance in this chapter, so we are now able to look at aspects of our game design and ways to refine and improve the gameplay.

There are several elements of game balance:

Difficulty: The level of challenge that a player will face. We explored a number of aspects of difficulty:

- **Flow:** The channel of flow that prevents players from being bored or frustrated. Too little challenge will result in boredom, too much in frustration.
- **Difficulty setting and dynamic difficulty:** The use of particular difficulty settings as opposed to a system that automatically adjusts to suit the player's skill.
- **Difficulty parameters:** The elements that will affect difficulty, namely combat, item placement, puzzles, and traps.
- **Difficulty ramping:** The increase in difficulty over the course of the game.

- **Learning:** The psychology of learning as well as the learning curve that might be employed in a game.

Motivation: The rewards handed out to the player to keep them motivated in moving toward the final goal. Rewards can take the form of glory, sustenance, access, and facility.

- **Scheduled reward:** The spread of reward across the game to keep the player interested.
- **Risk and reward:** The potential risks posed to the player to match the reward that might be offered. This encourages the player to make a choice.

Component balance: The relationship between game elements will have a dramatic impact on the playability of the game.

- **Dominant strategies:** Imbalanced systems will have exploits that enable one strategy to win out over the others.
- **Component relationships:** The system of what relationship one component has to another.
- **Redundancy:** The process of one component making a previously useful component redundant and the steps that can be taken to avoid this.
- **Player relationships:** The relationships of players in multiplayer games—either symmetrical or asymmetrical.
- **Economic balance:** A look at ways of determining component worth and cost as well as looking at economic feedback loops.

In the next chapter we will look at ways of applying these basic principles to the game to perform the act of balancing.

THE ACT OF BALANCING

In This Chapter

- Preparation
- Game Walkthrough
- Spreadsheet Modeling
- Paper Prototyping
- Playtesting

Knowing the principles of how to balance a game is all well and good, but when it comes to practical application of these principles, it can be uncharted territory. Different designers will use their own techniques for establishing game balance. Much of the process may be determined by the game's target audience.

Luckily there are a number of tried and tested techniques for ensuring that the balancing process goes as smoothly as possible:

- Preparation
- Game walkthrough
- Spreadsheet modeling
- Paper prototyping
- Playtesting

PREPARATION

The bulk of balancing work is often done once content has been completed, but long before the final balancing process even begins, it is helpful to make sure that the game is ready to be balanced.

During production there will inevitably be tweaks made here and there to make the game feel right. With different members of the team working on different aspects at any one time, the result is a mishmash of balance ideals. They may get the game into a state where it feels right, but each element may be totally out of balance with everything else.

Establishing early balance values and keeping them consistent across elements will ensure a clean slate from which to balance and a good idea of exactly how each gameplay segment is working.

Game elements do not generally exist in isolation. They are interrelated with many other game elements. Changing one element has a knock-on effect, which might not even be known about. Establish early what knock-on effects there will be and huge problems in the later stage of development will be avoided.

Another important issue concerns inconsistent abstractions and runaway complexity. Often, over the course of the project, little elements are studied in isolation or simply built in as the game progresses. The result is a mess of different elements that do not work well together or are inconsistent. Good communication is an essential part of making sure everyone on the team knows exactly how elements should work together and ensures that there aren't multiple solutions to the same problem.

GAME WALKTHROUGH

The game walkthrough is a technique we have used when balancing games in the past, which involves mapping out the whole game and determining targets for specific sections of the game. This process is used to build the first balancing pass of the game in order to get an initial structure in place. This technique works particularly well when a level of character progression is involved.

First, the game is broken down into every possible stage—every quest, mission, and combat encounter. These are all written out in summary form. Next, target values are assigned across the game, such as the desired character level, score, commodity amount, or items at particular points in the game. This is especially important for doling out experience points. With these targets set, the sharing of values can be made over each combat encounter, puzzle, and so on. With a rough value for each element, the individuals in a scene can then be attributed with values, such as applying experience values to each type of monster. This should indicate the increase in difficulty as the game progresses. There is likely to be a lot of number juggling on paper at this point before anything is even implemented.

The next task is to imagine playing the game as the absolute best player and the worst, to see how distribution of rewards occurs for each of them. It is likely that high-scoring players will be well ahead of lower-scoring players at this point. This may be fine in an arcade experience, but not as good in a character-leveling environment. In this sort of situation, the best players will quickly outclass the challenge of the game.

The solution is to stagger the targets for character levels, so that each successive level requires ever more points to achieve. Each section of the game provides points that allow players to access the desired level fairly easily, but makes it difficult to achieve the next stage. Players will need to move on to the next stage to progress more quickly. This prevents reliance on farming—continually replaying an easier section of the game to build up points and progress further. Another technique for making farming less rewarding is to offer less and less reward each time the same section is replayed. It soon becomes futile to remain in that section and forces the player to move on. Bear in mind, though, that some players do find farming rewarding, so don't be overzealous in trying to crack down on this practice.

The game walkthrough should never be taken as gospel and set in stone, as there will be a mass of issues that come out of playtesting. No one is able to balance an entire game in their head—at least not a complex computer game.

Spreadsheet Modeling

Spreadsheet modeling is the act of creating prototypes of various game systems to get a view of how data behaves with different values plugged in. Any numerical systems can be tested in this manner, though it may require a little bit of spreadsheet knowledge to get up and running. This technique allows the designers to have an overview of every variable and tweak numbers to create a result. It allows the designers to easily compare numbers and different results. The result of this is the ability to fine-tune aspects of the game without having to load the game each time.

The technique's restriction to numeric values means its use is limited. It's not viable or even desirable to try to model the whole game. It is most suited to the following types of system:

Combat: Setting attack damage values against health values or enemies
Character progression: Calculating damage and so forth as attributes increase
Experience: Calculating experience values of enemies for the game walkthrough
Economy: Calculating prices of goods and distribution of wealth across the game
New stat-based systems: Prototyping new game mechanics that use numeric values

We highly recommend using this kind of approach, as it allows balancing to be done with a very quick turn around, but it must be remembered that it is not a suitable substitute for playtesting!

PAPER PROTOTYPING

Paper prototyping is extremely useful for strategy-based games as a method of testing underlying mechanics, but it has rather a limited use for action–adventure games. The concept is to create a board, card, dice, token, or similar game that represents much of the underlying mechanics. You can probably see why it is not so suited to action–adventure, as it does not represent any of the interaction mechanics that make such games fun. However, it can be useful to create paper prototypes for specific systems such as combat or magic. Basically, the paper prototype can represent different attacks with cards or tokens, use dice to represent random numbers, and use the underlying formulas that drive these systems (as long as they are not too complex).

The advantage of a paper prototype is quick, cheap iteration that allows the designer to get an idea of how well the system works and how well any formulas hold up. It is unlikely that such a prototype will be great fun to play like a strategy prototype, but it does give the designers a good base to build from.

PLAYTESTING

Playtesting is the real meat of game balancing. This is where the vast majority of data will be collected for the designers to use and abuse as they deem necessary.

We talked earlier about two forms of playtesting: internal and formal. Internal playtesting has a huge impact on game balancing, as the designers need to repeatedly play the game to get a feel for it. However, they are often so deep in the development of the game that they don't spot some of the glaring problems of game balance. Plus, most game developers are pretty competent gamers. It is becoming more and more indispensable to have a formal playtesting procedure to gather a lot of data.

The types of data that come out of playtesting that are useful for balancing are extensive. They are split into two types: empirical and player feedback.

Empirical Data

Empirical data is gleaned from observing and recording player actions. This provides a lot of potential data:

Death hotspots: Areas where the players die often

Low-health hotspots: Places where players struggle to find health or other replenishments

Attack usage: Which attacks are used most often

Weapons: Which weapons are used most

Experience: How much experience a player has by a certain point

Area time: The amount of time a player spends in each area

Cash: How much money players spend and accumulate and what they spend it on

Potentially limitless amounts of data could be exhumed, but it is the use of this data that is important. Each of these data types can provide a view of a different aspect of game balance However, the manner in which a designer reacts to this data is also important.

Looking at weapon or attack usage can very quickly point out areas of imbalance or indicate possible dominant strategies. Generally a good spread of use will indicate they are well balanced in regard to each other and people will naturally have favorites. However, if there is a very large bias to the use of a particular attack or weapon, it is fairly safe to assume that it is too powerful. This is not always so easy to determine.

At first glance, a section where the player is dying a lot would seem to be too hard, and often this will be the case. However, this is not a problem if the challenge is particularly enjoyable. The key here is that we also need to look at user feedback in regard to any decisions we make that aren't immediately obvious.

One very important aspect of a formal playtest is to not offer the player hints or advice. The whole point is to determine how the player who buys the product will cope with the game without any external intervention.

Player Feedback

Formal playtests are a pretty time-consuming task. This shouldn't be done by designers, as they will be far too busy to be able to sit through reams of videos. Many top publishers have entire departments dedicated to producing "usability" studies on games that are then presented to the development team. Some publishers use this data to force changes onto the game. This can be dangerous. Designers should have the final say on this score and be able to use the data to balance without being forced just because data might indicate a trend—unless, of course, these data point out blatant flaws in the current balancing scheme. It is also vital that formal playtesting is performed on the target audience, not an audience that will not identify with the product.

Two forms of feedback can be useful: observed feedback and interviewed feedback. Observed feedback is taken by filming the subject playing the game. This can elicit a lot of information about how players are feeling when playing the game by their body language and the way they react. Interviewed feedback is taken by asking the players how they feel about certain aspects of the game—if they found a certain section enjoyable and why they found it so. The problem with interviewed feedback is that responses from people tend to be rather ambiguous. They may be trying to please or may be being purposely obtuse in their answers.

With both user feedback and empirical data, the designer should be able to make informed decisions about balancing choices. It is advisable to have a number of successive formal playtesting sessions to refine the balance of the game.

SUMMARY

The act of balancing can initially be daunting to the new designer, but once you have balanced a few games you start to create your own methods and style of game balance. We examined a number of ways of balancing during the course of this chapter:

- **Preparation:** Much of the initial game balance may be performed as the game is slowly being developed. However, most games don't really come together until the very end of the project.
- **Game walkthrough:** A method of performing a virtual playthrough and setting desired targets at particular points. The elements needed to get to these points can then be adjusted across the game.
- **Spreadsheet modeling:** The use of spreadsheets to set up simulations of game systems and get an idea of the numbers that will provide the desired results.
- **Paper prototyping:** The act of building a model of the game or a particular aspect of the game on paper so that it can be played out.
- **Playtesting:** The act of getting information from playtesters to get data that will improve the game. This will come from empirical evidence and player feedback.

At some point the balancing must stop and the final bugs will have been fixed. Now you have a finished game in your hands. Designers are generally never 100% happy with the final product. There is always something more they wanted to tweak or an extra feature or element of content that they wanted to squeeze in. This is a perfectly reasonable emotion, as it drives designers to create ever better designs. Don't throw these ideas away. They may find a use in a future project.

ABOUT THE CD-ROM

The CD-ROM contains a number of files you should find useful as reference. Please also refer to the system requirements contained in this document to ensure that your system meets these requirements.

FOLDERS

The files on this disc are organized into folders as follows:

Figures: All of the figures from the book, organized in folders by chapter.

Examples: A number of documents that can be used for ideas, layout, and so on. These documents follow the design of a fictitious game called *Soul Thief.*

- *Balance-LevelPace.xls:* An example spreadsheet that shows how pace can be estimated over the course of a level. This is also shown in graph form in a separate worksheet for easy viewing. This file requires Microsoft Excel® 2002 or later.
- *Balance-Worth.xls:* The balance sheet shows how to use various calculations for determining the worth of various game elements. There are several worksheets for different aspects of the game systems. This file requires Microsoft Excel 2002 or later.
- *Design-Database.mdb:* The design database is a repository for all level design information in the game. There are two main areas of the design database: Data Entry and Reports. Data Entry allows the user to fill in all pertinent data in an easy manner. Reports shows some examples of reports that might be generated from the data in the database. The underlying tables allow the user to change further data behind the scenes to adjust the database to their own needs. This file requires Microsoft Access® 2002 or later.

- *Design-GameProposal.doc:* The game proposal shows how a document can be laid out and what kind of information should be imparted to the reader of the document. This file requires Microsoft Word® 2002 or later.
- *Design-LevelDesign.doc:* The level design document shows an example layout and sample content of what should be included in the document. This file requires Microsoft Word 2002 or later.

SYSTEM REQUIREMENTS

133 MHz Pentium® III processor; 128 MB RAM; Microsoft Windows 2000, XP Home or Professional Editions; Microsoft Office® 2002.

REFERENCES

[Adams02] Adams, Ernest, "Balancing Games with Positive Feedback." Available online at *http://www.gamasutra.com/features/20020104/adams_01.htm*, January 4, 2002.

[Adams03] Adams, Ernest, "The Designer's Notebook: Defining the Physical Dimension of a Game Setting." Available online at *http://www.gamasutra.com/features/20030430/adams_01.shtml*, April 11, 2003.

[Adams05] Adams, Ernest, "Interactive Narrative Revisited: Ten Years of Research." Available online at *http://www.designersnotebook.com/Lectures/Interactive_Narratives_Revisit/body_interactive_narratives_revisit.htm*, 2005.

[BatemanBoon05] Bateman, Chris and Boon, Richard, *21st Century Game Design*. Charles River Media, 2005.

[Booth04] Booth, Michael, "The Making of the Official Counter-Strike Bot." Presentation at GDC 2004.

[Brownlee] Brownlee, Jason, "Finite State Machines (FSM)." *Available online at http://ai-depot.com/FiniteStateMachines/*

[Campbell49] Campbell, Joseph, *The Hero with a Thousand Faces*. Princeton University Press, 1949.

[Carless03] Carless, Simon, "Marc Laidlaw on Story and Narrative in Half-Life." Available online at *http://www.gamasutra.com/features/20030808/carless_01.shtml*, August 8, 2003.

[ChenBrown01] Chen, Steven and Brown, Duncan, "The Architecture of Level Design." Presentation at GDC March 2001.

[ConwayRoenisch94] Conway, Hazel and Roenisch, Rowan, *Understanding Architecture: An Introduction to Architecture and Architectural History*. Routledge, 1994.

[Dunniway00] Dunniway, Troy, "Using the Hero's Journey in Games." Available online at *http://www.gamasutra.com/features/20001127/dunniway_01.htm*, November 27, 2000.

529

[Edge04] Author uncredited, "Different Strokes." *Edge* 133 (2004): p, 60–67.

[Felluga03] Felluga, Dino, "Modules on Barthes: On the Five Codes." Available online at *http://www.cla.purdue.edu/academic/engl/theory/narratology/modules/barthescodes.html*, Nov. 28, 2003.

[Field72] Field, Syd, *Screenplay: The Foundations of Screenwriting; A Step-by-Step Guide from Concept to Finished Script*. Dell Publishing, 1972.

[Freeman02] Freeman, David, "Four Ways to Use Symbols to Add Emotional Depth to Games." Available online at *http://www.gamasutra.com/features/20020724/freeman_01.htm*, July 24, 2002.

[Gard00] Gard, Toby, "Building Character." Available online at *http://www.gamasutra.com/features/20000720/gard_01.htm*, June 20, 2000.

[Hancock02] Hancock, Hugh, "Better Game Design Through Cutscenes." Available online at *http://www.gamasutra.com/features/20020401/hancock_01.htm*, April 2, 2002.

[Hopson01] Hopson, John, "Behavioral Game Design." Available online at *http://www.gamasutra.com/features/20010427/hopson_01.htm*, April 27, 2001.

[Jak04] Jak, Sable, *Writing the Fantasy Film: Heroes and Journeys in Alternate Realities*. Michael Wiese Productions, 2004.

[Leonard03] Leonard, Tom, "Building AI Sensory Systems: Lessons from Thief and Half-Life." Presentation at GDC 2003.

[Liden] Lidén, Lars, "The Use of Artificial Intelligence in the Computer Game Industry." Presentation at GDC.

[MalimBirch98] Malim, Tom and Birch, Ann, *Introductory Psychology*. Palgrave, 1998.

[Newman02] Newman, James, "The Myth of the Ergodic Videogame." Available online at *http://www.gamestudies.org/0102/newman/*, July 2002.

[Pagan01] Pagán, Tito, "Where's the Design in Level Design? Part One." Available online at *http://www.gamasutra.com/resource_guide/20010716/pagan_01.htm*, July 2001.

[Pinter01] Pinter, Marco, "Towards More Realistic Pathfinding." Available online at *http://www.gamasutra.com/features/20010314/pinter_01.htm*, March 14, 2001.

[PratchettWhitta04] Pratchett, Rhianna and Whitta, Gary, "The Write Stuff." *Develop* 39 (May 2004): p. 34–35.

[Reynolds99] Reynolds, Craig, "Steering Behaviors for Autonomous Characters." Available online at *www.red3d.com/cwr/steer/*, 1999.

[RollingsAdams03] Rollings, Andrew and Adams, Ernest, *Andrew Rollings and Ernest Adams on Game Design*. New Riders Publishing, 2003.

[SalenZimmerman04] Salen, Katie and Zimmermann, Eric, *Rules of Play: Game Design Fundamentals*. MIT Press, 2004.

[Smith02] Smith, Harvey, "GDC 2002 Web Lecture: Systemic Level Design for Emergent Gameplay." Available online at *http://www.gamasutra.com/features/slides/smith/index.htm*, June 12, 2002.

[Song05] Song, Jiesang, "Improving the Combat 'Impact' of Action Games." Available online at *http://www.gamasutra.com/features/20050428/sang_01.shtml*, April 28, 2005.

[Spoors] Spoors, Glen R, "Narrative and Interaction in Computer Games: Codes of Computer Gameplay." Available online at *http://www.upnaway.com.au/~waldemar/Research/ANZCA%202001.doc*

[Tapper03] Tapper, Paul, "Personality Parameters: Flexibly and Extensibly Providing a Variety of AI Opponents' Behaviors." Available online at *http://www.gamasutra.com/features/20031203/tapper_01.shtml*, December 3, 2003.

[TVTropes] TV Tropes Wiki, "Narrative Devices." Available online at *http://tvtropes.org/pmwiki/pmwiki.php/Main/NarrativeDevices.*

[Valve04] Valve, *Half-Life 2: Raising the Bar.* Prima Games, 2004.

[Vogler98] Vogler, Christopher, *The Writer's Journey: Mythic Structure for Writers* (2nd Edition). Michael Wiese Productions, 1998.

[Wikipedia] Author uncredited, "Dramatic Structure." Available online at *http://en.wikipedia.org/wiki/Dramatic_structure.*

INDEX

3D environments, 478
3D render engines, 98

A
A* algorithm, 382–383
A-plot, 63
abstract entities, 350–351
abstraction and simulation, 28–30, 48
acceleration movement, 144
accuracy
    character, 268
    weapon, 225–228
achievements or rankings, online, 297
acquisition
    See also collection
    and economic conflict, 35
    of objects, and replayability of games,
      43
acrobatics
    gameplay type, 33–34
    movements, 122–124
action
    -based events, 353–354
    -adventure games, 5
    mechanics of AI, 376–392
    and proairetic codes, 59
    reaction, and feedback in gameplay,
      31
    rising and falling, in narrative struc-
      ture, 62
actions
    and materials (AI), 388
    and reactions (AI), 364–366
    and sounds, 454–455

Adams, Ernest, 70
advertising and localization, 17–18
ageia (type of play), 27
agility, 268
agon (type of play), 27
AI (artificial intelligence)
    actors. *See* AI actors
    communication, 366–367
    components of, 364–366
    construction methods, 374–376
    and difficulty balancing, 502–505
    group management, 392–394
    mechanics of action, 376–392
    methods of choice, 367–374
    system component of game, 95
AI actors
    allies, 427–433
    Bot AIs, 433–434
    enemies, 399–414
    nonplayer characters (NPCs),
      414–427
    player expectation and feedback,
      398–399
aiming and targeting, 180–189, 190
air control character movement, 118
algorithms, AI, 382–383
allies (characters), 77–78
    AI actors, 427–433, 434–435
    inventory, 293
alpha testing, 19
ammunition, 221–222, 286–287
amnesia of avatars, 70
analog controllers, range of movement,
    115

analog sticks, 107, 143
Androcles and the lion, 68
anger in gameplay, 42
animated cameras, 164
animation
    of actions, reactions, 365–366
    blending, 211
    character, 380
    flow in combat moves, 209–212
    ranged combat, 233–235
    system component of game, 94–95
    windows, 199–200
animations
    incidental, 407–408
    playing, 381
antagonist character, 76–77
appearance of characters, 78–79
arcade modes, 87
architecture in world building, 315–317
Aristotle, 61
armor, 267
art mockup, 340–341
artificial intelligence. *See* AI
assault games, multiplayer, 47
atmospheric sounds, 454
attack windows, 199–202
attacks
    attack windows, 199–202
    damage and impact, 240–262
    defense against ranged, 233
    enemy strategies, 400–405
    linked, in cooperative gameplay, 44
    parameters, 196–199
    QTE, 125–129
    skill, 180
attributes in character economies, 266–270
audio
    designing with, 452–453, 461–462
    as diegetic story element, 74
    engine component of game, 99
    settings, 469–470
auto look, 148–149
auto-mapping, map screen, 490
auto targeting, 185
avatars (character type), 76
awareness, 270

B

back story, 54, 75, 80
background sequences, 72
backtracking, 325
balancing (game balance)
    described, 497

component balance, 511–520
    difficulty, 500–509
    level design, 342–343
    melee combat, 194–195
    motivation, 509–510
    movement, 123
bars (HUD component), 483
Barthes, Roland, 59
bases, respawning, 47–48
beam weapons, 229–231, 236–237
beat 'em ups (games), 5
behaviors. *See specific behavior*
beliefs and customs in story-based games, 56
bending time, 299
bespoke peripherals, 22, 110
beta testing, 19–20
binary code, and level design, 357
Black & White, 37
blades (weapons), 195
blending, animation, 211
blocking defensive moves, 213–214
blood, 261
bludgeons, 196
blur, motion, 142
book, this
    CD-ROM, about, 527–528
    scope and organization of, xiii
Bot AIs, 433–434
bounce of projectiles, 228–229
bounding boxes and collision detection, 245
brainstorming, 6, 23, 339
branching
    combat moves, 210–211
    narrative structure, 65, 87, 90–91
    QTE (quick time event) sequences, 128
broadcast standards and localization, 13
budget, game restrictions, 29
buffering during combo moves, 207–208
bug testing, fixing, 19–20
buildings, architecture in world building, 315–317
buoyancy, 443–444
buttmonkey, 68
buttons
    See also specific control device
    context sensitivity, 125
    joypad, 107–108
    one-button combat controls, 192–194
    third-person action adventure control devices,
        112–113
buying items, 494

C

Caillois, Roger, 27

calculating damage and impact, 247–255, 262–263
calibration of peripherals, 22
camera AI, 159, 167
camera system component of games, 95–96
cameras
   See also viewpoints
   animated, 164
   basics of, 139–142, 166
   in character-based games, 115
   and combat cinematics, 177–178
   as entities, 346–347
   game, 142–164
   multiplayer game, 164–165
   using in game control, 110
camouflage, 387
Campbell, Joseph, 63
Canadian game market, 14
capture the flag games, 47
career modes, 87
Carmack, John, 98
CD-ROM, about, 527–528
censorship, 16–17
center of mass, 440
cerebral obstacles, 34–35
challenge modes, 88
challenges, time-based, 298–299
character-based games, 4–6, 52
character control
   advanced movement, 115–124
   control input, control schemes, 106–114
   object interaction, 124–125
   quick time events, 125–129
   standard movement, 114–115, 129
character economies, 266–273, 303
character growth, and gameplay, 37
character-relative movement, 115
characters
   See also AI actors, players
   controlling. *See* character control
   creating, 270–273
   depth of, 406–414
   player expectation and feedback, 398–399
   progression, 274–279
   ragdoll, 261–262
   selection, creation, 471
   skeletons, 95
   speaking different language, 56
   in story-based games, 75–81, 83
   supporting (allies), 77–78
   as symbols, 81
   types in stories, 68–69
charging movement, 119
charisma, 268–269

chase-camera systems, 146–147, 153
checkpoints, 301
Chekhov's gun, 68, 69
choice
   and gameplay, 31
   moral, and gameplay, 37
Chronicles of Riddick, The, 143
chronology of story, 66–67
cinematics, 136, 177–180
ciphers as cerebral obstacles, 34–35
clarity and abstraction, 30
class
   in character creation, 271
   in economies, 285
   and role-playing games, 291–292
cliff-hangers, 70
climax of story, 62
clothes
   apparel, 289–290
   costumes, 79–80
   in story-based games, 56
clues, 504
codes
   as cerebral obstacles, 34–35
   hermeneutic, semantic, symbolic, cultural,
      59–60
coding, hard
   AI construction, 374
   level construction, 356
cohesion in world building, 314
collection
   and economic conflict, 35
   in economies, 280
   and gameplay, 291
   of goods by players, 283
   and replayability of games, 43
collisions
   and response, 442–443
   target collision types, 243–246
combat
   See also conflict
   action control devices, 113–114
   AI (artificial intelligence), 390–392
   basics of, 170–172, 189
   cameras, 162–163
   control systems, 215
   difficulty, 502
   dynamics, 176–180, 189
   and economic conflict, 35
   melee combat dynamics, 192–215
   procedure, 172–176
   turn-based, 34
comedy in gameplay, 41

command attacks, 202–203
commander AI, 394
commands, user, 430–432
communication, AI, 366–367
compass, 485–486
competition
    See also conflict, combat
    ageia, 27
    competitive gameplay, 44–48
complexity, and level design methodologies, 334
component-based camera systems, 152
conflicts and gameplay, 33–36
conquest games, 46
consistency
    in gameplay, 32
    interactive storytelling issue, 70
console design
    conception aspect of, 4–7, 23
    console submission process, 20–23, 24
    game production process, 1, 10–20
    game proposal and preproduction, 7–10
construction, and economic conflict, 35
construction methods
    AI (artificial intelligence), 374–376
    level design, 356–357
content
    documenting, 23
    gameplay, 11–12
    locking, unlocking, 275–277
    structure, 89–93, 101
context sensitivity, 125, 203–204
continuity in narrative, 52–53, 82
continuous environments, 92
control devices, 106–110
control systems, combat, 192–194
controllers
    and game requirements, 21–22
    and localization, 14
    movement, 94
controls, object, 125
conversations, 32, 416–420
cooperation
    and gameplay in multiplay games, 44
    and player abilities, 35
cost of items, 518–519
costumes, 56, 79–80
counterattacking, 214
counters (HUD component), 483
courage, 270
courage, modeling, 423–425
crosshair
    accuracy, 225
    aiming, 182

crouching stance, 120
cultural code, 60
culture
    gaming, and localization, 17
    and setting, 54–55
cursor (HUD component), 484–485
customs and beliefs in story-based games, 56
cutscenes, 73
cycling, targets, 183–184

D
damage, and difficulty, 502
damage and impact
    calculating, 247–255, 262–263
    hit test, 240–247
    impact and hit reactions, 255–262
dancemat control devices, 110
data
    controller, 350
    -driven level design, 357
    for playtesting, 524–525
    saving game, 493
    storage and game requirements, 21
    types in game system, 97
databases and level design, 359–360
dead-eye skill, 189
dead zones, first-person camera, 143–144
death matches, 45
Deathmatch, 327
debugging, level design tools for, 358–360
decision trees (AI), 367–368
deduction in puzzle-solving, 36
defectors, 77
defense
    combat AI, 390–392
    combat systems, 193
    defensive combat moves, 212–214, 217
    against ranged attacks, 233, 237
defining gameplay, 26–33
delay, spawn, 47
dénouement of story, 62–63
departure, in hero's journey, 63–64
depth of field (focus), 140–141
designing
    with audio, 452–453, 461–462
    culture for story-based games, 54–55
    games. *See* game design
    levels. *See* levels
    with music, 456–459
destruction of buildings, 318–319
detecting hits, 240–247
deux ex machina, 63, 70
development kits, 8

development testing, 19
devices
    bespoke, 22, 110
    control, 106–111
    targeting, 185–187
dexterity, 268
diegesis and mimesis, 58–59
diegetic story elements, 74–75
difficulty
    and game balance, 500–506, 519–520
    selection, 467
digital pads, 107
dilation, time, 30
disbelief, suspension of, 52–53
disconnection of peripherals, 22
disposition of characters, 81
distances, attack parameters and, 198
distortion, time, 30
documents
    functional specification, 11
    level design, 339
    macro design, 8–9
    paper prototyping, 524
domain-based worlds, 92–93
dominant strategies, 511
drawing on targets, 189
driving games, 46, 52
dropping movement, 118–119
DS handheld system (Nintendo), 110
Dunniway, Troy, 63
duration of games, 42–43
dynamics
    combat, 176–180, 189
    fluid, 443–444
    melee combat, 192–215
    physics simulation, 438–440

E
economies
    character, 266–273
    economic balance, 513
    economic conflict categories, 35
    inventory, 282–295
    lives and saves, 300–303
    player rating, 295–297
    progression, 273–279
    wealth, 279–282
editing
    live, 360
    visual, 375
effects. See specific effect
Elite, 87
embedded narrative, 52

emergent
    behaviors (AI), 375
    gameplay, 33
    narrative, 52
emotions
    See also motivation
    allies (characters), 433
    in gameplay, 39–42
    modeling, 409–414
    and reactions, 420–426
enemies
    AI actors, 399–414, 434
    in games, 76–77
    inventory, 293
engines, physics, 94
Entertainment Software Ratings Board (ESRB),
    censorship, ratings, 16–17
entities
    combat, 170–172, 189
    game, 97
    and logical structures, 343–351
    persistence, 351–352
environment inventory, 294–295
environmental
    damage and impact, 250
    structure, 91–92
environments, 3D, 478
episodic structures, 91
equipment selection (HUD component), 485
ergonomic control devices, 106–108, 111
error messages, game requirements, 21
ESP (extra sensory perception), 390
European market for games, 12
evasive movement, 119, 214
event devices, 67–68
event message system, 99–100, 366–367
events, types of, 353–354
evil
    and good, scale, 422–423
    in gameplay, 41
expansion of game spaces, 314–315
expectations of player, and feedback, 398–399
expectations in games, 28
experience, in gameplay, 36–37
exploration cameras, 161
exposition of story, 62
Extensible Markup Language (XML), 357
extra sensory perception (ESP), 390
extras (non-player characters), 78

F
face buttons on joypads, 107–108
facial motion capture, 461

falling movement, 118–119
fantasy games, 57–58
fashion, in story-based games, 56
fast forward time, 300
fear, in gameplay, 41, 413–414,
    423–425
F.E.A.R. game, 67
feedback
    action and reaction in game-
        play, 31–32
    and difficulty, 505–506
    economic loops, 519
    force, and control scheme,
        109
    player, 398–399, 525–526
feel of control devices, 108
field of view (FOV), 140,
    142–143
Field, Syd, 61
fiero, 40
fighting. *See* combat, conflict
Final Fantasy, 279
finale of story, 70
finite state machines (FSMs),
    371–373
fire effects, 222–223
firing projectile weapons,
    220–229
first-person aiming, 181
first-person cameras, 142–145
first-person shooter games, 6,
    112
first person viewpoint, 134–135,
    165
five-act narrative structure,
    61–62
fixed cameras, 150
flashback techniques, 66, 67, 71
flight of projectiles, 223–224
flocking (AI), 384
flow
    and game balance, 500–501
    ludic, in level design,
        319–331
    narrative, 70, 89, 324, 331,
        332
    schemas for front end,
        473–476, 480
    summary about, 331–332
fluid dynamics, 443–444
FMA, FMV game sequences,
    73–74
focus (depth of field), 140–141

focus groups, focus testing, 7, 18
folders on CD-ROM, 527–528
foley sound, 453–454
forced game pacing, 38
foreshadowing, 67, 71
formations (AI), 393–394
fourth wall, 53
FOV (field of view), 140,
    142–143
framing, camera, 160–161
free-for-all matches, types of,
    45–46
freeze framing, 178
French language games, 14
Freytag, Gustav, 61
friction, 439
front end (user interface)
    elements of, 466–473, 480
    flow schemas, 473–476
    technical requirements,
        478–479
    visual style, 476–478
frustration, modeling, 412–413
FSMs (finite state machines),
    371–373
functional specifications, 11
funny cheat modes, 43

G
gambling
    and economic conflict, 35
    in economies, 282
game balance
    balancing process, 522–526
    component balance, 511–519
    described, xiii
    difficulty, 500–506, 519–520
    learning, 506–509
    motivation, 509–510
game balancing, 19
game cameras, 142–164,
    166–167
game design
    concepts of, xiii, 26
    console. *See* console design
    game vs. story, 52–53
game entities, 97
game logic, 96
game mechanics
    described, xiii
    game implementation and,
        11–12
    generally, 103

game modes, 86–89, 101
game over screen, 479
game proposals, 7
game relationships, 96
game structure
    logical, 86–93
    physical, 93–100
Game Studio Express
    (Microsoft), 8
gameplay
    content, 11
    defining, 26–33
    described, 1, 48
    emergent, 334–335
    game duration, 42–43
    goals of, 38–39
    multiplayer, 43–48
    pace, 37–38
    physics in, 444–449
    types, and level design,
        311–312
    types of, 33–37, 48–49
games
    See also gameplay
    balancing. *See* game balance
    character-based. *See* charac-
        ter-based games
    console design. *See* console
        design
    defined, 26
    design, of, xiii, 26, 52–53
    hints, 348, 470, 491–492
    licensed, 4
    logical structure, 89–93
    physical structure, 93–100
    playtesting, 20, 341–342,
        524–526
    replayability, 43
    rules of, 27
    system components of,
        94–99, 101
    testing, 18–20
    translation elements, quality,
        15–16
    walkthrough, 522–523
Garb, Tony, 80
Gauntlet, 89
gender, 271
geography and setting, 54
Germany, censorship and rat-
    ings, 16–17
gliding movement, 124
glory in gameplay, 40

goals
  of gameplay, 38–39
  of simulation, 28
Goddard, Jean-Luc, 66
good and evil, scale, 422–423
gore, 261
Grand Theft Auto, 16–17, 37, 57, 90–91, 301
graphics, and render engines, 98–99
grappling, throws, 205
gravity, 439
ground attacks, 204
group management (AI), 392–394

H
Half-Life 2, 72, 76–77, 92
Halo, 183
HDTV (high-definition TV), 14
heads up display (HUD), 482–488
health, 267
  of combat entities, 170–172, 189
  difficulty, 502
hearing, 387–389
hermeneutic codes, 59
Hero with a Thousand Faces, The (Campbell), 63
hero's journey, 63–65
high-definition TV (HDTV), 14
highlighters (HUD component), 485
hints, 348, 470, 491–492
history, in story-based game narrative, 57–58, 82
hit class, attack parameters, 199
hits
  critical, calculating damage, 248–249
  detecting, 240–247, 262
  effects, impact reactions, 255–262
  reactions, 256–262
hold the flag games, 45
homing weapons, 223–224
HUD (heads up display)
  component positioning, 487–488, 494–495
  components of, 482–487
HUD manager, 349–350
humor in gameplay, 41

I
Ico, 56–57
icons (HUD component), 484
ilinx (type of play), 27
impact
  and damage, 240–262, 263
  hit effects, reactions, 255–262
  projectile, 228–229
implementation, game, 11–12
infiltration games, multiplayer, 47
initiation, in hero's journey, 64
interactions
  with objects, 124–125, 130
  player abilities, 32
interactive
  cinematics, 180
  cutscenes, 73
  storytelling, 70–75
interactivity and gameplay, 31
interfaces
  front end. *See* front end
  QTE (quick time event), 128–129
  user. *See* user interfaces
international market and localization, 12–13
interrogation and interview in puzzle-solving, 36
interrupt windows, 201
intro movies, 470
inventory
  player, 278–279, 282–295, 303–304
  screen, 489–490
inverse kinetics (IK), 95
isometric viewpoint, 137–138, 165
Italian language games, 14
items
  See also objects
  as plot devices, 69
  progression, 274
  selling, buying, 494
  support, 287–288

J
James Bond: Everything or Nothing, 182
Japanese market for games, 12, 14
joy, modeling, 426
joypads, 106, 136

juggernaught games, 45
jump attacks, 203
jumping movement, 116–118

K
keyboards as control devices, 109
kinematrics, 440
kinetics, inverse (IK), 95
knowledge, conflicts of, 35–36
Kojima, Hideo, 53
Korean market for games, 12

L
ladders, 122
landscape in world building, 317–318
languages
  and localization, 14–15
  selection, 466–467
  in story-based games, 56–57
Lara Croft, 80
last man standing, 45
laws in story-based games, 57
layers
  level design tools, 359
  sound, 458
leader following (AI), 384
learning
  and game balance, 506–509
  systems (AI), 373–374
LeBlanc, Marc, 52
ledges, 122–123
legend, map, 490–491
length of games, 42–43
lens, camera, 140–142
lens controllers, 154–155
lens flares, 141
level-design tools, 358–360
level-design principles
  flow, 319–331
  form, 312–319
  function, 310–312
level implementation
  design methodologies, 334–336
  level design pipeline, 336–343
  logical structures of, 343–356
  tools for, 358–360
levels
  cameras and, 158–159

designing. *See* level-design principles
distinct, 92
in gameplay, 31
of goal in gameplay, 39
implementation. *See* level implementation
logical structures of, 343–356
selection menu, 468
licenses, render games, 98
licensed games, 4
light gun control devices, 109
lights
levels, 387
types, adjusting, 346–347
limpet mines, 231
linear chronology, 66
linear games, 89–90
linking entities, tools for, 358
live editing, 360
lives and saves, 300–304
localization, 12–13, 24
lock-on attacks, 203
lock target, 183
lockdown sequences, 72
locking, unlocking content, 275
LOD (level of detail), and AI, 375–376
logic
entities, 351
game, 96
in puzzle-solving, 35
logical
game structure, 86–93, 100–101
level structures, 343–356, 361
logo screens, 466
look-at controllers, 154
look control, first-person camera, 143
love, in gameplay, 40
luck, 269
ludic flow, 323–330
ludic function, 310–312
ludologists vs. narratologists, 52–53

M
MacGuffin, 69
macro design documents, 8–9, 23
magic, 269
magical damage, 250–251

management and economic conflict, 35
manager entities, 348–349
manner of characters, 80
market research for game concepts, 6–7, 23
markets
in game economies, 281–282
and localization, 12–13
masterminds, 77
match mode, 88
match mode, multiplayer, 88
material hit-effect matrix, 256
materials
actions and, 388
and object behavior, 442
Max Payne game, 67
melee combat games
AI (artificial intelligence), 390
collision, hit detection, 241–243
combat dynamics, 188, 192–215
impact and damage, 247–248
Memento (film), 59, 66
memory-based puzzles, 36
menus, 476–477
meshes
complex collision, 246
navigation, 380
messaging, event, 366–367
Metal Gear Solid 2, 53
metaphors
front end (user interface), 477–478
save game, 493
Metroid Prime, 142
micro design, 11, 23
Microsoft
See also specific products
and console development, 8
middleware, 93, 98
mimesis and diegesis, 58–59
mimicry (type of play), 27
mine weapons, 231–232, 237
mini game modes, 88
minions, 77
mission-based games, 46–47
mockups, art, 340–341
modeling, spreadsheet, 523–524
modes
combat, engaging, 176–177
firing, 221

modes, game, 86–89, 101
modifiers, damage, 252–254
momentum, 439–440
money in game economies, 280, 288
monitoring, in multiplayer games, 44
monomyth (hero's journey), 63–65
moral choices and gameplay, 37
morale, 409–411
morals in story-based games, 57
motion
blur, 142
sensing, 109
sickness with first person viewpoint, 135
slow, 179
motivation
of characters, 81
and game balance, 509–510
in gameplay, 38–39
in NPCs, 427
risk and reward, 510
mouse as control device, 109
movement
actor parameters (AI), 381–382
advanced character, 115–124, 129–130
animation flow in combat moves, 209–212
attacks. *See* attacks
camera, 139–140
of characters, 81
of chase cameras, 147–148
controllers, 94, 152–154
defensive combat moves, 212–214
detection (AI), 386
first-person camera, 144
jumping, 116–118
in melee combat, 202–206, 216
quick time events, 125–129
set and player abilities, 32
standard character, 114–115, 129
during target locking, 184–186
vibration, 108–109
movies, intro, 470
multiplayer

arcade/narrative modes, 89
differencing, 290
gameplay, 43–48
match menu, 471–473
modes, game, 88–89
options, 475–476
ratings, 295–297
story in games, 58
music
designing with, 456–459
and localization, 17

N

names of characters, 270–271
narrative
in character-based games, 52
elements of, 58–60
flow, 70, 89, 324, 331, 332
function in level-design, 312
interactive storytelling, 70–75
modes, 87
plot, 65–70
progression and gameplay,
36–37
and setting, 54–58
structure, 60–65, 82
text display, 74
types, aspects of, 52–53
National Television System
Committee (NTSC), 13–14
natural game pacing, 38
navigation
with AI, 376–392
in level flow, 321–322
negative emotions in gameplay,
41–42
network system, component of
game, 98
Ninja Gaiden, 124
Nintendo Wii (pointing wand),
110
Nintendo DS handheld system,
110
node linking games, 46
nodes, waypoint, 378–379
nonplayer characters (NPCs)
AI actors, 414–427, 434–435
extras (allies), 78
and interactive choice, 31
inventory, 294
North American market for
games, 12, 14
NPCs. *See* nonplayer characters

NTSC (National Television System Committee), 13–14

O

objects
game impact, 513–519
interactions with, 124–125,
130
picking up, throwing,
445–446
structure of, 441–444
obstacles, skill-based and cerebral, 33–35
occlusion in level design,
320–321
offensive combat AI, 392
one-button combat controls,
192–194
online rankings, achievements,
297
outcomes of QTEs, 128
over-the-shoulder aiming, 181
over-the-shoulder viewpoint,
137

P

pace of gameplay, 324–325
painting, target, 189
PAL (Phase Alternation Line), 13
panic, in gameplay, 42
paper prototyping, 524
parrying weapons, 214
party games, 89
pass the bomb games, 45
pathfinding (AI), 382
patrols, 326
patrols of NPCs, 415
pause menu, 488–489
peripherals and game requirements, 21–22
persistence
of entities, characters, 420
entity, 351–352
of virtual objects, 30–31
personality of characters, 80
Phase Alternation Line (PAL), 13
phoneme matching, 461
physical
flow in space, 319–323
game structure, 93–100, 101
structure of objects, 441–444
physics
in gameplay, 444–449

ragdoll, 261–262
simulation, 438–444
sounds, 455
of virtual worlds, 30
pickups, and player abilities, 32
picture sizes, refresh rates, 13
pinpoint aiming, 182
pipeline, level design, 336–343,
361
platformers (games)
control schemes, 111–112
described, 5–6
play, and gameplay, 27
player
expectation and feedback,
398–399
health, 170–172
inventory, 282–295
profiles, 468
ratings, 295–297
player abilities, 32
player-controlled cameras,
149–150
player-guided projectiles, 224
player input systems, QTE (quick
time event), 126–129
players
See also AI actors, characters
learning from, 374
trade with other, 282
PlayStation 3 (PS3) and HD
images, 14
playtesting, 20, 341–342,
524–526
plot
See also narrative
continuity, 53
elements of, 65–70, 82
pointing wands, 110
poles, ropes, 123
polling system, 100
Polti, Georges, 66
positive emotions, in gameplay,
40–41
post-structuralism, 60
postmortems of products, 23
power, in gameplay, 40
preproduction process of game
development, 8–10, 23
Prince of Persia: Sands of Time, 300
Prince of Persia: Warrior Within,
163
proairetic code, 59

procedures, combat, 172–176, 189

product placement and localization, 17–18

production (game process), 10–20

products, postmortems of, 23

profiles, player, 468

progression
in economies, 273–279, 303
in space, 322–323

projectile weapons, 236, 240–262

prone stance, 120

proposal, game, 7

protagonist character, 76

prototyping games, 9–12, 23

prototyping on paper, 524

psychology of learning, 507–510

puzzles, 34–35, 444–445, 504

Q

QTE (quick time event) sequences, 125–131

quality control of console games, 18–19

quest items, 288

quest log, 491

quick time event (QTE) sequences, 125–131

quicksaves, 301–302

R

race (character), 271

race (driving) games, 46, 52

ragdoll physics, 261–262

random systems, weighted (AI), 368–369

ranged combat animation, 237

rankings, achievements online, 297

ratings
and censorship, 16–17
player, 295–297, 304

reaction, and player abilities, 34

reactions
actions and (AI), 364–366
emotions and, 420–426
hit, 256–262

real-time
combat, 175–176, 177
conflict, 33

realism

in games, 28
ultra-, 302–303
verisimilitude in narrative, 53

recharging weapons, 222

recoil, gun, 226

Red Dead Revolver, 189

redundancy
and game balance, 512
in simulations, 29

refresh rates, 13

registry windows, 200–201

render engine component of game, 98–99

replayability of games, increasing, 43

replays, performing, 179

replenishing player health, 170–172

reputation, 417, 422

researching game concepts, 6, 338–339

Resident Evil, 150, 471

resource manager (system component of game), 97–98

respawning, methods of, 47–48

response
collisions and, 442–443
mechanisms, 354–355
windows, 201–202

responsiveness of control system, 111

restart points, 301

resume game, 488

return, in hero's journey, 64–65

reverse, time, 30, 66

rewards. *See* motivation

rewind time, 300

rhythm-based challenges, 33–34

rigging animation, 94–95

roaming chronology, 66

robots. *See* Bot AIs

role-playing games, 6

ropes, poles, 123

rounds in multiplayer games, 45

rules
of games, 27, 48
of games in virtual worlds, 31–33
in multiplayer games, 45
territorial, in multiplayer games, 46
of virtual worlds, 30–33

Rules of Play: Game Design Fundamentals (Salen, Zimmermann), 26

S

S/Z (Barthes), 59

sandbox, and gameplay, 37, 87

savepoints, 302

saves (lives), 300–304

saving games, 492–493

scale, world building, 313

scaling (distance), 388

scatter, weapons, 223

scenery, 346

schedules, 354

schemes, control, 111–114

scoring
achievements, rankings, online, 297
and game balance, 517
system (AI), 369–371

screen effects, combat cinematics, 179–180

screen-relative movement, 114

screens
loading, 470
split, 164

scripted sequences, 71–72

scripting
for AI construction, 374
for level construction, 356–357
level design tools, 358
speech, 459

scripts, user, 430–432

searching (AI), 384–385

SECAM (Systeme Electronique Courleur avec Memoire), 13

seeking (AI), 384

selling items, 494

semantic code, 60

sensory AI, 385–390

sequences
entities and events, 352–354
in games, 71

setting
and costumes, 79–80
difficulty, 501
and narrative, 54–58, 82
scene, 71
and sound, 452–453

shoulder buttons, triggers, 108

Shyamalan, M. Night, 67

side-on viewpoint, 138
sign-off phase, 343
signposting, 312
simulation
    and abstraction, 28–30, 48
    physics, 438–444
single-player modes, 86–89
skill attacks, 180
skill-based obstacles, 33–34
skills of players, 32
skip time, 30
slow motion, 179
smell (AI), 389–390
Smith, Harvey, 334
smoothers (cameras), 155
sneaking movement, 121–122
sorrow, modeling, 426
sounds
    See also audio, music
    basic hearing (AI), 387–389
    types of, 453–456
space
    -based events, 354
    -filling volumes, 379–380
    and sound effects, 455–456
    spatial puzzles, 34
    in virtual worlds, 31
    in world building. *See* level-
        design principles
Spanish language games, 14
spears, 196
specialized level design, 335–336
specifications
    functional, 11
    level, 339–340
speech, using, 459–461
speed
    attack parameters, 196–199
    character, 267–268
    gameplay pace, 37
    kill, 295–297
    projectile velocity, 225
spline cameras, 151, 153–154,
    156–157
Splinter Cell: Pandora Tomorrow,
    292
split body animation system, 235
split screen cameras, 164
Spoors, Glenn R., 60
spreadsheet modeling, 523–524
sprinting movement, 119
SQL (Structured Query Lan-
    guage), 360

stances, combat, 206–207
standing stance, 120
states (AI), 364–365
status effects, 251–252, 255
stealth, and player abilities, 34
steering, camera, 159–160
storage of data, and game re-
    quirements, 21–22
store screens, 494
story
    See also narrative, plot
    elements of narrative, 58–60,
        83
    interactive storytelling, 70–75
    time line, 75
    vs. game, 52–53, 82
story-based games
    characters in, 75–81, 83
    game vs. story, 52–53
    setting, 54–58
    story, narrative elements,
        58–75
Street Fighter 2, 207
Street Fighter Alpha 3, 180
strength, character, 267
structuralism, post-structuralism,
    60
structure
    content, 89–93
    game. *See* game structure
    level, 343–356
    narrative, 60–65
    of objects, 441–444
Structured Query Language
    (SQL), 360
styles
    building, 316
    front end visual, 476–478
    movement, 114–115
    music, 456
    visual, 312–313, 480
supporting characters (allies),
    77–78
surveys, market research, 7
suspension of disbelief, 52–53
sweep selection (targeting),
    188
swimming movement, 121
symbols
    and buildings, 317
    characters as, 81
    as plot devices, 69
    symbolic code, 60

system components of games,
    94–99
system level design, 334–335,
    360–361
system requirements
    CD-ROM, 528
    and game requirements, 21
Systeme Electronique Couleur
    avec Memoire (SECAM), 13
systems. *See specific system*

T
taboos, cultural, 17
talking, speech, 459–461
target, collision types, 243–246
target painting, 189
targeting, combat basics, 180,
    183–189, 190
tasks and schedules, 381
team death matches, 45
teams, group management (AI),
    392–394
technical limitations of games,
    29
technical requirements
    for console development,
        20–21
    for user interface, 478–479
Technique of Drama (Freytag), 61
technology
    localization and, 13
    in story-based games, 55
Tekken, 113
territorial conflict (gameplay
    type), 33
testing
    hit detection, 240–247
    playtesting, 20, 341–342,
        524–526
    types of game, 18–20, 24
text
    as diegetic story element, 74
    display as narrative, 74
themes, plot, 65–66
third-person action adventure
    control devices, 112–113
third person aiming, 181–182
third person viewpoint,
    135–139, 165
Thirty Six Dramatic Structures
    (Polti), 66
threat weighting, 187–188
three-act narrative structure, 61

6/07

throws, grappling, 205
time
    altering to highlight action, 178
    game duration, 42–43
    gameplay pace, 37–38
    line, story, 75
    period of story-based games, 55
    for puzzle-solving, 34
    QTE (quick time event) sequences, 125–129
    seasons, challenges, manipulations, 298–300
    in virtual worlds, 30
timing-skill obstacles, 33–34
Tolkien, J.R.R., 57
Tomb Raider, 184
tools
    in economies, 290
    level design, 358–360
    for level implementation, 358–360
top-down viewpoint, 139
touch (AI), 389
touch screens, 110
toyplay, and gameplay, 27, 37
tracking (AI), 382–383
tracking movement system, 148–149, 151
trade, 281–282
trading
    and economic conflict, 35
    items, value of, 518
traditions and customs in story-based games, 56
trails, weapon, 215
training mode, 88
traitors, 77
transitions, camera, 157
translation elements, quality of localization, 15–16
traps, 447, 504
traverser, 346
treasure, valuables, 490
turn-based combat, 34, 173–175
TVTropes Web site, 67
tweakers (cameras), 155

twists, plot, 67

U
U-571 (film), 57
uberjoypads, 106–107
user commands, scripts, modes, 430–432
user interfaces
    back end, 479
    described, xiii
    front end, 465–480
    game requirements, 22
    in-game interface, 481–495
    prerequisites for good, 463
    system component of game, 95

V
verisimilitude in narrative, 52–53, 82
vertical slice described, 10, 23
vibration in control schemes, 108–109
video as diegetic story element, 74
viewpoints
    first person, 134–135, 165
    switched-view approach, 224
    third person, 135–139, 165
violence, censorship and ratings, 16–17
VIP multiplayer games, 47
virtual worlds
    rules of, 30–33
    world building, 307
viscosity, 443
vision (AI), 386
visual continuity, 53
visual settings, 469–470
Vogler, Christopher, 63
voice acting, 408–409, 460–461
voice pools, 459–460
volumes, space-filling, 379–380
vulnerability, and collision detection, 246–247

W
walkthroughs, game, 522–523

walls
    movement along and up, 124
    sneaking movement along, 121–122
WalMart, censorship and ratings, 16–17
wealth, 279–282, 303
weapon trails, 215
weapon wheel, 485–486
weaponry
    See also specific weapon
    beam weapons, 229–231
    in economies, 286
    makeshift, 445
    melee weapons, 195–196
    mine weapons, 231–232
    parrying weapons, 214
    projectile weapons, 220–229
    targeting and aiming, 180–189
weather, 298
weighting
    threat, 187–188
    weighted random systems, 368–369
windows, attack, 199–202
wisdom, 269
Wizard of Oz, The, 68
world building
    described, xiii
    tools, 358
    and virtual worlds, 307
Worms 3D, 18
wriggle (hit recovery), calculating, 260
Writer's Journey, The (Vogler), 63

X
Xbox 360 and HD images, 14
Xbox Live Arcade, 8
XML (Extensible Markup Language), 357
XNA (Microsoft), 8

Z
zombies, 261
zones, damage, 252
zooming cameras, 165